GENERAL JOHN LAMBTON.

By G. Romney.

The Durham Light Infantry

PREFACE

The general plan on which this history has been written is the simple one of a statement of facts in chronological order; no attempts at elaboration or expansion have been made; details of campaigns, except when they are intimately connected with the regiment, have been avoided.

Tradition has been brushed aside; if anything traditional is mentioned, the fact of its being traditional is expressly stated.

Dates, figures, etc., have all, with a few trifling exceptions, been obtained from official documents.

When information has been obtained from non-official sources, the source from which it has been obtained is mentioned.

As far as can be ascertained, all documents, books, etc., which might have thrown light upon the history of the regiment, have been most thoroughly searched in (i.) the War Office Library, (ii.) the Public Record Office, London, (iii.) the India Office, (iv.) the British Museum, and (v.) the Public Record Office, Dublin.

Much information has been derived from (i.) "A Soldier's Journal" (published 1770), anonymous, (ii.) "Vicissitudes of a Soldier's Life" (published 1827), by John Green, (iii.) Outram's "Persian Campaign" (printed for private circulation 1860), (iv.) the late Colonel W. Gordon's "History of the Durham L.I." (published 1894), and from a variety of books relating to the British Army generally. Free use has, of course, been made of the regimental records of the 1st and 2nd Battalions.

It is not possible for me to mention here by name all the many friends who have kindly assisted in searching for information, but I now tender them all my most sincere thanks.

My correspondence on this subject—much of it with strangers—has been enormous; out of the many people to whom I wrote, only one ignored my letter; all the others did their best to assist me.

PREFACE

I cannot overstate the debt of gratitude which I owe to Mr. A. D. L. Cary, librarian at the War Office, and to his two most able assistants, Messrs. Fyfe and Govier, for all the trouble they have taken on my behalf; without their willing co-operation many interesting facts would never have been brought to light.

Mr. R. H. Headley, of the Military Department, India Office, has given much valuable assistance in the compilation of the list of officers of the 2nd Bombay European L.I., and also in connection with many other details concerning that corps.

The particulars concerning ships of the Royal Navy in which the 1st and 2nd Battalions embarked on different occasions were kindly provided from the library at the Admiralty by Rear-Admiral W. C. Pakenham, C.B., M.V.O.

My thanks are due to the Earl of Durham, K.G., etc., for permission to insert a photograph of his picture of General John Lambton, and also to Colonel H. C. Surtees, C.B., etc., for allowing me to have the old 68th (grenadier company) cap-plate, in his possession, photographed.

It may perhaps be well to state that this book is primarily a history of the two Regular Battalions, the idea having been originated, and the necessary funds for compilation having been mostly provided, by officers, past and present, of those battalions.

Names of places have been spelt, as far as possible, in accordance with the spelling in "The Times" Atlas.

The lists of officers of the Regular Battalions are believed to be complete, although it is possible that occasionally the name of an officer, whose sojourn in the regiment did not extend beyond a few days or even a few weeks, may have escaped notice. A few notes regarding nearly all the officers are given, but neither time nor circumstances have permitted of a complete biography of each officer being made; in some cases it has not been possible to ascertain Christian names, in others names are not always spelt in the same manner, and in a few instances dates of commission could not be traced.

W. L. VANE.

Haughton Hall, Darlington.
May, 1914.

CONTENTS

PAGE

CHAPTER I
The 68th Light Infantry (1756-1785) 1

CHAPTER II
The 68th Light Infantry (1785-1809) 24

CHAPTER III
The 68th Light Infantry in Walcheren and the Peninsula (1809-1814) 41

CHAPTER IV
The 68th Light Infantry (1814-1854) 65

CHAPTER V
The 68th Light Infantry in the Crimea 82

CHAPTER VI
The 68th Light Infantry (1856-1881) 93

CHAPTER VII
The 106th Light Infantry (1839-1862) 106

CHAPTER VIII
The 106th Light Infantry (1864-1881) 118

CHAPTER IX
1st and 2nd Battalions The Durham Light Infantry (1881-1898) 121

CHAPTER X
The South African War (1899-1902) 135

CHAPTER XI
1st and 2nd Battalions The Durham Light Infantry (1903-1914) 157

APPENDICES

		PAGE
APPENDIX	I—Roll of Officers, 68th Regiment of Foot ...	168
	Roll of Officers, 2nd Bombay European Light Infantry	214
	Roll of Officers, 106th Bombay Light Infantry	222
	Roll of Officers, 1st and 2nd Battalions The Durham Light Infantry	230
APPENDIX	II—List of Colonels and Colonels-Commandant, 68th Regiment	242
	List of Colonels, 2nd Bombay European Light Infantry	251
	List of Colonels, Durham Light Infantry	257
APPENDIX	III—Lieutenant-Colonels and Adjutants of the 68th Regiment, 68th Light Infantry, 2nd Bombay European Light Infantry, 106th Bombay Light Infantry, Durham Light Infantry	260
APPENDIX	IV—Regimental Music	268
APPENDIX	V—Freemasonry	271
APPENDIX	VI—Durham Light Infantry Club	272
APPENDIX	VII—Durham Light Infantry Cottage Homes ...	273
APPENDIX	VIII—"The Durham Light Infantry Gazette" and "The Bugle"	274
APPENDIX	IX—The 2nd Battalion Durham Light Infantry Polo Club in India, 1888-1899 ...	275
APPENDIX	X—Memorials to those who have lost their lives on active service	281
APPENDIX	XI—The 3rd and 4th Battalions Durham Light Infantry	288
APPENDIX	XII—The 5th, 6th, 7th, 8th, and 9th Battalions Durham Light Infantry	304
POSTSCRIPT	... ...	314
INDEX	... ...	315

ILLUSTRATIONS

	PAGE
General John Lambton	Frontispiece
Grenadier's Cap-Plate	facing 13
Officer's Breast-Plate	,, 38
Lord William Paulet, Captain Cross, etc.	,, 76
Officers of the 68th Light Infantry, 1855	,, 87
Crimean Colours (68th)	,, 90
Officers' Waist-Plates, 2nd Bombay European Light Infantry and 106th Light Infantry	,, 118
Memorial at Vaal Krantz	,, 138
Durham Light Infantry South African War Memorial	,, 284
William Harry, 1st Duke of Cleveland	,, 291

INTRODUCTION

Considering the distinguished services that have been rendered to the State by the Durham Light Infantry, it is remarkable that the literature dealing with the regiment is so meagre, and, even in some cases, of such a poor quality. In the few accounts of the regiment that do exist, the records of the earlier years of the 1st Battalion must (except in the case of the late Colonel Gordon's excellent little book) be studied with great caution, as they are not always accurate; certain errors crept in many years ago, and have been accepted as true statements for so long, that it is now a difficult matter to prevent their being perpetuated. In the case of the 2nd Battalion also, the year mentioned as that in which the battalion was raised varies in different accounts.

In spite of most careful research, the compiler of this book has not been able to present as full an account of the 1st Battalion during the first fifty years of its existence as he would have liked to have done—those interested will understand the difficulties of the situation; he hopes, however, that readers will look leniently on this and on other shortcomings.

The compiler also hopes that this book will not only interest those who are serving, or who have served, in the several battalions of the Durham Light Infantry, but that it will also stimulate a greater interest among all classes of the community of the county of Durham in their county regiment.

The Durham Light Infantry, as at present constituted, consists of nine battalions: two Regular Battalions of the Line, two of Special Reserve, and five of the Territorial Force.

These nine battalions did not spring from a common origin, and consequently are not yet so closely connected with each other as is desirable, but the affinity between them is rapidly growing. Unfortunately, there is not any station for a battalion of Regular Infantry in the county of Durham, so far too little is known in it

INTRODUCTION

about the two Regular Battalions. The 1st Battalion has not been in the county since the year 1800, and the 2nd has never yet been in it; the other seven, being far more local, are consequently better known.

Then, again, owing to the fact that there is not any large training centre in the county of Durham, these several battalions have little opportunity of meeting; in fact, none of the battalions of the Territorial Force have ever been trained in conjunction with either of the Regular Battalions, although this is not the case with the two battalions of the Special Reserve.

The relationship of the two Regular Battalions to each other is very close; the other seven are practically separate units, but all the nine are animated by the same spirit, by the same pride in their county name, and in each other's records, and by the same determination to uphold the honour of their King, and their country, and their county.

THE
DURHAM LIGHT INFANTRY

CHAPTER I.

THE 68TH LIGHT INFANTRY (1756-1785).

As the two Regular Battalions came into existence at different periods, and under such widely different circumstances, it is necessary to deal with them separately until they became closely associated in July, 1881, after which date their records are given together.

1756 — In the year 1756, after the loss of Minorca, and in consequence of the threatening state of affairs in Europe, which led to the "Seven Years' War," the British Government decided on an increase to the forces. Among other augmentations, fifteen regiments of infantry were authorised, by an order dated 29th September, 1756, to raise second battalions, as from 25th August, 1756.

These fifteen regiments were:—

    (i.) Colonel Howard's, or 3rd Regiment of Foot.
    (ii.) Colonel Duroure's, or 4th Regiment of Foot.
    (iii.) Lieut.-General Wolfe's, or 8th Regiment of Foot.
    (iv.) Major-General Bocland's, or 11th Regiment of Foot.
    (v.) Lieut.-General Skelton's, or 12th Regiment of Foot.
    (vi.) Lord George Beauclerk's, or 19th Regiment of Foot.
    (vii.) Colonel Kingsley's, or 20th Regiment of Foot.
    (viii.) Lieut.-General Huske's, or 23rd Regiment of Foot.
    (ix.) Colonel Cornwallis's, or 24th Regiment of Foot.
    (x.) Major-General Holmes's, or 31st Regiment of Foot.

THE DURHAM LIGHT INFANTRY

(xi.) Colonel Leighton's, or 32nd Regiment of Foot.
(xii.) Lord Charles Hay's, or 33rd Regiment of Foot.
(xiii.) Earl of Effingham's, or 34th Regiment of Foot.
(xiv.) Lord Robert Manners's, or 36th Regiment of Foot.
(xv.) Major-General Stuart's, or 37th Regiment of Foot.

Each of these fifteen new battalions was to be composed of 1 major, 1 adjutant, 1 quartermaster, and 2 surgeon's mates, and to have 10 companies, each composed of 1 captain, 1 lieutenant, 1 ensign, 3 serjeants, 3 corporals, 2 drummers, and 70 private men.

The daily rates of pay and subsistence were to be as under:—

Rank.	Pay.	In lieu of his Servant.	Subsistence.
Major, as Major	5/-	—	11/6
Adjutant	4/-	-/8	3/-
Quartermaster	4/-	—	3/-
Surgeon's Mates, each	2/6	—	2/-
Captain	8/-	2/-	7/6
Lieutenant	4/-	-/8	3/6
Ensign	3/-	-/8	3/-
Serjeant	1/6	—	1/-
Corporal	1/-	—	-/8
Drummer	1/-	—	-/8
Private Man	-/8	—	-/6

These amounts, with certain small allowances for various purposes, amount to a total of £40 4s. 8d. for the total pay of each battalion for one day.

It may be noted that the above rates were the normal daily rates of pay, at that time, for regiments of foot on the British establishments; the rates for regiments on the Irish establishments in a few instances differed slightly.

These fifteen new battalions were in 1758 constituted into

THE 68TH LIGHT INFANTRY (1756-1785)

separate regiments, and numbered from 61 to 75; the 2nd Battalion of the 23rd (Royal Welch Fuzileers) thus became the 68th Regiment; those that were numbered from 61 to 70 (inclusive) exist to this day; the remainder—71st to 75th (inclusive)—were disbanded, after the Peace of Paris, in 1763, at the conclusion of the " Seven Years' War."

But to return to the year 1756; the 23rd (Royal Welch Fuzileers) had formed part of the unfortunate garrison of Minorca that had been obliged to capitulate to the French in the month of June; it was sent to Gibraltar, and in due course home, disembarking at Plymouth early in the month of October, and marching at once to Leicester, where its 2nd Battalion was being raised. The earliest extant " marching order" concerning the 2nd Battalion is dated the 4th October, 1756; the substance of it is that the battalion is " to remain at Leicester until further orders," and has nothing whatever to do with marching.

1757 The two battalions remained together at Leicester until the end of April, 1757, when the 1st was moved to Market Harborough and adjacent towns, the 2nd remaining at Leicester. In the following month the two battalions moved to Berkshire, the 1st to Newbury, Ellsley, and Hungerford, the 2nd to Henley, Reading, and Ockingham [sic]. They were shortly afterwards again together at Chatham, and in September proceeded, still together, from Chatham to Dover, with a detachment at Folkestone.

1758 An order was issued from Army Headquarters on 15th April, 1758, for both battalions of the Royal Welch Fuzileers to march from Dover, each battalion in three divisions, by different routes to the Isle of Wight. It was the second division of the 1st Battalion that the anonymous author of " A Soldier's Journal" joined, together with other recruits, at Kingston-on-Thames on 11th May, 1758; he had enlisted in the previous month, but unfortunately he does not name the place of his enlistment; he was under fifteen years of age at the time, but, in spite of his youth, was accepted for duty in the ranks and was on active service in the early part of June.

In the course of a few days both battalions reached the Isle of Wight, and were encamped at King's Forest between Cowes and Newport.

THE DURHAM LIGHT INFANTRY

It was during their stay in this camp that the two battalions were separated, and the 2nd Battalion became the 68th Regiment, but the exact date is not clear; the letter of service to Colonel John Lambton, which is given here, authorises him to raise recruits from 13th May, 1758.

GEORGE R.

These are to Authorize you by Beat of Drum or otherwise to raise so many Men in any County or part of our Kingdom of Great Britain as are or shall be wanting to recruit and fill up the respective companies of our 61st Regiment of Foot under your command to the numbers allowed upon the Establishment. And all Magistrates, Justices of the Peace, Constables and other our Civil Officers whom it may concern are hereby required to be assisting unto you in providing Quarters, impressing carriages, and otherwise as there shall be occasion. And for so doing this our order shall remain in force for Twelve months from the date hereof and no longer.

Given at our Court at Kensington this 13th day of May, 1758, in the Thirty-first year of our Reign.

By His Majesty's command,

BARRINGTON.

To our Trusty and well-beloved Granville Elliot, Esqre., Major General of our Forces, and Colonel of our 61st Regiment of Foot, or to the officer appointed to raise men for our said Regiment.

Like orders of the said Date for Recruiting the following Regiment, viz.:

* * *

68th. Colonel John Lambton.

* * *

THE 68TH LIGHT INFANTRY (1756-1785)

But Colonel Lambton's and Lieutenant-Colonel Adey's commissions in the 68th were dated 22nd April, 1758; and in the warrant (dated Kensington, 4th August, 1758) for the pay of these officers from 22nd April, 1758, to 24th June, 1758, it is expressly stated that the second battalions were "formed into regiments separate and apart from the old battalions from and after the 25th day of June last."

On the other hand, the author of "A Soldier's Journal" states that the recruits, who had arrived in the Isle of Wight with the regiment, were not allotted to battalions until the third day after their arrival (i.e., on 19th May); then the two Majors drew lots, and "it happened to be my chance to be drawn for the 2nd Battalion, which was the sixty-eighth Regiment" [sic]. Also, in the orders for sailing on 1st June, the 23rd is described as the "Welch Fuzileers" and the 68th as "Lambton's," which style of description seems to indicate that the separation had, in fact, already taken place.

The uniform of the Royal Welch Fuzileers was "red, faced blue; white lace, with red, yellow, and blue stripes."

The uniform, facings, and colours of the newly-constituted 68th Regiment were:—Uniform: Red, faced deep green; deep green lining; white lace, with one black and two yellow stripes; white buttons; drummers' coats, deep green; the King's colour to be the Union, with the rank of the regiment in the center, within a wreath of roses and thistles.

The second colour to be deep green, Union in the canton, rank in the center, the rank of the regiment to be in gold characters on a crimson ground within a wreath of roses and thistles on the same stalk as the King's or first colour.

There is not, unfortunately, any record of the presentation of these colours.

This concentration of troops in the Isle of Wight was the result of a suggestion of Frederick the Great of Prussia that, as the British Government did not feel disposed to attach an army to his own, useful diversions might be made by the British on the French coasts. Accordingly, in May, 1758, about 14,000 soldiers and 6,000 Marines were collected there, while fifteen ships of the line and some frigates were in close proximity; in addition to these forces Admiral Sir E. Hawke, with twenty ships of the line, cruised before Brest. Charles, third Duke of Marlborough, was in command of the land forces, with Lord George Sackville as second in command; Admiral Lord Anson was in command of the whole fleet, and Commodore Howe directed the transports.

The detail of the troops was as under:—

Guards' Brigade (Major-General Dury): The first battalion of each of the three regiments of Foot Guards.

1st Brigade (Major-General Mostyn): 5th, 25th, 36th, and 74th Regiments of Foot.

2nd Brigade (Major-General Waldegrave): 20th, 30th, and 67th Regiments of Foot.

3rd Brigade (Major-General Boscawen): 23rd, 33rd, and 68th Regiments of Foot.

4th Brigade (Major-General Elliot): 24th, 34th, and 72nd Regiments of Foot.

In addition to the above there were the light troops of nine Dragoon Regiments, three companies of Artillery, and a large siege train.

On embarkation, however, the 74th Regiment was left in camp. The establishment of each battalion of Foot Guards was nine companies, each company to consist of three serjeants, three corporals, two drummers, and seventy private men; the establishment of each regiment of Foot was nine companies, each company to consist of four serjeants, four corporals, two drummers, and one hundred private men.

Two transports were provided for each battalion of Foot Guards, and three transports for each regiment of Foot.

The troops embarked on 28th May; the author of "A Soldier's Journal" was on the "Constant Jean, about 300 tons burthen, in which was stowed 400 private soldiers, besides officers, serjeants, drums, and women" [sic].

The fleet sailed in two divisions, each in two lines, with fireships, bombs and their tenders, ordnance transports, and baggage and train horse ships between the two divisions. The transports of the 68th were on the right of the second line of the second division, with

THE 68TH LIGHT INFANTRY (1756-1785)

H.M.S. "Success" on their right and H.M.S. "Saltash" in their rear.

The expedition anchored on 5th June in Cançale Bay, near St. Malo, and after pillaging that village and attempting Cherbourg, returned on 1st July to St. Helen's Bay in the Isle of Wight.

For a second expedition to the coast of France, Lieutenant-General E. Bligh (or Blighe), then in his seventy-fourth year, was appointed to command in the place of the Duke of Marlborough; the troops embarked on 23rd July, the author of "A Soldier's Journal" on the "Friends' Good Will," also about 300 tons.

On this occasion only twelve battalions of infantry were embarked, viz., the same three battalions of Foot Guards, the 5th, 24th, 30th, 33rd, 34th, 36th, 67th, 68th, and 72nd Regiments of Foot. The fleet sailed, as before, in two divisions, the 68th (now conveyed in only two transports, the "Isobel and Mary" and the "Friends' Good Will") being in the centre of the first line of the second division.

The actual numbers of the 68th on board these two transports were only 25 officers and 534 non-commissioned officers and men (besides 3 servants and 16 women), out of a total strength of 37 officers and 811 non-commissioned officers and men; the majority of those left behind being sick and unfit for active service. Colonel Lambton was on board the "Isobel and Mary," and Lieutenant-Colonel Adey on the "Friends' Good Will."

The troops disembarked on 7th August in the bay of Ureville, and marched on the following day towards Cherbourg. As the British largely outnumbered the French, the town was taken with little resistance; the harbour basin and forts at Cherbourg were then demolished, and after a few trivial skirmishes the troops re-embarked on 16th August, and sailed for England. The 68th apparently did not land in England, but remained on board ship cruising about in the Channel until it took part in the third expedition, landing for the third time on the French coast at Lunaire Bay on 3rd September.

This third expedition was a complete failure; the British suffered a severe defeat, with heavy losses in killed, wounded, and prisoners, at St. Cas on 11th September, and immediately sailed for England. On this occasion the French force, under the Duc d'Aiguillon,

Governor of Brittany, consisted of nine battalions of infantry, together over 6,300 men, several squadrons of cavalry, the "Garde de Cote," and armed peasants and militia.

General Bligh estimated his losses as between 600 and 700 officers and men, of whom between 300 and 400 were taken prisoners by the French. In the 68th no officers were killed, but Captain Revell and Lieutenant Grant were taken prisoners, as also were several men, probably most, if not all, of Captain Revell's company. The loss of arms and equipment in the 68th was very great, no less than 99 firelocks were taken; of this number 73 were from Captain Revell's company, which appears to have been the grenadier company.

The grenadiers of the whole army, together with four companies of the 1st Regiment of Guards, had been drawn up on the beach, under Major-General Dury, to cover the embarkation of the troops, and this covering force was severely handled by the French.

The 68th disembarked at Cowes on 19th September, and proceeded to its former camping ground at King's Forest. The prisoners were not kept long by the French, as on 15th of the following December "Marching Orders" notify that the prisoners of war of the 68th were to march to Rochester on their arrival from France.

In October in the same year the regiment proceeded by flying camp to Rochester, with detachments at Stroud, Finsbury, and Brompton, and at once began to recruit, as owing to losses in the French expeditions and to drafting—173 men had been transferred to the 61st Regiment—it was now very weak in numbers.

1759 — On 14th February, 1759, the company at Finsbury rejoined head-quarters at Rochester, where guarding French prisoners of war was the principal duty.

On 23rd March orders were issued for the regiment to march in two divisions from Rochester to Southampton (four companies), Gosport (three companies), Fareham (one company), and Bishop's Waltham (one company) to reach their destinations on 10th April, but this order was in a few days varied by detailing one company for Romsey instead of for Fareham. In a few days after its arrival one of the four companies at Southampton was ordered to Fordingbridge and Romsey.

THE 68TH LIGHT INFANTRY (1756-1785)

On 2nd June the regiment embarked on three transports for Jersey, but was wind-bound for fifteen days at Yarmouth, Isle of Wight, and did not reach Jersey until 21st June.

An estimate, still in existence but unsigned, for clothing Colonel Lambton's regiment in 1759 gives the following prices:—

A serjeant's coat and breeches ...	...	... £3	0 0
A serjeant's shirt and neckcloth ...	...	... 0	6 0
A serjeant's pair of hose ...	...	... 0	3 0
A drummer's coat and breeches ...	...	... 2	15 6
A grenadier's coat and breeches ...	...	... 1	5 11
A centinel's coat and breeches ...	...	... 1	5 6
A centinel's shirt and neckcloth ...	...	... 0	3 10
A centinel's pair of hose ...	...	... 0	1 2
Laced hat	...	... 0	2 6
Pair of shoes	...	... 0	3 8

The strength on 31st July, 1759, was 33 officers and 785 non-commissioned officers and men.

In September orders were issued for the 68th, on disembarkation from Jersey, to march to Southampton (four companies), Romsey (three companies), Ringwood (one company), and Fordingbridge (one company), but the regiment did not leave Jersey until 1760 February, 1760, and after a passage of thirty hours, disembarked at Southampton on the 8th February, and proceeded to the allotted stations.

During the first week in March, 600 men of the 68th embarked at Portsmouth to be drafted, in three parties of 200 men each, into regiments serving in the West Indies; this fact is no doubt the origin of the misstatement that the regiment took part in the capture of Dominica in 1761.

On the 18th March the 68th started from Southampton to march to Leeds, and on the 27th passed through Hatfield (strength 43 officers and 208 non-commissioned officers and men); on the 10th May orders to march from Leeds to Newcastle were issued; and in July we find the regiment at Tynemouth Barracks (strength, nine companies, 41 officers and 239 non-commissioned officers and men, out of an establishment of 1,034 all ranks).

THE DURHAM LIGHT INFANTRY

1761   In February, 1761, two companies marched from Tynemouth to Durham in aid of the civil power, and in April, 95 private men started from Tynemouth to march to Canterbury to join Colonel Trapeaud's regiment (70th Foot); in May a detachment was sent to Hexham, and head-quarters were moved to Morpeth, the detachment at Durham rejoining at Morpeth; returns compiled at Morpeth in July shew a strength of 42 officers and 289 non-commissioned officers and men. The estimate for the pay of Major-General Lambton's regiment (1034) for the year 1762 was £18,365 11s. 8d.

1762   In January, 1762, the regiment, 415 non-commissioned officers and men, marched in two divisions from Morpeth to Berwick, "there to receive orders from Lord George Beauclerk, commanding in North Britain, for their further march"; this further march finally took the regiment to Fort George, where it was quartered in August and remained without any detachments, until 26th April, 1763, and probably to a somewhat later date. On 6th July, 1762, the regiment was reviewed at Dundee by Major-General the Marquis of Lorne; it was still at Dundee on 14th July, 1762.

1763   In January, 1763, a party under Lieutenant Haste—presumably a recruiting party—at Colchester was ordered to march to Scotland to rejoin head-quarters. The exact date and place of embarkation in Scotland have not been found, but as a supplementary estimate for 1763 provided pay for Major-General Lambton's regiment up to, and including, 11th July, the regiment was on the British establishment up to that day. The regiment landed at Donaghadee on 12th July, (strength, 9 companies, 29 officers, 18 serjeants, 18 corporals, 9 drummers, and 233 privates), and marched on the same day to Belfast; the establishment at this time was 1034 all ranks.

After a few days in Belfast the regiment was distributed as under—

    3 companies at Dungannon.
    3   ,,   ,, Omagh.
    2   ,,   ,, Stewartstown.
    1 company at Cookstown.

The distribution of companies on subsequent dates was, on 10th October—

THE 68TH LIGHT INFANTRY (1756-1785)

        4 companies at Omagh.
        1 company at Stewartstown.
        1   ,,   ,, Newtown Stewart.
        1   ,,   ,, Cookstown.
        1   ,,   ,, Strabane.
        1   ,,   ,, Dungannon.

1764 On 10th January, 1764.
        3 companies at Strabane.
        1 company at Dawson Bridge.
        1   ,,   ,, Newtown Stewart.
        1   ,,   ,, Magherafelt.
        1   ,,   ,, Cookstown.
        1   ,,   ,, Stewartstown.
        1   ,,   ,, Dungannon.

On 11th April the nine companies were all at Cork, evidently in preparation for sailing to the West Indies: there were then 250 privates in the regiment, the numbers of other ranks being the same as in the previous July. The establishment of privates was now 47 in each company, making 423 in the regiment. Again, unfortunately, the date of sailing from Ireland cannot be found; the journal of the House of Commons for 1765 informs us that provision had been made for Major-General Lambton's regiment from 2nd June, 1764, and that it had been ordered from Ireland to North America*; it looks therefore, as if the regiment had come back on the British establishment and sailed from Ireland on that date; if so, the voyage must have been very quickly accomplished, as the 68th landed in Antigua on 21st June, 1764.

This tour of service in Antigua, which lasted for eight years, does not appear to have been marked by any incidents worthy of special mention.

The following certificate, which was of the usual form at that period, is interesting:—

"These are to certify that the cloathing of His Ma'ties 68th Regt. of Foot for the year 1765, comanded by Majr. Genl. Jno. Lambton,

---

* The West India islands were at this time included in the general term "North America."

THE DURHAM LIGHT INFANTRY.

arrived here 1st Augt. in good order, and was deld. and put on the Men's Backs 3rd Apr. follow^g., and they appeared compleatly Cloath'd.

"As witness my hand at Antigua 3rd April 1766.

"Geo. Thomas,

"Geo. Munro, Capt. 68th Regt."

(Note.—Geo. Thomas was Governor of Antigua.)

1770 On 12th May, 1770, there were 401 non-commissioned officers and men in the regiment; their classification was as under:—

Age.	Height.	Nationality.
55 years ... 1 man	6' 1" ... 3 men	
50 ,, ... 4 men	6' 0" ... 1 man	
45 ,, ... 10 ,,	5' 11" ... 9 men	
40 ,, ... 22 ,,	5' 10" ... 17 ,,	English ... 196
35 ,, ... 54 ,,	5' 9" ... 27 ,,	Scotch ... 106
30 ,, ... 91 ,,	5' 8" ... 60 ,,	Irish ... 71
25 ,, ... 122 ,,	5' 7" ... 79 ,,	Foreigners 28
20 ,, ... 71 ,,	5' 6" ... 74 ,,	
18 ,, ... 26 ,,	Under 5' 6" 131 ,,	
Total 401	Total 401	Total 401

Numbers did not appear upon regimental buttons until 1767; and in 1768 elaborate clothing regulations were issued from Army Head Quarters; amongst these orders it is laid down that—

(i.) No colonel is to put his arms, crest, device, or livery on any part of the appointments of his regiment.

(ii.) The number of the regiment is to be upon the buttons of officers and men.

(iii.) The uniform of the 68th to be: Red, faced deep green; silver lace for officers' hats; waistcoats, breeches, and lining of coats, white; white lace, with yellow and black stripes; coats of drummers and fifers to be deep green, faced red.

GRENADIER'S CAP-PLATE.

THE 68TH LIGHT INFANTRY (1756-1785)

The first of these orders here quoted cannot have been very strictly obeyed, for Colonel H. C. Surtees, C.B., of Mainsforth Hall, possesses the plate of a grenadier's cap which bears the Lambton crest, the initials " J.L." and the motto " FAITHFUL "; so, if the tradition as to the origin of the motto is correct, this plate cannot have been designed until a later date than 1768.

In 1759 a light infantry company had been added to the 60th Royal American Regiment, but this had only been a tentative measure; the regular institution of light infantry companies did not take place until eleven years later; the following is the Royal Warrant whereby light infantry companies were for the first time added to the establishment of certain regiments of foot.

GEORGE R.

ORDER FOR RAISING MEN IN NORTH AMERICA FOR THE AUGMENTATION OF THE 8TH REGT. OF FOOT.

Whereas we have thought fit to add one Company of Light Infantry consisting of three Serjeants, three Corporals, two Drummers, and sixty-two Private Men, besides Commissioned officers to our 8th Regiment of Foot under your Command, as also to augment each of the old Companies of our said Regiment with twenty Private Men per Company, These are to authorize you by Beat of Drum or otherwise, to raise so many men in any part of our Dominions in North America, as shall be wanted to compleat the said Augmentation. And all Magistrates, Justices of the Peace, Constables, and other our Civil officers, whom it may concern, are hereby required to be assisting unto you in providing Quarters, impressing Carriages, and otherwise as there shall be occasion. Given at our Court at St. James's, this 25th Day of December, 1770, in the Eleventh Year of our Reign.

By His Majesty's Command,
BARRINGTON.

Our Trusty and well beloved Daniel Webb Esq., Lieut. General of our Forces, and Colonel of our 8th Regiment of Foot, or to the officer appointed by him to raise men for our said Regiment.

THE DURHAM LIGHT INFANTRY

Like orders for augmenting the following Regiments in North America, viz. :—

10th Regiment of Foot.	36th Regiment of Foot.
14th ,, ,, ,,	52nd ,, ,, ,,
16th ,, ,, ,,	59th ,, ,, ,,
18th ,, ,, ,,	60th Sir Jeffrey Amherst's.
21st ,, ,, ,,	64th Regiment of Foot.
26th ,, ,, ,,	65th ,, ,, ,,
29th ,, ,, ,,	66th ,, ,, ,,
31st ,, ,, ,,	68th ,, ,, ,,
32nd ,, ,, ,,	

1772   New colours were provided in September, 1772, but there is not any record of where, or by whom, they were presented; the receipted bill, still in existence, is as under :—

The Commander of the 68th Regt. Foot
                               to Robt. Horne.

1772
Sept. 24.

	£	s.	d.
To Six Ydd. ½ Deep Green Mantua Silk at 8. 6.	2	15	3
To Six Ydd. Blew and White	2	11	0
To three ydd. ½ Crimson in Grain	1	13	3
To making the Union and Regt. Sheets of Colours	1	8	6
To two Pair of Crimson and Gold Tossells and Cords	2	12	6
To two Colour Cases and Painted and Copper Caps	1	5	0
Lineing the Hose		2	0
To Embroidering the Rank of Regt. in Gold Characters with a large Ornament of Roses and Thistles	9	9	0
To 2 Colour Staves with Spears Gilt, etc.	1	1	0
To a Deal Packing Case		5	0
	£23	2	6

THE 68TH LIGHT INFANTRY (1756-1785)

Reced. 24th Sept., 1772, from Lieut. Genl. Lambton by the hands of James Meyrick Esqre., Twenty-three Pounds 2s. 6d. in full of the above for Colours for 68th Regt.

£23 2. 6.

(sd.) ROBT. HORNE.

In July, 1772, six companies of the 68th were moved from Antigua to St. Vincent to take part in the operations against the Carribs; this detachment on 15th December of same year was under the command of a captain, and consisted of only 8 officers, 7 drummers, and 228 rank and file; on 20th December the remaining four companies were also moved from Antigua to St. Vincent; the effective strength of the regiment on 1st January, 1773, is given as 10 officers and 383 non-commissioned officers and men.

Major W. Dundas, then in command of the 68th, writing from Macariacou Camp, St. Vincent, on 18th January, 1773, complained that there were on that date only two captains, five lieutenants and two ensigns to do the duty of the regiment, and that, even from that small number, one lieutenant was employed on the staff.

Although the Carribs were supposed to number only about 1500 men, they made a stubborn resistance before they were subdued: the British force employed to subdue them numbered about 2,500 men, and included six battalions and parts of two others besides some artillery and marines.

The casualties in the 68th, from the time of taking the field against the Carribs on 26th September, 1772, to the conclusion of the campaign on the 20th February, 1773, were:—

    1 Subaltern (Ensign G. Mackay) killed.
    2 Serjeants died, and 1 serjeant wounded.
    Privates: died 16, killed 9, wounded 11, deserted 3, sick 63.

It was during this campaign that the motto "FAITHFUL" is supposed to have been gained on account of distinguished service; it is believed to have been borne on the colours.

The Legislative Assembly of St. Vincent voted silver medals to commemorate this campaign, but for distribution only to local troops.

THE DURHAM LIGHT INFANTRY

In due course Lieutenant-General Lambton was credited by the State with £180 8s. 3d., "to replace sundry accoutrements, etc., lost by the 68th upon reduction of Charribs in St. Vincent in 1772."

1773   In March, 1773, the regiment fell to a strength of 235 non-commissioned officers and men, and embarked for England; on 8th April orders were issued for the 68th on disembarkation at Portsmouth to go to Alresford (three companies), Alton (three companies), and Farnham (four companies); on 28th April orders were given for the ten companies, in all only 308 non-commissioned officers and men, to assemble on Saturday, 8th May, at Farnham, where the regiment was reviewed on 2nd June by Lieutenant-General Irwine. On 12th June a detachment, consisting of 2 captains, 4 subalterns and 86 private men, with non-commissioned officers and drums (in proportion) was ordered to arrive at Portsmouth on Sunday, 20th of the same month, and to return to Farnham after His Majesty the King had left Portsmouth.

While at Portsmouth His Majesty King George III. reviewed this detachment, with other troops, one day, while it was on the usual morning parade, without arms.

His Majesty had started from Kew at 4 a.m. on 22nd June for Portsmouth, and accomplished the journey in seven hours; the object of this journey was an inspection of the fleet assembled at Spithead; the King returned to Kew on the 26th.

On 9th July the 68th commenced to march from Farnham to Norwich, and on 5th August was at Yarmouth with a strength of 35 officers and 277 non-commissioned officers and men.

On 12th August the regiment received orders to be ready to move to any part of Norfolk in aid of the civil power, and a detachment of 1 captain, 2 subalterns, and 60 non-commissioned officers and men was sent to Fakenham.

On Monday, 4th October, the regiment marched from Norwich en route for Newcastle (six companies), and Tynemouth and *Clifford's Fort (four companies).

On 4th November two of the companies at Newcastle were ordered

---

*Clifford's Fort is on the north bank of the Tyne, close to the mouth of the river, between North Shields and Tynemouth.

THE 68TH LIGHT INFANTRY (1756-1785)

to Tynemouth, and shortly afterwards two more proceeded to Tynemouth.

1774 On 3rd May, 1774, orders were issued for the 8 companies at Tynemouth to march in 2 divisions to Berwick and there receive orders from the officer commanding the troops in North Britain; a further order on the 17th May stated that the "8 coys., 68th, on arrival at Berwick are to be enlarged with Tweedmouth."

The detachment at Newcastle was at the same time ordered to proceed to Berwick.

Before starting on its march northwards the regiment was reviewed at Newcastle on 16th May, by Major-General Evelyn.

In July the regiment was for a second time in its career at Fort George, but on this occasion only 7 companies were at head-quarters; of the remaining three, two were at Aberdeen and one at Banff; this distribution remained unaltered until July, 1775, when there

1775 were 6 companies at Fort George, 2 at Fort Augustus and 2 at Fort William.

In December the regiment was moved to Ireland and on the 6th of the month was at Donaghadee; on the 3rd January, 1776, the distribution of companies was as under:—

3 at Armagh, 2 at Drogheda, 2 at Hamilton's Bawn, 2 at Fews, and 1 at Charlemont.

On 16th December, 1775, the establishment was laid down to be:—

Eight ordinary companies, each consisting of 1 captain, 1 lieutenant, 1 ensign, 3 serjeants, 3 corporals, 2 drummers, and 56 private men. One grenadier company, consisting of 1 captain, 2 lieutenants, 3 serjeants, 3 corporals, 2 drummers, 2 fifers, and 56 private men; and 1 company of Light Infantry, consisting of 1 captain, 2 lieutenants, 3 serjeants, 3 corporals, 2 drummers, and 56 private men. These numbers, together with five staff officers, make a total of 677 all ranks, and the pay of the whole, including an allowance of 4s. per company for widows, agent, etc., amounts to £37 4s. 6d. for one day.

It was at this time that Lieutenant James Hackman, who was on duty at Huntingdon with a recruiting party, made the acquaintance

THE DURHAM LIGHT INFANTRY

of Miss Martha Ray. The story of this romance is too sad and too well-known to need repetition here; it will suffice to recall the fact that James Hackman—then a clergyman—shot Miss Ray dead outside Covent Garden Theatre on 7th April, 1779, and was himself hanged at Tyburn on the 19th of the same month.

In March, 1776, new hats were supplied as under:—

68th Regiment.
Dr. to Benjn. Page.

1776.

March 25th.

			£	s.	
To one hat for the musick master	11	4½	1	10	10½
scarlet feather for Do.	19	6			
paid for a Hat for the Serjiant major			—	18	0
three Serjiants Hats at 8s.			1	4	0
60 plain Hats the same kind of the 66th regt. at 3s.			9	0	0
one Hat for a Musition	4	0			
five Hats of my own to compleat the number wanted at 2s. 6d	12	6			
one hat, cap, made with a comb	3	3			
	19	9	—	19	9
Altering 350 hats at 3d. p. hat			4	7	6
Cash pd. for 4 yd. of Looping for Do.			—	10	0
Altering 19 Serjiants at 3d. p.			—	4	9
6 caps and combs at 10½d. each			—	5	3
Altering 60 hats into Caps	15	0			
paid for tape and thred for Do.	17	4			
			1	12	4
porterage to the Barrack Sundry times			—	8	8
			21	1	1½

THE 68TH LIGHT INFANTRY (1756-1785)

March 12th, 1777.

SIR,

Three days after sight pay to Mr. Benjn. Page or order twenty-one pounds, one shilling, and one penny half-penny, being the amount of within account, and charge the same to General Lambton's Clothing account.

(sd.) LAW REYNOLDS,
Lieut.-Col. 68th Regt.

To
Sir Willm. Montgomery, Bart.

Received the contents in full the 24th March, 1777.

(sd.) BENJ. PAGE.

1776 In July, 1776, the regiment was moved from the North of Ireland to Dublin and stayed there, without any detachments, for exactly a year; it then returned to the North of Ireland.

The distribution of companies for the following six years was:—

1777 July—Belfast 2, Armagh 2, Drogheda 2, Killough 2, Charlemont 1, Carrickfergus 1.

1778 April—Belfast 5, Armagh 2, Killough 1, Charlemont 1, Dundalk 1. July—Dublin 9, Kinsale 1.

1779 July—Waterford 5, Carrick-on-Suir 3, Camp near Carrigaline 1. (The station of the 10th Company is not mentioned in the muster roll of this date.) October—Rathkeale 4, Clare Castle 2, Askeaton 1, Cahircon Camp 2, Camp near Carrigaline 1.

1780 January—Rathkeale 3, Clare Castle 2, Cahircon 1, Askeaton 1, Innes 1, Kilkenny 1, Newcastle 1. April—Galway 7, Clare Castle 2, Kilkenny 1. October—Limerick 6, Clare Castle 2, Camp near Cashell 1, Foynes Island 1.

1781 February—Limerick 6, Clare Castle 2, Ross Castle 1, Rathkeale 1. July—Limerick 8, Ross Castle 1, Rathkeale 1. October—Cork 9, Crosshaven 1.

1782 January—Cork 8, Cove 1, Crosshaven 1. April—Cork 9, Ross Castle 1. July—Youghal 4, Cloyne 2, Carlisle Fort 2, Middleton 2.

THE DURHAM LIGHT INFANTRY

On 31st August, 1782, regiments were attached to counties with a view to stimulate recruiting, and the 68th was allotted to the county of Durham.

On 8th September the regiment was mustered on board the transports "Friendship" and "Prosperous Amelia" at Cove of Cork and showed a strength of 45 officers, 40 serjeants, 40 corporals, 22 drummers and fifers, and 646 private men; it then proceeded to Hilsea; on 16th November one company was sent, on detachment, to Fareham.

Early in December the 68th received orders to be ready for immediate foreign service and to be completed by drafts from the 75th Foot up to the following establishments, viz.: 10 companies, 45 officers, 40 serjeants, 40 corporals, 20 drummers, 2 fifers, and 700 private men. The total pay for this establishment, including allowances for agent, widows, etc., amounted to £45 9s. 6d. for one day.

Further orders were given in a few days for a recruiting company (4 officers, 8 serjeants, 8 corporals, 4 drummers, and 30 private men), to be formed in addition to the ten service companies.

On 24th December a route was issued for the 68th, "destined for Jamaica," to march from Hilsea and "embark upon the Vessels destined for their acception."

1783 — How far these vessels proceeded down the channel is not clear, but on 25th January, 1783, a route was issued for "the 68th, on arrival at Spithead to disembark, and march to Petersfield (4 coys), Alton (1 coy), Alresford (1 coy), Andover (2 coys), and Basingstoke (2 coys)."

This cancelling of the voyage to Jamaica was due to the Peace of Versailles, signed on 20th January, 1783.

There was much discontent, and even mutinous conduct, in the Army at this time; it appears that a large number of men had been enlisted to serve only for three years or during the American war, and they claimed that, with peace, their agreed term of service had expired.

In the "Gentleman's Magazine" for January, 1783, it is stated that the 77th (Atholl Highlanders) at Portsmouth, ordered to the East Indies, had revolted on the 27th of the month, and that the 83rd at Guernsey, had also revolted against going to the East Indies; in the same magazine for February, 1783, it is stated, in news from

THE 68TH LIGHT INFANTRY (1756-1785)

Portsmouth, that "on the 31st past, the 77th, or Scotch regiment, continued to parade the streets attended with their serjeants and corporals, but without their officers; they appeared entirely free from intoxication and behaved with so much decency as to remove from the inhabitants every apprehension of danger. Since which the 68th regiment, embarked on board the transports for the West Indies, hearing that the Highlanders were not to be sent to the East Indies, made a determination that they would disembark, and in consequence, very early in the morning of the 30th past, they were discovered getting the transports under way to run them in to the harbour, but they were all prevented by a man-of-war firing on them, except one transport, the master of which was compelled by the soldiers, amounting to about 300, to bring his vessel so near the southern beach that they all got on shore, marched towards the town with an intention to demand quarters of Lord George Lennox who met them and ordered them to return, which they refused; his lordship would not permit them to have quarters but sent them to Hilsea Barracks, where they are to remain till orders are received from London." The whole of the regiment was subsequently disembarked.

In the "Scots' Magazine," Vol. 45, 1783, it is stated that there has been similar trouble with the 81st which was also at the same time at Portsmouth under orders for foreign service.

To allay these discords, a proclamation was inserted in the "London Gazette" on 14th February, explaining that there was no intention of breaking faith, and that, when the treaty of peace was accomplished, all men who had completed three years would be entitled to discharge; and, further, early in March, it was notified from Army Head-quarters, that those men who had been enlisted for three years, or during the war, although not entitled to discharge until the treaty had been ratified, might be discharged at once; at the same time the establishment for battalions, not for foreign service, was reduced to forty private men per company, but the 68th was not included amongst those to be placed on the reduced establishment.

This last mentioned allocation of companies only lasted for a few weeks, as early in March the regiment was quartered at Winchester, where it was employed in guarding prisoners of war, and where it remained for eight months.

THE DURHAM LIGHT INFANTRY

On 17th October a route was issued for the "68th to march from Winchester to Hilsea Barracks, and to remain there until the transports are ready to convey them to Guernsey and Jersey."

On 9th August the standard of height for recruits for regiments of foot was 5ft. 7in. for men under 25 years of age, and 5ft. 5in. for men under 18.

1784   The regiment remained at Jersey and Guernsey—a half battalion in each island—until June 1784; on the 15th of this month it was ordered back to Hilsea Barracks; and after a brief stay of three months at Hilsea was again, on 29th September, ordered to embark on the "Brittannia" and to return to Jersey and Guernsey, a half battalion to each island as before.

This return from the Channel Islands for such a short period was evidently brought about by the contemplated disbandment of the regiment, for Sir George Yonge, Secretary for War, wrote as under:—

"War Office,
"7th June, 1784.

"Sir,—

"I have the honour to acquaint you it has been thought fit to disband the 68th Regiment of Foot, under your command, and that the official orders for that purpose will be sent to the regiment as soon as they can be prepared.

"I have the honour to be,
"Sir,
"Your most obedient and most humble servant,
"GEO. YONGE.

"General Lambton,
"Colonel of the 68th Regt. of Foot."

All interested must be thankful that this contemplated disbandment was never carried out.

On 20th March, 1784, a general order was issued that "waist-belts are to be worn over the right shoulder instead of round the waist," and on 3rd December there was an order that "the shoulder

THE 68TH LIGHT INFANTRY (1756-1785)

straps of the Regiments of Foot shall, for the future, be made of cloth, of the same colour with their Facings."

After an uneventful year's stay in the Channel Islands, varied only by serious disagreement between Captain C. W. Este, commanding the half-battalion in Guernsey, and the Lieutenant-Governor of that island, the regiment sailed early in October, 1785, for Gibraltar, where it remained for no less than nine years.

1785

CHAPTER II.

THE 68TH LIGHT INFANTRY (1785-1809).

THIS long period of garrison duty at Gibraltar was singularly devoid of any interesting occurrences. During the first few years the establishment of rank and file was only 400, and the strength was very slightly under that figure; in 1790 the establishment
1790 was increased to 27 serjeants, 20 drummers, and 600 rank and file, but the actual strength remained the same as before. This increase of establishment was again reduced in January, 1791; in a couple of months' time it was again increased; on 1st March, 1793, the strength had fallen to 21 sergeants, 11 drummers, and 369 rank and file, and of the rank and file two were returned as being "sick in Barbary."

1792 Black stocks were introduced in the place of rollers or neckcloths in 1791, and on 4th April, 1792, serjeants were ordered to carry pikes instead of halberds.

1793 On 1st December, 1793, the strength was 28 officers (of whom six were absent), 31 serjeants, 21 drummers, and 555 rank and file.

1794 In December, 1794, the regiment proceeded to the West Indies; it arrived at Martinique on Christmas Day, and on the 1st January, 1795, was at St. Lucia with a strength of
1795 (ten companies), 25 officers, 31 serjeants, 21 drummers, and 536 rank and file; by the 1st February there were already 94 men sick. Shortly after this a body of runaway negroes and other men of colour, stated to number about 7,000, and called brigands, became a daring and troublesome enemy; the brigands were assisted by the French.

Early in April, Colonel J. Stewart, of the 68th, who commanded in St. Lucia with the rank of brigadier-general, sailed for Vieuxfort at the southern extremity of the island with the following force:—

(i.) The 61st Regiment;
(ii.) The flank companies of the 9th and 68th Regiments; and
(iii.) A black regiment;

the whole numbering about 600 whites and 400 negroes.

Colonel Stewart landed his force on 16th April in a neighbouring bay, and advanced upon Vieuxfort, which, after a slight skirmish, was abandoned by the brigands. In the "London Gazette" of 30th June, 1795, three rank and file of the 68th are reported as having been wounded in St. Lucia while serving under Colonel (Brigadier-General) Stewart, on the 14th of the previous April; it appears probable that there is an error in the date, and that they were wounded in the skirmish on the 16th.

Having left a garrison in Vieuxfort, Colonel Stewart followed the enemy on the 18th, and reached Choiseul on the evening of the next day.

On the 22nd, Colonel Stewart came in sight of the enemy's position about 11 a.m.; the enemy advanced in dense columns, and at first were driven back by the light companies of the 61st and 68th, but these two companies were eventually repulsed with heavy losses. In the light company of the 68th, Captain D. Waugh and one man were killed, and Lieutenant F. H. Malet, one serjeant, and ten rank and file were wounded.

Colonel Stewart retreated that evening to Choiseul, and eventually to Vieuxfort, having lost in these few days nine officers and over one hundred and sixty men killed and wounded.

After further losses in the next two months, Colonel Stewart, who had been besieged in the fort Morne Fortuné, embarked his force unperceived on 18th June, and took it to Martinique. St. Lucia was, thus, for a time lost to the British; it was, however, recovered on 25th May, 1796.

General the Hon. Sir John Vaughan, in a despatch dated Martinico, 28th June, 1795, concerning affairs in St. Lucia, states: "It appears that a party of Brigands, consisting of picked men, with their chief, Fedon, at their head, had been routed with considerable slaughter by a detachment of His Majesty's troops, under the command of Lieutenant Hinuber, of the 68th Regiment"; but the actual date of this action is not mentioned in the despatch.

Yellow fever had accentuated the difficulties of the situation; on 1st May the 68th had no less than 174 men sick, and in July headquarters at Martinique had only 95 men fit for duty.

On 2nd March, 1795, a revolt took place in the island of Grenada, and on the 14th a re-inforcement of 120 men of the 68th arrived there from St. Lucia; in June a further part of the regiment was sent from Martinique, and the remainder followed in August.

On 22nd March, Lieut.-Colonel Schaw was directed to maintain the post at Belvidere until some other troops arrived, and he was then to send thirty men to reinforce Goyave.

On 18th April, sad to relate, two men of the 68th, named Dailey and Welsh, deserted to the enemy, but it is some satisfaction to know that, to their great disappointment, they were treated by the rebels as common prisoners and sent to gaol.

On 6th July, thirty of the 68th, under Ensign Leigh, were foraging in the valley of Grand Pauvre, attended by 200 negroes to carry the plantains; they were attacked in rear, and fifty of the negroes were captured by the enemy.

On 8th August the enemy attacked Belvidere, and the British retreated, covered by Major McLean, of the 68th.

The garrison of Goyave, which was considered next of importance to St. George's, consisted of 100 effectives of the 68th (besides convalescents), 55 Black Rangers, and 83 of the St. John's Militia; 60 of the 68th were stationed at the principal post, the Upper Battery, to which a brass 6-pr. gun had been moved, 15 of the 68th were on a saddle of a hill below the Upper Battery with a 6-pr. gun, while Lieutenant-Colonel Schaw, with the reserve, one French 14-pr. and two 6-pr. guns, was at a dwelling house a little above the works. On the night of 15th October the brigands carried this post, and Lieutenant-Colonel Schaw, with the 68th, at the rear of the retreat, retired from Goyave on to St. George's, twelve miles distant, where he arrived at 8 a.m. on the following morning.

As Lieutenant-Colonel Schaw's report on the evacuation of Goyave was considered of sufficient importance to be printed in full

THE 68TH LIGHT INFANTRY (1785-1809)

in the "London Gazette" 29th December, 1795, to 2nd January, 1796, it is now given here:—

Copy of letter from Lieutenant-Colonel Schaw, 68th Regiment, to Brigadier-General Nicholls, dated St. George's, 17th October, 1795.

"Sir,—

"In obedience to your desire I should have earlier given you an account of the particulars which obliged me to evacuate the Post of Gouyave, but waited to ascertain our loss, which I find to be Two serjeants and Thirty-four rank and file missing with one Lieutenant (Carr), supposed to be mortally wounded.

"The insurgents attacked a strong Picquet, consisting of a captain, two subalterns, four serjeants, and sixty rank and file, posted on the hill commanding the town of Gouyave, one subaltern, of which, with twenty men, were detached along the ridge running West, about 200 yards from Captain Hamilton's post, in order to prevent their approach from coming up a valley in their front, which had the desired effect, as Ensign Connor, of the 68th Regiment, a very steady and brave officer, checked a column intended against him by the vigilance and fire of his advanced sentries. The column then (as he supposes) directed their route towards the captain's post, as a hot firing soon after commenced there, during a very heavy shower of rain.

"This circumstance induced Ensign Connor to march to the support of that post, but on his arrival fell in with Captain Hamilton, who told him he had been surrounded with a very superior body of the enemy, which had penetrated and driven his party from the works, and that Lieutenant Carr, with several of his men, were badly wounded; all which circumstances were confirmed to me by the arrival of Captain Hamilton at Gouyave House, who made me a similar report.

"During this transaction a report prevailed that the Insurgents were advancing from our rear and the part of the works below; and I was confirmed in it by firing being heard from the latter mentioned place.

"This prevented me from calling up Colonel Webster's Black Corps, who had the defence of the town and the protection of the hospital; as also Captain Angus' Black Corps, which had been posted to defend the sugar works (and, as I had been informed, had perceived an enemy approaching), to make an attempt on the hill again.

"An attempt, however, was made by all the men I could muster of the 68th Regiment, but they were not able to advance further than the post already mentioned on the left of the ridge, which was gained with great difficulty, from the very steep and slippery state, occasioned by the constant rains, and finding the enemy so superior in numbers and in possession of a field piece, from which they fired grape, as to make it too hazardous, and no probability of success.

"It was then the general sense of the officers under my command, whose opinion I severally took, to retreat to Sauteur, but that afterwards being found impracticable it was resolved to march to St. George's.

"This, Sir, is a detail of facts, as nearly as I can state to you, of this unfortunate business, but which, however to be lamented, will not, I trust, appear to you either to have proceeded from any want of vigilance, or neglect of duty, on my side.

"I have the honor to be, etc.,
"JOHN B. SCHAW,
"Major of the 68th Regt.,
"and Lieut.-Colonel.

"I have the honour herewith to send you a state of the 68th Regiment.

"Return of the 68th Regiment of Foot, of officers, non-commissioned officers, and rank and file on the 16th of October, 1795.

"Present, 10 officers, 17 serjeants, 15 drummers, 107 rank and file.
"Missing, 2 serjeants, 34 rank and file.
"Sick at Gouayrve, 29 rank and file.
"Total, 10 officers, 19 serjeants, 15 drummers, 170 rank and file.
(Sd.) "JOHN B. SCHAW, Major,
"68th Regt."

NOTE.—The above state as given by Lieutenant-Colonel Schaw is palpably not a state of the whole regiment, but only of the head-quarters at Goyave.

THE 68TH LIGHT INFANTRY (1785-1809)

In November there were only 296 non-commissioned officers and men in the regiment, and by 1st December this number had shrunk to 174.

1796 — The state of affairs in Grenada then became worse. On 29th February, 1796, the blockhouse at Labay was evacuated, and its garrison retreated to Sauteur, which was under the command of Major O'Meara, of the 68th; and then, having destroyed their artillery, they all fell back on St. George's.

However, on 25th March, Brigadier-General Nicholls defeated the brigands at St. Andrew's Bay, and inflicted a final defeat on them near Goyave on 18th June; but the now attenuated and sickly 68th does not appear to have taken a very prominent part in these final operations.

All the available rank and file were now drafted into the 63rd Regiment; the regiment, a mere skeleton, embarked in the end of July, and landed at Portsmouth on 23rd September, consisting, besides the commissioned officers, of only twenty-one non-commissioned officers and men. On 27th September a route was issued for the 68th to proceed to Chatham, but in a few days its destination was altered to Durham; accordingly, after several of the non-commissioned officers and men had been discharged, and all the officers had been granted leave of absence, the remainder, now only seven in number, under the command of a serjeant, by name Preston, commenced to march to the North of England. On 15th October, however, a fresh route was issued directing this party on arrival at Stamford to proceed to Leeds instead of to Durham.

On 24th November routes were issued for parties to proceed from Leeds to Derby and Shrewsbury for recruits; on 7th December recruiting parties were ordered to proceed to Cambridge, Huntingdon, Northampton, Oakham, Oxford, Bedford, Hertford, and Folkingham; and on the same day a route was issued for the 68th to march from Leeds to Colchester. On 10th December the party at Shrewsbury was ordered to move to Oxford.

About this time regimental chaplains disappeared from the Army List, and a chaplain-general was first appointed. Parochial clergy were then employed for troops at home, and chaplains were hired for any particular expedition when the army went abroad.

THE DURHAM LIGHT INFANTRY

An exception was made for garrisons and fortresses, and in 1798 there were fifteen such stations at home and thirteen abroad to which chaplains had been appointed.

1797 — On 4th February, 1797, the "parochial recruits" were ordered to march from Colchester Barracks to Chatham Barracks, and on 18th February orders were given for the 68th to march from Colchester on Friday, 24th February, for Liverpool, to arrive there on 16th March, and to embark for Ireland.

Returns compiled at Bedford on 1st March give a strength of 12 officers present (out of a nominal 48) and 84 non-commissioned officers and men; but the strength of the regiment on landing in Ireland on the 18th of the same month is returned as 202 of all ranks, including only 54 rank and file; this increase was probably accounted for by recruiting parties, the numbers of which were not previously known, rejoining head-quarters on the line of march.

Having landed at Dublin, the regiment proceeded to Malahide, where it remained for about a year. The muster-roll for the 23rd March gives the strength as 52 officers, 37 serjeants, 14 corporals, 11 drummers, and 103 privates. By September the number of privates had fallen to 35, and on 13th March, 1798, the regiment consisted of 52 officers, 33 serjeants, 8 corporals, 23 drummers, and 23 privates—an almost incomprehensible proportion of the different grades.

1798

In April the regiment was moved to Dublin, and the regimental records state "when it was necessary to call out the whole Dublin garrison against the rebels, the post of the 68th—then 36 firelocks—was guard to the advance guns."

The regiment only stayed in Dublin for a few months, and when the rebellion was suppressed was moved in September to Granard, and in October to Boyle, where it remained for a little over a year.

1799 — During the year 1799 efforts were made to obtain recruits, but with very little success, as in December the strength, excluding officers, was only about 120.

A return compiled in the office of the Muster-Master-General in Dublin, on 9th May, 1799, gives the establishment of the 68th as ten companies—

THE 68TH LIGHT INFANTRY (1785-1809)

Officers.	Staff-Serjts.	Serjts.	Corpls.	Drummers and Fifers.	Private Men.
55	2	51	50	22	550

and the annual charge for the regiment as £23,559 7s. 2d.

On 12th August, 1799, serjeants' sashes were ordered to be of crimson worsted, intermixed with the colours of the facings, and not plain crimson.

1800 On 10th February, 1800, the regiment was at Trim. On 24th February the use of hats for non-commissioned officers and men of infantry was abolished and caps were substituted. In the beginning of the year 1800 volunteering from the Irish Militia to the Regular Army took place, and the 68th received about 2,600 men.

The regiment then embarked at Warrenpoint, near Newry, landed at Liverpool, and marched to Sunderland, where it arrived at the end of March.

On 25th May the 68th was divided into two battalions. On 4th June orders were given for "both battalions to embark at Sunderland for the Downs"; and on 30th June a route was issued for "the detachment 68th, lately disembarked at Portsmouth from the 'Ariadne' and 'Active Endeavour' transports, to march to Dover to join the regiment"; but there is not any indication as to where this detachment came from.

The regimental records give Shields, not Sunderland, as the place of embarkation in June.

The 1st Battalion proceeded to Dover, the 2nd to Deal.

On 9th July routes were issued for both battalions to march to Swinley Common, near Bagshot, where a considerable force was being assembled; the 1st Battalion to march from Dover in four divisions, and to arrive at Swinley on 21st, 22nd, 23rd, and 24th July; the 2nd Battalion to march from Deal in four divisions, and to arrive at Swinley on 21st, 22nd, and 23rd July; but on 10th July the dates of arrival of the 2nd Battalion were altered to 19th, 21st, and 22nd July.

On 19th August a detachment 68th on the "Edminston" tender was ordered to disembark at Sheerness, and proceed to Chatham; but, as in the case of the detachment at Portsmouth in the previous June, there is again no intimation as to where it came from.

When the camp at Swinley was broken up about 1st September, the 1st Battalion marched to Canterbury, the 2nd to Ashford; a detachment at Wrotham (probably that from the "Edminston" tender) joined the 2nd division of the 2nd Battalion at Maidstone on 6th September, and proceeded with it to Ashford Barracks.

On 4th October, the light companies of the 68th were ordered to Guildford; on 7th November they were ordered to march, on the 10th inst., to Godalming, Monsel, and Milford; and on 14th November the light company of the 1st Battalion was ordered to march to Gosport, and the light company of the 2nd Battalion to remain at Godalming.

On 31st October, the remaining nine companies of the 1st Battalion were ordered to march from Canterbury as under, in four divisions:—

    3 companies to Guildford, Stoke, Shalford, and Catherine Hill.
    2 companies to Dorking, Capel, Wooten, and Abinger.
    2 companies to Godstone, Bletchingley, Ostend, and Lampsfield.
    2 companies to Sevenoaks, Seal, and Minehead.

And on 14th November they were ordered to march as under:—

    1st Division from Guildford to Gosport, to arrive 18th November.
    2nd Division from Dorking to Gosport, to arrive 19th November.
    3rd Division from Godstone to Gosport, to arrive 20th November.
    4th Division from Sevenoaks to Gosport, to arrive 21st November.

On the same date orders were issued for the 1st Battalion, on reaching Portsmouth, to embark; and for the 2nd Battalion at Ashford to march in four divisions to Portsmouth, to arrive 28th and 29th November, 1st and 2nd December.

On 20th November further orders for the 2nd Battalion were as under:—

    Light Infantry Company from Godalming to Portsmouth, to arrive 23rd November.
    1st Division from Sevenoaks to Portsmouth, to arrive 24th November.

THE 68TH LIGHT INFANTRY (1785-1809)

2nd Division from Sevenoaks to Portsmouth, to arrive 25th November.

3rd Division from Maidstone to Portsmouth, to arrive 26th November.

4th Division from Maidstone to Portsmouth, to arrive 27th November.

1801   The 1st Battalion, strength 45 officers, 44 serjeants, 21 drummers, and 795 rank and file, arrived at Martinique and remained there. Four companies of the 2nd Battalion arrived at Martinique on 24th January, and proceeded at once to Barbados; a further detachment, four companies, of the 2nd Battalion reached Martinique on 3rd February.

A return dated 1st March, 1801, gives the following distribution:

1st Battalion at Martinique.
2nd Battalion, 4 companies at St. Anne's Barracks, Barbados.
  ,,   ,,   4 companies at the Saints.
  ,,   ,,   2 companies missing.

These last two companies, strength, 7 officers, 5 serjeants, 3 drummers, and 171 rank and file, were on the "Devon," which parted off Madeira, and up to 1st March had not been heard of; however, they reached Martinique on 8th March in the "Bryan." Unfortunately, no mention is made as to when and where they were transhipped from the "Devon" to the "Bryan."

The total strength of the 2nd Battalion was 47 officers, 40 serjeants, 17 drummers, and 851 rank and file, making a total of 1,860 of all ranks in the regiment on its arrival in the West Indies.

Drafts for the regiment began arriving at once in the West Indies, the first one arriving as soon as 15th March; nine others, totalling altogether 238 men, arrived in 1801; one, in particular, is described as consisting of "deserters, recruits, and culprits."

On 1st April both battalions were at Martinique; on 1st May the first was at Martinique, the second at Dominica; on 1st August the first was at Barbados, the second still at Dominica.

The mortality in the regiment at this time was appalling; out of one hundred and twenty officers no less than thirty-four died in 1801.

THE DURHAM LIGHT INFANTRY

1802

On 9th April, 1802, the 8th West India Regiment, quartered at St. Ruperts, in the north-west of the island of Dominica, mutinied and murdered three of their officers and several other Europeans. This alarming piece of information reached Brigadier-General the Hon. A. J. Cochrane-Johnstone, who was governor of Dominica, as well as colonel of the 8th West India Regiment, by express at Roseau on the following day. The mutineers had also fired upon H.M.S. "Magnificent" lying at anchor in Prince Rupert's Bay.

Brigadier-General Cochrane-Johnstone assembled the following force, and sailed with it for Prince Rupert's on the 11th, arriving there the same evening:—

    (i.) 360 men of the 2/68th, then quartered at Morne Bruce under Majors G. Scott and A. M. K. Hamilton.
    (ii.) Two companies of Militia; and
    (iii.) A detachment of artillery.

On landing he was joined by—

    (i.) Major Gordon, of the 8th West India Regiment, with 50 men of that regiment;
    (ii.) Captain Puxley, with 80 men of the Royals (1st Foot), from the Saints;
    (iii.) The St. John's Company of Militia; and
    (iv.) A party of seamen and marines from H.M.'s ships.

At 1.30 p.m., on the 12th, Brigadier-General Cochrane-Johnstone marched into the garrison and found the mutineers drawn up.

Regimental records state that the mutineers gave a general salute, which was returned by the 68th.

The General then ordered the 8th West India Regiment to ground arms, which they were about to do, when a black serjeant told them to take them up again and to fire. The firing at once became general, and the 68th charged; the mutineers then dispersed and ran, and in half an hour's time Majors Scott and Hamilton carried both the outer and inner cabrits.

The mutineers, who numbered about 700, had over 100 killed and about 50 more died of their wounds; most of the remainder were taken prisoners.

THE 68TH LIGHT INFANTRY (1785-1809)

The victims of the mutiny were:—

Killed on April 9th: One captain, two subalterns, and the serjeant-major of the 8th West India Regiment; Mr. Laing, assistant commissary; Serjeant McKay, 68th (attached to the Quartermaster-General's department at Prince Rupert's Bay); Mrs. McKay (wife of Serjeant McKay); a bombardier, R.A.; one rank and file, 68th.

Wounded on 9th April: Two white serjeants, 8th West India Regiment; Mr. Barron, clerk of ordnance.

Killed on 12th April: One serjeant and three rank and file, 68th; one rank and file, Militia.

Wounded on 12th April: One serjeant and ten rank and file, 68th; three rank and file, Royals (1st Foot); two marines and one seaman, R.N.; five rank and file, Militia.

In the regimental records it is stated that an unfortunate incident followed the suppression of the mutiny; after the 68th had obtained possession of the fort all was quiet, but one man of the guard, which had been mounted in the fort, unaware that there was a quantity of ammunition under the guard bed, began to smoke, and was the cause of the ammunition being blown up and of several of the guard being severely injured, in some cases fatally. This incident is not mentioned by Brigadier-General Cochrane-Johnstone in his report on the suppression of the mutiny.

At the subsequent Court-Martial, of which Major G. Scott, 2/68th, was president, seven men of the 8th West India Regiment were sentenced to death; the sentence was confirmed and carried out.

A detachment of 100 men of the 68th remained at Prince Rupert's; in a short time, after the arrival of four companies of the 4th West India Regiment, the detachment was reduced to fifty men.

In this year several alterations in clothing were made; the coats of serjeants were ordered to be made of scarlet cloth, while those of corporals and private men were to be of red cloth; the coats of drummers and of fifers were to be deep green, faced with scarlet; a queue was to be worn by all non-commissioned officers and men except grenadiers, light infantry, and drummers, who were to wear their hair short at the hind part as well as at the top and sides; also non-commissioned officers of the guards and line were in future to be distinguished by chevrons instead of by epaulettes and shoulder-knots; the chevrons to be worn on the right arm;* (i.) the serjeant-major and quartermaster-serjeant to wear four, (ii.) other serjeants to wear three, and (iii.) corporals to wear two.

On 1st September, the 1st Battalion at Barbados had fallen to a strength of 14 officers, 23 serjeants, 14 drummers, and 570 rank and file; the 2nd Battalion at Dominica had fallen to 20 officers, 45 serjeants, 11 drummers, and 487 rank and file.

On 24th September, the 2nd Battalion was incorporated into the 1st at Barbados.

By the Peace of Amiens, 28th March, 1802, all the French Colonies acquired during the war were restored to France; accordingly St. Lucia and Martinique ceased to be British possessions; but war was again declared between Great Britain and France in May, 1803.

1803   In February of this year the standard for infantry was reduced to 5ft. 5in. An expedition against St. Lucia was at once organised, under Lieutenant-General W. Grinfield, who sailed from Carlisle Bay, Barbados, on 20th June, with the following force: Staff, 17; 2/1st Royal Scots, 487; 64th, 744; 68th, 765; 3rd West India Regiment, 744; R.A., artificers, etc., 422, making a total of 3,149, all ranks.

The exact detail of the 68th was 22 officers, 54 serjeants, 17 drummers, 672 rank and file, and two light 6-pr. guns.

The British landed on the evening of 21st June, and at 4 a.m. on the morning of the following day took the fortress Morne Fortuné; the British troops were formed into three columns with a reserve; the third column, under Colonel Shipley, Royal Engineers, was a feint only, and consisted of one company 68th, and one company 3rd West India Regiment; the reserve, under Brigadier-

---

* Non-commissioned officers of Light Infantry, and certain other distinguished corps, at a later period wore the chevrons on both arms; the date on which this practice was introduced into the 68th has not been ascertained.

THE 68TH LIGHT INFANTRY (1785-1809).

General T. Picton, consisted of the remainder of the 68th; the third column made a demonstration on the left, while the fortress was carried by the other two columns in half an hour. The Royal Scots and 64th bore the brunt of the work. The casualties for the whole force were 20 men killed, 9 officers and 109 men wounded; the 68th was not actively engaged, and had only one casualty, viz., one drummer missing.

St. Lucia thus was once again a British possession.

On 25th June, General Grinfield sailed for Tobago, leaving Brigadier-General Brereton with the 68th and three companies of the 3rd West India Regiment to garrison St. Lucia.

In June, 1803, the rank of "captain-lieutenant and captain" ceased to exist, as from this date companies were no longer held by field officers, and each company was commanded by a captain.

1805 The regiment, which in August, 1803, had a strength of 806 all ranks, remained in St. Lucia until February, 1805, when it was sent to St. Vincent; while in St. Lucia it suffered severely from sickness, losing over 500 men dead and 170 invalided to Europe during the last six months of 1804. Lieutenant J. C. Stewart, Private E. Farrell, and several others are reported to have died in St. Lucia from the effect of snake-bite.

On 1st April, 1805, the regiment was ordered to proceed from St. Vincent to Antigua, where it remained until June, 1806.

In the latter part of 1805, Jerome Bonaparte, with five sail of the line, visited the West India Islands, and landed troops in some of them; on his approach to Antigua the troops marched across the island to oppose a landing, but no attempt to land was made; the troops were then ordered by Brigadier-General Vandeleur to march back to their quarters, and although the distance was only twelve miles, five men are stated to have dropped dead on the road owing to the extreme heat.

1806 On 1st May, 1806, there were only 304 rank and file in the regiment, and during the month 188 of these were transferred to other regiments in the West Indies; many of them were culprits, who had not any choice in the matter, but others, who wished to volunteer, were allowed to do so, and were paid a bounty of three guineas each; they went to the 70th and the 96th.

THE DURHAM LIGHT INFANTRY

The regiment, now numbering only about 140 men, embarked for England on 9th and 12th June, whether on two ships or all on one is not recorded; the regimental records state that the regiment landed at Portsmouth on 16th August, but the routes issued about this date are rather confusing, and do not give any clear indication as to where head-quarters were; a detachment 68th on the "Carysfort" frigate was ordered on 16th August to disembark and march to Faversham, and on 19th August a detachment 68th at Bluetown, Sheerness (presumably the same detachment), was ordered to march to Dartford; on 23rd August two routes were issued to detachments 68th at Dartford and Hilsea; these parties were both ordered to march to Hatfield, and, having met there, to proceed to Durham, to reach Stamford on 11th September and Durham on 25th September. There is not any clue as to where the detachment on the "Carysfort" came from.

On 30th August a fresh route was issued for "the 68th to proceed to Leeds instead of to Durham, to arrive 23rd September." On 1st September the regiment was at Staines, with a strength of 142 non-commissioned officers and men. It is a peculiar coincidence that these orders, first to proceed to Durham, and then to proceed to Leeds instead of to Durham, were similar to those issued to the regiment on its return from the West Indies in September, 1796.

Recruiting in Leeds must have been singularly unsuccessful as John Green, author of "Vicissitudes of a Soldier's Life," who enlisted on 24th October, 1806, when he was only sixteen years of age, and only five feet one inch and a half in height, states that he was the first recruit to join the 68th since the regiment had returned from the West Indies.

On 27th November the regiment commenced to march to Ripon. Recruiting in the course of the next few months appears to have been more successful, and in August, 1807, drafts were received 1807 from Ireland as well as from the Durham and 2nd West York Militias. In September and October several parties of volunteers from various Militia regiments joined the regiment at Ripon from Stowmarket, where there was a depot for Militiamen volunteering into the line.

On 5th November, 1807, the 68th marched from Ripon through

OFFICER'S BREAST-PLATE.

Worn about 1796—1810.

THE 68TH LIGHT INFANTRY (1785-1809)

Boroughbridge to Wetherby, on 6th to Ferrybridge and Pontefract, and on 7th to Doncaster, where it remained for three months; on 1st December the strength was 465 non-commissioned officers and men.

1808   In February, 1808, the regiment marched to Malton, and seven days after its arrival there detached three companies to Pickering; on 15th March the regiment commenced to march to York, where it stayed until 14th July; it then proceeded to Doncaster, arriving on 18th. Early in August it marched to Hull, arriving on 16th, and was quartered in the ropery barracks at Wincolmlee.

The 68th was now made a light infantry regiment; the following is a copy of the letter notifying the fact.

"Horse Guards,
"14th September, 1808.

"Sir,—

"I have received H.R.H. the Commander-in-Chief's directions to acquaint you that His Majesty has signified His Royal Pleasure that the 68th Regiment shall be forthwith formed into a Light Infantry Corps, and that the clothing, arming and discipline of the Regiment shall be the same in all respects as the 43rd and 52nd Regiments.

"I have accordingly made application to the Board of Ordnance for the arms now in possession of the 68th Regiment to be exchanged as early as possible for those of the Light Infantry Pattern.

"I have the honor to be, etc.,
"H.C.,
"A.G.

"General Sir Thomas Trigge, K.B.,
    "etc.,   etc.,   etc.,
      "Colonel of the 68th Regiment."

N.B.—"H.C., A.G.," is Lieutenant-General Sir H. Calvert, K.C.B., Adjutant-General of the Forces, subsequently created a baronet.

THE DURHAM LIGHT INFANTRY

On 12th September a route was issued for the 68th to march in two divisions from the York district to Hithe [sic] Barracks, to reach Brigg on the first day of the march, and Hithe on 7th and 8th October; this route was varied on 4th October by the destination being altered to Brabourne Lees instead of Hithe.

The regiment accordingly crossed the Humber by Barton and proceeded on its march to the South of England.

On Saturday, 1st October, the regiment, now numbering 595 non-commissioned officers and men, reached Highgate where headquarters halted; five companies were sent on to Hampstead; on 3rd October the march was resumed; the regiment marched through London, crossing the Thames by Blackfriars bridge, and halted at Bromley where Sir Thomas Trigge, the Colonel, resided; Sir Thomas, dressed in uniform, met the 68th on its arrival at Bromley, and entertained all the officers at dinner. In due course Brabourne Lees was reached, and here the necessary alterations in clothing were made; here also the 68th and 85th were taught the light infantry exercise by Major-General Baron de Rottenburg. At Christmas the new clothing was ready. "It was completely altered, having instead of shoulder knots, wings, green tufts in the place of white ones, and bugles in front of our caps instead of plates. We also gave in our arms and accoutrements, and received in return japanned muskets with double sights, and a complete set of new accoutrements." (John Green.)

The buttons in use up to this period were flat and of white metal; the device on them was the number "68" above which was a crown, and below which there was an heraldic wreath.

While at Brabourne Lees, where the barracks were capable of containing three thousand men, various parties of recruits arrived from Lichfield and other places.

CHAPTER III.

THE 68TH LIGHT INFANTRY IN WALCHEREN AND THE PENINSULA.

1809
ON 24th June, 1809, a route was issued for the "68th at Brabourne Lees to march to Portsmouth, to arrive 4th July";
the urgency of this march was so great that halting on Sunday was not allowed, and the distances covered in a day were so great that when the regiment reached Gosport, where it encamped, nearly all the men were lame.

On Sunday, 16th July, the regiment embarked on H.M.S. "Cæsar," 80 guns, 2,003 tons, commanded by Captain Charles Richardson, but the "Cæsar" did not sail until the morning of the 26th; the return of the regiment compiled on the "Cæsar" at Spithead on 25th July gives the number of non-commissioned officers and men on board as 39 serjeants, 22 drummers, and 760 rank and file, total 821; the "Cæsar" arrived in the Downs on the evening of the following day, and on the morning of the 28th the whole fleet collected there sailed for the mouth of the Scheldt.

The fleet arrived off the island of Walcheren on the evening of the 29th and anchored; here the "Cæsar" met with two accidents, first of all during the night another vessel ran foul of her, fortunately without serious results, and on the following morning when sailing towards the northern part of the island she ran aground; fortunately, again in this instance, she was refloated with nothing worse than a severe straining.

The force embarked on the fleet for this expedition amounted to very nearly 40,000 officers and men, exclusive of officers and men of the Royal Navy; it was organised in two wings; Brigadier-General de Rottenburg's brigade of light troops was in the left wing and consisted of 68th (775), 1/71st (934), 85th (970), and two companies of 2/95th (200); these numbers refer to rank and file only, but, in the case of the 68th, the number does not agree with that quoted above, nor with that quoted by John Green.

The troops landed in the afternoon of the 30th, and on the following day there was a new distribution of the troops; two companies of the 68th were now in Major-General Graham's brigade in the right wing, the remaining eight companies of the regiment being still in the 5th (Brigadier-General de Rottenburg's) brigade, but in the centre. On 1st August both portions of the regiment were actively engaged; a small body of the enemy was dispersed by Brigadier-General de Rottenburg's brigade and pursued to the gates of Flushing by the 68th and 85th, both of which suffered severely for their rashness.

Then followed the siege of Flushing, which capitulated on 15th August.

A few days after this the 68th was moved to the island of South Beveland; fever and ague made their appearance, and in a short time about half the men were sick in hospital.

On 4th September the 68th left South Beveland and returned to the island of Walcheren, being quartered for about a week at Middleburg and then at Tervere.

The design upon Antwerp had now been abandoned, and the 68th remained as parts of the army of occupation in Walcheren, until the treaty of Schönbrunn was considered by the British Government to have caused further occupation to be of no advantage.

From the return of 1st October it appears that there were four women and one child present with the 68th at Walcheren.

During the operations in Walcheren, leading up to the capitulation of Flushing, the following casualties occurred in the 68th:—

Killed: 15 rank and file.
Wounded: 7 officers, and 43 rank and file.
Prisoners: 2 rank and file, and 1 bugler.

The officers wounded were:—Major R. Thompson, right arm amputated; Captain G. C. Crespigny, slightly; Captain M. Soden, slightly; Lieutenant J. Menzies, severely; Lieutenant J. Hinds, severely; Ensign J. Thomson, severely; Lieutenant W. Smyth, slightly.

THE 68TH LIGHT INFANTRY (1809-1814)

In addition to the above casualties in action, no less than 5 officers and 384 men are stated in the regimental records to have died from the Walcheren disease; the officers were:—Captain J. Somers, Lieutenant J. Nixon, Ensign J. Jenkins, Ensign A. Todd, Ensign W. Reid.

The number of deaths among the men is probably exaggerated; regimental returns between 25th August and 25th December only account for about 100 deaths; but as over 500 men were invalided home during the same period, it is probable that there were a large number of deaths among them, some, possibly, after some time had elapsed.

The regiment returned to England in December, was on the "Nile" in the Downs on Christmas Day, and shortly afterwards landed at Deal and marched to Brabourne Lees; the regimental records state that there were only fifteen rank and file present on this march, but the return compiled on the "Nile" gives the strength of the regiment as 141 non-commissioned officers and men, of whom 18 were sick and 11 were on command; there were on this date 637 non-commissioned officers and men, mostly invalids, at the depôt at Brabourne Lees. At this period there were recruiting parties at Durham, Ashford, Aberdeen, and also in Ireland.

1810   In March, 1810, the regiment proceeded from Brabourne Lees to Hythe, and in April was under orders to march to London to assist in quelling the disturbances arising out of the committal of Sir Francis Burdett, Bart., to the Tower; its services, however, were never required for this unpleasant duty.

By a general order of 20th October, trumpet, drum, and bugle majors were appointed with the rank and pay of serjeant; and stoppages from the pay of buglers, etc., hitherto made for remunerating bugle majors, etc., were ordered to be discontinued; also, in this year regimental schools were first established.

On 24th November a route was issued for "the 68th to proceed in two divisions—five companies in each division—to Littlehampton barracks and Bognor barracks, to arrive 4th and 5th December."

1811   John Green states that head-quarters and five companies were located at Littlehampton, three companies at Arundel, and only two at Bognor; this undoubtedly was the actual

43

distribution; the three companies at Arundel were under the command of Major and Brevet-Lieutenant-Colonel A. Hinuber, and made their mark there by a most regrettable proceeding on the night of Sunday, 3rd February, 1811; it appears that some of the townspeople had insulted some of the officers on several occasions, so on this particular Sunday night a captain, two subalterns, a corporal, and several privates sallied forth armed with thick sticks and administered some severe punishment to several of the townsmen; this highly improper proceeding was followed by courts-martial, civil proceedings, and much unpleasantness. The regiment was at once moved to Lewes, marching by way of Shoreham and Brighton; while at Lewes great efforts were made in all directions to obtain recruits, with the result that by the end of May the regiment was about 850 strong. Two routes issued at this time are interesting; the first, dated 24th April, 1811, orders "a party of invalids from the 68th, from Sussex, to proceed to the York Hospital, Chelsea; a cart to be hired for those unable to walk"; the second, dated 8th May, 1811, orders "one captain and twenty-four men, 68th, to proceed from Okehampton to Lewes; to avoid all places where Local Militia may be assembled for permanent duty."

On 29th May a route was issued for the 68th to march in two divisions to Portsmouth, to arrive 6th and 7th June. The regiment accordingly marched to Portsmouth, and immediately embarked upon the "Melpomene" for conveyance to Lisbon; the depot remained at Lewes.* The "Melpomene" did not actually sail from Portsmouth until 18th June, and reached Lisbon on the 27th, the voyage having been accomplished with a most favourable wind, and without any untoward incident.

A noticeable point is that the 68th did not take its colours to the Peninsula.

The 68th landed at Lisbon on 28th June, 1811, and marched

---

* Both Colonel Gordon and John Green state that the name of the ship was the "Amphitrite," but in the monthly return for June, 1811, now in the Public Record Office in London, it is distinctly stated that the return was compiled on the 25th of the month at sea on board the "Melpomene."

THE 68TH LIGHT INFANTRY (1809-1814)

to the St. Domingo convent where it stayed for seven days; on 5th July the regiment started in boats to proceed up the Tagus, but owing to various delays did not reach Valada until the following morning; it then landed and marched to Santarem; continuing its march it reached Abrantes on the 10th, Portalegre on the 15th, and Arronches on the 17th, returning to Portalegre on the 20th. On 19th July the 68th was posted to the 1st Brigade, 7th Division, which had been about thirty miles in advance at Campo Mayor, and joined it in the course of a day or two on its arrival at Portalegre; the next move was to Niza, which was reached on 23rd, and where a halt was made until the 31st. Ensign Forbes died of disease at Niza on 6th August. The 7th Division at this time was commanded by Major-General W. Houston, and consisted of two British brigades and Coleman's Portuguese brigade; the 1st Brigade under Major-General Sontag, was composed of the 51st, 68th, 85th and the Chasseurs Britanniques, the 2nd, under C. Von Alten, was composed of the 1st and 2nd light battalions (King's German Legion) and the Brunswick Oels; the Portuguese brigade composed of the 7th and 19th Line, and the 2nd Caçadores.

The return of the 68th at Niza, on 25th July, gives the strength of the regiment as 39 officers and 769 non-commissioned officers and men; a return of the same date at Lewes gives the strength of the depot as 14 officers and 84 non-commissioned officers and men. About 1st August Major-General Houston was invalided home, and Major-General Sontag assumed temporary command of the 7th Division.

On 31st July the Division left Niza, and marching by way of Castello Branco and Penamacor reached Villar Maior on 10th August, and halted there until the 17th September.

The return, of 15th September, 1811, of Wellington's army on the Beira frontier gives the strength of the British brigades of the 7th Division as under:

THE DURHAM LIGHT INFANTRY

Officer commanding 7th Division, Major-General Sontag.

Sontag's Brigade	51st Foot	309
	68th Foot	479
	85th Foot (5 Companies)	166
	Chasseurs Britanniques	671
Von Alten's Brigade	1st Light Battalion, King's German Legion	602
	2nd ,, ,, ,, ,, ,,	516
	Brunswick Oels (9 companies)	536
	Total	3,279

Included in the above figures are 161 officers. In addition to the above number the 68th had a very large number of men sick in hospital, and absent from the regiment from various causes.

In consequence of some hostile movements of the enemy the 7th Division then crossed the frontier into Spain, but was compelled to retire, and on 27th September the 68th experienced a little skirmishing with the French near Sabugal, after which the 7th Division on the 30th of the same month went into quarters at Penamacor, and remained there until 19th November.

On 3rd October the 85th was ordered home to recruit.

In October Major-General Sontag was invalided and C. Von Alten assumed temporary command of the 7th Division; the 1st Brigade was without a general officer commanding until Major-General H. de Bernewitz was appointed to the command on 23rd December; Colonel Halkett, 2nd Light Battalion King's German Legion, assumed temporary command of the 2nd Brigade. The return of the 68th at Penamacor, on 25th October, gives the strength of the regiment as 39 officers and 752 non-commissioned officers and men, but this is not by any means a true indication of the effective strength of the regiment in the field, as at this time, besides other absentees, there were nearly 250 men sick. At this time the depôt had left Lewes and was at Silverhill.

On 8th October a general order directed that the clothing of buglers was in future to be of the same colour as that worn by serjeants and their regiments, but distinguished by the lace.

On 11th November the depôt was ordered to march from Silver-

THE 68TH LIGHT INFANTRY (1809-1814)

hill Barracks to Brabourne Lees, where it stayed for over two years.

On 19th November the 68th was moved back to Pedrogos, about two leagues from Penamacor, on the road to Castello Branco, and remained there until 10th January, 1812; on 26th and 27th December part of the army in front was sharply engaged, but the 68th does not appear to have taken any part in these actions; while at Pedrogos there was a great deal of sickness.

1812 — On 10th January, 1812, the 68th returned to Penamacor and rejoined the 7th Division, which marched for the neighbourhood of Ciudad Rodrigo, and reaching Peneparda on 14th January, halted there, guarding the passes of the Sierra de Gata, and covering the besieging army; a few days after the storming of Ciudad Rodrigo, on the night of the 19th January, the 7th Division returned to Portugal, and on 4th February the 68th was once more at Pedrogos, where it stayed until the 20th.

The march towards Badajoz now began; on 28th February the 68th crossed the Tagus at Villa Velha, reached Estremoz on 4th March, and Borba on the next day; halted there for ten days, then crossing the river Guadiana on the 16th, entered Spain, and moved on to Lorena; the 7th Division was included in the force under Lieutenant-General Sir T. Graham, which covered the siege of Badajoz from Lorena to Albuera; so, again, as in the case of the storming of Ciudad Rodrigo, the 68th had the misfortune of not being actively engaged.

On 6th April, the actual night of the storming of Badajoz, the 68th was at Albuera, and remained there until the 9th, when the return journey to Portugal was commenced; Castello Branco was reached on 21st April, and St. Estevan on the 25th, but the regiment returned to Castello Branco on 30th April and remained there until 2nd June. Paymaster J. Wood died at Lisbon on 31st March, and Brevet-Major M. Soden died of disease at Elvas on 21st April.

On 2nd May Major-General C. Von Alten was transferred to the Light Division, and Major-General John Hope was given the command of the 7th, which he held until the 23rd of the following September.

On 17th May, 1812, the 68th was inspected by Major-General Henry de Bernewitz, commanding 1st Brigade, 7th Division Infantry,

THE DURHAM LIGHT INFANTRY

at Castello Branco; the following extracts from the report are worthy of notice.

Total in Portugal, 34 officers, 34 serjeants, 29 corporals, 18 buglers, and 527 privates.

CLASSIFICATION OF N.C.O.'S AND MEN.

Height. Ft. Ins.	Serjts.	Corpls.	Buglers.	Privates.
6	1	2	0	1
5 11	7	3	0	30
5 10	8	3	0	15
5 9	6	4	2	52
5 8	7	9	1	113
5 7	2	4	2	142
5 6	3	4	9	148
5 5	0	0	4	26
	34	29	18	527

Nationality.	Serjts.	Corpls.	Buglers.	Privates.
English	10	10	13	219
Scotch	9	9	0	91
Irish	15	10	5	217
	34	29	18	527

Age.	Serjts.	Corpls.	Buglers.	Privates.
40 years	2	1	0	9
35 ,,	2	1	0	7
30 ,,	10	5	1	139
25 ,,	20	21	1	189
20 ,,	0	1	8	133
18 ,,	0	0	8	48
Under 18	0	0	0	2
	34	29	18	527

THE 68TH LIGHT INFANTRY (1809-1814)

Service.	Serjts.	Corpls.	Buglers.	Privates.
30 years	1	0	0	0
25 ,,	2	0	0	0
18 ,,	3	1	0	6
14 ,,	11	0	3	29
12 ,,	4	0	1	6
8 ,,	0	0	0	1
5 ,,	4	9	7	112
4 ,,	5	5	5	124
3 ,,	1	10	2	84
2 ,,	0	0	0	65
1 ,,	1	3	0	52
Under 1 year	2	1	0	48
	34	29	18	527

The Major-General's remarks for this year are unfortunately, in some instances, very uncomplimentary; a few of his observations are here quoted:

"No striking unanimity between the commanding officer and the officers."

"Only one man per company in the band according to regulation."

"The privates not so clean or healthy as could be wished; not well set up; several serious excesses have been committed by the men since they have been in this country."

"The junior officers do not possess that activity and intelligence which is required of a light infantry officer."

"The regiment has no colours in the country."

At the time of this report there were recruiting parties at Dublin, Armagh, Durham, Knaresborough, Ipswich, and Southampton.

Up to the present time the 68th had been singularly unfortunate in its experiences of active service; the regiment as a collective body, as well as the individuals composing it, had invariably fought gallantly and maintained the best traditions of British courage and endurance, but it had had the bad luck to have taken part in several unsuccessful operations, such as the third descent on the coast of France in 1758, and the expedition to Walcheren in 1809; and, on the other hand, when it had taken part in more brilliant undertakings, such as the capture of St. Lucia, in 1803, and the sieges of Ciudad Rodrigo and Badajoz in 1812, its lot had been to be in reserve, or to form part of the covering force; now, however, this spell was broken, and the 68th was about to take a prominent part in a series of brilliant military events.

On 2nd June the 7th Division marched from Castello Branco in the direction of Salamanca, arriving there on the 17th; while on this march, on the 10th, when close to Ciudad Rodrigo, the Earl of Wellington made a close inspection of the 7th Division, three regiments of cavalry, and a brigade of flying artillery; this parade was a very long one and was of a purely ceremonial nature.

On the 16th contact with the enemy took place, but after a little skirmishing the French moved away.

On 20th June Marmont took up a position about six miles from Salamanca, and the British, with the exception of the 6th Division, which was engaged in the siege of the forts of Salamanca, occupied some rising ground, known as the heights of Villares, facing the French; just before dusk the 68th was ordered to descend the hill and take possession of the village of Moresco, which was on the enemy's left flank; owing to the numerically weak state of the regiment, about seventy of the Brunswick Oels were sent in support; the 68th accordingly advanced and occupied the village from which the French had retreated, but the latter soon returned in force and were twice driven back; as it was now quite dark the regiment received orders from Lieutenant-General Graham to retreat to the top of the hill; the retreat was conducted in good order; in this engagement Captain J. Hawkins was severely wounded, and Captain W. Mackay received no less than twenty-two bayonet wounds, but he recovered and continued to serve; Lieutenant G. Macdonald and Private Joseph Baker were taken prisoners; no operations took place on the following day, and in the evening the 68th was relieved by a Portuguese brigade, and retired about a mile to the rear; on the 22nd the French advanced to attack the heights of Villares above Moresco, and the 68th was again in action; the 7th Division drove

THE 68TH LIGHT INFANTRY (1809-1814)

off the French, who eventually gave up the attempt to capture that important position; the casualties among the non-commissioned officers and men of the 68th on the heights of Villares, 20th to 22nd June (inclusive), were two serjeants and four rank and file killed, two serjeants, one bugler and twenty-eight rank and file wounded, and two privates taken prisoners; nearly all these casualties took place on the 20th. Lieutenant G. Macdonald, who had been wounded, was released on the 12th of the following September, but he is not recorded in regimental returns as having rejoined his regiment until May, 1813. With reference to the second action the Earl of Wellington wrote in his despatches, 25th—30th June, 1812, "I therefore requested Lieutenant-General Sir T. Graham to attack them (the French) in that post on the 22nd with the troops on the right, which he did with those of the 7th Division, which were the reserve of the right, under the command of Major-General Hope and Major-General de Bernewitz. The enemy were driven from the ground immediately with considerable loss; our troops conducted themselves remarkably well in this affair; which took place in the view of every man of both armies."

The forts of Salamanca having surrendered to the 6th Division on 27th June, the army moved on the 29th; the 68th arrived at Medina del Campo on 2nd July, and remained there until the 12th.

On the 12th the 7th Division moved to Nava del Rey, and after two or three days commenced to march back to Salamanca, arriving there on the 21st; during a part of this march the allies and the French were marching, in sight of each other, in two parallel lines not more than one mile apart.

Early on the morning of the 22nd July the 68th had a sharp skirmish with the French, who, after trying to drive in the British piquets, retired; Brevet-Major Miller and several privates were wounded; Major Miller's wounds were so severe that he subsequently died from them; after this the 68th remained on its ground until relieved in the afternoon, about 3 p.m., by the 95th, when it rejoined the 7th Division; about this hour the action became general; in the first instance the 7th Division was in reserve in the centre, but about 4.30 p.m. it was ordered to advance and was soon engaged; after the issue had remained doubtful for sometime the French gave way in all directions and were beaten with great loss; the casualties in the 68th on this day, at the memorable battle of Salamanca, were, besides Major Miller mortally wounded, Lieutenant F. Finucane killed, Captain W. North slightly wounded, Serjeant Dunn and two rank and file killed, and fourteen rank and file wounded. On the following morning the allies started in pursuit of the French, and continuing to march, passed Segovia on 7th August, and reached Madrid on the 12th; the Earl of Wellington entered the city at the head of the 7th Division, and the 68th was the first British infantry regiment to enter Madrid.

On the following night the 68th took part in the attack on the fort El Retiro, which was girt with a triple wall; the main body of the regiment was allotted the task of breaking in the large outer gates. This was accomplished with hatchets, and by midnight the British were in possession of the outer works, one man of the 68th being wounded. Early next morning an attack on the fort itself was commenced, and the Earl of Wellington came to superintend the operations; about 10 a.m., when everything was ready for a general storm, the French surrendered; about 2,000 prisoners, 200 pieces of cannon, and a large amount of stores of all sorts were taken; every man of the 68th was served out with a pair of French shoes.

On 19th August the regiment marched for El Escurial, 32 miles north-west of Madrid, arrived there the following day, and halted there until 1st September, when the Earl of Wellington, having left two divisions for the protection of Madrid, set off with the rest of the army northwards; Valladolid was reached on 7th September, and after a halt of three days, as the French retired, the march was continued, and Burgos was reached on the 18th; the siege of Burgos was begun by the 1st Division and after two or three days the 7th Division was moved round the city and encamped near Olmos, covering the siege of Burgos; on 14th October the 68th and 51st left Olmos and advanced to Upper and Lower Monasterio, where they constructed a breastwork; on 19th October the 68th returned to the heights above Olmos, where on the following day the 7th Division had a brisk skirmish with the enemy; the French had advanced to attack but were eventually driven back, the guns of the 5th Division

THE 68TH LIGHT INFANTRY (1809-1814)

assisting in repulsing them; six men of the 68th were reported wounded in this affair.

Major-General John Hope having to give up the command of the 7th Division on 23rd November, owing to his health, the division was without a G.O.C. until the 25th October, when George, 9th Earl of Dalhousie, was appointed to the command.

The retreat from Burgos was now begun; on 26th October the 68th was at Valladolid, where there was a halt for two days, and on the 29th was at Tordesillas, where there was a halt for eight days; then, in consequence of the attempts of the French to outflank the British, the retreat was continued; on 17th November, when near Juan Manoz, the 68th and 51st were, after much skirmishing, subjected to a severe cannonading, but did not suffer any loss; at night the regiment, drenched to the skin and famished, was on outpost duty.

When near Ciudad Rodrigo the French, having failed to intercept the retreat of the British, gave up the attempt; the retreat was then continued, and on 3rd December the 68th reached the neighbourhood of Santo Martinho, and went into winter quarters.

Thus ended the campaign of 1812.

On 28th November the 1st Battalion 6th Foot, from England, was added to Colonel Halkett's brigade, and the 1st Battalion 82nd Foot was transferred from the 4th Division to Major-General de Bernewitz's brigade. On 6th December Major-General E. Barnes assumed command of Colonel Halkett's brigade; at the same time the 3rd Provisional Battalion, consisting of the second battalions of the 24th and 58th, was added to it, and the two light battalions of the King's German Legion were transferred from it to the 1st Division; the Portuguese brigade in the 7th Division remained unaltered.

The retreat from Burgos had the most disastrous effect on the health of the troops as at the end of November the 68th had no less than 247 men sick; this number, no doubt, was rapidly reduced by rest in cantonments.

Between 25th December, 1811, and 25th December, 1812, 122 men of the regiment died in the Peninsula.

1813   Although the regiment was at rest from 4th December, 1812, to 29th January, 1813, it would appear that it was not actually at Santo Martinho but about two leagues distant at Cassios de Baxo; but on 31st January it was moved to Santo Martinho and remained there until the middle of May.

During this winter two drafts arrived from the depot, but in spite of great efforts sufficient recruits could not be obtained, and the actual strength of the regiment, throughout the Peninsular War was considerably less than the establishment; in February, 1813, it was notified in General Orders that fifty boys were allowed to be enlisted in each regiment of infantry.

On 9th February, 1813, Major-General H. de Bernewitz inspected the 68th at Santo Martinho.

The totals in the Peninsula were:—38 officers, 31 serjeants, 32 corporals, 19 buglers, and 525 privates.

There were also 23 women, legally married, and 8 children under 10 years of age (3 boys and 5 girls).

It is gratifying to notice that Major-General de Bernewitz's remarks are a very pleasant contrast to his remarks of the previous year; he states,

"The regiment is particularly well drilled in the light manœuvres.

"The privates are much improved in health, cleanliness, and conduct.

"The buglemen are acquainted with the sounds used by light infantry."

There are also the same remarks about the band, and the colours, as were made in May, 1812.

Quartermaster J. Wilson died at Santo Martinho on 23rd March. On 14th May, the 7th Division, in Sir Thomas Graham's column, left Santo Martinho and commenced its long march towards the Pyrenees; there was a five days' halt near Miranda; a return of the regiment compiled there on 25th May gives the strength as 38 officers, and 594 non-commissioned officers and men; of the non-commissioned officers and men 253 were English, 64 were Scotch, and 277 were Irish; at this time the depot was still at Brabourne Lees, but there were recruiting parties at Dublin, Armagh, and Durham.

During this halt the division was reviewed on different days by the Earl of Dalhousie and Sir Thomas Graham. Major-General de Bernewitz gave up the command of the 1st Brigade, 7th Division,

THE 68TH LIGHT INFANTRY (1809-1814)

in April, and Major-General W. Inglis was appointed in his place on 21st May, but the latter did not actually assume command until after the battle of Vittoria, when Colonel Grant of the 82nd had been in temporary charge. On the 2nd or 3rd June (accounts differ as to the exact day) the Marquis of Wellington reviewed the 6th and 7th Divisions while on the march between Toro and Tordesillas; the troops were drawn up in two lines, the 6th Division in the first line, the 7th in the second; after a general salute and an advance in line, the different regiments marched past his lordship in column.

Owing to the necessities of the situation this march was conducted with great rapidity; and the troops suffered severely from lack of halts and from want of food; the Ebro was crossed on 16th June, and on the 20th the army encamped within about sixteen miles of Vittoria.

The battle of Vittoria was fought on the following day. Sir Rowland Hill commanded the column on the right, Sir Thomas Graham the column on the left, and the Marquis of Wellington himself directed the movements of the 3rd, 4th, 7th and Light Divisions in the centre; at 1 p.m. the 3rd and 7th Divisions crossed the river Zadora, the 7th following the 3rd and forming up on its right; the light and 4th Divisions were further to the right. A general advance then took place, and John Green states, "I don't know that I ever saw the 68th regiment march better in line than they did into the battle of Vittoria; every man was as steady as possible."

The French, who were driven back, reached their last defence one mile in front of Vittoria at 6 p.m.; as is well known they were soon forced from this position, were defeated all along the line, and retreated in the greatest confusion.

After the battle the 7th Division encamped about two miles beyond Vittoria, towards Pamplona.

The actual numbers of the 68th in action on this day were:— 3 field officers, 4 captains, 17 subalterns, and 1 staff officer; 15 serjeants, 13 buglers, and 340 rank and file. Total—393 all ranks.

The casualties were:—Killed: Captain H. Anderson, Lieutenant J. H. Perwin, 2 serjeants, and 21 rank and file. Wounded: Lieutenant-Colonel W. Johnston (severely), Captain W. Gough (severely), Captain J. Reed (slightly), Lieutenant S. Sorlie (slightly), Lieutenant H. Mackay (slightly), Ensign R. Ball (severely), Ensign J. Fowke (severely), Ensign D. J. Skene (slightly), Ensign S. W. L. Stretton (severely), Lieutenant and Adjutant J. Hinds (severely), 3 serjeants (including Serjeant-Major Kearns) and 87 rank and file.

By a general order of 6th July, 1813, the serjeant-majors' pay was raised to three shillings a day, and by the same order it was laid down that one serjeant was to be selected from each company, to be termed "Colour-Serjeant," and to receive two shillings and fourpence a day.

In the afternoon of 22nd June, the 7th Division followed the French in their retreat towards Pamplona, and proceeding in due course to the Pyrenees occupied a chain of mountains running by Echalar to Vera; from 8th to 25th July the 68th was in the neighbourhood of Maya and Zagaramurdi.

In consequence of the plundering of Joseph Bonaparte's baggage and treasure by the British after the battle of Vittoria, all the men were searched, and the money found on them was taken away; according to John Green, the amount recovered from the 68th averaged over thirty-two pounds per man.

On 25th July, Marshal Soult having attacked Sir Rowland Hill's division in great force, Major-General Barnes's brigade was detached from the 7th Division and sent to Sir Rowland Hill's assistance; this brigade was restored to the 7th Division in the course of two or three days.

On 26th July owing to the French having succeeded in turning the right of the British, the 7th Division abandoned Echalar and retired; it continued to retreat for the following three days, so as to still cover the siege of San Sebastian and the blockade of Pamplona, but on the morning of the 30th July, when in the neighbourhood of Pamplona, again advanced and greatly distinguished itself that day at the battle of Ostiz (called by Sir W. Napier the second battle of Sauroren); Major-General Inglis was ordered by the Earl of Dalhousie to possess himself of the crest of a high mountain occupied by the enemy, commanding the main road which passed between that mountain and their main body; according to

THE 68TH LIGHT INFANTRY (1809-1814)

their own report the strength of the enemy amounted to 2,000 men, whilst, from the occupation of a part of his force elsewhere, the force which Major-General Inglis could employ did not exceed 445 bayonets; in spite of this inequality of numbers the enemy's position was carried by storm, and they themselves were driven down the opposite side of the hill by which the right of the French Army was turned.

Concerning this affair, Sir W. Napier says:—"General Inglis, advancing with only 500 men of the 7th Division, broke at one shock two French regiments."

The total loss of the 1st Brigade on this day was 145 killed and wounded; the killed included Major G. C. Crespigny; the wounded included Captain Irvine, Lieutenant Leith, and Ensign O'Connell, who lost an arm; one man of the 68th, who was taken prisoner, had been placed as sentry on an advanced post before daylight, and unfortunately had not been withdrawn in time.

Lieutenant-Colonel Hawkins himself led the skirmishing party, every officer of which, except himself, was killed or wounded; Major-General Inglis's horse was shot under him.

On the following day the 7th Division was again engaged at the combat of Doña Maria; the 1st Brigade lost 1 officer and 116 men killed and wounded. Volunteer Browning, of the 68th, was wounded on this day.

On these two days the 68th lost one serjeant and seven men killed, and forty-one wounded; seven of the latter died from their wounds in the course of the next few days.

The next day the 7th Division moved off in pursuit, and encamped near Vera.

On 2nd August the division was again engaged near Echalar, and the vigorous attack of Major-General Barnes's brigade elicited from the Marquis of Wellington the statement that it was "the most gallant, the finest thing he ever witnessed."

In the regimental records it is stated that "a great proportion of the 68th formed the advanced guard of General Barnes's brigade in the action above alluded to."

On this day the principal attack was made by the 2nd Division; Major-General Inglis's brigade was on the right of that division, and was detailed to keep the enemy in play until the arrival of Sir William Stewart.

On 3rd August the division encamped on the same ground that it was on on 25th July, and remained there until 30th July, when the 1st Brigade marched to the neighbourhood of Lazaca; a draft of sixteen men from England joined this day.

In divisional orders of 3rd August, Lieutenant-General the Earl of Dalhousie highly commended the gallant conduct of the 1st Brigade under Major-General Inglis on 30th July, and also that of the 2nd Brigade under Major-General Barnes on 2nd August.

On 31st August Major-General Inglis received orders to move to the support of the 9th Portuguese Brigade in Sir G. Lowry-Cole's division, which was posted in a strong position between Lazaca and the convent of St. Antonio, but finding that position untenable from the superior numbers of the enemy who were getting round his left flank, he ordered the Portuguese to take up another position in its rear, and the 51st to form across an isthmus at the foot of the new position; as soon as the 51st was in its place, he ordered the 82nd and Chasseurs Britanniques to retire behind the 51st; these movements were alternately covered by the 68th under Brevet-Lieutenant-Colonel Hawkins, and the light companies of the brigade under Lieutenant-Colonel de Hautois; these two corps, fighting face to face with vastly superior numbers, with difficulty effected the movement behind the 51st; in this severe engagement, known as the combat of Vera, Major-General Inglis's brigade lost 22 officers and 271 men killed and wounded; in the 68th Lieutenant D. J. Skene was severely and Ensign J. Gibson slightly wounded, one serjeant and eight men were killed, and three serjeants and fifty-eight men were wounded. Of the latter, one serjeant and five men died in the course of a day or two. John Green was on this day severely wounded and incapacitated from further service in the Peninsular War. Also, Major-General Inglis had again a horse shot under him.

The Marquis of Wellington, in a despatch of 2nd September referring to this action, stated, " Major-General Inglis and the regiments of his brigade of the seventh division conducted themselves remarkably well. The 51st regiment, under Colonel Mitchell, and

THE 68TH LIGHT INFANTRY (1809-1814)

the 68th, under Lieutenant-Colonel Hawkins, covered the change of position by the troops from the heights, between the Bidassoa and Lazaca, to those of San Antonio; and these two corps were distinguished."

After this the brigade remained in, or in the neighbourhood of, Echalar until 7th October, when it advanced, and for the first time the piquets of the 68th were in France, then in the course of a few days, it returned to Echalar where it remained until in due course it again advanced and performed a brilliant part at the battle of Nivelle on 10th November.

Between the 25th September and 25th October twelve men of the 68th died from wounds, received probably on 31st August.

By this time the regimental depot had moved from Brabourne Lees to Hythe.

The Earl of Dalhousie went home early in October, and Major-General Le Cor, commanding the Portuguese brigade, was in temporary charge of the 7th Division until 18th November, when Major-General G. T. Walker was appointed to command in the Earl of Dalhousie's absence.

On 10th November the Marquis of Wellington attacked in four columns; Sir Rowland Hill was on the right with the 2nd and 6th divisions; Marshal Beresford came next with the 3rd, 4th, and 7th Divisions; Major-General C. Von Alten came next with the Light Division; and Sir John Hope was on the left with the 1st and 5th Divisions.

Marshal Beresford's objectives, in the first instance, were the redoubts in front of the village Sarre, and Sarre itself.

Before daybreak the 7th Division marched to the *embouchere* of the Puerto d'Echalar, and remained in column until the enemy advanced; the 68th then took possession of the left hand redoubt, which the enemy, observing that their flanks were turned, had soon evacuated. Shortly after this, Major-General Inglis's brigade advanced, and, moving through the village of Sarre, proceeded to the attack of the heights beyond that village, carrying everything before it. On arriving in front of the village of St. Pie, which by this time was in the possession of the 3rd Division, Major-General Inglis received orders from Marshal Beresford to cross the Nivelle by a wooden bridge on his left, and to attack the heights above that village, which were occupied by the enemy in great strength.

Major-General Inglis reported that "the 68th made the attack with its usual vivacity, supported by the 51st, and carried the heights after a severe struggle." He also added that it was justice to state that these two regiments were gallantly supported by the 82nd, and the Chasseurs Britanniques, without whose assistance they could neither have succeeded nor maintained themselves.

Night ended the contest; the two armies then bivouacked convenient to each other, but Marshal Soult withdrew his forces before daylight on the following morning.

In this battle the 68th lost Captain H. B. Irvine, Lieutenant R. Stopford, one serjeant (Luke Deery), and five privates (B. Larkin, W. Jefferies, W. Kelly, T. Minahan, and R. Bargate), killed. The wounded were: Captain N. Gledstanes (severely), Captain H. M. Archdale (slightly), Lieutenant R. Clarke (severely, leg amputated), Lieutenant W. Mendham (severely), Ensign J. Gibson (slightly), Ensign T. Browning (severely), four serjeants, two buglers, and twenty-six rank and file; nine of the last mentioned died from their wounds. On this day Major-General Inglis received a severe contusion on the foot by a musket ball.

Referring to the battle of Nivelle Sir W. Napier states that the Marquis of Wellington "drove Maransin from his new position after a hard struggle, in which General Inglis was wounded, and the 51st and 68th Regiments were handled very roughly."

On the following day the Marquis of Wellington again threatened the enemy with Beresford's and Hill's columns, but Marshal Soult shifted his ground and fell back towards Bayonne.

The 68th then encamped near St. Barbe; on 25th November it was at D'Arbonne, where it remained until 12th December.

On the 25th December the 68th was at Ustaritz, the nominal strength being 32 officers and 478 non-commissioned officers and men, but a considerable number of men were non-effective from sickness.

On 8th January, 1814, the regiment arrived at Halso, and remained there until 12th February.

THE 68TH LIGHT INFANTRY (1809-1814)

1814   The state of the 7th Division on 16th January, 1814, is quoted in "Wellington's supplementary despatches" as under.

G.O.C., MAJOR-GENERAL G. T. WALKER.

                                                                                Effective Rank and File.

....	6th Foot, 1st Battalion	709
	24th, 2nd Battalion } 3rd Prov. Battalion ...	271
	58th, 2nd Battalion }	184
	9 companies Brunswick Oels	250
Major-General W. Inglis.	51st Foot	268
	68th Foot	238
	82nd Foot	489
	Chasseurs Britanniques	288
Colonel Doyle.	7th Portuguese	684
	19th Portuguese	854
	2nd Caçadores	374

                Sick, absent of the division 1707

                Total of the division (all ranks) 7756

On 12th and 13th February the 68th was on outpost duty on the river Adour, covering the siege of Bayonne, and was in contact with the French; there was much firing especially at night, but no casualties are reported.

On 23rd February, Marshal Beresford led the 3rd and 7th Divisions; the enemy's outposts were attacked and driven through the village of Oeyreguave; the 68th lost on this day Captain Leith, and one man killed; Lieut. H. Stapylton was mortally wounded and died three days later; one serjeant and seven men were wounded.

On 24th February Marshal Beresford kept Foy in check at Peyrehorade with the 7th Division; and on the 27th the battle of Orthes was fought at which Major-General Inglis's brigade had a considerable share of the fighting; the Major-General's horse was wounded; the casualties in the 68th were Ensign T. Sheddon severely wounded, three men killed, twenty-seven men wounded, and Adjutant Hinds's horse killed. From 1st to 8th March the 68th were at St. Sever, which was at that time the head-quarters of the army.

Marshal Beresford was then detached with the 4th and 7th Divisions and Vivian's cavalry against Bordeaux; by this time the Earl of Dalhousie had once more assumed command of the 7th Division in the place of Major-General Walker who had been wounded at Orthes.

On reaching Langon, Marshal Beresford left the Earl of Dalhousie with the bulk of the force, and pushing on with his cavalry entered Bordeaux.

On 11th March, near Langon, Major Winnett of the 68th crossed the river Garonne at night with a strong piquet in boats, but as the enemy became aware of his presence, he retired again.

On 21st March the 68th entered Bordeaux and remained there until the 26th when it returned to Langon.

On 28th March the 68th was engaged in driving back a party of the enemy on the right bank of the Garonne, the enemy were pursued through the village of La Réole, but without effect; one man of the regiment was wounded.

On 4th April the enemy were driven through Marmande; the next day the regiment returned to La Réole and on 10th April moved to Sauveterre and remained there until the 18th.

On 12th April a *feu de joie* was fired to celebrate the conclusion of peace, and a grand ball was given on the following evening. After this the 68th oscillated between Langon and La Réole until 25th June, when it moved towards Bordeaux; the next day it passed through Bordeaux, and on 4th July reached Paullac, where it remained for four days and then embarked for Ireland.

As previously stated, the strength of the regiment throughout its career in the Peninsula never approximated its establishment of 961, all ranks (at an annual estimated charge of £30,116 16s. 6d.); in January, 1814, H.R.H. the Duke of York wrote to the Marquis of Wellington that there were only twenty-four rank and file at the depot at Hythe, but "exertions will be made to augment its numbers"; at this period there were recruiting parties at Durham and Carlow.

THE 68TH LIGHT INFANTRY (1809-1814)

Lieutenant-Colonel W. Johnston and Brevet-Lieutenant-Colonel J. P. Hawkins were both awarded medals and the C.B.* for their services in the Peninsula; as is well known, the medal for general distribution for service in the Peninsular War was not issued until 1848. Permission to bear the word "Peninsula" on the colours was granted soon after the conclusion of the war.

Owing to the different numbers quoted in various accounts it is difficult to arrive at the correct number of casualties in the regiment in the Peninsular War, but from the "London Gazette" and from regimental monthly returns—the latter series not being complete—the numbers are:—

Officers killed in action, 7.

Officers wounded, 27; of this number two died from their wounds, two were subsequently killed in action, and two were wounded on two different occasions.

Non-commissioned officers and men killed in action, 59.

Non-commissioned officers and men wounded, 312; of this number at least 35, and probably more, died from their wounds.

Deaths from all causes in the Peninsula, 12 officers, 11 serjeants, 4 buglers, and 337 rank and file.

The numbers given by John Green, and in the regimental records exceed the above considerably.

The following non-commissioned officers and men, several of whom were killed, are recorded as having signalised themselves in action with the enemy during the Peninsular War.

---

* These were the first personal honours gained by the regiment, but it must not be forgotten that membership of the Order of the Bath was extremely limited up to 2nd January, 1815, when the Order was enlarged and divided into three classes in commemoration of the auspicious termination of the war.

Colonel (as he then was) W. Johnston and Lieutenant-Colonel J. P. Hawkins were included in the first list of Companions of the Bath, which bore the date 4th June, 1815, although it was not announced in the "London Gazette" until the following September.

THE DURHAM LIGHT INFANTRY

Colour-Serjeant J. Duff.	Serjeant J. Loughlin.
,, ,, L. Currie.	,, E. Delang.
,, ,, G. Hinds.	Private T. Minahan.
,, ,, T. Hynes.	,, M. McGready.
,, ,, W. Kelly.	,, T. McCallum.
,, ,, T. Haggerty.	,, O. Sweeny.
,, ,, R. Baker.	,, E. Sweeny.
,, ,, W. Seery.	,, M. Cavioll.
,, ,, L. Deery.	,, T. Kelly.
,, ,, D. Sullivan.	,, T. Lee.
Corporal W. Tothwell.	,, R. Mitchell.
Bugler T. Staro.	,, C. Hurrell.
,, J. Forge.	,, W. Starkey.
Serjeant R. Duncan.	,, P. Wheeler.
,, T. Hoole.	,, G. Browne.
Private T. Murrey.	,, P. Corkvey.
,, J. Reilly.	,, T. Creilly.
,, T. Rea.	,, E. Murphy.
,, P. Sheridan.	,, J. McGlenchy.
,, T. Kaine.	,, M. McEwen.

Colour-Serjeant J. Duff was present in every action in which the regiment was engaged in the Peninsula and was specially signalized on all occasions; he was subsequently serjeant-major, and eventually adjutant.

On 8th July the regiment was embarked on H.M.S. "Dublin," 74 guns, 1,766 tons, Captain T. Elphinstone, but, for some reason which has now been lost sight of, was shortly afterwards transferred to H.M.S. "Bedford," 74 guns, 1,606 tons, Captain J. Walker, and in due course sailed in that ship to Ireland, disembarked at Cove on the 26th, marched to Cork, and on the 29th to Fermoy; it is recorded that the greatest unanimity prevailed between all ranks of the sea and land forces during the voyage from Paullac to Cove.

CHAPTER IV.

THE 68TH LIGHT INFANTRY (1814-1854).

THE regiment was not allowed much rest on its arrival in Ireland as, after a stay of only eight days in Fermoy, it was on the march again on 6th August, 1814, and arrived at Clonmel on the following day; exactly a month afterwards, on the 7th September, it again was on the road, this time for the North of Ireland; Belfast was reached on 22nd September, and here at last it was allowed to remain for nearly a year and a half.

The depot, which had been at Hythe (with a permanent recruiting party at Durham) for some considerable time, was moved in August, 1814, to Ashford, and in the following month to Brabourne Lees; thence after a short stay it marched to Portsmouth, halting on the way for about a week at Chichester, and embarked on a transport on 19th October. The ship did not sail until the 29th, and, owing to storms and delays, did not reach Dublin until 24th November; the depot then marched to Belfast and rejoined head-quarters; according to John Green "the appearance of the regiment was much better than could be expected," and its strength after the depot had joined was nearly five hundred.

After the Peninsular War it did not fall to the lot of the 68th to be on active service again for forty years, when it took part in the Crimean War, but during this long period it did useful work on garrison duty in various places, chiefly abroad; of these forty years only three were spent in England.

Soon after reaching Belfast, many men who were found unfit from wounds and disease contracted in the Peninsula were discharged; John Green, who was both wounded and time-expired, was one of them.

1815 In October, 1815, "small books" were instituted.

THE DURHAM LIGHT INFANTRY

1816　　On 27th February, 1816, the regiment left Belfast and started to march to Enniskillen; having remained a few days at the latter place, it again moved on, and on 19th March reached Castlebar, where it remained for a year and two months.

The facings are now described in the "Army List" as being "bottle green" instead of "deep green," and the lace as being "silver"; this description continues until 1832.

1817　　On 14th May, 1817, the regiment left Castlebar, and, having reached Dublin on the 22nd, was quartered in George Street Barracks, near the Castle, and stayed there for nearly a year. The establishment of the 68th was now 726, all ranks, at a total charge for one year of £23,534 18s.

1818　　On the 16th March, 1818, a move was made for Fermoy, and after a short stay there the regiment embarked at Cove on 15th and 16th May on five transports, viz., "Albury," "Alfred," "Wyton," "Sir George Osborne," and "Lady Hamilton." Quebec was reached on 3rd and 4th July, and there the regiment was quartered until May, 1819.

1819　　A change of stations was then made to Upper Canada; the regiment moved in two divisions, at an interval of some days, and reached its destination in June and July; head-quarters were located at Fort George, Niagara, and several detachments were sent out; Brevet-Lieutenant-Colonel Hawkins, with only one company, was sent to the important point of Amherstburg; Major Winnett, with two companies, to Drummond Island; Major Gledstanes, with one company, to York; Lieutenant Menzies, with twenty men, to Penetanguishene; Ensign Carson, with eighteen men, to Grand River; and Serjeant Lynch, with sixteen men, to Queenstown Heights.

In December prize money for the detention of French ships at St. Lucia in 1803 was paid to all ranks who were entitled to it.

1820　　On 1st January, 1820, all ranks subscribed one day's pay to create a fund for distressed widows and orphans of soldiers of the regiment.

On 16th May the regiment embarked on the steamboat "Frontenac" at Fort George, Niagara, and disembarked at Kingston on

THE 68TH LIGHT INFANTRY (1814-1854)

the evening of the following day; it is very gratifying to be able to record that Colonel W. Johnston, C.B., received a highly complimentary letter from the magistrates and responsible inhabitants of the Niagara district expressing regret at the departure of the 68th for another station.

1821   While at Kingston the establishment was reduced, by a general order of 6th August, 1821, from ten to eight companies of 72 rank and file each, or, including officers and non-commissioned officers, a total of 650, all ranks.

In the following November permission was given in a general order for one serjeant to be employed as master of the band, and ten men as musicians in each battalion, regardless of the number of companies, instead of one serjeant as master and one man per company as had been hitherto allowed.

1823   The regiment stayed at Kingston until the end of May, 1823, when it proceeded in four divisions to Quebec; the first division embarked on 23rd May, and proceeded down the St. Lawrence to Lachine, where it arrived on the 26th; then, having marched on the following day to Montreal, embarked on the steam vessel "New Swiftsure," and arrived at Quebec on the morning of the 28th; the remaining three divisions shortly followed.

Although trousers of a dark grey colour had been substituted for breeches and gaiters as service dress in 1808, and seem to have been generally worn after that date, commanding officers were reminded in September, 1819, that non-commissioned officers and men must possess a pair of white breeches and long black gaiters, but that they might be supplied with a pair of grey pantaloons instead of a second pair of breeches; in 1820 the colour of the pantaloons was altered from dark grey to blue grey; it was not until June, 1823, that breeches and leggings were officially discontinued. In the same month the 68th was authorized to bear on its colours and appointments the words, "Salamanca, Vittoria, Pyrenees, Nivelle, and Orthes"; and in August of the same year the establishment of the band was increased to one serjeant, as master, and fourteen musicians.

THE DURHAM LIGHT INFANTRY

1824   On 9th June, 1824, a terrific thunderstorm passed over the city of Quebec; Ensign J. D. Cogan, who had only joined in the previous October, was killed in his own quarters; Corporal Nattrass, with his child, aged 20 months, in his arms, were both killed; so also was Bugler H. Brown; several others, men, women, and children, were severely injured.

1825   By an order, dated Horse Guards, 26th April, 1825, the establishment of the regiment was augmented to ten companies, of which six, at a strength of eighty-six rank and file each, and a total of 26 officers and 556 non-commissioned officers and men were to be stationed abroad; and the remaining four, at a strength of 56 rank and file each, under a field officer, and a total of 13 officers and 240 non-commissioned officers and men, were to be formed into a depot at home.

On 24th September in this year the regiment paraded on the plains of Abraham before the Earl of Dalhousie, G.C.B., now Governor-General, and formerly G.O.C. the 7th Division in the Peninsula, and new colours were presented by the Countess of Dalhousie.

The regiment was moved from Quebec in two divisions on 27th September and 1st October, and arrived at Kingston on 12th and 19th October.

1826   By a general order, dated 10th April, 1826, officers of light infantry regiments were instructed to wear coatees corresponding with those of the rest of the line, so that the only distinctions of light infantry officers were wings, bugle ornaments, and green feathers.

While at Kingston the usual half-yearly inspections were made by Major-General Sir Peregrine Maitland, K.C.B.; the number of privates in the service companies varied from 359 in May, 1826, to 448 in May, 1827; there were also about 200 on both the above dates in England at the depot at Devonport; a rather peculiar circumstance, for which no explanation is given, was that "The Musicians" at this time were not with the service companies, but at the depot.

THE 68TH LIGHT INFANTRY (1814-1854)

1827 On 31st July, 1827, head-quarters arrived at York (in 1834 renamed Toronto) by the steamboat "Queenstown," detachments having been sent during the month to Drummond Island, Amherstburg, Fort George, Grand River, and Penetanguishene. In December of this year the standard for infantry of the line was raised to 5 ft. 7 in., or, when a regiment was within fifty of its establishment, to 5 ft. 8 in.; this high standard, however, was not long maintained, as in March, 1829, it was 5 ft. 7 in. without any limitations.

1828 In a Horse Guards order of 22nd December, 1828, concerning the head-gear of the infantry, the following appears:—

"It is understood that the cap-line is to be worn on parade occasions only, and it is to be white for all the men, except Light Infantry, who are to wear green. That of the officers is to be gold for all regiments, whether wearing white or yellow buttons; scales the same."

Further orders on the subject of dress were issued on 10th February, 1829, and these include:—

(i.) In future all officers of infantry are to wear a coatee without lappels.

(ii.) The blue-grey trousers now worn by the infantry are to be discontinued, and trousers of the Oxford mixture are to be adopted in place of them for officers and men.

(iii.) A forage cap as described in the margin to be worn at all times by officers with the great coat, or off parade.

* * * *

For light infantry, green, with a band of the colour of the facings of the regiment; regiments wearing green facings to have a red band.

* * * *

(iv.) The chaco to be the same throughout the infantry; the feather to be white for the grenadiers and battalions, and green for light infantry as before.

(v.) Epaulettes are not to be worn on any uniform over wings; field officers of fusiliers and light infantry and rifle corps, as a distinction, to wear epaulettes only.

THE DURHAM LIGHT INFANTRY

A few days later a new pattern pouch for serjeants of light infantry was approved.

1829 It was again notified in the following April that field officers of fusiliers, light infantry, and highland regiments were to wear epaulettes only, and that a pattern wing for other officers of these corps had been approved.

In the following August orders were issued for the forage caps of privates of light infantry regiments to be green, with a band as detailed for the officers' caps in the preceding February.

On 12th May, 1829, the first division of the regiment left York for Montreal, and the second division followed on 4th June; this move was preparatory to returning to the mother country, and was the occasion of complimentary letters to the commanding officer from the inhabitants of both York and Kingston.

On 12th October the regiment left Montreal for Quebec, where, on the 18th, it embarked on board three transports, viz., "Countess of Harcourt," "Kaines," and "Sylvia"; these three transports reached Cove of Cork, on 15th, 16th, and 18th November, and on the 19th the 68th marched to Fermoy.

1830 The regiment moved from Fermoy to Athlone on 4th, 5th, and 7th June, 1830, and arrived at its new quarters on 12th, 14th, and 15th of same month; detachments were sent to Roscommon and Shannon Bridge.

By a general order of 2nd August, officers and men of the light infantry, throughout the army, were ordered to wear a green tuft instead of a feather; and the bands of infantry regiments were ordered to be dressed in white clothing with the regimental facings.

1831 On 6th, 8th, 10th, and 11th October, 1831, the regiment marched from Athlone for Limerick, and arrived on 10th, 12th, 13th, and 14th of the same month; detachments, which had been at Roscommon, Gort House, and Corroboy, marched under Captain Gibson, Lieutenants North and Bouchette on 12th October, and reached Limerick on the 17th.

After a two months' stay in Limerick the regiment marched in December to Galway, arriving on the 15th and 17th; detachments were now sent out to the following eleven places: Gort, Ardrahan, Tubber, Mr. Alexander's house at Loughrea, Kilcriest, Prospect Cot-

THE 68TH LIGHT INFANTRY (1814-1854)

tage (Ardfrey), Kilcolgan Castle, Kinvarra, Curranrue, New Quay, and Oughterard.

1832   In February, 1832, head-quarters marched from Galway to Clare Castle, arriving on the 9th; no less than eighteen detachments were now supplied, viz., Ennis, Clifton House, near Corofin, Kilfenora, Tulla, Tomgraney, Killaloe, Mount Shannon, Kilrush, Scattery Island, Kilcredaun Point, Donaha, Kildysart, Ennistymon, Miltown Malbay, Six-Mile Bridge, and three of the former detachments, which remained stationary, namely, Gort, Tubber, and New Quay.

In the "Army List" for 1832 the facings are still described as bottle green, but the lace has been changed from silver to gold.

Head-quarters suffered severely from cholera while at Clare Castle; between 9th and 29th June there were 122 cases and 22 deaths.

The detachments at Six-Mile Bridge, Ennistymon, Tulla, Tomgraney, Clifton House, Mount Shannon, and Kilrush were withdrawn and encamped with head-quarters. Surgeon James Reid died on 11th June.

There were also eleven cases and four deaths at Gort, three cases and one death at Ennis, and two cases and one death at Six-Mile Bridge.

The regiment marched from Clare Castle on 12th, 15th, and 17th October for Dublin, and arrived on 20th, 23rd, and 25th of the same month, occupying quarters in Richmond Barracks.

1833   On 10th April, 1833, a change of quarters in Dublin was made from Richmond Barracks to the Royal Barracks.

On 6th and 7th July, the regiment marched from Dublin for Newry, arriving 9th and 10th; detachments were sent to the following places: Armagh, Aughnacloy, Carrickmacross, Louth, Crossmagien, Newtown-Hamilton, and Keady.

Head-quarters marched in two divisions from Newry for Belfast on 11th and 12th December; detachments at Louth, Carrickmacross, Armagh, and Castlewellan marched on the 17th; these various parties embarked at Belfast on 18th, 19th, 22nd, and 23rd December, disembarked at Glasgow, and marched to Edinburgh, arriving there on 23rd, 24th, 26th, and 27th of the same month.

THE DURHAM LIGHT INFANTRY

1834   The strength of the 68th at Edinburgh Castle on 1st January, 1834, was 38 officers (of whom eight were absent), 42 serjeants, 13 buglers, and 714 rank and file.

In February, Major Lord William Paulet went to Glasgow with 13 officers and 316 non-commissioned officers and men in aid of the civil power there; Lord William Paulet returned with his party to Edinburgh in the following month, having received the thanks of the magistrates and factory owners for the assistance given in suppressing the riots at Glasgow.

On 3rd September the regiment, having been divided into service and depot companies, embarked at Leith on H.M.'s troopship "Romney," 30 guns, 1,227 tons, master commanding, James Wood, and sailed on the 7th, arriving at Portsmouth on the 14th.

Major Lord W. Paulet disembarked with the depot companies on the 15th, and remained at Portsmouth; the service companies sailed from Portsmouth on 21st September, arrived at Gibraltar on 10th October, and disembarked on the 12th.

This tour of service in Gibraltar, which lasted over three years, appears to have been as devoid of interesting occurrences as the tour of nine years' duration which took place there about forty years before.

In May, 1834, there were again alterations in the officers' forage cap; that for light infantry was henceforth to be dark green with a black silk oak leaf band, instead of the coloured band ordered in 1829, unless the regiment was styled "Royal."

In the "Army List" for 1834 the facings are no longer described as bottle green, but simply as green.

1837   In January, 1837, bandsmen of infantry regiments were ordered, in reference to the order of August, 1830, to wear white in undress, as well as in full dress.

1838   In January, 1838, the regiment embarked, in two divisions, at Gibraltar, and sailed to Jamaica. The head-quarters division, consisting of 8 officers, 18 serjeants, 2 buglers, 266 rank and file, 48 women, and 89 children, embarked on the "Maitland" transport on the 11th, and arrived off Port Royal on 20th February; 2 officers, 88 non-commissioned officers and men, 15 women and 22 children disembarked at Port Royal on the following day; the remainder, which constituted head-quarters, disembarked at Kingston on 23rd February, and marched on the same day to Stony Hill Barracks; during the voyage five children, one of whom died, were born at sea. The second division, 4 officers, 8 serjeants, 6 buglers, 149 rank and file, 23 women, and 38 children, under Major Lord William Paulet, embarked on the "Nurna" transport on the 13th, and arrived off Port Royal on the 20th March; 3 officers and 71 non-commissioned officers and men disembarked at Kingston on the 21st and proceeded to Up Park; Lord William Paulet disembarked with the remainder on the 22nd, and rejoined head-quarters at Stony Hill.

1839 In April, 1839, the 68th moved from Kingston and Port Royal to the north side of the island, and was quartered as under:

head-quarters and three companies at Maroon Town, now known as Trelawny, two companies at Falmouth, and a field-officer with one company at Lucea; this change of quarters was effected by sea, head-quarters having been conveyed to Montego Bay in H.M.'s frigate "Pique," and Captain Smyth's company to Lucea in H.M.'s frigate "Andromache."

Lieutenant James Duff died on 16th April, 1840.

1840 On 11th September, 1840, the regiment was inspected at Maroon Town by Major-General Sir W. M. Gomm, K.C.B., commander of the forces in Jamaica, and new colours were presented on this day by Lady Gomm; at the conclusion of the ceremonial parade the regiment gave an exhibition of light drill, with an unlimited expenditure of blank ammunition, which, according to the local newspaper, created a great impression on the minds of the spectators.

While at Maroon Town much hard work was performed by the men in extending the parade ground and improving the roads; a sum equal to the cost of five hundred pairs of ankle-boots, at 5s. 6d. a pair, was granted for the men who had been employed on this work.

1841 On 23rd January, 1841, the detachment at Lucea, having been relieved by a company of the 82nd Regiment, joined the detachment at Falmouth.

The death roll in Jamaica from 1838 to 1841 included 9 serjeants, 1 bugler, and 94 rank and file.

THE DURHAM LIGHT INFANTRY

On 23rd June, the regiment, strength, 16 officers, 26 serjeants, 8 buglers, 386 rank and file, 53 women, and 112 children, embarked on H.M.'s troopship "Apollo," 46 guns, 1,086 tons (launched in 1805), master commanding, William White, and sailed on the 26th for Quebec, arriving there on 5th August; during this voyage five men, two women, and three children died, and three children were born.

On arriving in the St. Lawrence, off Quebec, a wing, under Captain Smyth, consisting of 9 officers and 306 non-commissioned officers and men, was transhipped and landed at Riviere-du-Loup (Fraserville) on 8th August; a subaltern's detachment having been left there, the remainder occupied Fort Ingall, St. Rose du Dégelé, and Blockhouse Fort at the Little Falls, Madawaska, then in dispute between Great Britain and the United States.

On 6th August head-quarters proceeded to William Henry, now known as Sorel, where they found 160 men, a draft from the depot, and 140 volunteers for permanent service in Canada from other regiments going home. The boundary between New Brunswick and the state of Maine, as well as other matters, having been settled by the Ashburton treaty, which was concluded at Washington, 9th August, 1842, by Alexander, Lord Ashburton, and John Tyler, president of the United States, the troops were withdrawn from the Madawaska country, and the detachments arrived in Quebec on 29th September, 1842; on 6th October head-quarters arrived at Quebec, from William Henry, to relieve the 2nd Battalion Coldstream Guards, and occupied the Jesuit Barracks.

1842

The strength of the regiment was now 16 officers, 33 serjeants, 9 buglers, and 590 rank and file.

In August, 1843, the regiment was encamped for a month, with the 81st and 82nd Regiments, on the plains of Abraham, and was inspected by Sir J. Hope, K.C.B., commanding the Eastern Division of Canada.

1843

In this month the coloured stripe in serjeants' sashes was ordered to be discontinued; the serjeant's sash was "henceforth to be manufactured of the national crimson colour throughout, uniformly for the whole army (including rifle corps)."

THE 68TH LIGHT INFANTRY (1814-1854)

1844   On 4th May, 1844, the regiment marched to the citadel of Quebec to relieve the 82nd Regiment, and, having embarked on the 23rd of the same month on H.M.'s troopship "Apollo," sailed for England on the 28th; strength, 16 officers, 29 serjeants, 9 buglers, 415 rank and file.

Having disembarked at Chatham on 23rd June, the regiment occupied Brompton Barracks, and then marched in three divisions on 24th June and two following days for Canterbury; the depot from Dover rejoined head-quarters at Canterbury on 6th July.

On 30th August percussion arms, 800 muskets and 40 fusils, were supplied.

On 6th September there was an inspection by Major-General Browne, C.B., D.A.G. to the Forces. Strength (besides officers), 49 serjeants, 17 buglers, 794 rank and file.

On 2nd October the regiment marched from Canterbury to Walmer, and on the 7th a detachment of one serjeant and twenty-seven rank and file was despatched to Sandgate for the protection of the military lunatic asylum; a subaltern officer was subsequently added to this detachment.

On 11th November the regiment was reviewed by Field-Marshal the Duke of Wellington; His Grace expressed himself to Lieutenant-Colonel Lord William Paulet in the following terms:—

"The 68th has always been a good regiment; I am happy to find it so now, and I feel certain that it will continue to be so."

He also spoke of the movements, conduct, and general appearance of the corps in the most flattering terms, and desired that his sentiments might be communicated to the regiment.

1845   On 21st May, 1845, there was again an inspection by Major-General Browne, D.A.G. to the Forces, who said that he had never inspected a finer regiment.

In July the regiment moved in three divisions to Portsmouth; the first division marched on the 25th to Dover, and proceeded by rail on the same day to Reigate; on the following day it marched to Kingston-on-Thames, and on the same evening proceeded by rail to Gosport; Fort Monkton and Haslar Barracks were occupied.

On the 28th the second division (head-quarters) followed the same route, and occupied Colewort Barracks on the 29th.

THE DURHAM LIGHT INFANTRY

On the 29th the third division also followed the same route, and occupied the Victualling Store Barracks.

There was a detachment at Marchwood from 20th August until 27th December; there was also a detachment at Tipnor from 26th August until 27th January, 1846.

On 26th September two-and-a-half companies from Fort Monkton rejoined head-quarters, leaving one company at the fort until 4th November.

There was an inspection by Major-General Sir Hercules Pakenham on 4th October.

On 21st October one company was sent to Fort Cumberland, and a second company was sent to the same place on 27th December; both these companies remained there until the latter part of the following January.

1846 On 27th January, 1846, the first division of the regiment travelled by rail to Nine Elms Station, then, having marched across London to Euston Station, was entrained the same evening and conveyed by the London and Birmingham Railway to Weedon, where it arrived on the following morning; one company was sent to Birmingham and one to Wolverhampton.

The second division left Portsmouth on the 28th, and arrived at Weedon the same evening, detaching one company to Hanley and one to Burslem.

On 2nd March the company at Hanley was moved to Burslem, and the two remained there until the following August.

On 17th March three companies were moved by rail from Weedon; two of them constituted head-quarters and went to Chester, the third went to Liverpool; on 19th May two more companies were moved from Weedon and went to Stockport.

On 2nd April the establishment of the band in an infantry regiment was raised to one serjeant and twenty privates.

On 23rd May, one company from Chester was sent, at two hours' notice, to Bangor, North Wales, in aid of the civil power; it returned to head-quarters on 2nd June.

On 17th August head-quarters, having been conveyed by railway to Birkenhead, embarked on H.M.'s steam transport "Rhadamanthus," 813 tons, master commanding, Jonathan Aylen; the detachments

LORD WILLIAM PAULET, CAPTAIN CROSS, ETC.

THE 68TH LIGHT INFANTRY (1814-1854)

from Liverpool and Stockport also embarked on the same ship; this party reached Kingstown on the following day, and proceeded to Palatine Square, Royal Barracks, Dublin.

On the 18th of the same month, the last remaining company at Weedon and the company at Birmingham were conveyed by railway to Liverpool, and embarked there on H.M.'s steam transport "Dee," 704 tons, master commanding, Thomas Driver; the detachments from Wolverhampton and Burslem joined them on the following day; the "Dee" sailed on the next day, and reached Kingstown on the 21st; this party at once disembarked and rejoined head-quarters at the Royal Barracks.

The strength of the regiment was now 38 officers, 47 serjeants, 40 corporals, 17 buglers, 757 privates.

There was an inspection by Lieutenant-General Sir E. Blakeney, commanding the forces in Ireland, on 12th September, and an inspection by Major-General Wyndham on 14th October.

Shortly after this 2 officers and 33 non-commissioned officers and men were sent on detachments to Navan, and 2 officers and 42 non-commissioned officers and men to Oldcastle; and on 28th December 1 officer and 42 non-commissioned officers and men were sent to Kells. In addition to these detachments, parties numbering, in the aggregate, 12 officers and 377 non-commissioned officers and men, were sent to Naas, Rathangan, Robertstown, Maryborough, Athy, and Mountmellick, to furnish escorts for provision boats.

On 18th December, head-quarters were transferred from the Royal Barracks to Ship Street Barracks in Dublin, and were struck off garrison duty for canal escort duty.

Lieutenant-General Morant notes in his diary that "in 1846 troops carry their muskets to church in Ireland."

In 1847 the following movements took place:—

1847 1st January—2 officers and 54 non-commissioned officers and men to Trim; this party was withdrawn at the end of March.

20th March—Head-quarters from Ship Street Barracks to Royal Square, Royal Barracks, and two companies from Ship Street Barracks to Beggars' Bush Barracks.

29th and 31st July—(a) 8 officers and 247 non-commissioned

officers and men to Dundalk, and (b) 4 officers and 116 non-commissioned officers and men to Drogheda; these two parties, which were in aid of the civil power during the elections, returned on 5th and 7th August respectively.

22nd September—2 officers and 59 non-commissioned officers and men to Strokestown; this party was reinforced on 6th December by 2 officers and 43 men.

22nd September—2 officers and 60 non-commissioned officers and men to Castlereagh; relieved by a detachment from the 38th Regiment on 24th November.

27th September—2 officers and 43 non-commissioned officers and men to Longford; this party was moved on 14th December to Boyle, and on 12th January, 1848, to Elphin.

28th September—2 officers and 64 non-commissioned officers and men to Edenderry.

11th October—5 officers and 199 non-commissioned officers and men Dublin to Mullingar; and two companies (4 officers and 127 non-commissioned officers and men) to Carrick-on-Shannon; these two latter companies rejoined head-quarters at Mullingar on 20th November.

13th October—2 officers and 107 non-commissioned officers and men, Dublin to Mullingar.

14th October—Head-quarters (8 officers and 160 non-commissioned officers and men), Dublin to Mullingar.

12th November—The regiment was inspected at Mullingar by Major-General Sir G. Campbell, Bart., commanding Athlone District.

During November and December detachments were sent to Tullamore, Philipstown, Kilbeggan, Oldcastle, and Longford.

The following movements took place :—

1848 6th February—The detachment at Elphin rejoined head-quarters at Mullingar.

13th March—The detachment at Kilbeggan joined the detachment at Tullamore.

15th March—A reinforcement of one officer and thirty-one non-commissioned officers and men proceeded to Tullamore from Philipstown.

THE 68TH LIGHT INFANTRY (1814-1854)

22nd March—A reinforcement of thirteen non-commissioned officers and men proceeded from Mullingar to Granard.

3rd April—The detachment at Edenderry proceeded to Trim.

2nd May—The detachment at Longford proceeded to Castlereagh.

26th May—Major-General Sir G. Campbell, Bart., inspected the regiment.

30th May—A detachment was sent to Clonmellon; it remained there until 1st June, 1848.

4th September—A detachment was sent to Oughterard.

8th September—The detachment at Castlereagh proceeded to Ballinrobe.

11th September—The detachments at Granard and Philipstown proceeded to Tuam and Galway respectively.

13th September—Head-quarters arrived at Galway from Mullingar.

13th October—Major-General Sir G. Campbell, Bart., inspected the regiment, and on the same day the detachment at Tuam proceeded to Dunmore.

7th December—A detachment was sent to Spiddle in aid of the civil power.

27th December—A further detachment was sent to Spiddle, and thence to Cashla Tower; it returned 15th February, 1849.

1849   In January, 1849, officers' blue frock coats and frog belts were discontinued, and scarlet shell jackets and black sling belts substituted.

In February the establishment was reduced to 47 serjeants, 17 buglers, 40 corporals, and 710 privates.

There were eighteen cases of cholera in April, ten of these (seven men and three women) were fatal.

On 10th April a detachment was sent to Westport, and on the 14th the detachment at Tuam rejoined head-quarters.

There were inspections during this year in May and October by Major-General T. J. Wemyss, and in September by Lieutenant-General Sir E. Blakeney.

THE DURHAM LIGHT INFANTRY

1850
On 12th April, 1850, the regiment marched from Galway and arrived at Limerick on the 17th; detachments as under were sent out:—

To Clare Castle, 6 officers and 127 non-commissioned officers and men.

To Kilrush, 2 officers and 64 non-commissioned officers and men.

To Killaloe, 2 officers and 64 non-commissioned officers and men.

These three detachments rejoined head-quarters at Limerick in the following October.

There was an inspection by Major-General T. E. Napier on 3rd May; and again another by the same officer on 10th January, 1851.

1851
Early in 1851 the regiment was divided into service and depot companies; the latter marched on 10th and 12th February for Birr, there to be stationed; the service companies, 23 officers, 31 serjeants, 23 corporals, 11 buglers, 535 privates, 36 women, and 52 children proceeded to Cork by rail on 22nd February, and on the 27th embarked on H.M.'s troopship "Resistance," 10 guns, 1,081 tons, master commanding, Manser Bradshaw; the "Resistance" sailed on the following day, and reached Malta on 19th March. The regiment disembarked at Malta on 20th March, and was quartered at Fort Ricasoli until the following April, when it moved to Lower St. Elmo Barracks; one company, however, was in the first instance detached for about a month to St. Salvador Barracks.

In May and November inspections were made by Lieutenant-General Sir R. Ellice.

1852
In March, 1852, the establishment was raised to 47 serjeants, 16 buglers, 40 corporals, and 810 privates. The usual inspections in this and the two following years were made by Lieutenant-General T. Fergusson, C.B.

On 12th October, 1852, head-quarters and three companies were moved to Isola, two companies to St. Francisco di Pasto Barracks, and one company to Zeitun Gates.

1853
On 2nd April the regiment was once more united, this time in Floriana Barracks; but in the middle of October it was again split up, head-quarters going to Strada Forré Barracks,

THE 68TH LIGHT INFANTRY (1814-1854)

three companies to Lower St. Elmo Barracks, and one company to Marsamusetto Barracks.

1854   In February, 1854, and again in the following June, the establishment was raised; by the last order there were to be 47 serjeants, 50 corporals, 17 buglers, and 1,140 privates.

In February the detachment at Lower St. Elmo Barracks rejoined head-quarters, and on 13th July the regiment returned to its original quarters at Fort Ricasoli.

About this period the regimental depot was at Belfast.

CHAPTER V.

THE 68TH LIGHT INFANTRY IN THE CRIMEA.

On 7th August, 1854, the 68th, composed of 24 officers, 48 serjeants, 18 buglers, and 777 rank and file, embarked on the Cunard s.s. "Cambria," and arrived at Beikos Bay, on the eastern shore of the Bosporus, on the 12th; three companies landed at Unkiar-Skelessi on the 14th, and the remaining five companies landed at the same place on the following day. On 30th August the whole re-embarked at Unkiar-Skelessi, reached Varna 1st September, Baltchik Bay the next day, Eupatoria 13th September, and landed on the next day close to Lake Touzla.

Cholera had unfortunately made its appearance on the "Cambria," and there were ten deaths from it while at Varna and Baltchik Bay.

At daylight on 19th September the regiment, which was now in the 2nd Brigade, 4th Division, although it had originally been destined for the 1st Brigade, under the command of Lieutenant-General the Hon. Sir G. Cathcart, K.C.B., marched about ten miles, and bivouacked near the Bulganak river.

Two companies (Captains Macbeth's and Blount's), 6 officers and 174 non-commissioned officers and men, were detailed as personal escort to General Lord Raglan; they remained on this duty until 5th April, 1855, when they rejoined head-quarters.

The composition of the 4th Division was:—

1st Brigade,
Brig.-General T. L. Goldie.
- 20th Regiment.
- 21st Fusiliers.
- 57th Regiment.

2nd Brigade,
Brig.-General A. W. Torrens.
- 46th Regiment (two companies only).
- 63rd Regiment.
- 68th Light Infantry.
- 1st Battalion Rifle Brigade.

68TH LIGHT INFANTRY IN THE CRIMEA

But the 57th had not yet arrived, and head-quarters of the 46th did not join the brigade until three days after the battle of Inkerman.

Also, the 63rd and the two companies of the 46th remained under Brigadier-General Torrens at the place of disembarkation on the 19th as rear guard, and did not reach the field of action at the Alma until 6 p.m. on the following day.

On the 20th September, at the battle of the Alma, the somewhat attenuated 4th Division was in reserve, and there were not any casualties in the 68th, although the regiment was at one time shelled by the Russians.

After a couple of days' delay, the allies marched daily round towards Balaklava, and on 28th September occupied the southern heights above Sevastopol. During this period the 68th suffered severely from cholera; fifteen men died at the Alma and twenty-nine were lost on the march; there were not any tents, and water was scarce.

Preparations for the siege of Sevastopol were then made; but the actual bombardments did not commence until 17th October; on this day Assistant-Surgeon J. F. O'Leary was killed while on duty in the trenches, and Colour-Sergeant H. Sladden was conspicuous by his bravery. Captain Morant was severely wounded on the 21st October.

On 25th October the battle of Balaklava was fought; when the 4th Division arrived on the scene of action the enemy were retiring; one man of the 68th was killed and one was wounded; only two companies of the 68th were in action on this day, the remainder were on duty in the trenches.

On 5th November, at the battle of Inkerman, the 68th, which was the only regiment in red, without great coats, was, from various causes, very weak in numbers; the actual strength going into action was 16 officers, 15 serjeants, 14 buglers, and 198 rank and file.

In the course of the day Major H. G. Wynne, Lieutenant F. G. Barker, and seventeen privates were killed; Brevet-Lieutenant-Colonel Harry Smyth, who shortly afterwards died from his wounds. Lieutenant J. Cator, two buglers, and thirty-one privates were wounded; two serjeants and one private were missing; and Lieutenant-Colonel Henry Smyth's horse was shot under him.

THE DURHAM LIGHT INFANTRY

The strength of the 4th Division in action on this day was as under:—

1st Brigade.	20th Regiment	340
	21st Fusiliers	402
	57th Regiment	347
2nd Brigade.	63rd Regiment	466
	Two companies 46th and four companies 68th	384
	1st Battalion Rifle Brigade	278

Two companies of the 68th were, as before mentioned, on Lord Raglan's guard, and the other two were on duty in the trenches on this day.

Sir George Cathcart was killed; Brigadier-General Goldie was severely wounded and died the same night; and Brigadier-General Torrens was severely wounded, was invalided home, and died in August in the following year.

The explanation of the fact that the 68th was the only regiment in red on that day was given by Lieutenant-General Morant to Mr. A. W. Kinglake in June, 1870, in the following words:—

"The 68th at guard-mounting used to wear the great coat over the accoutrements, and this was the manner in which the 68th marched down to the great fight on the morning of Inkerman; of course, it was soon found necessary to halt the regiment in order that the men might throw off their great coats to get more easily at their ammunition on the field of battle. The 68th then, appearing in their red coats, drove a vast body of Russians pell-mell into the valley of the Tchernaya on the right of the British attack, etc."

In his diary also Lieutenant-General Morant states:—

"The French Zouaves saved the 68th from being totally annihilated; the Light Bobs, having followed the Russians into the valley, on ascending found the Russians on their right flank, ten yards above them, etc."

A. W. Kinglake, in his "History of the Crimean War," makes the following remarks about the regiment at Inkerman, vol. vi., pages 234 and 235:—

"The four companies of the 68th, under Colonel Henry Smyth, with two companies of the 46th, under Captain Hardy, formed up on their left, had already deployed on a front towards the body marked out for attack; and the brigadier, General Torrens, now placing himself at their head, these 400 men in line, closely followed by Cathcart and his staff, began to move down the steep. Cathcart some time before had caused them to leave their great coats, and they were the only considerable body of infantry who on this day disclosed their red uniforms. Traversing difficult, obstructed grounds, and incurring after a while heavy fire from artillery, as well as from the troops in their front, they still worked their way down with a keenness which—even in the eyes of the enemy looking up from some distance below—was expressive, it would seem, of a resolute purpose, for the troops which this attack threatened were presently seen to waver, if not indeed to give way, and our people then no longer firing, but setting their hearts on the bayonet, descended with impetuous haste to strike at the shaken mass. Colonel Henry Smyth, commanding the 68th men, had his horse shot under him, and Captain Wynne fell dead in the midst of this charge, being struck through the head by a musket ball whilst leading forward his company and striving to keep it united; but if less than 400, the English, extended in line and yet further disparted in moving by the roughness of the ground, had, by this time, spread out a great front, and already the huddled and clustered aggregate below was shrinking under this onset as from the cast of a net, and flying down the hillside."

Mr. Kinglake also adds a note: "Their red jackets drew fire from sixteen guns on East Jut."

This charge took place between 7.30 and 8.30 a.m., in what Mr. Kinglake calls the second period of the battle.

The Russian regiment which the 68th charged was the "Regiment of Jakutsk (Yakutsk)."

In describing the fourth period (9.15 to 10 a.m.) of the battle, Mr. Kinglake says, vol. vi., page 364:—

"Haines had placed an officer and some men of the 68th under the shelter of a stone wall, to the left front of the Barrier, to watch the enemy on Shell Hill, and harass the artillery there by a well sustained fire."

And vol. vi., page 365:—

"The presence of 68th men in an organised state near the Barrier so soon after the false victory of the second period is obviously highly creditable to the regiment."

With reference to the battle of Inkerman, Sir C. A. Windham, A.Q.M.G., 4th Division, made, amongst others, the following entries in his diary:—

"I then continued . . . in rear with the four companies of the 68th Regiment, who were lower down the hill than the right wing of the 20th Regiment. The 68th were led into action by Brigadier-General Torrens, who fell severely wounded when in the act of trying to restrain their ardour, after driving the enemy before them.

"I did all I could to get back the men of the 20th and 68th, but it was a work of time, as the ascent was almost perpendicular, and the men were mixed with the Guards and others, who had pursued the enemy even into the meadows.

"I took them (i.e., the 20th and 68th) to the rear of the 2nd Division camp.

"I placed myself under Major-General Pennefather in front of the camp of the 2nd Division . . . sending Lieutenant-Colonel Smyth with the 68th still further to the front."

And, with reference to the death of Sir George Cathcart, Sir C. A. Windham writes:—

"It is thought great blame attaches itself to Sir George's having descended the hill.

"The 68th were almost the only men of our division that did go down."

On the death of Sir G. Cathcart, Brigadier-General Goldie commanded the 4th Division, and when the latter was wounded Colonel F. Horn, 20th Regiment, was the senior officer; when Brigadier-General Torrens was wounded, Lieutenant-Colonel Horsford, 1st Battalion Rifle Brigade, was the senior officer in the 2nd Brigade.

The 14th November had unpleasant reminiscences for those who were in the Crimea, for there was a tremendous hurricane on that day, as well as an absence of rations.

OFFICERS OF THE 68TH LIGHT INFANTRY.
CRIMEA, SPRING, 1855.

Lieut. Vaughan.   Bt.-Maj. Lewis.   Capt. Hamilton.   Lt.-Col. Macbeth.
        Bt.-Maj. Finch.   Maj. Blount.   Lt.-Col. Smyth.

68TH LIGHT INFANTRY IN THE CRIMEA

1855   Early in January, 1855, Lieutenant H. Battiscombe was wounded.

In February the silver medal for distinguished conduct in the field, with an annuity of £20, was awarded to Quartermaster-Serjeant Sant; and the medal, with gratuities, was awarded as under:—£15 to Colour-Serjeant H. Sladden, £10 each to Corporals J. Coughlan, J. Dutton, G. Harrington, and W. Starkie, £5 each to Bugler H. Sanderson, Privates M. Cormick, J. Deacon, W. Fletcher, J. Harwood, C. Hutchinson, S. Lucas, A. Moulton, J. Ogden, and W. Tame. Medals, with gratuities, according to the above scale and numbers in each rank, were awarded to each infantry battalion in the Crimea. Lieutenant Harry E. Smyth died from fever at Balaklava on 14th March.

The health of the regiment, which had been very bad during the severe winter, was beginning to improve, but the number of sick was still abnormally high, as Colonel Smyth, in a private letter, dated 2nd March, gave the strength as—

Men fit for duty	212
Sick (present and absent)	300
Lord Raglan's guard	140
Servants, etc.	70
Total	722

The establishment was at this time raised to sixteen companies, with 67 officers and 2,150 non-commissioned officers and men.

Early in 1855 the 63rd Regiment was moved from the 2nd Brigade, 4th Division, and was replaced in April by the 48th Regiment.

After the battle of Inkerman, Lieutenant-General Sir H. J. W. Bentinck, K.C.B., was appointed to the command of the 4th Division, but he was prevented, by a wound which he had received at Inkerman and by ill-health, from joining until 1st June, 1855; in the meantime the division was commanded by Major-General Sir John Campbell, Bart., who was subsequently killed in the attack on the Redan on

THE DURHAM LIGHT INFANTRY

18th June. During this period Colonel McPherson, C.B., 17th Foot, was brigadier of the 1st Brigade, and Colonel R. Garrett, 46th Foot, of the 2nd Brigade.

In August the 4th Division was constituted as under:—
G.O.C., Lieutenant-General Sir H. J. W. Bentinck, K.C.B.

1st Brigade,
Brigadier-General
the Hon. A. Spencer, C.B.
{
17th Regiment.
20th Regiment.
21st Fusiliers.
57th Regiment.
63rd Regiment.
}

2nd Brigade,
Colonel R. Garrett, K.H.
{
46th Regiment.
48th Regiment.
68th Light Infantry.
1st Battalion Rifle Brigade.
}

In October, 1855, for a very brief period, Major-General C. A. Windham, C.B., commanded the division; and in November, 1855, Colonel R. Garrett, now a Major-General, was appointed to the command of the 4th Division, which position he held until the end of the war, and Colonel G. Staunton was appointed to the command of the 2nd Brigade, which position he also held until the conclusion of the war.

On the night of 11th May, in the midst of an awful storm of wind and rain, the Russians made a sortie from Sevastopol, which was most successfully resisted by about 200 of the 68th; regimental records state that Lieutenant-Colonel Macbeath was in command, but there is now some doubt as to whether he was actually on the spot at the time of the Russian attack or not.

The Russians were believed to have been about eight times the number of the 68th; Captain Edwards and 5 rank and file were killed, 22 rank and file were wounded, and one man was missing; Captain Hamilton was awarded the Victoria Cross for his gallant conduct on this occasion; Colour-Sergeant H. Sladden was also recommended for it, but his claim was not considered to be sufficiently strong; however, he was subsequently awarded the Cross of the Legion of Honour, 5th Class, for his conduct on this night.

68TH LIGHT INFANTRY IN THE CRIMEA

Concerning this affair, Lord Raglan wrote on 12th May to Lord Panmure :—

"Last night a very determined sortie was made upon the advance of our left attack. The enemy moved forward in two columns from the Woronzoff road. Our advanced sentries having slowly retired, the guard of the trenches was prepared to receive them, and consequently drove them back in the most determined manner. A few Russians only got into the parallel, and five were left dead close outside. The conduct of both officers and men was admirable, and it is with deep concern that I have to report the death of Captain Edwards, of the 68th Foot, and that of five men. I have also the pain of saying that the wounded amount to thirty."

And Sir C. A. Windham writes, in his diary :—

"May 12th; just after I had coiled myself up in my blankets a sapper came and stated that there had been a heavy attack on the Green Hill advance, and asked for an ambulance wagon. I turned out and got on my horse (1.30 a.m.), went to Major Grant, and ordered one. I then returned and went to the trenches, and found there were thirty-six killed and wounded on our side, and about twelve Russians killed in the trenches. Macbeth was much pleased with the conduct of the men. Shocking wet night, and some of the men severely wounded. Captain Edwards, of the 68th, killed."

As regards the operations on 7th June, Sir C. A. Windham writes :—

"At a quarter past six the signal went, and they (i.e., the French) attacked the Mamelon and carried it with little or no opposition. Previous to the attack, I accompanied Norcott and 300 of the 68th to the Woronzoff road and placed them in reserve, and, I hoped, in safety. I took Hamilton with me and left him there. On our way down a 42-pounder came slap into the middle of the men, but, thank God, hurt no one."

According to Lord Raglan's despatches, Lieutenant John Marshall was killed on this day, but according to the regimental records he was killed on 8th June, on which latter day repeated attempts were made by the Russians to regain possession of the Quarries. During this summer cholera again made its appearance, and the 68th lost six men from it.

THE DURHAM LIGHT INFANTRY

During the siege of Sevastopol there were frequent casualties in the regiment, but no considerable number occurred on any one day.

In the final assault upon Sevastopol on 8th September the 4th Division was in reserve, and the 68th was not called upon to take an active part in the closing act of the eleven months' siege.

In October "Alma, Inkerman, and Sevastopol" were ordered to be borne upon the colours.

An interesting fact connected with this year is that a private of the 68th, Robert Robinson, who had been invalided early in the war, was selected in January to be personal attendant upon Miss Florence Nightingale, and that he accompanied her from Scutari to the Crimea, and during her sojourn in the latter place. It is gratifying to learn that he performed his duties so well that on his return to England Miss Nightingale took steps to have his education improved, obtained employment for him, and continued in after years to be his benefactor in many ways.

1856   The regiment was inspected by Brigadier-General Staunton, commanding 2nd Brigade, 4th Division, on the Sevastopol Heights, on 8th February, 1856, and three days afterwards, at the same place, by Major-General R. Garrett, commanding 4th Division.

On 17th May the regiment (28 officers, 47 serjeants, 18 buglers, 694 rank and file) embarked at Balaklava on the P. and O. s.s. "Rippon" for Corfu, and sailed the same evening; 4 serjeants and 22 men, included in the above figures, were taken on board at Scutari.

The casualties in the Crimean war were:—

	F.O.	Capts.	Subalterns.	Staff.	Serjts.	Buglers.	R. & F.
Killed	1	1	2	1	—	—	32
Wounded	1	1	2	—	2	2	68
Died	—	—	1	—	6	4	205
Total	2	2	5	1	8	6	305

Of the wounded, one officer, Brevet-Lieutenant-Colonel Harry Smith, and nineteen men died from their wounds.

The above figures, quoted from the regimental records, differ

CRIMEAN COLOURS (68TH).

Monument in Leeds Parish Church.

slightly, as regards rank and file, from the figures on the Crimean monument in Durham Cathedral.

The regiment arrived at Corfu on 23rd May, disembarked on the next day, and encamped on the esplanade until the 29th, when it marched into the Citadel Barracks.

Notification was shortly afterwards made that the Emperor of the French had awarded the Legion of Honour to Lieutenant-Colonel H. Smyth, C.B., Captain T. de C. Hamilton, Lieutenant A. H. Tucker, Colour-Serjeant H. Sladden, Privates W. Fletcher, and J. Ogden.

At the conclusion of the war twelve names were submitted for the Victoria Cross, but the much prized honour was only awarded to Captain T. de C. Hamilton and Private W. Byrne.

The award was notified in the "London Gazette" in the following words:—

Victoria Cross.

"Captain T. de Courcy Hamilton, 68th Light Infantry.

"For having on the night of 11th May, 1855, during a most determined sortie, boldly charged the enemy with a small force from a battery, of which they had obtained possession in great numbers, thereby saving the works from falling into the hands of the enemy. He was conspicuous on this occasion for his gallantry and daring conduct.

"Private John Byrne, 68th Light Infantry.

"At the battle of Inkerman, when the regiment was ordered to retire, Private J. Byrne went back towards the enemy, and, at the risk of his own life, brought in a wounded soldier under fire. On 11th May, 1855, he bravely engaged in a hand-to-hand contest with one of the enemy on the parapet of the work he was defending, prevented the entrance of the enemy, killed his antagonist, and captured his arms."

In addition to the Legion of Honour, the Emperor of the French sent the French Crimean Medal for distribution to a proportion of the British Army; nine non-commissioned officers and men of the 68th were recommended to His Majesty to receive the medal, but the names of the last two are not mentioned in regimental records as having received it. Their names are:—

THE DURHAM LIGHT INFANTRY

Serjeant-Major John Gibbons; wounded at Inkerman; particularly distinguished for discipline.

Serjeant Peter Delany; twice wounded at Inkerman.

Corporal Patrick Finns; received two musket balls through the jaw at Inkerman.

Private James Sims; gallantry in action on 22nd November, 1854, on the Woronzoff Road.

Serjeant Thomas Watson.
Private William Ferris. } Distinguished conduct 11th May, 1855.
Private Charles Ross.

Private Joseph Mitchell; wounded at Inkerman, and wounded a second time after his return from hospital at Scutari.

Corporal Donohue; wounded 11th May, 1855.

The King of Sardinia presented four hundred medals for military valour to the British Army; the following were the fortunate recipients of this honour in the 68th:—

Lieutenant-Colonel Henry Smyth, C.B.; commanded the regiment throughout the campaign.

Lieutenant-Colonel George Macbeath, C.B.; present at the Alma, Inkerman, and the Siege of Sevastopol.

Lieutenant Sheffield Grace; distinguished conduct on the Woronzoff Road, 22nd November, 1854.

Lieutenant Francis de Luttrell Saunderson; distinguished conduct, 11th May, 1855.

Private Samuel Burrows; rescuing a wounded officer under heavy fire, 22nd November, 1854.

Private J. Magner; distinguished conduct, 11th May, 1855; and on other occasions.

The Sultan of Turkey distributed the Turkish Crimean Medal generally to the allied forces; the device on the medal varied slightly according to whether it was intended for the British, French, or Sardinians; but some of the medals intended for the Sardinians were accidentally distributed to the British Army.

CHAPTER VI.

THE 68TH LIGHT INFANTRY (1856-1881).

In 1856 the following movements took place in the Ionian Islands:—

2nd June—1 officer and 34 non-commissioned officers and men to Cerigo.

13th June—The reserve companies from Malta, under Major Lewis, rejoined head-quarters.

15th August—4 officers and 204 non-commissioned officers and men embarked on the transport "Mauritia" for Zante; and a detachment also embarked on the same vessel for Cephalonia.

28th August—Head-quarters and remaining three companies (13 officers and 460 non-commissioned officers and men) embarked on the transport "Prince Arthur," and, having disembarked a detachment of 1 officer and 43 non-commissioned officers and men at Ithaca, reached Cephalonia on the 30th. This party occupied Argostoli, and detachments, each numbering about fifty of all ranks, were sent to Lixuri and the Castle of St. George.

On 10th November the establishment was reduced to 43 officers and 1,091 non-commissioned officers and men.

1857 There was an inspection by Major-General Sir C. Butler, C.B., on 15th May, 1857.

Towards the end of July, 1857, the detachments in the islands of Zante, Ithaca, and Cerigo, now numbering altogether 376 all ranks, were collected by the transport "Dutchman" and conveyed to Portsmouth, where they disembarked on 15th August, and proceeded to Colewort Barracks. Head-quarters at Cephalonia, 603 all ranks, embarked on the transport "Lebanon" on 7th September, and having disembarked at Portsmouth on the 22nd proceeded to Anglesey Barracks, where the wing from Colewort Barracks joined them. There was an inspection by Major-General the Hon. Sir J. Y. Scarlett, K.C.B., on 17th October.

On 5th November new colours were presented by H.R.H. the Duke of Cambridge to the regiment, over one thousand strong on parade, on Southsea Common; the old colours were subsequently deposited in the Parish Church of Leeds.

On the 12th of the same month, the regiment was entertained at the Crystal Palace, Sydenham, by the officers; the band of the Grenadier Guards attended specially for this occasion.

In the same month the establishment was raised to 48 officers (including two lieutenant-colonels) and 1,291 non-commissioned officers and men.

In December the regiment sailed for Madras; the left wing, 18 officers and 371 non-commissioned officers and men, on s.s. "Argo," 2,249 tons, on the 19th; the right wing, 21 officers and 434 non-commissioned officers and men, on s.s. "Australian," 1,351 tons, on the 22nd.

1858 The "Australian" reached Madras first, on 5th March, 1858; the party on board disembarked on the following day, and was quartered at Government House. The "Argo" arrived on 9th March; the party on board was transhipped on the 12th to the freight ship "Minden" for conveyance to Burmah.

On 13th March head-quarters and two companies, 12 officers and 240 non-commissioned officers and men, embarked on s.s. "Viscount Canning," and sailed with the "Minden" in tow; both ships reached Rangoon on the 22nd. The three companies, 10 officers and 212 non-commissioned officers and men, of the right wing, which had been left at Madras, rejoined head-quarters at Rangoon on the 30th of the same month.

Detachments were sent in October to Meaday and Thayetmyo, and remained there until 17th November.

There was an inspection by Major-General J. Bell on 30th October.

1859 Early in 1859 two large drafts, numbering together 393 men, joined from home; the strength of the regiment was in consequence brought up to a total of 1,258 all ranks.

On 27th May one company was sent to Meaday and one to

THE 68TH LIGHT INFANTRY (1856-1881)

Thayetmyo; and on 16th June two more companies were despatched to Thayetmyo.

The distribution of companies was then, six at Rangoon, three at Thayetmyo, one at Meaday, and two at the depot in Ireland.

1860 During 1860 there were several changes of companies between head-quarters and the two detachments.

1861 On 1st January, 1861, the state of the regiment was—

Head-quarters, Rangoon, seven companies	818	all ranks.
Thayetmyo } Three companies	226	,, ,,
Meaday }	75	,, ,,
Depot at Poonamalee	48	,, ,,
Depot at Fermoy	248	,, ,,
Total service and depot companies	1415	,, ,,

In March the facings were changed from green to dark green.

1862 In March and November, 1862, the regiment was inspected by Major-General M. Carthew.

1863 On 1st April, 1863, a trained bandmaster from Kneller Hall was added to the establishment.

The service of non-commissioned officers and men on 1st July, 1863, was:—

	Serjts.	Buglers.	Corpls.	Privates.	Total.
19 to 21 years	—	—	—	1	1
15 to 19 years	—	—	—	3	3
10 to 15 years	—	—	—	5	5
5 to 10 years	41	12	31	427	511
Under 5 years	5	8	9	380	402
	46	20	40	816	922

Of the above number, 598 were members of different branches of the Protestant religion, and 324 were Roman Catholics.

There were 120 women on the strength of the service companies on this date.

In the late autumn of this year the regiment embarked at Rangoon for New Zealand in three divisions; the first, on s.s.

THE DURHAM LIGHT INFANTRY

"Armenian," 789 tons, 7 officers and 349 non-commissioned officers and men, on 29th October; the second, on s.s. "Australian," 1,351 tons, head-quarters, 12 officers and 299 non-commissioned officers and men, on 21st November; and the third, on s.s. "Light Brigade," 9 officers, 298 non-commissioned officers and men and families, on 29th November. These three ships arrived at Auckland on different dates in the middle of January, 1864; one man on the "Australian" died during the voyage.

1864

Shortly before the departure of the regiment from Burmah the inhabitants of Rangoon presented the officers with a handsome piece of plate, in the shape of a large Burmese silver bowl, which is now used as the centre piece on the mess table; they also presented the non-commissioned officers with a testimonial.

On 20th January head-quarters and six companies, 14 officers and 406 non-commissioned officers and men, of the 68th, and 120 of the 43rd, embarked on H.M.S. "Miranda," 15 guns, 1,039 tons, captain, Robert Jenkins, and landed at Tauranga, Bay of Plenty, on the following day.

Detachments were supplied to Rangariri and Razorback on the 23rd January by the party on the "Armenian," which had been the first ship to sail from Rangoon, and had only reached Auckland on the previous day; also a detachment of 67, all ranks, was stationed at Maketu from 10th March to 9th April.

By 25th April all detachments had rejoined head-quarters, and the ten service companies were again together.

The knapsack carried by the 68th at this time, with the regulation articles of kit inside it, weighed 20 lbs.

On 29th April the attack on the Gate Pah took place; although it was not successful great heroism was displayed by the British.

However, the Maoris, in spite of the failure of the British attack, evacuated the stockade during the night, before operations could be resumed on the following morning.

The part played by the regiment in this action is thus described in Sir James Alexander's "Bush Fighting—The Maori War":—

"On the 27th (April) the General moved the 68th Regiment, under Colonel Greer, and a mixed detachment of 170 men of the

THE 68TH LIGHT INFANTRY (1856-1881)

12th, 14th, and 65th Regiments, under Major Ryan, of the 70th, towards the Maori entrenchments.

"The 68th Regiment and Major Ryan's detachment were encamped about 1,200 yards from the enemy's position on the 27th.

"Strength of the 68th, 732 officers and men.

"Colonel Greer and the 68th started at 6.45 p.m. (after dark), 28th April, to get in rear of the enemy by a flank march; to accomplish this it was necessary to cross part of a mud flat at the head of the bay, about three-quarters of a mile long, only passable at low water, and then nearly knee deep, and within musketry range of the shore.

"Each man carried one day's cooked rations and a great coat.

"The rest of our troops made a feigned attack to divert the enemy's attention, and the 68th reached the top of the ridge unopposed; at 1.30 a.m. (29th April) Colonel Greer advanced, and at 3 a.m. was 1,000 yards directly in rear of the pah; he sent Major Shuttleworth forward with three companies to the left rear of the pah, and at daybreak detached three companies, under Major Kirby, to the right, and put sentries round the pah.

"There was bombardment from the rest of the troops on the next day (29th) until 4 p.m., when it ceased, and a rocket signal told Colonel Greer that the assault on the pah was about to take place, when he moved up close round the rear. The Maoris made a determined rush for the right rear of the pah, but were met by three companies of the 68th, and after a skirmish the main body were driven back into the pah; about twenty got past on the right of the 68th, but they received a flank fire from Lieutenant Cox's party; sixty men of the 68th, and Lieutenant Hotham's thirty men of the Naval Brigade, and sixteen of the Maoris were seen to fall, and a number of men pursued the remainder. The men were collected again and posted. Captain Trent, 68th, and Lieutenant and Adjutant Covey gave valuable assistance, also Mr. Parris, who had volunteered as guide.

"The officers and men of the 68th were accorded the greatest credit for the cheerfulness and zeal with which they performed very harassing duties."

In this action the 68th lost one serjeant and one man killed and one serjeant and seventeen privates wounded; one of the privates subsequently died from his wounds.

Colonel Greer, Major Shuttleworth, Captain Trent, Lieutenant Cox, and Lieutenant and Adjutant Covey were mentioned in despatches for their conduct on this day.

On 23rd May a redoubt was thrown up at Judea, and a detachment, 107 all ranks, was left there.

Two companies, 165 all ranks, were detached to Maketu, and two companies, 162 all ranks, to Gate Pah.

Colonel Greer having been informed on 20th June at Te Papa that the Maoris were erecting a new pah on a place called Te Ranga, so situated as to cut off his communications, started on the following morning with a force of 600 officers and men, made up from the 43rd, 68th, and 1st Waikato Militia; he had also one 6-pounder gun with a few artillerymen, and some cavalry of the Colonial Defence Force; the information given to him was correct, and Colonel Greer, finding the Maoris in great strength, sent back to Te Papa for reinforcements; however, he commenced the attack before his reinforcements arrived, and in the course of the afternoon gained a complete victory; over 100 of the enemy were killed, several were captured, and the pah was destroyed. The casualties in the 68th in this affair were four rank and file killed, Captains Trent and Casement, Lieutenant Stuart, Ensign Palmer, two serjeants, and eighteen rank and file wounded; two of the wounded rank and file died from their wounds.

Serjeant-Major Tudor, Serjeant J. Murray, Corporal J. Byrne, V.C., Private T. Smith, and Private Caffrey were conspicuous for their gallant conduct on this day.

Colonel Greer was awarded the C.B., and Major Shuttleworth and Captain Trent were given brevet promotion.

In August the detachments at Maketu and Judea were both reduced to about 80, all ranks.

1865 On 10th January, 1865, a detachment was sent to Auckland on H.M.S. "Esk," 21 guns, 1,169 tons, Captain J. P. Luce, and thence to Onehanga, where it embarked for Wanganui on 19th February; after a few days it proceeded to Patea, and on 13th March formed part of a force which, under Lieutenant-Colonel

THE 68TH LIGHT INFANTRY (1856-1881)

Morant, had a brisk skirmish with the Maoris; Serjeant Castles was on this day severely wounded in the chest; this detachment returned to Wanganui on 17th June.

During the remainder of 1865 and the first two months of 1866 there were many moves of detachments; finally in March, 1866, the regiment was concentrated at Otahuhu, near Auckland, and was inspected there by Major-General Ireton Chute on the 9th, previous to embarkation for England.

The regiment then embarked on three ships, the "Ballarat," "Percy," and "Maori," which reached Portsmouth on 12th June, 30th June, and 7th July respectively.

The total casualties in the Maori war were four officers wounded, six non-commissioned officers and men killed, and thirty-nine (three of whom died from their wounds) wounded; in addition to the above, there were twenty-five deaths from disease in New Zealand.

Serjeant-Major Tudor, Lance-Serjeant J. Castles, and Lance-Corporal J. Byrne were awarded the medal for distinguished conduct in the field.

Serjeant John Murray was awarded the Victoria Cross—

"For his distinguished conduct at Te Ranga on the 21st June, 1864, when the enemy's position was being stormed, in running up to a rifle pit containing from eight to ten of the enemy, and, without any assistance, killing or wounding every one of them. He is stated to have afterwards proceeded up the works, fighting desperately, and still continuing to bayonet the enemy."—"London Gazette."

Sir James Alexander gives another version of Serjeant Murray's heroism. He states:—

"Serjeant Murray, 68th, was recommended for the V.C. for saving the life of Corporal J. Byrne, V.C., 68th, who was the first man of his company into the rifle pits, and was going to be tomahawked by a Maori, whom he had transfixed with his bayonet."

1866 In March, 1866, the establishment was reduced to ten companies, 49 serjeants, 21 buglers, 40 corporals, and 640 privates. The depot companies rejoined head-quarters at the Clarence Barracks shortly after the latter had arrived at Portsmouth.

There was a detachment of two officers and sixty non-commissioned officers and men at Tipnor from 26th October to 15th November.

There was an inspection by Lieutenant-General Sir G. Butler, K.C.B., on 17th October.

1867   The regiment proceeded to Crewe, on special service, on 15th March, 1867, and returned to Portsmouth on the 22nd of the same month.

In April the establishment was reduced by 80 privates.

On 30th May the regiment was moved to the North Camp, Aldershot, and was inspected by Brigadier-General Sir A. Horsford, K.C.B., commanding 3rd Brigade, on the following day.

1868   On the night of 31st January, 1868, the regiment left Aldershot, and arrived at Manchester on the following morning.

There was a detachment of varying strength at Wigan from 31st March to 19th May; and again on 17th November a detachment, 38 all ranks, was sent to Wigan for special duty, but it rejoined head-quarters the same day. The usual half-yearly inspections were made by Major-General Sir J. Garvock, K.C.B.

1869   In April, 1869, the establishment was further reduced by 40 privates. On 10th September the regiment embarked at Liverpool on H.M.'s troopship "Himalaya," 2 guns, 3,453 tons, Captain Shute B. Piers—this ship was originally built for the P. and O. Company—and arrived at Queenstown on the 12th; on the next day, three companies proceeded to Tralee, two to Fermoy, two to Ballincollig, and one to Killarney; head-quarters and two companies were transhipped and conveyed by river steamer to Cork on the 14th.

Early in October the detachments at Tralee and Killarney rejoined head-quarters at Cork, and the detachment at Ballincollig was moved to Fort Elizabeth and Cat Fort in the city of Cork.

On 13th October there was an inspection by Major-General G. Campbell, C.B.

In 1870 the following movements took place:—

1870   5th January—One company to Youghal.

6th January—Four companies to Fort Camden, and two companies to Fort Carlisle in Cork Harbour.

THE 68TH LIGHT INFANTRY (1856-1881)

5th April—The company at Youghal was sent to Forts Camden and Carlisle.

8th, 11th, and 12th July—The regiment was moved from Cork and quartered as under:—

Head-quarters and three companies at Kilkenny, two companies at Birr, two companies at Templemore, two companies at Tipperary, and one company at Portumna.

6th August—The detachment at Tipperary was moved to Templemore.

14th September—Two companies were sent from Templemore to Galway.

21st, 22nd, and 23rd September—Head-quarters and two companies proceeded by march route from Kilkenny to Templemore.

28th December—The two companies at Birr rejoined head-quarters at Templemore.

29th December—The detachment at Portumna was moved to Galway.

In May, 1870, authority was given for "New Zealand" to be borne on the colours; and in August the establishment was augmented to 800 rank and file.

1871   In February, 1871, the establishment was again augmented by an additional 50 rank and file.

After an inspection by Major-General G. Campbell, C.B., on 6th May, the following movements took place in 1871.

20th May—Five companies, under Major Trent, to Fort Carlisle, Cork Harbour, for engineering work.

9th June—The detachment at Galway rejoined head-quarters at Templemore.

29th June—One company from Templemore to Fort Carlisle to relieve men for musketry.

10th July—One company from Templemore to Kilkenny.

26th July—One company from Templemore to Birr.

12th August—One company from Fort Carlisle to Templemore.

18th September—One company from, and one to, Fort Carlisle from head-quarters.

18th September—One company to Waterford.

THE DURHAM LIGHT INFANTRY

2nd October—The detachment at Waterford returned to Templemore.

3rd October—The detachment at Kilkenny returned to Templemore.

18th October—The detachment at Fort Carlisle proceeded to Cork.

20th October—One company from Templemore to Youghal.

24th October—Head-quarters and two companies from Templemore to Cork.

25th October—One company, Templemore to Cat Fort, Cork.

26th October—The detachment at Birr to Fort Elizabeth, Cork.

On 2nd August Her Majesty approved of the following proposals that were submitted to her by H.R.H. the Duke of Cambridge:—

(i.) That a universal pattern button bearing the Royal Arms be substituted for the present button bearing the number of the regiment, which in future will be shown on the shoulder strap.

(ii.) That the facings be removed from the cuffs, but retained on the collars.

(iii.) That the colour of the tunics for the band be scarlet instead of white.

(iv.) That the number of patterns of lace on the drummers' coats be reduced to one.

(v.) That the Army be dressed in scarlet instead of red.

Amongst the reasons quoted in favour of these changes when they were laid before Her Majesty are:—

As regards (iii.), "The proposal to change the colour of the tunics for the band from white to scarlet has often been recommended by the medical officers, as the white cloth must be cleaned with pipeclay, which, if put on dry, causes the soldier to inhale a quantity of dust, and if applied wet renders the tunic damp and unhealthy. It has also been found that the enemy at a distance can easily distinguish the number of battalions in the opposing force by merely counting the bands," etc. As regards (iv.), "There are at present about 250 different patterns of lace on the drummers' coats," etc.

THE 68TH LIGHT INFANTRY (1856-1881)

On 1st September the establishment was augmented to 1,032, all ranks.

1872 On 9th February, 1872, the regiment embarked at Queenstown on H.M.'s Indian troopship "Euphrates," 3 guns, 4,173 tons, Captain St. George C. D'A. Irvine, and, having reached Bombay, via the Suez Canal, on 13th March, proceeded on the following day to Poona, and was quartered in the Wanowrie lines; strength, 30 officers and 890 non-commissioned officers and men.

1873 In 1873, Major-General J. T. Grant, C.B., was the inspecting officer. In April this year the depot was established at Sunderland with the depot of the 106th Light Infantry; it had, on the departure of the regiment for India, been attached successively to the 43rd Light Infantry at Cork, to the 98th at Templemore, and from October, 1872, to the 35th at Sheffield. In December the regiment attended a camp of exercise at Chinchwud.

1874 On 9th February, 1874, four companies were sent, under Major Trent, to Bombay, in consequence of riots there; this party returned to Poona on 15th March.

In November the regiment left Poona in two divisions; the first, consisting of head-quarters and four companies, 510 all ranks, was conveyed by rail to Deolali on the 7th, and thence by rail to Khandwa on the 8th; it then marched to Mhow, arriving on the 18th; the second division, four companies, was conveyed to Deolali by rail on the 30th, and thence by rail to Khandwa on 1st December; the journey was then continued by march route, and the allocation of companies was, one at Asirghar, one at Indore, and two at Mhow.

1875 During the year there were some interchanges of companies between head-quarters and the different detachments; and towards the end of August there was an outbreak of cholera at Mhow; head-quarters went into cholera camp at Husora on 23rd August, and returned to Mhow on different dates in September; during this outbreak 12 men, 4 women, and 11 children died. Captain A. F. Marshall also died from cholera at Ahmedabad, where he was D.A.Q.M.G.

On 23rd December the regiment, 20 officers and 826 non-commissioned officers and men, marched from Mhow, en route for Nasirabad and Nimach; three companies arrived at Nimach on

THE DURHAM LIGHT INFANTRY

1876 — 11th January, 1876, and head-quarters with the remaining five companies arrived at Nasirabad on 29th January; during this march fine weather was experienced, and the troops enjoyed excellent health. In February, as well as in February of the following year, there were inspections by Major-General G. S. Montgomery, C.S.I. In December there was an interchange of companies between Nasirabad and Nimach.

A medal to commemorate the proclamation of H.M. the Queen as Empress of India at Delhi on 1st January, 1877, was granted to every regiment in India; that granted to the 68th was presented to Orderly Room Colour-Serjeant T. Lambert.

1877 — Captain Leonard Bolden was killed by a tiger when shooting near Mandalgarh on 22nd April, 1877.

In this year the helmet was adopted in lieu of the shako for infantry of the line on home service.

In December, 1877, there was again an interchange of companies between Nasirabad and Nimach.

1878 — On 19th February, 1878, there was an inspection by Major-General T. Forbes, C.B. There were severe cholera epidemics at both Nasirabad and Nimach in the early autumn of this year; twenty-five men and one woman died from this disease.

On 2nd November head-quarters and the five companies, 380 all ranks, at Nasirabad left that station by rail, and arrived at Mian Mir on the 8th; they remained in camp until the 15th, when they moved into barracks; one company was detached on the 11th to Fort Lahore.

On 21st November one company was detailed as guard to H.E. the Viceroy, the Earl of Lytton, at Bhawulpur House, Lahore, and remained on that duty until 18th December.

On 25th November the three companies, 210 all ranks, at Nimach left that station by march route for Nasirabad, and were conveyed from the latter place by rail to Mian Mir; they rejoined head-quarters on 19th December.

While at Mian Mir the usual inspections were made by Brigadier-General Murray, C.B.

THE 68TH LIGHT INFANTRY (1856-1881)

1879   In April and May, 1879, over 230 men were sent to Banikhet and Dalhousie for the hot weather.

There was a severe cholera epidemic in May, which resulted in the death of twelve men and two children; the regiment went into camp at Changa Manga, and returned to Mian Mir on 21st June. In September one company was sent to Multan Fort; it returned on 11th November.

During this year two very large drafts, amounting together to 450 men, were received from the 106th Light Infantry, the consequence was that at the end of October there were 1,011 non-commissioned officers and men in the regiment.

1880   In April and May, 1880, 400 men were sent to Banikhet and Dalhousie for the hot weather.

At the conclusion of the Afghan war there was a considerable concentration of troops at Mian Mir in the autumn, and H.E. the Marquis of Ripon held a durbar at Lahore.

On 1st December the regiment commenced to march to Meerut, and, having been joined at Amritsar by a party of convalescents from Dalhousie, arrived at Meerut on 5th January, 1881, with a

1881   strength of 761 non-commissioned officers and men; twelve days after this a detachment of about 220, all ranks, proceeded to Fatehgarh; this detachment was augmented in the following August by an additional 100 men. During the stay of the regiment at Meerut the usual inspections were made by Lieutenant-General Sir R. O. Bright, K.C.B.

On 1st July, 1881, the numbers of line regiments were abolished; the 68th on this date became the 1st Battalion Durham Light Infantry, and the 106th became the 2nd Battalion Durham Light Infantry, the 68th lost its dark green facings, and the Durham Light Infantry, in common with other English regiments not designated "Royal," was ordered to assume white facings; badges, buttons, etc., being similar in both battalions; at the same time the distinctive privilege, enjoyed by the non-commissioned officers, of wearing their chevrons on both arms was taken away; from this date they were to be worn on the right arm only. The rank of second-lieutenant was abolished; and there were numerous other changes.

CHAPTER VII.

THE 106TH LIGHT INFANTRY (1839-1862).

THREE separate regiments have borne the number "106," but, although the first two had not any connection with each other nor with the present 2nd Battalion of the Durham Light Infantry, a few remarks on them may not be considered to be out of place.

The first 106th Regiment was raised by that brave soldier and fiery politician, Lieutenant-Colonel Isaac Barré; it existed from 17th October, 1761, to 24th April, 1763; its establishment was, at the commencement of its career, five companies, each consisting of 4 serjeants, 4 corporals, 2 drummers, and 100 private men, with 2 fifers in addition for the grenadier company, besides the commissioned officers; the establishment was later raised to ten companies, 1,034 all ranks. On 3rd November, 1761, His Majesty King George III. was pleased to order Lieutenant-Colonel Barré's regiment to be named "The Black Musqueteers"; this name is supposed to have been derived from the black facings and black belts worn.

The regiment was raised in London, but recruiting was not very brisk at the start, as by 1st December, 1761, the regiment only consisted of 8 officers, 14 serjeants, 10 drummers, and 26 rank and file; matters however rapidly improved, and when the regiment proceeded from London to Devizes in March, 1762, it numbered 499 rank and file; it was quartered at Winchester in November, 1762, and in the following December was at Plymouth, over 600 strong; it was disbanded at Exeter in April, 1763, being one of several regiments that were reduced after the Peace of Paris (10th February, 1763) at the conclusion of the Seven Years' War.

The second 106th regiment came into existence on 17th May, 1794; it was formed from the Norwich Royal Regiment of Volunteers, which had been raised, at his own expense, by William Earle

THE 106TH LIGHT INFANTRY (1839-1862)

Bulwer, father of the distinguished novelist E. G. Bulwer-Lytton, afterwards the first Baron Lytton. W. Earle Bulwer was only "major commanding," although there were two other majors. This regiment had a very brief life and very little can be found out about it now; it was disbanded early in 1795.

Two interesting circumstances connected with this regiment are, that Major Bulwer had been at one time a lieutenant in the 68th, and that the celebrated admiral, Thomas Lord Cochrane, afterwards 10th Earl of Dundonald, was a captain in it.

The late Colonel William Gordon states, in his book, that this regiment was raised at Norwich, and was called "The Norfolk Rangers"; his authority for the latter statement cannot be traced; the possibility of a misconception on this point is raised by the fact that in 1794 there was a regiment of volunteer cavalry in Norfolk, of which the Marquis of Townshend was "Major Commandant," called "The Norfolk Rangers"; the 106th in one of its returns is called the "Norwich Regiment."

The third 106th Regiment is the present 2nd Battalion of the Durham Light Infantry, which in its earliest days was known as the "2nd Bombay European Regiment," and later for about twenty years as the "106th Bombay Light Infantry."

As, however, previous to the year 1839 there had been more than one regiment of European infantry in the service of the Hon. East India Company in the Bombay Presidency, it is necessary, to avoid confusion, to state a few facts concerning these previous "2nd Bombay Europeans," before commencing to record the history of the present 2nd Durham Light Infantry. On three different occasions second battalions had been raised for the Bombay Regiment of European Infantry, but none of them existed for more than ten years; these second battalions were frequently alluded to, even in official documents, as if they were separate regiments, and this fact no doubt gave rise to the confusion as to the date of the origin of the present 2nd Durham Light Infantry. Assuming this to be the case it is still difficult to understand why the year 1826 is given in some accounts as the date of origin; on the first occasion there was a second battalion from August, 1768 to 1778; there was also a third battalion from 1768 to 1770.

THE DURHAM LIGHT INFANTRY

On the second occasion there was a second battalion from September, 1788, to July, 1796; on the third occasion there was a second battalion from June, 1824, to October, 1829.

1839   By an order of the Governor-General of India, dated 29th July, 1839, it was notified that the Hon. East India Company had resolved to add an additional regiment of European infantry to each of their armies in the presidencies of Bengal, Madras, and Bombay; each of these regiments was to consist of ten companies, was to have an establishment of 1 colonel, 2 lieutenant-colonels, 2 majors, 10 captains, 16 lieutenants, 8 ensigns, and 920 non-commissioned officers and men, and was to date from 8th October, 1839. On 8th October, Lieutenant-Colonel G. B. Brooks (Brevet-Major-General) was appointed to be the Colonel; and in Bombay orders of 16th December, it was notified that the new regiment in the Bombay Presidency was to be a light infantry regiment, that its uniform was to be red, facings pale buff, lace white with a black worm, that it was to be armed with the new double-sighted musket, and that its head-quarters were to be established at Poona on the 1st of the following February.

1840   In January, 1840, the order as to the new regiment being made light infantry was suspended, but in the following November it was confirmed.

On 3rd January, 3 colour-serjeants, 10 serjeants, 15 corporals, 2 drummers, and 21 privates were transferred from the 1st European Regiment, as from 8th October, 1839.

It is worth noting that, while numerals were placed on the buttons of native regiments, the crest of the East India Company was originally the only design on the buttons of the European regiments, but when it was finally decided that the 2nd Bombay European Regiment was to be light infantry the device on the buttons was a bugle horn with a "2" inside it.

The officers, unless promoted on transfer, were gazetted with the dates of their commissions in their former regiments in the Bombay Army.

During the year 1840 various parties of recruits joined from England, including one, on 29th July, of 87 men who had been saved from the wreck of the "Lord William Bentinck" on the rocks off

THE 106TH LIGHT INFANTRY (1839-1862)

Colaba; and by the end of the year the regiment was over the established strength. The regiment was then denominated "The Second Regiment Bombay European Light Infantry."

At this period the depot of the East India Company's European forces was at Chatham.

1842 — On 6th April, 1842, the left wing of the regiment left Poona by march route for Bombay in relief of the 1st regiment which was then quartered there. During this year the facings were changed from pale buff to white, which latter continued to be the colour for sixty years.

On 17th November the left wing was relieved by the right wing, and shortly afterwards the regiment received orders to join the force under Sir C. Napier in Sind; the left wing, with which were the head-quarters, then returned to Bombay. On approaching that city, head-quarters were at once transferred to the right wing, which embarked without delay for Cutch, and, having landed at Mandvi, marched for Bhuj, and arrived there on 16th March, 1843; the left wing remained at Bombay until 8th May, 1843, when it

1843 — embarked for Karachi; but the strength of the Amirs had been broken by Sir C. Napier at Dubba on 24th March, so the regiment did not have the good fortune to be actively engaged. It was, however, the recipient of a very flattering message from Sir C. Napier on quitting his command in January, 1844, for Belgaum; head-quarters and the right wing arrived at Bombay about 25th January, and then sailed for Vengurla; the left wing sailed direct from Karachi to Vengurla, and then rejoined head-quarters at Belgaum.

Late in 1843 the depot of the East India Company's European forces was moved from Chatham to Warley.

1844 — In September, 1844, a detachment of the regiment, consisting of 9 officers and 200 non-commissioned officers and men, under Captain Gillanders, formed the European portion of a "Field Detachment" sent, under the command of Lieutenant-Colonel J. Wallace, 20th Madras Native Infantry, to quell an insurrection that had broken out among the Ghadkarries in the Kolhapur district. The inhabitants of the state of Sawant Wari also joined in the insurrection.

THE DURHAM LIGHT INFANTRY

The town of Samanghur was stormed early in the morning of 13th October; there were two columns of attack, the first, under Captain Jones, included eighty men of the 2nd European Light Infantry; the second, under Captain Gillanders, included seventy men of the 2nd European Light Infantry. Everything was ready at 4.30 a.m., and the storming only occupied half an hour; the enemy's losses were 500 to 600 killed, and 500 to 600 prisoners; the casualties in the 2nd European Light Infantry in the actual storming were: Killed, nil; wounded, four privates; but there were several casualties during the siege, including Lieutenant W. P. Shakespear, who died from a gunshot wound on 30th September; Private W. Ward, who was killed on 27th September; another private, whose name cannot now be traced, killed; and some men wounded.

On 1st December the fortress of Panhala was captured; on this occasion Major-General P. de Lamotte, C.B., was in command, and the detachment of the 2nd European Light Infantry was in the 1st Brigade, under Lieutenant-Colonel Wallace; the storming party, under Lieutenant-Colonel R. W. Brough, included 100 men of the 2nd European Light Infantry, under Captain Gillanders; the storming occupied one hour, and about 2,000 prisoners were captured; the casualties in the regiment on this day were: Killed, two privates (D. McLeod and H. White); wounded, Lieutenant Aitchison and ten privates.

On 8th December the Pettah of Rangna was stormed; the centre column of attack consisted of Captain Gillanders, with three other officers and 100 men of his regiment; the only casualty in this party was one private wounded.

Also, in the defile of Sassadroog on 31st December, Lieutenant Campbell and four privates (C. Mutlow, M. Corcoran, T. Reilly, and D. Breslin) were killed, and Lieutenant Tyacke and four privates were wounded; Lieutenant Thompson was wounded at Sarapur; Ensign Faure was killed while passing along the road between Sassooly and Banda with a mounted escort on 31st December; and two privates (W. Fogarty and A. Beauchamp) were killed and five were wounded on other occasions.

The total casualties in the campaign were: Killed, three officers and ten privates; wounded, three officers, three serjeants, one corporal, and twenty-four privates.

The following were honourably mentioned:—Lance-serjeant E. Leek (Sassadroog), Private W. Noble (Samanghur), Private E. Forrest (Panhala), and Private W. Nicholson (Panhala). Also Corporal T. Thacker, Private W. Walsh, and Private D. Desmond, for bringing in Lieutenant Campbell's body under a heavy fire at Sassadroog.

1846 On 22nd January, 1846, the regiment was presented with its first colours by Major-General Morse at Belgaum; these colours, which were replaced in 1860, were recovered from the Bombay Arsenal in July, 1887, and restored to the 2nd Battalion Durham Light Infantry at Poona.

On 22nd October in the same year the regiment marched from Belgaum and sailed from Vengurla on 8th, 9th, and 10th November in the transports "Recovery," "Eliza," and "Larkins" for Aden, where it disembarked on 22nd November; great discomfort was experienced at Aden owing to the insufficiency of the accommodation in barracks for the number of men quartered there.

1848 On 16th January, 1848, the right wing embarked on s.s. "Queen," and proceeded to Poona, where, in the course of a few weeks, 399 recruits joined from England in three parties; in the following September and January two parties, 100 men in each, were transferred as volunteers to the 1st European Regiment, which was then on active service in the Punjab; four non-commissioned officers of the 2nd European Regiment, Serjeants A. Fletcher and W. Noble, and Corporals A. Bright and J. Lancaster, accompanied the latter party, and were awarded the medal.

1849 The right wing marched from Poona on 1st November, 1849, and arrived at Belgaum on the 29th; a month later it was joined by the left wing, which had arrived at Vengurla from Aden on 15th December.

1850 The strength on 1st January, 1850, was 1,048 non-commissioned officers and men.

1853 In November, 1853, the Hon. East India Company resolved to raise a third European regiment in each of the three presidencies, and a party, consisting of 3 serjeants, 11 corporals, 10 lance-corporals, 2 buglers, and 50 privates from the 2nd, as well as a party from the 1st European Regiment, was drafted to form the nucleus of the new regiment.

During the cold weather, 1853-54, the regiment marched from Belgaum to Karachi; the conduct of the men during this long march elicited much praise from Lord Frederick Fitzclarence, commanding the forces in the Bombay Presidency. There was a detachment at Shikarpur.

1854 In December, 1854, the regiment was moved to Haiderabad (Sind), where it suffered severely from malarial fever, no less than 560 men being sick at one time.

1855 On 14th December, 1855, the name of the regiment was altered to the " 2nd European Regiment, Bombay Light Infantry."

1856 In October, 1856, the Bombay Government organised an " expeditionary field force for foreign service beyond sea," under the command of Major-General F. Stalker, C.B.; the 2nd European Light Infantry was included in this force, and embarked on the river steamers " Indus," " Satellite," and " Jhelum " for conveyance to Karachi, when it was inspected by Major-General Scott. Seventy-four men volunteered from the 1st European Regiment, which was then at Karachi, and 120 more were attached; these men brought the 2nd European Light Infantry up to a total of 929, all ranks, for field service.

On 18th and 19th November, the 2nd European Light Infantry embarked for the Persian Gulf on four steamers, " Punjab," " Ajdaha," " Chusan," and " Victoria," and on 7th December landed at Hallilah Bay, twelve miles south of Bushire, with little opposition; the island Karrak had been occupied by the British three days previously.

The infantry were in two brigades; the 2nd Brigade was under Brigadier R. W. Honner, and was composed of 2nd European Light Infantry, 4th Regiment Native Infantry (Rifle Corps), and 2nd Belooch Battalion. After an advance of two miles the force bivouacked until the 9th, when the old Dutch fort of Reshire, which was garrisoned by 1,000 of the Tungastoon Hill Tribe, was taken; the 2nd European Light Infantry lost two men, M. Daly and J. Doyle, killed, and one serjeant and five men, of whom one belonged

THE 106TH LIGHT INFANTRY (1839-1862)

to the 1st Regiment, wounded in this affair. On the following day an advance was made on Bushire, which the ships of the Indian Navy bombarded for two hours with such success that the town was promptly surrendered; there were not any casualties in the regiment on this day; Lieutenant-Colonel Ramsey is included in those mentioned in Major-General Stalker's despatch, reporting the successes of these two days.

1857 No further operations were carried out until Sir James Outram arrived on 27th January, 1857; in the meantime considerable reinforcements had arrived, and the troops were newly organised, the first division being composed of the original force in the field except the cavalry, under Major-General F. Stalker; the second of the reinforcing troops under Brigadier-General H. Havelock, C.B.; the cavalry division was under Brigadier-General J. Jacob, C.B.

On 3rd February Sir J. Outram marched with 5,000 men, including the 2nd European Light Infantry (693 all ranks), with 18 guns, without tents, etc., to attack the Persians who had occupied an entrenched post near Borasjoon, 46 miles from Bushire. The march was a most fatiguing one owing to the harassing nature of the soil and the incessant rain; the Persians were surprised on the 5th, and fled almost without striking a blow.

On the 7th, after two days' rest, Sir J. Outram set out on his return to Bushire; and at 11 p.m. on the same night his rear-guard was attacked, and the action soon became general; Sir J. Outram was unfortunately thrown from his horse, and was disabled for some hours, but he recovered in time to resume command at daybreak on the 8th, when the action re-commenced and the battle of Kooshab was fought; in about an hour from the time the first shot was fired, the Persians were flying in every direction, leaving 700 dead on the field, 100 prisoners and two guns. In this action the casualties of the 2nd European Light Infantry were: Killed, three men, Privates T. Deveran, T. Galahar, and M. Shield; wounded, Ensign E. M. Woodcock and eight privates; Lieutenant A. D. Frankland, also of the 2nd European Light Infantry, who was brigade-major of cavalry, was killed.

THE DURHAM LIGHT INFANTRY

The same night the troops marched twenty miles, and after a rest of six hours resumed the march and reached Bushire at midnight on 9th February.

The 2nd European Light Infantry did not take part in the expedition to Mohumra, but remained at Bushire until 15th May, when it embarked for Karachi on the ships "Morse," "Nadir Shah," and "Madge Wildfire," which reached their destination on the 29th and 30th of the same month.

Lieutenant-Colonel J. S. Ramsey was again mentioned in despatches.

On 1st June, 118 men volunteered to the 1st European Regiment, which was under orders for Multan.

On 29th July a wing of the 2nd European Light Infantry was ordered to proceed from Karachi to Bombay on s.s. "Berenice"; on arriving at Bombay three companies were transferred to s.s. "Victoria" for conveyance to Goa, where they landed and proceeded to Belgaum, under Major Jones; these three companies reached Belgaum on 11th August, and one of them was at once sent to Dharwar; the remainder of the party which had arrived at Bombay on the "Berenice" proceeded to Kolhapur, with the exception of forty men who were sent, under Major Saunders, to Ratnagiri.

Head-quarters and the other wing of the regiment remained at Karachi until the end of the following November.

One of the first acts of the detachment at Kolhapur on its arrival there was to be present at the disarming of the 27th Native Infantry.

On the night of 13th September head-quarters of the regiment at Karachi were present at the suppression of the intended mutiny and the disarming of the 21st Native Infantry; 200 men, accompanied by a troop of Bombay Horse Artillery, were marched to the lines of the 21st Native Infantry, which was then fallen in; there was not any resistance, but when the 21st Native Infantry had been disarmed about fifty muskets were found to be loaded; the owners of the loaded rifles were made prisoners, the remainder were dismissed, and the European troops returned to their barracks about 5 a.m.

The detachment at Kolhapur was present at the suppression of the rising there on the night of 6th December.

THE 106TH LIGHT INFANTRY (1839-1862)

On 22nd November head-quarters embarked at Karachi and reached Vengurla on 28th, and Belgaum on 8th December.

On 30th November the two companies, which had been at Belgaum since the previous August, proceeded, under Captain Aitchison, to suppress an insurrection that had broken out in the state of Shorapur, and were present, in Colonel G. Malcolm's force, at the taking of the fort of Shorapur on 9th February, 1858; two officers, Captains Aitchison and Jessop, and 91 non-commissioned officers and men of the regiment, were present at this affair, and in due course the officer commanding 2nd European Light Infantry was requested to forward medal rolls, but enquiries on the subject were instituted in 1909, and no correspondence as to whether the rolls had ever been forwarded or not could be traced.

1858

Head-quarters marched early in February, 1858, from Belgaum to join the force in Shorapur; they arrived as far as Danur on the Kistna, as a support to Colonel Malcolm's force, but, as the insurgents had then been defeated, they returned to Belgaum.

On 13th October permission was given for "Persia," "Reshire," and "Kooshab" to be borne on the colours.

On 2nd August the Bill for the extinction of the Hon. East India Company received the Royal Assent, and was entitled "An Act for the Better Government of India"; it was to come into operation on 1st September, 1858; on 1st November a public proclamation was made at Allahabad that Her Majesty the Queen had assumed the direct control and sovereignty of India; that the Company's troops were disbanded, and that those men who continued to serve in their regiments, which now became part of Her Majesty's Forces, were granted a boon of two years' service. The Governor-General now became the Viceroy.

On 1st January, 1859, the strength was 699 non-commissioned officers and men.

1859

In the 2nd European Light Infantry 1 serjeant, 12 corporals, 9 buglers, and 357 privates decided to go home, under G.G.O., 26th July, 1859, and proceeded to Goa for embarkation to England.

In 1859 wicker helmets were supplied to European soldiers in India.

THE DURHAM LIGHT INFANTRY

1860   In January, 1860, the regiment was moved from Belgaum and Kolhapur to Bombay; and on 21st November was presented with new colours in Bombay by Sir William Mansfield, K.C.B., Commander-in-Chief in the Bombay Presidency.

1861   Early in December the regiment left Bombay, and, having been conveyed by rail to Mhow, marched thence to Nimach, where it arrived on 28th January, 1861.

On 11th of April permission was granted for "Bushire" to be borne on the colours. In this year the British and Indian armies were amalgamated; the local European regiments in India now became part of the Imperial Forces; it was optional for all ranks to remain for local employment in India, or to volunteer for general service.

1862   One captain, 9 lieutenants, 1 ensign, 47 serjeants, 29 corporals, 17 buglers, and 397 privates belonging to the 2nd Bombay European Light Infantry became the 106th Bombay Light Infantry on 30th July, 1862; the remainder elected for local service. The establishment at this time was:—1 colonel, 1 lieutenant-colonel, 2 majors, 12 captains, 15 lieutenants, 10 ensigns, 1 paymaster, 1 adjutant, 1 quartermaster, 1 surgeon, 3 assistant surgeons, 1 serjeant-major, 1 quartermaster-serjeant, 1 serjeant-instructor of musketry, 1 paymaster serjeant, 1 armourer serjeant, 1 schoolmaster, 1 bandmaster serjeant, 1 hospital serjeant, 1 orderly-room clerk, 12 colour-serjeants, 38 serjeants, 1 bugle-major, 24 buglers, 50 corporals, and 900 privates.

Of the above establishment 6 officers and 104 non-commissioned officers and men were to be the depot; the remainder formed the ten service companies.

Major and Brevet-Colonel R. W. Disney-Leith, from the 1st Bombay European Regiment (Fusiliers), was appointed to the command of the 106th; Colonel Leith, who was then a captain in the 1st Bombay Fusiliers, led the storming party at the storming of Multan on 2nd January, 1849, and was severely wounded, losing his left arm. At the time of his appointment to the command of the 106th in 1862, Colonel Leith was on leave in England; his place was accordingly filled, until his arrival, by Major and Brevet-Lieutenant-Colonel the Hon. E. C. H. Massey, of the 95th Regiment, who had

THE 106TH LIGHT INFANTRY (1839-1862)

at one time been an ensign in the 68th Light Infantry, and who subsequently, as Lord Clarina, became colonel of the Durham Light Infantry.

1863
The depot, which for the past twenty years had been at Warley, was in 1863 at Birr, where it formed part of the 13th Depot Battalion.

CHAPTER VIII.

THE 106TH LIGHT INFANTRY (1864-1881).

1864
THE 106th marched from Nimach on 9th January, 1864, and arrived at Nasirabad on the 23rd.

On 27th May, Captain Wilmot was killed by a tiger when shooting in the same district in which Captain Bolden, of the 68th, was also killed by a tiger.

1865
1866
In 1865 there were outbreaks of cholera in June and October; ten men, seven women, and fourteen children died from this disease. In November this year the depot, which had been at Limerick, was moved to Mullingar, where it remained until September, 1866.

1867
Early in 1867 the regiment marched to Mian Mir, 600 miles, via Delhi and Ambala, and reached its destination on 25th March; there were two outbreaks of cholera this year; during the first there were ten deaths, and during the second, which was in June, there were sixty-six deaths, including six women and seven children.

1868
On 31st March, 1868, the regiment marched from Mian Mir, and arrived at Ambala on 18th April; strength, 19 officers and 633 non-commissioned officers and men.

1869
In 1869, beside two drafts from England, numbering together 190 men, the regiment received 72 men from various regiments leaving India. The depot, which had been at Chatham for nearly three years, was in July moved to Shorncliffe, where it remained for a year.

1870
In 1870 the establishment was reduced by two companies, and the medical officers were removed from the regimental establishment; the numbers were now to be:—Service companies, 30 officers and 885 non-commissioned officers and men; depot, 4 officers and 112 non-commissioned officers and men.

In November the regiment was conveyed by rail to Jhansi, and

TWO OFFICERS' WAIST PLATES
(a) *2nd Bombay European L.I.*
(b) *106th L.I.*

THE 106TH LIGHT INFANTRY (1864-1881)

in the following month two companies were detached to Nowgong. The depot was now attached to the 22nd Foot at Kinsale.

1871 In February, 1871, two companies were detached to Gwalior, and in October the Snider rifle was issued with sword-bayonets for serjeants; in the same month the rank of ensign was abolished.

1872 In 1872 a new universal mess dress for officers was introduced, and boots, pantaloons, and sabretaches were ordered to be worn by mounted officers. The depot was attached to the 1st Battalion 20th Foot, at the Curragh, until December, when it was attached to a detachment of the 35th Foot at Sunderland, where it remained for eleven years.

1873 On 12th August, 1873, Lieutenant-Colonel W. M. S. Bolton died at Morar; on 12th December the regiment, strength 20 officers, 672 non-commissioned officers and men, 52 women, and 102 children, embarked on H.M.'s troop-ship "Euphrates," 3 guns, 4,173 tons, Captain St. G. C. D'A. Irvine, at Bombay, and reached Portsmouth on 12th January, 1874. Two serjeants,

1874 1 corporal, and 162 privates had been left behind as volunteers to different regiments in India; of these numbers both the serjeants and four of the privates were transferred to the 68th Light Infantry.

On arrival in England the 106th was quartered at Parkhurst, Isle of Wight. On 14th August new colours were presented to the regiment by H.R.H. the Princess Royal of England, who was accompanied by her husband, the Crown Prince of Germany; on the same day the old colours were deposited in the church of St. Thomas, Newport, Isle of Wight. At the close of the ceremony in the church, the regiment, headed by Lieutenant-Colonel Gillespie, marched past the colours as they lay on the communion table, every officer and man saluting as he passed.

In November the Snider rifle was replaced by the Martini-Henry rifle.

1875 In February, 1875, the new valise equipment was taken into use. On 25th June, the 106th proceeded from Parkhurst to Aldershot; it was at first under canvas, and later in huts in the South Camp.

THE DURHAM LIGHT INFANTRY

1876   On 28th July, 1876, head-quarters and three companies proceeded to Chester, two companies to Bootle and Liverpool, two to Weedon, and one to Castleton, Isle of Man.

1877   On 27th July, 1877, the regiment was once more united in Salford Barracks, Manchester.

1878   In April, 1878, the Reserves were called out; 664 men were in the first instance sent to the 106th, but later they all, except 131, who were posted to the regiment, were sent to other regiments; in May, 295 men of the Militia Reserve joined from Barnard Castle; in July the Reserves were demobilised.

On 28th May a detachment, consisting of 3 officers and 112 non-commissioned officers and men, was sent to Ashton-under-Lyne in aid of the civil power; this detachment rejoined head-quarters on 18th June.

On 9th August a company was detached to Tynemouth Castle.

On 5th October the regiment proceeded from Manchester to Preston.

In April of this year a new pattern kersey frock was issued to the men, and in June the shako gave place to the helmet.

1879   In the course of the year 1879, the 106th sent no less than 455 men to its linked regiment, the 68th Light Infantry, in India.

1880   On 16th March, 1880, the regiment, now consisting of only 16 officers and 381 non-commissioned officers and men, left Preston for Liverpool by rail, and was conveyed thence in H.M.'s troopship "Assistance," 2 guns, 2,515 tons, Captain Claude E. Buckle, to Kingstown; from Kingstown the regiment marched to Dublin, where it was quartered in the Royal Barracks until 20th April; it was then conveyed by rail to Athlone; after a stay of eight months at Athlone, it was on 20th December moved to the Curragh.

1881   On 21st June, 1881, one company was sent to the Royal Barracks, Dublin, the remaining seven companies following three days later. On 1st July, as has been previously stated, the 106th Bombay Light Infantry became, under the new organisation, the 2nd Battalion Durham Light Infantry.

CHAPTER IX.

1ST AND 2ND BATTALIONS THE DURHAM LIGHT INFANTRY (1881-1898).

WHEN the new organisation of the infantry of the line, introduced by the Right Hon. H. C. E. Childers, Secretary of State for War, took effect on 1st July, 1881, the two regular battalions of the Durham Light Infantry were, as has been already stated, stationed: the 1st Battalion at Meerut and Fatehgarh, India, and the 2nd Battalion at the Royal Barracks, Dublin.

1881

Lieutenant H. P. O'Callaghan, 1st Battalion, died at Fatehgarh on 10th November, 1882.

1882

On 28th January, 1882, the 2nd Battalion was conveyed by rail from Dublin to the Curragh, detaching one company to Belturbet; in February it received 415 men as volunteers from various corps; of this number no less than 100 were from the 3rd Battalion Rifle Brigade, and 71 from the 2nd Battalion Royal Scots. On 1st July the company at Belturbet rejoined head-quarters, two companies, under Major Triphook, proceeded to Galway, and one company to Oughterard; on 7th July a company was sent to Naas.

All detachments having rejoined head-quarters two days previously, the battalion was conveyed by rail on 7th August to Dublin, where it embarked for Holyhead; thence it was conveyed by rail to the Albert Docks, London, where it embarked upon two ships for duty in the Mediterranean. Head-quarters and four companies, strength, 10 officers and 449 non-commissioned officers and men, on P. and O. s.s. "Verona," proceeded to Gibraltar; the remaining four companies, strength, 8 officers and 358 non-commissioned officers and men, on the British India Company's s.s. "Rewa," proceeded to Malta.

The battalion remained divided until 2nd March, 1883, when the half-battalion at Malta rejoined head-quarters at Gibraltar; on 21st August the battalion, which was quar-

1883

tered in Buena Vista Barracks, was inspected by Major-General Adams; a few days later it moved to Town Range Barracks.

On 25th October, 1883, the 1st Battalion was entrained for Allahabad, and arrived there after a journey of two days; it was shortly afterwards inspected by Major-General Sir H. T. Macpherson, V.C., K.C.B.; one company was detached to Fort Allahabad.

1884 Early in 1884 the depot and head-quarters of the 68th Regimental District were moved from Sunderland to Newcastle-on-Tyne, where a double depot was formed jointly with that of the Northumberland Fusiliers.

In this year three officers of the 1st Battalion died in India; on 22nd March, Major C. Covey met with a fatal accident while pig-sticking at Mejah, near Allahabad; on 27th July, Lieutenant-Colonel G. K. Shaw died at Kasauli, where he was in command of the convalescent depot there; and on 21st November, Lieutenant C. G. Wells died at Allahabad.

In October there was an outbreak of cholera at Allahabad, four companies went into camp at Burgarh, and three companies at Shirajpur; they returned to Allahabad on 11th November; there were five deaths.

The 2nd Battalion remained throughout the year at Gibraltar, but early in December moved from Town Range Barracks to Casement Barracks.

1885 On 20th January, 1885, the 1st Battalion was inspected by Major-General Sir H. T. Macpherson, K.C.B.

In August there was another outbreak of cholera; two companies went into camp on the 6th at Burgarh, and five at Dabhaura on the 8th; there were two deaths; on 5th October the two companies at Burgarh were moved to Dabhaura, and on 13th November the battalion returned to Allahabad.

On 31st October one company was detached to Fatehgarh, and remained there until 27th February, 1886.

On 15th February, 1885, the 2nd Battalion, 22 officers and 863 non-commissioned officers and men, embarked at Gibraltar on s.s. "Deccan," and arrived at Alexandria on the 22nd; after disembarkation it was inspected by Major-General W. Lennox, C.B., and then proceeded to the Citadel Barracks, Cairo.

THE DURHAM LIGHT INFANTRY (1881-1898)

In September it moved to Abassiyeh, and remained there, under canvas, until 6th November, when it marched back to the Citadel Barracks, Cairo, en route for Upper Egypt.

After two days in Cairo it was entrained at Boulac Railway Station for Assiout; when the battalion was marching to the railway station, the colours were deposited at the house of Lieutenant-General Sir F. Stevenson, K.C.B., commanding in Egypt; from Assiout the journey was continued in barges, towed by steamers, and Assouan was reached on 20th November.

On 21st November the battalion disembarked, and marched up the Tagoog Heights and occupied huts; on the following day it was inspected by Brigadier-General Green.

On 5th December head-quarters and four companies embarked at Shellal on the river steamer "Tyums," and arrived at Wady Halfa on the 9th; on the following morning this party, except the band, which was left at Wady Halfa, went to Sarras Station in two trains, and encamped inside a zareba. After the remaining companies had rejoined head-quarters here, the battalion held the line of railway between Sarras Station and the terminus at Akasheh, being distributed as under:—

Head-quarters and four companies at Sarras;
Two companies at Ambigole Wells;
Twenty-men at Ellahoial Wells;
Two companies at Akasheh.

The Durham division of mounted infantry consisted of Lieutenant H. de B. de Lisle, Serjeant Stuart, and twenty-nine men; similar detachments were furnished by 1st Duke of Cornwall's Light Infantry, 1st Royal Highlanders, and 2nd Oxfordshire Light Infantry, and the whole formed one company under Captain Rathborne, 1st Royal Berkshire Regiment.

On 28th September the mounted infantry proceeded up the Nile to Assouan, whence the baggage was transported to Shellal, seven miles distant; after remaining there a short time the mounted infantry pushed on to Wady Halfa, whence the Durham division was sent on, firstly, to Sarras, and afterwards to Akasheh. Serjeant Stuart, who had been left at Sarras, on being ordered to rejoin at Akasheh saw some severe fighting at Ambigole Wells. Starting early in December with a few men of the Royal Highlanders and Duke of Cornwall's Light Infantry he found, on reaching Ambigole, that three miles of the railway had been torn up. A party had just started to repair the damage when an Arab sheikh appeared with about 600 men, and demanded the surrender of Fort Ambigole; the working party rushed to the fort and got inside without any casualties. The enemy had a 7-pounder camel gun in a natural embrasure about 400 yards away from the fort.

The garrison of the fort consisted of eighty-one men; there was desultory firing throughout the night; on the following morning the fort was invested on three sides, and on the fourth were a number of wagons; in one of these wagons there were 7,000 rounds of ammunition, which fortunately the enemy did not attempt to seize; this ammunition was brought in under a heavy fire by Serjeant Stuart on the top of the wagon and ten men on the ground.

Serjeant Stuart was subsequently awarded the medal for Distinguished Conduct in the Field.

Serjeant Stuart started with two privates for Akasheh for reinforcements, and when about nine miles from Akasheh met a party, consisting of four companies of the Berkshire Regiment, some cavalry, and mounted infantry, under Major Dixon; Lieutenant de Lisle at once proceeded with a patrol to see if the fort had been again invested; the enemy had returned in force, but Lieutenant de Lisle and his patrol cut their way through, and found the garrison in good spirits, but weary. Lieutenant de Lisle returned alone for Major Dixon's force, but on the arrival of the latter at the fort early next morning it was found that the enemy had withdrawn; Lieutenant de Lisle was recommended for the Victoria Cross for his gallant conduct, but the claim was not considered to be sufficiently strong.

The whole force then moved to Akasheh, and the Durham division of mounted infantry was posted to Firket, six miles below Kosheh. Kosheh fort, held by the Cameron Highlanders, was at this time completely surrounded; a force moved to the relief, but was obliged to retire, the retreat of the Camel Corps being covered by the Durham division of mounted infantry.

On 24th December the battalion was at Akasheh, and on the two following days proceeded by half-battalions to Firket, where

THE DURHAM LIGHT INFANTRY (1881-1898)

Lieutenant-General Sir F. C. A. Stephenson, K.C.B., concentrated the frontier field force; on 29th December the force moved to a place between Mograkeh and Kosheh. The British portion of Sir F. Stephenson's force consisted of 20th Hussars, Mounted Infantry, British Camel Corps, and the 1st Brigade of Infantry, under Brigadier-General W. Butler, C.B., composed of 1st Royal Berkshire Regiment, 1st Royal West Kent Regiment, 2nd Durham Light Infantry, and the Cameron Highlanders, less two companies which remained in the fort at Kosheh.

On 30th December the force paraded at 5 a.m., and marched with the Durham Light Infantry on the left; at 8 a.m., the first shots were fired in the battle of Ginniss, which lasted until 11 a.m., when the enemy broke and fled, leaving their guns, camp, and standards in the hands of the British; the Durham Light Infantry pursued as far as Kozak, the mounted infantry as far as Amri, carrying several villages at the point of the bayonet; five men of the Durham Light Infantry were wounded, one of whom, Private Mason, died two days afterwards; a noticeable point about the battle of Ginniss is that it was fought and won in the old English formation of line.

Two days later, at Said Effendi, Lieutenant de Lisle, with a dozen mounted infantry and some men from the camel corps, captured a large nuggar with a number of the enemy on board; alongside of the nuggar an infant boy, about two years old, was found; from a wounded Arab it was learnt that his father had been killed at Ginniss, and that his mother, with two children, had intended to go to Berber, but had been prevented by the attack on the nuggar; the infant, whose real name was Mustapha, was taken charge of, and was christened James Francies Durham; he was brought up in the battalion, in due course enlisted into it, became a bandsman, and died at Fermoy on 8th August, 1910.

1886 On 1st March, 1886, the 1st Battalion was inspected by Major-General Sir C. J. S. Gough, V.C., K.C.B.

In August there was an outbreak of cholera; the battalion went into camp at Dabhaura, and returned to Allahabad on 21st October.

On 2nd September one company was sent to Chunar Fort, and remained there until 2nd February, 1887.

THE DURHAM LIGHT INFANTRY

On 19th September, Lieutenant E. H. Stockdale died from typhoid fever.

The 2nd Battalion was detailed to hold the frontier post of Kosheh at the conclusion of active operations on 9th January, 1886, and the mounted infantry returned to Akasheh; sickness now, unfortunately, appeared in the battalion, which was inspected on 5th February by Brigadier-General W. Butler, C.B.

On 6th April the battalion left Kosheh, after the forts and huts had been blown up, and marched to Akasheh on the following day; three days later, a similar destruction of the fortifications at Akasheh having been completed, the battalion was moved to Wady Halfa, and on the 26th of the month arrived at Assouan, where it occupied lines on the Tagoog Heights; later in the year it proceeded down the Nile in two divisions, reaching Cairo on 30th November and 2nd December; it was then quartered in the Kasr-el-Nil Barracks.

The granting of the D.S.O. to Colonel Coker and Lieutenant de Lisle was notified in the "London Gazette" of 25th November.

There was an inspection by Major-General Wilkie, C.B., on 11th December, and on the 17th there was a presentation of Egyptian medals by General Sir F. Stephenson, G.C.B.

While in Egypt the battalion lost one officer (Captain R. B. Barker) and fifty-five non-commissioned officers and men from wounds and disease. In addition to Serjeant Stuart, Private J. Warberton was awarded the medal for Distinguished Conduct in the Field.

1887 On 1st February, 1887, the 1st Battalion was inspected by Brigadier-General H. Wilkinson, C.B., and on 10th March left Allahabad for Bombay; on the 19th of the same month it embarked on H.M.S. "Euphrates," and sailed from India, after a period of service in that country of fifteen years; Portsmouth was reached on 13th April, and Colchester on the following day. The battalion, on arriving at Colchester, was only about 200 strong, but its numbers were rapidly made up by about 400 men who had been sent home from the 2nd Battalion during the previous month, and by a strong draft from the depot.

On 6th January, the 2nd Battalion embarked at Suez on H.M.'s Indian troopship "Crocodile," 3 guns, 4,173 tons, captain, Henry J. Carr, for conveyance to India; there was a draft on board, which had arrived on the same ship from England, consisting of 3 officers and 148 non-commissioned officers and men; this draft brought the battalion up to a total of 473 all ranks; Bombay was reached after a voyage of thirteen days.

On 20th January, the battalion was conveyed by rail to Poona, and occupied Ghorpuri Barracks; a party of 201, all ranks, joined from the 1st Battalion at Allahabad, and shortly afterwards a second party of 228, all ranks, also from the 1st Battalion, joined.

A detachment, 55 men, was sent to Khandalla on 13th April, and remained there for about two months.

1888

In May, 1888, there was a detachment of 2 officers and 44 non-commissioned officers and men of the 1st Battalion at Harwich; it only remained there for a few weeks.

On 11th June new colours were presented to the 1st Battalion at Colchester by H.R.H. the Duke of Cambridge; the old colours were deposited in Durham Cathedral on the 9th of the following September.

There was an inspection by Major-General Sir Evelyn Wood, V.C., K.C.B., on 7th July.

After the arrival of a draft, 131 all ranks, at Poona on 6th January, the 2nd Battalion had a strength of 1,033, all ranks, i.e., 22 above the Indian establishment.

There was an inspection in February by Major-General Solly Flood.

On 4th July the Khedive's Star was presented to the battalion by H.R.H. the Duke of Connaught.

A detachment, 100 men, under Lieutenant Long, was sent to Khandalla on 1st November, and remained there for nearly eight weeks.

1889

On 6th May, 1889, the 1st Battalion left Colchester; head-quarters and three companies proceeded to Bradford, four companies and "the bugles" to Lichfield, and one company to Weedon; a sub-detachment, one officer and 25 non-commissioned officers and men, was sent to Birmingham from Lichfield in June, and remained there for two months. Head-quarters were inspected at Bradford by Major-General N. Stevenson on 31st May.

On 22nd June the battalion, except the company at Weedon, assembled at Strensall; head-quarters and three companies returned to Bradford at the end of July, and the remainder to Lichfield at the end of August.

In December the 2nd Battalion was singularly successful at the meeting of the Bombay Presidency Rifle Association. The following prizes were won:—

    (i.) Duchess of Connaught's Cup, by the officers' team.
    (ii.) Civil Service Cup, by non-commissioned officers' team.
    (iii.) Bombay Presidency Cup, by battalion team.
    (iv.) Revolver Cup (warrant officers and non-commissioned officers) by Serjeant-Major Francies.
    (v.) Silver tankard for highest aggregate in the Bombay Presidency, by Private Challis.

1890 On 1st February, 1890, the company of the 1st Battalion at Weedon was moved to York and Strensall; and on 26th April the detachment at Lichfield proceeded to Strensall, with the exception of one company, which went to Tynemouth; head-quarters arrived at Strensall on 23rd June; in the middle of August the former distribution of companies at Bradford and Lichfield was resumed; in October and November there was a sub-detachment at Chester from the detachment at Lichfield; at first it consisted of 2 officers and 60 non-commissioned officers and men, and latterly of only 1 officer and 35 non-commissioned officers and men.

On 28th February, the 2nd Battalion left Poona for Bombay en route for Quetta; it remained in Bombay for seven days, being encamped on the Marine Parade Ground, and took part, on the defending side, in some operations which represented an attack on the port from the sea; on 7th March it embarked on R.I.M.S. "Canning"; H.R.H. the Duke of Connaught came on board to bid farewell to the battalion; Karachi was reached after a voyage of three days; on 11th March the battalion disembarked, and was entrained for Quetta, where it arrived on the 14th.

1891 On 20th and 21st April, 1891, head-quarters of the 1st Battalion at Bradford were called out in consequence of riots there, but fortunately no actual collision took place between the troops and the rioters.

On 27th April, the Lichfield detachment, 8 officers and 237 non-commissioned officers and men, was conveyed by rail to Aldershot,

THE DURHAM LIGHT INFANTRY (1881-1898)

where it was quartered in huts in the North Camp, and formed part of the 3rd Brigade, under Major-General C. Mansfield Clarke, C.B. This detachment was the only unit of infantry in the Aldershot Division which was still armed with the Martini-Henry rifle; the Lee-Metford rifle was shortly afterwards issued to the battalion.

Head-quarters and the three companies, 10 officers and 278 non-commissioned officers and men, from Bradford, and the company, 2 officers and 64 non-commissioned officers and men, from Tynemouth, arrived at Aldershot on 28th August, and camped on Cove Plateau; the battalion then took part in the manœuvres in the Meon district of Hampshire.

On 19th September the troops returned to Aldershot, and the 1st Battalion was quartered in huts in the South Camp; it then formed part of the 1st Brigade, under Major-General C. F. Gregorie, C.B.; it shortly afterwards occupied the newly-built Corunna Barracks in Stanhope Lines.

The inspection of the battalion had been carried out in the earlier part of the year by Major-General H. C. Wilkinson, C.B., at Bradford, Lichfield, and Tynemouth.

The 2nd Battalion was inspected at Quetta on 1st May by Major-General Sir G. White, V.C., K.C.B.

In August it suffered from cholera, and moved into camp in the Hanna Pass, returning to Quetta on 19th September; there were in this outbreak twenty-four cases, fourteen of which were fatal.

1892 In August, 1892, the 1st Battalion was, with other troops, in standing camp on Frensham Common for manœuvres, after which it returned to Aldershot.

On 17th February, the 2nd Battalion left Quetta en route for Mhow, and arrived on the 28th of the same month.

1893 Lieutenant A. C. Lascelles, 1st Battalion, died on 12th February, 1893.

On 13th May, 1893, the 1st Battalion attended the funeral of Field-Marshal Lord William Paulet at Amport St. Mary's, near Andover, at the expense of the officers; the Marquis of Winchester entertained both officers and men with much hospitality; before leaving Amport St. Mary's the battalion was inspected by H.R.H. the Duke of Cambridge, who addressed it in the most gratifying terms.

THE DURHAM LIGHT INFANTRY

On 29th August, the battalion marched for the manœuvres on the borders of Berkshire and Wiltshire, and returned to Aldershot on 19th September.

Having been inspected by Lieutenant-General Sir Evelyn Wood, V.C., G.C.B., two days previously, the battalion was conveyed by rail to Portsmouth on 29th September, and embarked on H.M.'s troopship "Assistance," 2 guns, 2,515 tons, captain, J. E. Blaxland; Queenstown was reached early on 2nd October, and the disembarkation took place at once; head-quarters and six companies, 13 officers and 624 non-commissioned officers and men, proceeded by rail to Buttevant, and two companies, 3 officers and 148 non-commissioned officers and men, to Tralee.

On 21st January, 1893, the 2nd Battalion was inspected at Mhow by Lieutenant-General Sir George Greaves, K.C.B., Commander-in-Chief of the Bombay Army; and on 6th March was armed with the Lee-Metford rifle.

1894   In 1894, the 1st Battalion, which then numbered 748 non-commissioned officers and men, was inspected at Buttevant on 30th July by Major-General J. Fryer, C.B.; and the 2nd Battalion was inspected at Mhow on 15th January by Lieutenant-General Nairne, Commander-in-Chief of the Bombay Army, and on 22nd January by Major-General H. S. Anderson, C.B.

1895   On 16th May, 1895, the 1st Battalion was inspected at Buttevant by Field-Marshal Viscount Wolseley, commanding the forces in Ireland; and on 23rd July by Major-General J. Fryer, C.B.; on this latter date the battalion numbered 780 non-commissioned officers and men; their averages were as under:—

Age.	Service.	Height.	Nationality.
Serjts., 28 yrs. 7 mths.	10 yrs. 11 mths.	5ft. 8in.	English, 679. Irish, 71.
Rank and File, 21 yrs. 2 mths.	2 yrs. 5 mths.	5ft. $6\frac{1}{8}$in.	Scots, 29. Foreigners, 1.

THE DURHAM LIGHT INFANTRY (1881-1898)

On 11th October it proceeded to Dublin; head-quarters and five companies to Richmond Barracks, three companies to Portobello Barracks; there were inspections on 16th October by Major-General Viscount Frankfort de Montmorency, and on 18th November by Field-Marshal Lord Roberts, commanding the forces in Ireland.

On 18th December the three companies at Portobello Barracks moved to Ship Street Barracks, where Captain Gunning's company had proceeded on the previous day.

On 23rd October, the 2nd Battalion vacated the barracks at Mhow, but remained at that station for manœuvres; at the conclusion of the manœuvres it proceeded to Badnawar for field-firing, and did not return to Mhow until 17th January, 1896; there was an inspection by Major-General M. H. Nicholson in December, 1895.

1896 On 29th July, 1896, the 1st Battalion, having been inspected a fortnight previously by Major-General Viscount Frankfort de Montmorency, marched for manœuvres in Co. Kilkenny; on 1st August it formed part of a large force which was reviewed at the Curragh by Field-Marshal Lord Roberts; the battalion returned to Richmond Barracks on 22nd August; the troops were in marching order throughout these manœuvres.

On 1st July of this year there were several alterations in the officers' uniform; the round forage cap, and the braided blue cloth patrol jacket, which had been introduced in 1867, were discontinued; the field service cap and blue serge jacket being substituted; roll-collar mess jackets were revived; the bear skin flounce on the wallets of mounted officers was discontinued, and black sword-knots, previously worn, were now sanctioned for officers of light infantry regiments.

In August the detachment at Ship Street Barracks moved to Wellington Barracks, Dublin, and was joined there by head-quarters and the remaining companies of the battalion from Richmond Barracks in the first week in November.

The 2nd Battalion left Mhow on 22nd January, and three days later arrived at Poona, where it was quartered in the Wanowrie Barracks. Major H. D. Rosseter died on 24th August.

Towards the close of the year the bubonic plague broke out in the city of Poona, the infection having doubtless been brought from Bombay, and rapidly spread.

1897   On 3rd May, 1897, the 1st Battalion returned to Richmond Barracks with a strength of 25 officers and 697 non-commissioned officers and men.

There was an inspection by Viscount Frankfort de Montmorency on 6th July, and on 6th August the battalion marched from Dublin for manœuvres; eight days later it returned to Dublin, and was present on 17th August when Field-Marshal Lord Roberts reviewed the whole of the troops, then in Dublin, in the Phœnix Park; on the following day their Royal Highnesses the Duke and Duchess of York entered Dublin in state; the battalion on this occasion was on duty between Kildare Street and Dawson Street; on 30th September there was an inspection by Major-General M. M. E. Gossett, C.B.

In July the field service cap was authorised for wear by officers of light infantry regiments instead of the peaked forage cap.

In March, 1897, volunteers were called for from the 2nd Battalion, as well as from other British and native troops in Poona and Kirkee, to undertake the work of stamping out the plague in Poona; on the 12th a camp was formed at Parbatti, about three miles from cantonments and near the city of Poona, under Major A. de B. V. Paget, 2nd Durham Light Infantry, with Lieutenant E. A. Iremonger, 2nd Durham Light Infantry, as adjutant and quartermaster; the number of troops in this camp was 18 officers and 875 non-commissioned officers and men; eight days later there was an addition of 4 officers and 215 non-commissioned officers and men; of these numbers 6 officers and 135 non-commissioned officers and men belonged to the 2nd Durham Light Infantry, but more men could have been furnished by the battalion if necessary, as nearly 700 had volunteered for plague duty. The troops worked under the instructions of a plague committee, of which Mr. Rand, C.I.E., I.C.S., who was shortly afterwards assassinated, was chairman.

The British troops were chiefly employed in making house to house inspections, removing infected persons, fumigating and lime-washing infected houses, etc.; the native troops were chiefly employed as orderlies, night patrols, and guards, both in the streets and in segregation camps. The conduct of the troops was most

THE DURHAM LIGHT INFANTRY (1881-1898)

unjustly maligned, both in England and India, but their general good behaviour and the manner in which the work was done were the subjects of highly complimentary remarks not only from Mr. Rand, but also from His Excellency Lord Sandhurst, the Governor of Bombay; also, the troops at the conclusion of their operations received the thanks of the Bombay Government.

The plague operations were concluded at the end of May. Stringent precautions against infection were taken, and no case of plague occurred amongst the troops employed during this period.

In addition to the party employed at Poona, there was also a party of the 2nd Battalion, under Lieutenant H. R. Cumming, engaged on plague duty at Sholapur in this year.

Early in October the following members of the 2nd Battalion were selected for service with the Tirah Expedition:—

Major A. de B. V. Paget.

Lieutenant A. K. Robb.	2nd Lieutenant W. Gibson.
Serjeant Trimnell.	Serjeant Haigh.
Serjeant Wrightson.	Lance-Serjeant Myers.
Corporal Griffen.	Lance-Corporal Pegg.
Lance-Corporal Symonds.	Private McGowan.
Private Robinson.	Private Lindsley.

Major Paget was commandant of the depot for British troops at the base at Kohat, but his duties there were varied by his periodically proceeding to the front in charge of convoys; at the end of the year the base was changed to Peshawar.

Lieutenant Robb and 2nd Lieutenant Gibson were attached to the 2nd Battalion Yorkshire Light Infantry; this battalion formed part of the reserve brigade at Rawal Pindi, but later was moved to Mamanai in the Bara Valley; on 29th January, 1898, it formed part of a column, under Colonel Sepping, which, when operating with other columns from Jamrud and Ali Musjid, was heavily engaged and suffered serious losses; Lieutenant Robb behaved with great gallantry in this action, and was recommended for the D.S.O.; the recommendation was, however, not entertained.

The ten non-commissioned officers and men of the 2nd Durham Light Infantry were chiefly employed with field hospitals and the transport corps; Lance-Corporal Pegg died on 19th December, 1897; several of the others were present at all the important actions, and at the march down the Bara Valley.

1898 After an inspection by Major-General M. M. E. Gossett, C.B., in July, 1898, the head-quarters of the 1st Battalion, strength, 13 officers and 398 non-commissioned officers and men, left North Wall, Dublin, on 16th August for Holyhead, en route to Wareham for manœuvres; the remainder of the battalion, 4 officers and 160 non-commissioned officers and men, chiefly recruits under six months' service, with the women and children, left North Wall, Dublin, on 29th August, and arrived at Tournay Barracks, Marlborough Lines, Aldershot, on the following day.

On 9th September head-quarters arrived at Tournay Barracks from the manœuvres; the battalion then formed part of the 3rd Brigade, under Major-General W. O. Barnard, by whom it was inspected in the course of a few days.

The 2nd Battalion was inspected by Major-General J. Duncan on 12th January.

In February there was a fresh outbreak of bubonic plague in Bombay; a party of the battalion, numbering 3 officers and 100 non-commissioned officers and men, proceeded to Bombay on plague duty; this party, except Private W. Hagan, who, unfortunately, died from the plague, rejoined head-quarters at Poona on 13th and 20th May. There was also a party of the battalion, under Lieutenant W. J. Ainsworth, on plague duty at Sholapur.

At the end of the year the battalion commenced to move from Poona to Mandalay in several parties; on 20th October the advanced party, under Major Paget, embarked at Bombay on R.I.M.S. "Dalhousie," 1,524 tons, commander, St. L. S. Warden, and reached Rangoon on 29th October; on 19th November "B" Company, under Major Saunders, embarked on the "Dalhousie," being joined at Bombay by a draft of 75 men which had just arrived from England, and reached Rangoon on 30th November, and Mandalay two days later; on 17th December "E" Company, under Lieutenant Robb, left Poona for Calcutta, and, having embarked on the "Dalhousie," arrived at Mandalay on 3rd January, 1899.

CHAPTER X.

THE SOUTH AFRICAN WAR (1899-1902).

1899   On 15th February, 1899, H.R.H. the Crown Prince of Siam, accompanied by his A.D.C., Captain Sarasiddhi, was attached to the 1st Battalion, and remained with it throughout the summer.

Early in September orders to prepare for service in South Africa were received by the 1st Battalion; by 18th October 525 reservists had joined, bringing the strength up to over 1,200, all ranks. Of this number about 280 were left behind on 24th October, when the battalion embarked at Southampton on the Cunard s.s. "Cephalonia," 5,517 tons, captain, H. W. Pierce; the actual strength embarking was 26 officers and 920 non-commissioned officers and men; of the latter number about 500, or rather more than half the total, were reservists. The "Cephalonia" reached Capetown on 18th November, and Durban four days later.

The battalion, which was in the 4th (Light) Brigade, disembarked on 23rd November, and was conveyed by rail to Nottingham Road, where camp was pitched; two days later it was conveyed again by rail to Mooi River, where it remained for about ten days.

The 4th (Light) Brigade was commanded by Major-General the Hon. N. G. Lyttelton, C.B., and consisted of the following battalions:—

      2nd Battalion Scottish Rifles.
      3rd Battalion King's Royal Rifle Corps.
      1st Battalion Durham Light Infantry.
      1st Battalion Rifle Brigade.

It was in the 2nd Division, under Lieutenant-General Sir C. F. Clery, K.C.B. The other brigade in the division was composed of the 2nd Battalions of the West Surrey, Devonshire, West Yorkshire, and East Surrey Regiments, under Major-General H. Hildyard, C.B.

THE DURHAM LIGHT INFANTRY

On 6th December the brigade marched from Mooi River, and arrived at Frere on the 8th; five days later the march was continued to Chieveley.

The 4th Brigade supported both General Hart's and General Hildyard's brigades at the battle of Colenso on 15th December, the 1st Durham Light Infantry and the 1st Rifle Brigade being in support of the former, the other two battalions in support of the latter; of the 1st Durham Light Infantry, Serjeant Flower and one private were wounded. A retirement on to Chieveley was made in the afternoon, and six companies, 1st Durham Light Infantry, were at once detailed for outpost duty; on the 17th the retirement was continued to Frere, where a halt was made until 10th January, 1900.

On 5th March, head-quarters of the 2nd Battalion, under Major Davison, left Poona for Bombay, and, having embarked on the "Dalhousie," reached Rangoon on the 15th, and Mandalay on the 17th of the same month.

On 16th November, a party, consisting of Major Saunders and fifty-two non-commissioned officers and men of the 2nd Battalion, left Mandalay by march route for Kunlong Ferry, to form part of the escort for a commission sent by the Burmese Government, with the sanction of the Government of India, to delimit part of the eastern frontier of Burma in conjunction with the Chinese Government; this party was the personal escort of Mr. J. G. Scott, C.I.E., the Commissioner; the other troops of the escort were:—

(i.) 200 men of the 10th (1st Burma Battalion) Gurkha Rifles.
(ii.) 25 Burma sappers and miners.
(iii.) 50 Kachin Police and a party of native signallers.

The commission reached Hopang a few days before Christmas, and was joined there by General Liu, the Chinese Commissioner, with a strong escort of Chinese soldiers; there were sports and festivities in the camp, and General Liu was most friendly and hospitable towards the British troops.

The 2nd Battalion was inspected by H.E. the Commander-in-Chief at Mandalay on 16th December.

1900   On 10th January, 1900, the 1st Battalion, which had been at Frere for over three weeks, joined in the advance northwards. Springfield was reached on the 11th, and Spear-

THE SOUTH AFRICAN WAR (1899-1902)

man's Hill on the next day; after various operations and movements in the intervening days, during which the Tugela was crossed, the 4th Brigade took part in the battle of Spion Kop on 24th January; in the earlier part of the day the 1st Durham Light Infantry and 1st Rifle Brigade were occupied in making a demonstration; later in the day the 1st Durham Light Infantry replaced the 2nd Scottish Rifles in the reserve, and also provided an escort for the naval guns.

On 3rd February the Tugela was re-crossed, and on the 5th the battle of Vaal Krantz was fought.

Having paraded at 6.30 a.m., the 4th Brigade marched to Mungar's Farm Drift, where the Tugela had to be crossed by a pontoon bridge, as the river was too deep to admit of wading; here there was a long delay, as the bridge was not ready until 1.30 p.m.; at 2 p.m. the 1st Durham Light Infantry started, and was soon under fire; several men were wounded while crossing the bridge. Having proceeded up a donga, and reached the head of it, the first company came out into the open and wheeled to the left; the other companies then followed; the battalion then worked its way to the left, and gradually ascended the first hill, which it took, the Boers running down the opposite bank; three prisoners and several ponies were captured.

In a short time the second hill was taken without much loss or opposition, but the third hill presented an almost impossible task, as it was regularly trenched, and was commanded on both sides by the Boer guns; moreover, the Rifle Brigade and Major-General Hildyard's Brigade had not yet come round on the right as was expected. Lieutenant-Colonel Woodland then waited for further orders; these orders were to entrench his battalion to the best of his ability; this was done.

At daylight next morning the battalion was busy wall-building, but owing to the heavy fire from the enemy, every advantage had to be taken of cover, and the battalion remained in its position throughout the day; about 3.30 p.m. the Boers made a determined attack on the left of the position; the 3rd King's Royal Rifle Corps, which had been in reserve, came up at the double at this moment; the enemy were driven off; a hot fire was kept up until it was nearly dark, when the battalion was relieved by the 2nd Battalion Queen's Royal West Surrey Regiment, and, having re-crossed the Tugela, bivouacked.

With reference to this battle, Sir Conan Doyle, in his history of the war, writes:—

"The attack was led by the Durham Light Infantry of Lyttelton's brigade, followed by the 3rd Rifles, with the Scottish Rifles and the 1st Rifles [sic] in support. Never did the old Light Division of Peninsular fame go up a Spanish hillside with greater spirit and dash than these, their descendants, facing the slope of Vaal Krantz. In open order they moved across the plain, with a superb disregard of the crash and patter of the shrapnel, and then up they went, the flitting figures springing from cover to cover, stooping, darting, crouching, running, until with their glasses the spectators on Swartz Kop could see the gleam of the bayonets and the strain of furious rushing men upon the summit as the last Boers were driven from their trenches."

Also, Colonel A. L. Woodland, C.B., in his diary, writes:—

"The regiment behaved splendidly."

In this action Major T. R. Johnson-Smyth, 2nd Lieutenant C. Duncombe-Shafto, and 18 non-commissioned officers and men were killed; Brevet-Lieutenant-Colonel H. S. Fitzgerald, Captain W. C. Lascelles, Lieutenant E. A. Blake, 2nd Lieutenants R. Lambton, C. Matthews, and E. W. Appleby, and 70 non-commissioned officers and men were wounded; one of the last named died while on the voyage home.

On 8th February a retirement commenced, and Chieveley was reached on the 11th; three days later a general advance took place, and continued daily until the 18th, when the battle of Monte Christo was fought, and the Boers were defeated with the loss of their camp; seven men of the battalion were wounded on this day.

Colonel Norcott was now in command of the 4th Brigade, and Major-General Lyttelton, of the 2nd Division, owing to the illness of Sir F. Clery.

On the 20th the battalion occupied Green Hill, and on the 23rd, after crossing the Tugela, was in reserve to Major-General Hart's brigade; one man (Private Gettle) was killed, and several were wounded.

MEMORIAL AT VAAL KRANTZ.

THE SOUTH AFRICAN WAR (1899-1902)

On the 24th, having relieved the Irish Brigade on Inniskilling Hill, the day was spent in removing the wounded under heavy fire. Lieutenant L. Soltau-Symons was wounded on this day by a splinter from a shell.

On 27th February the battalion took its part in the important victory of Pieters Hill; nine men were wounded.

Ladysmith having now been relieved, a further forward movement took place, and on 9th March the battalion, as advanced guard to the 2nd Division, arrived at Sunday's River, where it remained until 10th April; while at Sunday's River, Major-General Lyttelton was succeeded in the command of the 4th Brigade by Colonel (local Major-General) C. D. Cooper, and the first " special service " company of Volunteers, under the command of Captain J. Turnbull, 4th Volunteer Battalion Durham Light Infantry, joined the battalion. The other officers of the company were Lieutenant H. Bowes, 1st Volunteer Battalion Durham Light Infantry, and Lieutenant J. R. Ritson, 4th Volunteer Battalion Durham Light Infantry. Lieutenant J. B. Bowman, 3rd Volunteer Battalion Durham Light Infantry, joined later.

On 10th April, while the battalion was drilling in extended order at about 7.30 a.m., it was shelled by heavy artillery fire from the hills facing the camp; four men were wounded; the camp of the whole force was struck, and at night a retirement was made to Krogman's Farm; a week later the camp was moved to Buy's Farm, Modder Spruit.

On 7th May, Sir Redvers Buller advanced with his whole force; Mount Prospect Farm, facing the Boer trenches on Laing's Nek, was reached on the 21st, and the 4th Brigade remained there until 12th June; while falling in, preparatory to marching off, at 7 a.m. on the 13th at Vermaak's Kraal, the battalion was shelled by the Boers, and two men were wounded.

The camp at Mount Prospect Farm was frequently shelled by the Boers, but there were not any casualties in the Durham Light Infantry.

The Boers, having been defeated at both Botha's Pass and Allemann's Nek by Sir Redvers Buller, evacuated Laing's Nek on the night of 11th June; on the afternoon of the following day the 4th Brigade advanced and occupied Laing's Nek.

The forward movement was resumed on 18th June, and Vlakfontein was reached on 4th July.

A few days later the battalion returned to Greylingstad, and from this time until the end of September formed part of a column, under Lieutenant-General Sir F. C. Clery, which was continually on the move in the district round Greylingstad and Standerton.

On 31st August, Brevet-Lieutenant-Colonel H. S. Fitzgerald assumed command of the battalion vice Lieutenant-Colonel A. L. Woodland, who was invalided.

From the end of September to the end of December the battalion remained at Standerton with some detachments in the immediate vicinity; then during the last few days of December it moved farther up the railway line, head-quarters and three companies proceeding to Eden's Kop, and detachments of varying strength being sent to Vlakfontein, Zuikerbosch Spruit, Rustfontein, Kilfontein, and two other small posts on the line; this allocation of the battalion continued, with a few variations, up to the autumn of 1901.

The first "special service" company of Volunteers left the battalion on 9th October, 1900, but it did not leave South Africa until May, 1901, having in the meantime formed part of the Drakensberg defence force.

During the year 1900 the following officers, non-commissioned officers and men were mentioned in despatches on different occasions:—

In Sir Redvers Buller's despatch of 8th February, 1900.

Lieutenant-Colonel A. L. Woodland.
Brevet-Lieutenant-Colonel H. S. Fitzgerald.
Captain B. W. L. McMahon.
Captain O. B. Harter.
Captain H. R. Cumming.
Lieutenant G. L. Cochrane.
Lieutenant J. J. W. Prescott, R.A.M.C. (attached).

"A" Company—Colour-Serjeant C. Waiton, Corporal Kelly.
"B" Company—Colour-Serjeant J. Crump, Private Hall.

THE SOUTH AFRICAN WAR (1899-1902)

"E" Company—Serjeant Johnson, Private Allen.
"G" Company—Colour-Serjeant Williams, Serjeant Iles.
"H" Company—Serjeant Thomas, Private Ismay.
"K" Company—Colour-Serjeant J. P. L. Shea, Private Mellor.
"L" Company—Colour-Serjeant A. Noble, Private Nicholson.
"M" Company—Colour-Serjeant H. Tilley, Corporal Pratt, Private Stansfield.

In Sir Redvers Buller's despatch of 30th March, 1900:—

> Lieutenant-Colonel A. L. Woodland.
> Major T. R. Johnson-Smyth (killed).
> Major G. C. Mansel.
> Captain L. E. C. Elwes.
> 2nd Lieutenant C. L. Matthews.
> Lieutenant and Quartermaster J. H. Liebrecht.
> Lance-Corporal A. Bultitude.
> Private F. Lucking.
> Private A. Franklin.
> Private M. Williams.
> Private W. Hibbert.
> Private W. Baker.
> Private J. Horton.
> Private A. Swann.
> Private J. Crawford.
> Private F. Davies.

In Sir Redvers Buller's despatch of 9th November, 1900:—

Lieutenant-Colonel A. L. Woodland, "Devoted to his battalion. Brave and resolute, he has commanded it thoroughly well."
Brevet-Lieutenant-Colonel H. S. Fitzgerald.
Major G. C. Mansel.
Captain and Adjutant B. W. L. McMahon.
2nd Lieutenant A. W. B. Wallace.
Lieut. A. H. Bridges (I.S.C., 16th B.I.) (attached).
Captain J. Turnbull (4th V.B. D.L.I.) (attached).
Captain E. St. G. Pratt (Provost Marshal).
Captain L. Parke, A.D.C.

THE DURHAM LIGHT INFANTRY

Lieutenant W. Northey (divisional signalling officer).

Lieutenant E. B. Thresher (Composite Regiment of Mounted Infantry).

Also Privates G. Bennett, J. Cottle, J. S. Parker, and J. Robson were recommended for the Distinguished Service Medal.

On 2nd March, 1900, head-quarters and six companies of the 2nd Battalion, 327 non-commissioned officers and men, left Mandalay by march route for Maymyo for manœuvres, and returned on 7th May.

The escort for the "Burma-China" boundary commission returned to Mandalay on 19th May.

In February, 1900, the commission had arrived in the country inhabited by the wild head-hunting tribe of Was; on the 9th, Major Kiddle, R.A.M.C., and Mr. Sutherland, the assistant commissioner, were brutally murdered near the Chinese-Shan village Mong-Tum, about five miles from camp; the troops were at once called out, and, with the Chinese troops, attacked and pursued the armed tribesmen, and recovered the bodies of the murdered officers; on 26th and 27th February the troops were, for two days, engaged with the tribesmen, who had taken up a formidable position on high ground; the troops drove them off and destroyed four or five villages.

The country in which the commission had operated was rugged, mountainous, and removed from all civilization; the troops had marched over 1,000 miles, and at the conclusion received the thanks of the Lieutenant-Governor in Council.

On 20th December the battalion left Mandalay, and, having embarked on the following day at Rangoon on the s.s. "Canning," reached Calicut on 29th December; two days later it arrived at Wellington, where it remained for nearly two years.

Although the 2nd Battalion was not, as a unit, sent to South Africa, it was well represented there during the war by several officers, non-commissioned officers and men, who added considerably to its reputation; a short account of their performances up to the end of the war is now given.

In the middle of January, 1900, a company of mounted infantry left the battalion at Mandalay, and, sailing from Rangoon in the s.s. "Palamcotta" on the 24th of the month, arrived at Capetown on

THE SOUTH AFRICAN WAR (1899-1902)

13th February; it consisted of Captain C. C. Luard, Lieutenants W. J. Ainsworth, L. R. Ashburner, A. S. Way, and Grover (Shropshire Light Infantry) attached, 5 serjeants and 98 men; this company, with similar parties from the 2nd Essex Regiment and 2nd West Riding Regiment, formed the " Burma Mounted Infantry," under Major Cruikshank, Essex Regiment.

The 2nd Durham Light Infantry Company of Burma Mounted Infantry was, in the first instance, in the 3rd Brigade of Mounted Infantry, under Lieutenant-Colonel C. G. Martyr, and in this capacity accompanied Lord Roberts in his advance on Bloemfontein. After the occupation of Bloemfontein on 13th March, 1900, the company was transferred to the 7th Regiment of Mounted Infantry, under Lieutenant-Colonel E. G. T. Bainbridge; it was specially distinguished at the unfortunate action at Sannah's Post on 31st March, 1900. In his despatch describing this action, Brigadier-General R. G. Broadwood writes:—"' Q ' Battery, owing to its losses in the retirement, was compelled to come into action within 1,200 yards of the spruit, and the Durham Light Infantry company of mounted infantry, which was acting as right flank guard to the retirement, promptly occupied a position on the right and left flank of the battery; this checked any intention the enemy had of advancing from the spruit." And, further on, he writes:—" The action of ' Q ' Battery, the company of Durham Light Infantry, and of Lieutenant-Colonel Pilcher's regiment of mounted infantry being specially worthy of notice." Brigadier-General Broadwood then proceeds to mention, amongst others, Lieutenants Ainsworth, Ashburner, Way, and Grover (killed) Lance-Corporal Steele, and Privates Pickford and Horton, both of whom were severely wounded; eight privates, who eventually rejoined the company at Pretoria, were reported missing after this action.

In the advance on Johannesburg and Pretoria, the company, as part of the 7th Mounted Infantry, was in Lieutenant-General Ian Hamilton's division, and during this period was engaged with the enemy on no less than twenty-eight occasions; the principal actions in which it took part being Thabanchu, Sannah's Post, Hout Nek, Zand River, Lindley, Dornkop, and Diamond Hill. Subsequently the company was engaged in the pursuit of General De Wet in 1900-1901, and various other operations.

THE DURHAM LIGHT INFANTRY

Lieutenant Ainsworth was captured, in a train, by the Boers in July, 1900, but eventually he made his escape after trekking from Kroonstad to the north of Rustenberg with General De Wet's troops.

The strength of the company by June, 1900, was reduced to four officers and ninety-nine non-commissioned officers and men; by February, 1901, it was further reduced to two officers and eighty-five non-commissioned officers and men. By December, 1900, only one Burmese pony was left.

On 29th January, 1901, Lieutenant A. C. Way was killed, and was buried at Kaffirs Kraal, near Winberg, O.R.C.

The total casualties in the company during the war were :—

Killed—2 officers, 5 other ranks.
Died from wounds—1 private.
Killed by lightning—1 private (Private Durkin).
Invalided (wounds)—5 privates.
Invalided (disease)—5 privates.

At the conclusion of the war the company did not rejoin the 2nd Battalion as a unit; the men were sent to England in batches with men from the 1st Battalion, and then rejoined the 2nd Battalion at Aldershot.

In addition to the company of the 2nd Battalion in the Burma Mounted Infantry, the regiment provided officers, and in some instances non-commissioned officers and men, to no less than four different corps of mounted infantry during the war, viz., the 13th, 23rd, 24th, and 26th Mounted Infantry; but as the numbering of these corps does not agree with their seniority as regards the dates on which they came into existence, they will now be dealt with in a different order.

1. In December, 1899, shortly after the battle of Colenso, a company of mounted infantry, called the " 4th Brigade " Company of Mounted Infantry, was formed of one section each from the four battalions in the 4th Brigade; the contingent from the 1st Durham Light Infantry consisted of Lieutenant E. B. Thresher and thirty non-commissioned officers and men; very soon after the relief of Ladysmith this company was incorporated into a battalion of mounted infantry, under Captain (local Major) H. De La P. Gough, 16th

THE SOUTH AFRICAN WAR (1899-1902)

Lancers, known officially only as "Composite Regiment of Mounted Infantry," but generally alluded to as "Gough's Mounted Infantry." On Lieutenant Thresher being appointed adjutant of the 1st Durham Light Infantry in November, 1900, 2nd Lieutenant R. R. Lambton was sent from the 1st Battalion to replace him. 2nd Lieutenant K. Leather joined the corps in July, 1901, and served with it until the following November, when he rejoined his battalion; on 2nd Lieutenant Lambton's death in September, 1901, 2nd Lieutenant Appleby was sent to replace him; 2nd Lieutenant Appleby and his party were transferred to the 26th Mounted Infantry about the end of November, 1901.

This battalion, which had neither an official name nor number for the greater part of its career, received the designation "24th Mounted Infantry" about July, 1901.

From April to July, 1900, Gough's Mounted Infantry was in the 3rd Mounted Brigade, under the Earl of Dundonald, and took part in Sir Redvers Buller's operations in Northern Natal and the battle of Alleman's Nek; on 4th August it distinguished itself at the attack on De Lange's laager; in the early part of 1901 it was in Colonel Spens's column in the Eastern Transvaal, and later in Colonel Bullock's column; on 5th August, 1901, it surprised a Boer laager, and captured forty-one Boers and a large number of horses and cattle, and for the rest of the month was very actively engaged in the neighbourhood of Kroonstad; early in September it was conveyed by rail to Newcastle, in Natal, and on the 17th had the misfortune, while trying to cut off a party of Boers, to be caught by General Louis Botha, who had about 2,000 men with him, at De Jager's Drift; the casualties on this day were 20 killed and 34 wounded; the killed included 2nd Lieutenant Lambton, Privates Budd, Frost, and Royal, the wounded included Serjeant Salmon, Privates Capon and Birbeck, all of the 1st Durham Light Infantry.

2. In the beginning of November, 1900, Lieutenants L. Soltau-Symons and C. L. Matthews, with fifty-six non-commissioned officers and men of the 1st Battalion, joined the 2nd Division Mounted Infantry, which in the autumn of 1901 received the designation "26th Mounted Infantry"; towards the end of 1901 this party was reinforced by Lieutenant Appleby and thirty men transferred from

THE DURHAM LIGHT INFANTRY

the 24th Mounted Infantry; it was further reinforced in March, 1902, by 2nd Lieutenant W. R. Lovering and thirty men from England; it was then composed of two officers (Lieutenant Appleby and 2nd Lieutenant Lovering) and 115 non-commissioned officers and men, under the command of Captain L. Soltau-Symons, who had in the meantime been promoted into the Royal Warwickshire Regiment. On disbandment in September, 1902, two officers and 110 non-commissioned officers and men rejoined the 1st Battalion at Standerton.

This battalion of mounted infantry, which was commanded by Major W. S. Kays, King's Royal Rifle Corps, from November, 1900, to April, 1901, and for the rest of the time by Major E. A. Wiggin, 13th Hussars, was for the greater part of its career in Colonel Colville's column, but for the last two or three months of the war was in Colonel Mills's column; it took part in General French's operations in the Eastern Transvaal in the early part of 1901, and later in General Elliot's operations in the north-east of the Orange River Colony; it was again in the Eastern Transvaal, from June to August, 1901, and back again in August and September in the Orange River Colony, where it was present at the action at Roberts' Drift on 6th September; it was then once more in the Eastern Transvaal and in Swaziland; in February, 1902, it was for the third time in the Orange River Colony, and, when the war came to an end, was in the vicinity of Vryheid.

Corporal S. Nicholson was killed at Kroomdrai on 25th July, 1901; Serjeant W. Sykes was killed, and Lieutenant Matthews and Privates White and Reid were wounded at Roberts' Drift on 6th September, 1901; Private Harris was wounded at Kalespruit on 4th May, 1901.

3. Major E. St. G. Pratt was appointed to the command of the "13th Mounted Infantry" on its formation at Pretoria in November, 1900, and commanded it to the end of the war; he was accompanied by Lieutenants W. Northey, J. S. Unthank, and J. W. Jeffreys; the first of these officers was adjutant, the last was quartermaster, as well as transport officer; the battalion consisted of four companies, each composed of four sections, drawn from various regiments, but none of the non-commissioned officers and men belonged to the Durham Light Infantry. In January, 1901, the 13th Mounted Infantry and

THE SOUTH AFRICAN WAR (1899-1902)

the 14th Mounted Infantry were formed into the 5th Corps of Mounted Infantry, under the command of Lieutenant-Colonel A. V. Jenner, Rifle Brigade.

The first service of the 13th Mounted Infantry was under Colonel E. A. H. Alderson in December, 1900, and January, 1901, in the Magaliesberg Valley; it then, still in Colonel Alderson's column, took part in General French's operations in the Eastern Transvaal and in Zululand; it then was with Colonel Bullock's column in the Eastern Transvaal and the north of the Orange River Colony; from 27th July, 1901, to the end of the war, it served under Colonel Spens in various operations in the Orange River Colony, on the borders of Zululand, and in the Eastern Transvaal; when peace was declared the 13th Mounted Infantry was at Heidelberg, and remained there until its disbandment in August, 1902.

The casualty list fortunately did not include any of the four officers of the Durham Light Infantry.

4. Among the contingents from different regiments that composed the " 23rd Mounted Infantry " were two sections of the Durham Light Infantry, which arrived in South Africa from England in the middle of June, 1901; these two sections formed half of a company that was commanded by Captain H. M. Trenchard, Royal Scots Fusiliers.

2nd Lieutenants H. J. Coddington, C. O. Rowlandson, J. G. Gillespie, and C. R. Shirreff—the three last being Militia officers at the time—served for varying periods with this mounted infantry, which was commanded at first by Major T. B. Ramsey, Rifle Brigade, and, after his death, by Major T. J. Marker, King's Own Royal Lancaster Regiment.

This battalion of Mounted Infantry was principally employed on intelligence service, under the officer commanding the Vereeniging District, and suffered the following casualties in the half-company of Durham Light Infantry:—Lance-Corporal M. Naitby, killed at Vereeniging; 2nd Lieutenant H. J. Coddington, wounded at Leeuw Kop; Lance-Serjeant Gaitenby, Lance-Corporal Galloway, and Privates Hedley and Suddes, wounded at Villiersdorp. Lance-Serjeant Gaitenby subsequently died of his wounds.

THE DURHAM LIGHT INFANTRY

The 23rd Mounted Infantry was present at Vereeniging during the Peace Conference.

Major W. C. Ross, having been appointed staff officer to Brigadier-General Hector Macdonald, accompanied the latter when he left India early in January, 1900, for South Africa to assume command of the Highland Brigade; these officers joined the Highland Brigade at Modder River on 23rd January; on 4th February, Major Ross was informed that he had been selected, with the local rank of lieutenant-colonel, for the command of the 8th Battalion of Mounted Infantry, consisting of one company each from the Cheshire, South Wales Borderers, East Lancashire, and North Staffordshire Regiments.

Lieutenant-Colonel Ross at once proceeded to Orange River to assume command of his battalion, and started with it on the night of 12th February to catch up Lord Roberts's force, which was advancing from Modder River. It was first in action at Waterval Drift on 15th February, and from that time accompanied Lord Roberts's force to Pretoria, taking part in the actions at Paardeburg, Poplar Grove, Driefontein, Karree Siding, Brandfort, Zand River, Klip River, and Pretoria, as well as in numerous small engagements.

At Bloemfontein, Lieutenant-Colonel Ross's command was increased, and became the 8th Corps of Mounted Infantry, and then consisted of:—(i.) The original 8th Battalion; (ii.) Lumsden's Horse; (iii.) Lock's Horse; (iv.) companies from the Oxfordshire Light Infantry, West Riding, and Suffolk Regiments, usually working as one battalion.

After the occupation of Pretoria, the 8th Corps of Mounted Infantry was mainly employed in guarding the line of communications from Kroonstad to Pretoria; it also took part in some of the chases after General De Wet, and in the relief of Ladybrand.

On 6th November, after chasing General De Wet and ex-President Steyn for some days, Colonel Le Gallais's force, including the 8th Corps of Mounted Infantry, came up with them near Bothaville in the Orange River Colony, and defeated them, capturing all De Wet's guns, seven in number, and wagons and about 150 prisoners; Colonel Le Gallais and two other officers were killed, and Lieutenant-Colonel Ross was dangerously wounded, his lower jaw being blown

THE SOUTH AFRICAN WAR (1899-1902)

away and his throat injured. Lieutenant-Colonel Ross, who was not expected to live, fortunately made a good recovery, but was unable to take any further part in the war; he was mentioned in despatches three times, and was given the C.B.

Captain H. de B. de Lisle, D.S.O., who was in England at the Staff College in 1899, left for South Africa in October in that year, in the s.s. "Cephalonia" with the 1st Battalion, with two companies of mounted infantry, and on arrival at Capetown on 19th November was despatched on the same day to garrison De Aar. On 1st January, 1900, he assumed command of the 2nd Battalion of Mounted Infantry at Colesberg, and at the end of the month was sent to Orange River, with the rank of local lieutenant-colonel, to raise and command the 6th Battalion of Mounted Infantry, which was composed of companies of the Bedfordshire, Welsh, Essex, and Wiltshire Regiments and of the Gordon Highlanders.

On arrival at Bloemfontein, Lieutenant-Colonel de Lisle was given the command of the 2nd Corps of Mounted Infantry, which consisted of :—(i.) The original 6th Battalion ; (ii.) a pom-pom section Royal Artillery ; (iii.) New South Wales Mounted Rifles ; (iv.) West Australian Mounted Rifles.

Lieutenant-Colonel de Lisle's mounted infantry took part in the relief of Kimberley, and the actions at Paardeburg, Poplar Grove, Karee Siding, Houtner, Vet River, Zand River, Pretoria, Diamond Hill, and many others. From July to September it was employed in the operations in the Transvaal to the west of Pretoria, and on 14th August, Lieutenant-Colonel de Lisle was severely wounded. On 15th September he was given the command of the first of the many mobile columns that were organised. This column consisted of :— (i.) One section "R" Battery, R.H.A. ; (ii.) two corps of mounted infantry ; (iii.) Kitchener's Horse.

Captain H. B. Des V. Wilkinson, also of the 2nd Durham Light Infantry, was staff officer of this column, which played a very important part in General De Wet's defeat at Bothaville on 6th November, 1900; the first gun in this action was fired at 6 a.m., when Lieutenant-Colonel de Lisle's column was ten miles away, but he arrived with it on the scene of action at 7.15 a.m.

Lieutenant-Colonel de Lisle commanded a mobile column, with

THE DURHAM LIGHT INFANTRY

various changes, until December, 1901, when he was placed in command of the 2nd Cavalry Brigade; in April, 1902, he was transferred to the command of a new brigade called the "Australian Commonwealth Brigade," and remained with it until the end of the war; from November, 1900, to the end of May, 1902, he was engaged in various operations in the Transvaal, Orange River Colony, and Cape Colony; he was mentioned in despatches four times, was promoted to the rank of brevet-lieutenant-colonel, and was given the C.B.

1901   On two occasions in February, 1901, while the 1st Battalion was holding the line at Eden Kop, attacks were made on trains by the Boers; the first was on the 6th, near Vlakfontein Nek, the second was on the 20th, near Steyn's Kraal; on both occasions the Boers were driven off. Again, on the 24th of the same month, a train was blown up between Zuikerbosch and Steyn's Kraal, but, strange to relate, no Boers came to attack it.

On 23rd April, Lieutenant E. B. Thresher died at Standerton from enteric fever, and the second "special service" company of Volunteers, under the command of Captain J. Cook, 4th Volunteer Battalion Durham Light Infantry, joined the battalion at Eden Kop. The other officers of the company were Lieutenant H. Ensor and Lieutenant F. S. Warwick, both of the 1st Volunteer Battalion Durham Light Infantry.

On 22nd June, Lieutenant R. E. Rasbotham, while patrolling near Eden Kop with nine men, was killed, and two of his men, Privates Moore and Sedgewick, were wounded; Lieutenant Rasbotham remained conscious for half an hour after being struck, and continued to encourage firing until he died; Privates St. Clair and Atkinson behaved particularly well on this occasion, and the former was specially promoted to the rank of corporal by the Commander-in-Chief for his gallantry.

On 25th July, Corporal S. Nicholson (then serving in the 26th Mounted Infantry) was killed in action near Standerton.

On 6th September, Lieutenant C. L. Matthews was dangerously wounded, and Serjeant W. Sykes was killed in action at Roberts' Drift, Vaal River; both were serving at the time in the 26th Mounted Infantry.

THE SOUTH AFRICAN WAR (1899-1902)

Head-quarters and two companies proceeded by rail from Fortuna Siding, near Eden Kop, to Heidelburg on 7th September.

On 17th September, Lieutenant R. Lambton, Privates Royal, Frost, and Budd were killed, Serjeant Salmon was dangerously wounded, and Privates Capon and Beabeck were slightly wounded at De Jager's Drift, Blood River, Natal; all were serving at the time in the 24th Mounted Infantry.

On 3rd October, head-quarters and "A" Company returned to Eden Kop, and Major G. C. Mansel, with 4 officers and 196 non-commissioned officers and men, joined Colonel Sir H. Rawlinson's column at Greylingstad.

Towards the end of October the battalion, with the exception of Major Mansel's party, was concentrated at Standerton, and on 7th November, numbering 19 officers and 625 non-commissioned officers and men, left that place with Colonel Campbell's column; Captain Bell, with the band and a portion of "H" Company, proceeded two days later to Middelburg to form a field base.

On 12th November the battalion was again divided, and on 23rd, with the exception of Captain Bell's party at Middelburg and "L" Company, which had been left for a few days at Rooi Poort, was once more united at Bethel.

In three or four days' time the battalion was again broken up. Headquarters proceeded to the field base at Middelburg; "A," "K," and "G" Companies, under Major Saunders, joined Colonel Allenby's column; "B" and "E" Companies, under Major Mansel, joined Colonel Sir H. Rawlinson's column; "M" Company, under Major Vane, joined Colonel Wing's column; "L" and the Special Service Companies were at Rooi Poort, but shortly joined Major Vane, and were subsequently divided between Colonel Wing's and Colonel Simpson's columns. This division continued until the end of January, 1902.

Lord Kitchener, in his despatch of 28th July, 1901, mentions 2nd Lieutenant R. E. Rasbotham, Lieutenant L. F. Ashburner, Lieutenant R. B. Lambton, Private L. St. Clair, and Private Quinn.

The following were mentioned in Lord Roberts's despatch of 4th September, 1901, which was in continuation of his despatch of 2nd April, 1901 :—

THE DURHAM LIGHT INFANTRY

Major the Hon. W. L. Vane.
Captain B. W. L. McMahon.
Captain W. C. Lascelles.
Lieutenant L. C. Soltau-Symons.

Captain L. E. C. Elwes.
Captain R. F. Bell.
Captain H. R. Cumming.
Lieutenant C. L. Matthews.

Quartermaster and Hon. Lieutenant J. H. Liebrecht.

Serjeant-Major J. Freel.
Colour-Serjeant J. P. L. Shea.
Colour-Serjeant C. Waiton.
Serjeant H. Littlejohn.
Serjeant J. Nightingale.
Corporal A. Neal.
Private C. McMahon.
Private W. Lovatt.

Colour-Serjeant A. Noble.
Colour-Serjeant W. Pendlebury.
Colour-Serjeant H. Tilley.
Serjeant J. Crump.
Serjeant J. Atkinson.
Private J. Bell.
Private E. Nicholson.
Private A. Miller.

Throughout the year 1901 head-quarters of the 2nd Battalion remained at Wellington, but on 22nd March detachments were sent to Calicut and Malapuram.

On 24th May one colour-serjeant and five serjeants proceeded to Trichinopoly for duty with the Boer prisoners there.

On 1st October, in accordance with an Army Order of the previous July, a bounty of £10 was offered to all men, with more than six years and three months' service, but with less than eleven years' service, with a furlough of two months in England, to extend their service to twelve years with the colours. In the first instance, 141 men accepted the bounty, and 26 took furlough to England; eventually 224 men accepted the bounty.

1902   On 19th January, 1902, head-quarters of the 1st Battalion left Middelburg for Standerton, and at the end of the month the battalion began to occupy the block-house line leading from Ermelo towards the Swazi border; on 1st May the battalion was holding that portion of the block-house line between Roodeval, on the Vaal River, and Athole, close to the Swazi border, a length of twenty-five miles, head-quarters being at Athole. During the month head-quarters moved gradually eastwards, being finally located at Camp Buchanan, fourteen miles east of Athole.

In March there was an interchange of 150 non-commissioned officers and men between the 1st and 2nd Battalions; Captain E. B.

THE SOUTH AFRICAN WAR (1899-1902)

Hales, 2nd Battalion, was in command of these parties on the voyage from India to South Africa and vice versa.

In April the second "Special Service" Company of Volunteers left for England, on being relieved by the 3rd Company, under the command of Captain E. S. Strangwayes, 3rd Volunteer Battalion Durham Light Infantry. The other officers of this company were Lieutenant H. Ensor, 1st Volunteer Battalion Durham Light Infantry, and Lieutenant P. P. Wilson, 3rd Volunteer Battalion Durham Light Infantry.

On 1st June it became known that peace had been signed on the previous night, and on the 3rd the following detachment left to represent the battalion at the Coronation of H.M. King Edward VII. :—

Major the Hon. W. L. Vane.	Private Braithwaite.
Serjeant Crump.	,, Acres.
,, Hargreaves.	,, Braid.
Corporal St. Clair.	,, Senior.
Private McMahon.	,, Chambers.
,, Moore.	,, Moran (26th M.I.).

This detachment was driven day and night, fresh carts and horses being provided at the different stations on the road; in spite of numerous delays, it arrived at Standerton at 11.30 a.m. on the following day; the distance was 111½ miles, and the time occupied was 31 hours; this detachment reached Southampton the morning before the day appointed for the Coronation, but, owing to the postponement of the ceremony on account of His Majesty's illness, was not in London when the Coronation actually took place.

Head-quarters of the 1st Battalion having arrived at Standerton on 30th June, the demobilisation commenced on the following day, and men were sent in batches of one hundred each to the Reservists' Camp at Eden Dale, Pietermaritzburg, to await passage home.

There was an inspection by Lieutenant-General the Hon. N. G. Lyttelton on 27th September, and on 26th October the battalion left Standerton; it arrived at Durban on the 29th, embarked on the P. and O. s.s. "Assaye," 7,376 tons, and sailed on the same day for India.

In Lord Kitchener's final despatch, dated 23rd June, 1902, the following names were mentioned:—Major the Hon. W. L. Vane,

THE DURHAM LIGHT INFANTRY

Brevet-Major E. St. G. Pratt, Captain W. Northey, Captain and Adjutant E. A. C. Blake, Colour-Serjeant H. Bedford, Colour-Serjeant R. Ward, Colour-Serjeant C. Waiton, Colour-Serjeant H. Tilley, Serjeant M. J. O'Brien, and Corporal W. Jones.

It is a peculiar fact that, as in the case of the Walcheren Expedition, the Peninsular and the Crimean Wars, so also in the case of the South African War it is a difficult matter now to state positively the exact number of casualties that occurred. In "The History of the South African War" (written by direction of H.M.'s Government), by Major-General Sir F. Maurice, the numbers given are:—Killed, 5 officers and 44 non-commissioned officers and men; died of disease, 1 officer and 57 non-commissioned officers and men; wounded, 10 officers and 155 non-commissioned officers and men.

In the penny official history of the regiment the numbers given are:—Killed, or died of wounds, disease, etc., 6 officers and 112 non-commissioned officers and men; wounded, 10 officers and 155 non-commissioned officers and men.

It will be observed that there is a difference of eleven in the number of deaths; this most probably is accounted for by deaths on the voyage home, or very shortly after arrival home.

The number of names on the monument in Durham Cathedral Churchyard, although approximate, does not agree exactly with either of the numbers given above.

The honours gained were:—

COMMANDER OF THE BATH.

Colonel A. L. Woodland, Lieutenant-Colonel H. S. Fitzgerald, Major (and Local Lieutenant-Colonel) W. C. Ross, Captain (and Local Lieutenant-Colonel) H. de B. de Lisle.

DISTINGUISHED SERVICE ORDER.

Major G. C. Mansel, Brevet-Major E. St. G. Pratt, Captain L. E. Cary-Elwes, Captain W. C. Lascelles, Captain L. F. Ashburner, Captain W. J. Ainsworth, Captain W. Northey, Lieutenant A. S. Way.

THE SOUTH AFRICAN WAR (1899-1902)

BREVET PROMOTION.

Lieutenant-Colonel H. de B. de Lisle, Major E. St. G. Pratt, Major C. C. Luard, Major B. W. L. McMahon, Major H. R. Cumming, Major E. A. C. Blake.

Captain H. B. Des V. Wilkinson was noted as being qualified for staff employment, in consequence of having been employed on the staff in the field.

Quartermaster and Hon. Lieutenant J. H. Liebrecht was granted the honorary rank of Captain.

The undermentioned warrant officer, non-commissioned officers and men were granted the medal for " Distinguished Conduct in the Field " :—

Serjeant-Major J. Freel.	Lance-Corporal C. Steele.
Colour-Serjeant A. Noble.	Private G. Bennett.
,, ,, J. P. L. Shea.	,, J. Cottle.
,, ,, R. Ward.	,, E. Horton.
Serjeant W. H. Littlejohn.	,, J. S. Parker.
,, M. J. O'Brien.	,, S. Pickford.
Corporal H. Hawkins.	,, J. W. Robson.
,, A. Neal.	,, J. Bell.

Privates L. St. Clair and Quinn were specially promoted to the rank of corporal for gallantry.

The 1st Battalion reached Bombay on 11th November, 1902, and was transhipped to R.I.M.S. "Clive" on the following day; the "Clive" then sailed down the Malabar coast, and arrived at Cannanore on the 15th, where one company was landed in relief of one company of the 2nd Battalion. Head-quarters and the remaining seven companies were then conveyed to Calicut, where they disembarked, and remained for the night, one company being detached to West Hill Barracks in relief of one company of the 2nd Battalion.

On 16th November the battalion was entrained in the evening and started for Wellington; one company was detached, while on the journey, for Malapuram, the remaining five companies arrived at Wellington in the course of the following day.

On 29th December His Majesty the King approved of the facings of the Durham Light Infantry being changed from " white " to " dark green."

Towards the end of February, 1902, practically the whole of the 2nd Battalion was employed in guarding 400 Boer prisoners who had been sent to Wellington from Trichinopoly.

There were inspections in March by Brigadier-General Sir J. Wolfe-Murray, and in November by Brigadier-General Harman; on the 15th of the latter month the battalion left Wellington for Calicut; the two battalions then met for the first time; on the following day the 2nd Battalion embarked on R.I.M.S. " Clive," and three days later disembarked at Bombay; on the 25th it embarked on P. and O. s.s. " Assaye," and, having reached Southampton on 16th December, proceeded to Aldershot, where it was quartered in Corunna Barracks. Strength, 18 officers, 1 warrant officer, 351 non-commissioned officers and men, 12 women, and 14 children.

Major-General C. Douglas, soon after its arrival at Aldershot, inspected the battalion, which had been augmented by 343 men, details of the Durham Light Infantry.

CHAPTER XI.

1ST AND 2ND BATTALIONS THE DURHAM LIGHT INFANTRY (1903-1914).

1903   THE year 1903 was a comparatively uneventful one in the life of both battalions; the 1st remained at Wellington, the 2nd at Aldershot.

1904   In October, 1904, the 1st Battalion proceeded in two parties to Secunderabad, arriving there on the 22nd and the 24th, but its stay there was a very short one, as on 24th December head-quarters and four companies were entrained for Lucknow, the remainder of the battalion following early in January, 1905.

In December permission was given by His Majesty to the regiment to bear the words "South Africa, 1899-1902," and "Relief of Ladysmith" upon its colours.

On 22nd March, 1904, 350 non-commissioned officers and men of the 2nd Battalion, with a due proportion of officers, proceeded from Aldershot to London for duty at the funeral of H.R.H. the Duke of Cambridge; in June, both in this and in the following year, the battalion was inspected by Brigadier-General T. D. Pilcher, C.B.

1905   On 6th January, 1905, head-quarters and four companies of the 1st Battalion arrived at Lucknow; four days later they were joined by the remaining four companies from Secunderabad.

On 20th October, 1905, the 2nd Battalion left Aldershot for Ireland; it was conveyed by rail to New Milford, and thence by City of Cork Steam Packet Company's s.s. "Inniscarra" to Cork, where it was quartered in the Victoria Barracks; Brigadier-General R. Lloyd-Payne, D.S.O., inspected the battalion shortly after its arrival. In the course of a few days 3 officers and 160 non-commissioned officers and men were sent to Fort Westmoreland, Spike Island, and Cork Harbour for three months.

THE DURHAM LIGHT INFANTRY

1906
On 12th March, 1906, the 1st Battalion was inspected at Lucknow by Major-General Sir E. Locke Elliott, K.C.B., on which occasion there were 22 officers and 874 non-commissioned officers and men present on parade. From April to October 100 men of the battalion were at Naini Tal and 80 at Kasauli.

1907
In May, 1906, the 2nd Battalion was armed with the short Lee-Enfield rifle. During 1907 the 1st Battalion remained at Lucknow and the 2nd at Cork; the former was again on 15th March inspected by Sir E. Locke Elliott, but the numbers present on parade were a trifle less than in the previous year; during the hot weather the battalion sent 154 men to Ranikhet; Brigadier-General M. Quayle Jones, C.B., inspected the 2nd Battalion on 3rd July.

1908
During 1908, the 1st Battalion remained at Lucknow, sending 103 men to Ranikhet for the hot weather; the 2nd Battalion remained at Cork.

1909
In 1909 both battalions changed their quarters; the 1st was entrained on 9th January for Nasirabad, with a strength of 29 officers and 953 non-commissioned officers and men, and detached two companies to Nimach.

The 2nd moved by rail to Fermoy on 20th January; in June the 2nd Battalion received a new sword bayonet, five inches longer than the previous one, and was also equipped with web infantry equipment, 1908 pattern.

The 1st Battalion won the Commander-in-Chief's Cup for rifle shooting, for British troops in India, for the year ending 31st March, 1909.

On 23rd August the 2nd Battalion, after having been inspected by Brigadier-General F. C. Carter, commanding 16th Infantry Brigade, marched from Fermoy, with the other battalions composing the brigade, to Aglish Camp, Co. Waterford, for manœuvres; it only had a strength of 430 all ranks, as 170 men were allowed to proceed on furlough previous to embarking to join the 1st Battalion in India.

1910
On 5th January, 1910, the 1st Battalion was inspected at Nasirabad by Brigadier-General K. S. Davison, C.B.

In August of this year the 2nd Battalion was issued with a light entrenching tool; and on 1st September encamped in Moore

THE DURHAM LIGHT INFANTRY (1903-1914)

Park, Fermoy, with the remainder of the 16th Infantry Brigade for divisional training; on 9th September, the 6th Division, consisting of the 16th, 17th, and 18th Brigades, marched, under Major-General W. P. Pulteney, C.B., from Moore Park and Kilworth for manœuvres in Cos. Kilkenny and Carlow; the 2nd Durham Light Infantry returned to Fermoy by rail on 17th September.

1911   In November, 1911, the 1st Battalion received the new short magazine rifle, and on the 24th of the same month left Nasirabad by rail for Delhi, under the command of Major C. C. Luard, with a strength of 22 officers and 742 non-commissioned officers and men; the battalion arrived at Delhi on the following day, and formed part of the 2nd Composite Brigade of the Composite Division; a depot was left at Nasirabad.

On 11th December, His Majesty King George V. presented new colours at Delhi to the following seven battalions of British infantry, which paraded together for the ceremony:—1st Battalion Northumberland Fusiliers, 1st Battalion Durham Light Infantry, 2nd Battalion Royal Highlanders (Black Watch), 1st Battalion Seaforth Highlanders, 2nd Battalion Gordon Highlanders, 1st Battalion Highland Light Infantry, and 1st Battalion Connaught Rangers.

His Majesty then presented new colours to the following two battalions of native infantry:—18th Infantry and 19th Punjabis.

As soon as the British battalions had received their new colours, the seven commanding officers advanced towards His Majesty, who handed to each of them an address. That presented to the commanding officer of the 1st Durham Light Infantry was as follows:—

"Lieutenant-Colonel Wilson, officers, non-commissioned officers, and men of the 1st Battalion Durham Light Infantry:

"I am very glad to have this opportunity of giving new colours to your battalion.

"The presentation of colours is a solemn occasion in the history of a regiment, for you then bid farewell to the old flag which bears upon it the records of past achievements, receiving in return a new flag, upon which it lies with you to inscribe the names of future victories.

"Recalling with pride the deeds of those who have gone before, you look forward with hope into the coming days.

THE DURHAM LIGHT INFANTRY

"Remember that this is no common flag which I am committing to your keeping; a colour is a sacred ensign, ever by its inspiration, through no longer by its presence, a rallying point in battle; it is the emblem of duty, the outward sign of your allegiance to your God, your Sovereign, and your country, to be looked up to, to be venerated, and to be passed down untarnished by succeeding generations.

"It is just one hundred years since you embarked for Portugal, and opened the proud record, begun with Salamanca, continued with Inkerman, and lately maintained at Vaal Krantz.

"Remember that though you no longer take your colours with you into action, it is still in your power to inscribe upon them memorable names.

"GEORGE R.I."

The battalion took part in the Durbar on the 12th, and in the Royal Review on the 14th; on the 16th it furnished a guard of honour at Semingarh station when His Majesty left Delhi; on the 24th of the same month it left Delhi, under Major C. C. Luard, by rail for Nowshera, where it arrived two days later, and was quartered in Khartoum Barracks; previous to leaving, it was inspected by Major-General K. S. Davison, C.B.

One hundred and four Delhi Durbar Coronation medals were issued to the battalion; of this number 7 were issued to officers, 2 to warrant officers, and 95 to non-commissioned officers and men.

On 18th January, 1911, the 2nd Battalion, having been previously inspected by both Brigadier-General F. C. Carter, C.B., and Major-General W. P. Pulteney, C.B., left Fermoy for Colchester; it travelled viâ Waterford, Fishguard, and Acton, and took up its new quarters in Hyderabad Barracks.

In June the battalion was on duty in London on the occasion of the Coronation of their Majesties King George and Queen Mary; on the 7th, 4 officers and 100 non-commissioned officers and men, Captain F. G. Maughan being in command, proceeded to Regent's Park, London, as an advanced party; head-quarters, 17 officers and 400 non-commissioned officers and men, arrived in Regent's Park on the 20th; on the 22nd the battalion was on duty in St. James' Street, and on the following day in the Strand, near St. Clement Danes Church; it returned to Colchester the same evening.

On 29th June the battalion was again in London, this time only for the day, and with a strength of 17 officers and 400 non-commissioned officers and men, inclusive of band and bugles; it was on duty in Finsbury Pavement during the royal drive in that part of London.

The battalion was inspected by Brigadier-General H. N. C. Heath, C.B., on 4th August, and on the 17th of the same month left Colchester for strike duty at Bradford; 19 officers and 588 men proceeded on this unpleasant duty, 100 rounds of ball ammunition per rifle being carried; the journey was performed by night; the battalion, which fortunately was not in collision with the strikers, was accommodated in Bradford Moor Barracks, and returned to Colchester on 27th August.

On the day following the return to Colchester, Captain J. W. Jeffreys was sent to Felixstowe with 45 men, and Lieutenant W. B. Twist with 30 men to Harwich; both these detachments rejoined head-quarters on 7th October.

1912   On 21st April, 1912, head-quarters and five companies of the 1st Battalion left Nowshera by rail for Rawal Pindi; head-quarters and two companies then proceeded by road to Ghora Dhaka, where they arrived on the 27th; the other three companies proceeded by road to Khanspur, where they arrived on the 28th; the remaining three companies stayed at Nowshera for the hot weather; the parties at Ghora Dhaka and Khanspur left their respective stations in the middle of October, and the battalion was once more united at Nowshera on 25th October.

The 2nd Battalion, together with the other battalions composing the 11th Infantry Brigade, was inspected in review order at Colchester by Lieutenant-General Sir J. M. Grierson, K.C.B., on 19th April, 1912.

On 9th July new colours were presented to the 2nd Battalion on the Abbey Field at Colchester by the Earl of Durham, K.G., Lord-Lieutenant of the County of Durham; in his address the Earl of Durham laid stress upon the particular smartness of the battalion on parade on that day, and also upon his family connection with the Durham Light Infantry; the state showed a strength of 20 officers, two warrant officers, and 500 non-commissioned officers and men on parade; the recruits of the battalion, together with those of other battalions at Colchester, were employed in keeping the ground; the precision with which the ceremony was conducted was most favourably commented upon by all those who were present.

On 11th August the battalion—20 officers, one warrant officer, and 500 non-commissioned officers and men—was conveyed by rail to Aldershot, where it encamped on Rushmoor for brigade and divisional training; on 9th September the 4th Division, which included the 2nd Durham Light Infantry, marched into camp at Longmoor, and, after an inspection by General Sir C. Douglas, K.C.B., was conveyed by rail to Hitchin on the 14th to take part in manœuvres; it was in the Blue Force, under Lieutenant-General Sir J. M. Grierson, K.C.B.; at the conclusion of the manœuvres the battalion marched back to Colchester, arriving there on 19th September. In December a new rifle, the short Lee-Enfield, Mark III, was issued to the battalion.

On 24th October in this year a most interesting ceremony took place at Durham, when the old colours of the 1st, 2nd, and 3rd Battalions of the Durham Light Infantry were deposited in Durham Cathedral; previous to entering the cathedral a wreath was presented by the Earl of Durham, K.G., Lord-Lieutenant of the county of Durham, to the Sub-Dean, the Venerable H. W. Watkins, D.D., to be placed upon the cross, erected in the cathedral churchyard, to the memory of those members of the Durham Light Infantry who lost their lives in the South African War, 1899-1902; the escort for the colours was drawn from the depot at Newcastle-on-Tyne, representing the 1st, 2nd, 3rd, and 4th Battalions, and each of the five Durham battalions of infantry of the Territorial Force sent a detachment of one officer and twenty men, so that on this day, for the first time in the history of the regiment, representatives of the nine battalions of the Durham Light Infantry were paraded together.

These three pairs of colours were on a subsequent date finally fixed in the chapter house at Durham, together with the colours of the 1st and 4th (formerly 3rd) Battalions, which had hitherto been fixed in the south transept of the cathedral.

THE DURHAM LIGHT INFANTRY (1903-1914)

1913   In January, 1913, the following letter was sent out from the War Office:—

"War Office,
"13th January, 1913.

"SIR,

"I am commanded by the Army Council to inform you that the King has been graciously pleased to approve of the 2nd (South Canterbury) Regiment, New Zealand, being shown in the War Office Army List as being allied to the Durham Light Infantry.

"A copy of this letter has been sent to the officers commanding 1st, 2nd, 3rd, and 4th Battalions, and to the officer in charge of infantry records, York.

"I am, Sir,
"Your obedient servant,
"E. W. D. WARD.

"To Major-General
  "R. UPCHER, C.B., D.S.O.,
    "Colonel, Durham Light Infantry,
      "Fritton Warren, Great Yarmouth."

"L" Company, 1st Battalion, having left Nowshera on 16th April, arrived at Khanspur on the 20th of the same month; "A," "B," "E," and "K" Companies left Nowshera on the last-named date and arrived at Ghora Daka and Khanspur a week later; headquarters, with "A" and "B" Companies, were stationed at Ghora Daka, the other three companies at Khanspur; the remaining three companies of the battalion stayed at Nowshera; the eight companies were again united at Nowshera on 27th October. Lieutenant-General Sir J. Willcocks, K.C.S.I., etc., inspected the battalion—strength, 974 non-commissioned officers and men—on 27th September.

The 2nd Battalion left Colchester by rail on 29th August for brigade and divisional training, and then took part in the Army Exercise in September; on the 27th of that month the battalion was conveyed by rail from Rugby to Lichfield, where it is now quartered without any detachments.

THE DURHAM LIGHT INFANTRY

1914

In February, 1914, the 1st Battalion took part in a short, but most successful punitive expedition across the frontier of India; on the 20th of the month Major-General R. Bannatine-Allason, C.B., issued orders for the Nowshera brigade to move out "on manœuvres," the ammunition being carried in the ammunition column as if for divisional field-firing; on the 21st the brigade marched 19 miles to a camp north-east of Mardan.

Strength—

    Two squadrons Guides Cavalry.
    30th Mountain Battery.
    A half-company of sappers and miners.
    1st Battalion Durham L.I. (500 men).
    Guides Infantry (400 men).
    24th Punjabis (500 men).
    46th Punjabis (250 men).
    82nd Punjabis (400 men).

The 3rd Brigade was in support.

On the 22nd the march was continued to Rustam, 18 miles, through deep mud, and shortly before midnight the force collected in the nullah south of Rustam, and started for the Malandri Pass, 12 miles distant.

The pass was secured at 8.15 a.m. on the 23rd; the 24th Punjabis, with a detachment of sappers and miners, then burnt Nawai Kili $3\frac{1}{2}$ miles beyond the pass, and the 82nd Punjabis, with a detachment of sappers and miners, destroyed Zangi Khan, 1 mile from the pass. Both these parties were back at the pass at 2 p.m., having killed 4 men, wounded 8 or 10 men, and taken 10 prisoners, with much cattle, sheep, goats, etc.

The pass was held by the Guides, the 1st Durham Light Infantry, with two guns, being in support.

The 46th Punjabis and 54th Sikhs were behind them with the other four guns, ready to support when the troops retired from the pass. At 3.45 p.m. the pass was clear, and the troops were back in camp at 8.30 p.m.; the retirement was followed by the tribesmen, but with no vigour.

There were not any casualties on the British side, except that two men were burnt, not dangerously, however, while taking part in the destruction of Zangi Khan. The British force fired over 2,000 rounds; the Buxerwals fired a great deal, but without effect.

The whole expedition was most successful, but time did not permit the British force to reach the worst offenders.

The following letter announces a fresh link between the forces of Great Britain and those of the Oversea Dominions:—

" War Office,
" London, S.W.,
" 13th May, 1914.

" SIR,

" I am commanded by the Army Council to inform you that His Majesty the King has been graciously pleased to approve of the 106th Regiment, Winnipeg Light Infantry, Canada, being shown in the War Office Army List as allied to the Durham Light Infantry.

" This will be published in Army Orders in due course.

" A copy of this letter has been sent to the officers commanding 1st, 2nd, 3rd, 4th, 5th, 6th, 7th, 8th and 9th Battalions, and to the officer in charge of Infantry Records, York.

" I am, Sir,
" Your obedient servant,
" R. H. BRADE.

" Major-General R. UPCHER, C.B., D.S.O.,
" Colonel, The Durham Light Infantry,
" Fritton Warren, Yarmouth."

Present establishment (May, 1914)—1st Battalion, 1,031 all ranks; 2nd Battalion, 802 all ranks.

Present strength.—1st Battalion, 1,053 all ranks; 2nd Battalion, 545 all ranks.

The pay of the 2nd Battalion amounts to £20,534 5s. 8d. for one year; in 1756 the establishment of a battalion on home service was practically the same, and the net pay amounted to £13,316 8s. 4d. for one year.

APPENDICES.

[APPENDIX I.

OFFICERS.—68TH REGIMENT OF FOOT.

22ND APRIL, 1758, TO 30TH JUNE, 1881.

N.B.—Those Officers who were appointed to the Regiment on its formation, and who came from the 23rd Royal Welch Fuzileers, were, unless promoted on transfer, appointed with dates of their ranks in their former regiment.

Dates of promotion after 30th June, 1881, refer to the Durham Light Infantry.

NAME.	Ensign or 2nd Lieut.	Lieutenant.	Captain.	Major.	Lieut.-Colonel.	Colonel.	REMARKS.
Lambton, John	...	...	...	...	22-4-1758	22-4-1758	(See Appendix II.)
Adey, William	...	...	...	...	...	...	From senior Major, 23rd R.W.F.; carried one of the 23rd colours at Fontenoy, 30-4-1745; resigned, 1762.
Napier, William	...	...	...	6-5-1758	...	...	From 23rd R.W.F.; to Lieut.-Col., 14th Foot, 1760.
Rowley, William	...	...	25-8-1756	12-6-1760	...	...	From 23rd R.W.F.; formerly in Marines; half-pay Lieut.-Col., 1762.
			24-12-1755				
Dundas, William	...	...	29-8-1756	6-10-1769	...	...	From 23rd R.W.F.; formerly in Montagu's; to Lieut.-Col., 1st Foot, 1776.
Hewitt, Peter	...	...	30-8-1756	...	...	...	From 23rd R.W.F.; retired, 1762.
Lloyd, Richard	...	...	31-8-1756	...	...	...	From 23rd R.W.F.; retired, 1762.
Revell, Tristram	...	...	1-9-1756	...	...	...	From 23rd R.W.F.; formerly in York's; taken prisoner at St. Cas, 1758; Captain, 24th Foot, 1761.
Blaquire, John	...	...	2-9-1756	...	...	...	From 23rd R.W.F.; formerly Cornet in Ancrum's; to 18th Light Dragoons, 1759.
Ridley, Richard	...	...	3-9-1756	...	...	...	From 23rd R.W.F.; formerly in 1st Foot Guards; to Major, 107th, 1761.
Leslie, Samuel	...	...	...	...	...	...	Capt.-Lieut., 29-5-1758. From 23rd R.W.F.; to Captain, 14th Foot, 1762.

APPENDIX I

Name			Date		Notes
Dacre, Joseph	...	...	30-8-1756	...	From 23rd R.W.F.; died, 1761.
Jenkins, Thomas	...	...	31-8-1756	...	From 23rd R.W.F.; to Captain of an independent company, 1760.
Bellew, Lewis	...	...	4-9-1756	...	From 23rd R.W.F.; formerly Serjeant, Royal Irish; to half-pay, 1763.
Evans, Edward	...	...	7-9-1756	...	From 23rd R.W.F.; formerly in 1st Troop of Horse Guards; exchanged with Lieut. Grant (23rd), 1758.
Haswell, John	...	...	8-9-1756	...	From 23rd R.W.F.; formerly in 1st Troop of Horse Guards; died on the Cherbourg Expedition, 1758.
Munro, George	...	...	25-2-1757 30-10-1764	20-11-1776	Capt.-Lieut., 12-2-1762. From 23rd R.W.F.; Adjutant, 22-7-1758; retired, 1778.
Hunt, John	...	...	2-10-1757	...	From 23rd R.W.F.; to 9th Foot, 1759.
Patriarche, Philip	...	...	4-10-1757	...	From 23rd R.W.F.; to half-pay, 88th Foot, 1765.
Alderton, William	...	...	5-10-1757	...	From 23rd R.W.F.; to Captain of an independent company, 1760.
Wilkie, Patrick	...	...	6-10-1757	...	From 23rd R.W.F.; to Captain of an independent company, 1761.
Armstrong, Thomas	...	...	7-10-1757	...	Capt.-Lieut., 30-10-1764. From 23rd R.W.F.; died, 1764.
Teasdale, William	...	...	8-10-1757	...	From 23rd R.W.F.; not in 1765 list.
Hopper, Humphrey	...	...	10-10-1757	...	Capt.-Lieut., 23-1-1767. From 23rd R.W.F.; formerly Serjt.-Major, 23rd; Adjt. 1765; died, 1767.
Pawlett, William	...	...	10-2-1758 13-2-1757	...	From 23rd R.W.F.; formerly in 38th Foot; to Captain of an independent company, 1760.
Brereton, Boulter	...	...	7-3-1758	...	From 23rd R.W.F.; formerly in 53rd Foot; to Captain, 112th Foot, 1761.
Nicholson, Thomas	...	...	8-3-1758	...	From 23rd R.W.F.; formerly in Cunyngham's; to Captain of an independent company, 1760.
Owen, Arthur	...	...	22-7-1758	...	From 23rd R.W.F.; not in 1765 list.

Name.	Ensign or 2nd Lieut.	Lieutenant.	Captain.	Major.	Lieut.-Colonel.	Colonel.	Remarks.
Stafford, Robert	2-10-1757 (2nd Lt.)	23-7-1758	...	...	...	...	From 23rd R.W.F.; died, 1764.
Brodie, William	3-10-1757 (2nd Lt.)	14-9-1758	...	...	...	...	From 23rd R.W.F.; to half-pay, 8th Foot, 1765.
Melville (or Melvill), William	4-10-1757 (2nd Lt.)	12-7-1759	...	...	...	...	From 23rd R.W.F.; died, 1764.
Upton, John	5-10-1757 (2nd Lt.)	12-10-1760	...	...	...	...	From 23rd R.W.F.; to Captain, 109th Foot, 1761.
Fallé, Philip		...	...	...	...	...	From 23rd R.W.F.; to Lieut. in Tyrwhitt's independent company in N. America, 1760.
Este, Chas. William	27-1-1758 (2nd Lt.)	25-1-1761	29-3-1775	...	...	...	From 23rd R.W.F.; Adjutant, 11-3-1767; to Lieut.-Colonel, 65th Foot, 1795; Major-General, 1805.
Crawley, James	22-7-1758 (Ensign)	26-1-1761	...	...	...	...	To half-pay, 1763.
Hastings, George	23-7-1758 (Ensign)	...	...	...	...	...	To 9th Foot, 1759.
	Ensign.						
Boisdaune, Lewis	...	...	...	...	...	...	Chaplain, 8-7-1758. Retired, 1766.
Munro, James (called George Munro in Army Lists, 1759-1760)	16-2-1763	...	...	...	...	...	Quartermaster, 25-8-1756. From 23rd R.W.F., 1758; promoted Quartermaster from Serjeant; then Ensign, and again Quartermaster in 1764; died, 1764.
Stewart, William	14-9-1758	...	...	...	...	...	To 62nd Foot, 1759.
Wood, Robert	7-10-1758	27-1-1761	...	...	...	...	To half-pay, 1763.
Sandys, George	20-1-1759	...	...	...	...	...	From 62nd Foot; to Crawfurd's, 1759.
Bailey, Richard	25-3-1758 26-1-1758	...	...	...	...	...	From 23rd R.W.F.; appointed Quartermaster (68th), 22-7-1758, but apparently declined transfer and became Quartermaster (23rd) — 15-7-1758.
Pearson, William	...	...	...	...	...	...	Surgeon, 24-9-1757 — 15-7-1758. From 23rd R.W.F.; appointed Surgeon (68th), 15-7-1758, but apparently declined transfer and remained in 23rd.
Bristowe, Thomas	...	...	...	...	...	...	Surgeon, 5-8-1758; to half-pay, 122nd Foot, on Irish establishment, 1764.

APPENDIX I

Name				
Grant, Thomas			29-9-1757	From 23rd R.W.F.; originally in Pepperell's; exchanged with Lieut. Evans, 1758; taken prisoner at St. Cas, 1758; died, 1760. To Napier's independent company, 1760.
Campbell, Charles Henning	12-7-1759			
Winslow, Josiah	13-7-1759	22-12-1761		To half-pay, 1763.
Harris, Thomas	27-8-1759	12-2-1762		To half-pay, 1763.
Baillie, Francis		18-3-1760		From 3rd Foot; to 70th Foot, 1760.
Cusack, James		25-4-1760		From 70th Foot; to Captain of an independent company, 1760.
Pujolas, Anthony			12-6-1760	From 32nd Foot; to 66th Foot, 1761.
Johnston, Robert		22-5-1761		From 24th Foot; to 13th Dragoons, 1767.
Haste, Philip		22-8-1760	25-5-1772	Captain-Lieut., 11-3-1767. From Ross's independent company; Quartermaster, 1764; Captain-Lieut., 1767; to 36th Foot, 1780.
		23-2-1760		
Nestor, John	12-10-1761			From Volunteer; died, 1761.
Atkinson, John	27-1-1761	30-12-1763		To half-pay, 51st Foot, 1766.
Stainforth, John		4-5-1761		From 57th Foot; to half-pay, 1763.
Russell, Charles	11-6-1760	2-4-1762		To half-pay, 1763.
Gildart, John	12-6-1760	16-2-1763		To half-pay, 1763.
Beatson, James	21-2-1761			Not in 1765 list.
Hill, Foster	28-2-1761			Not in 1765 list.
Roche, David	17-3-1761			To 108th Foot, 1761.
Wedderburn, David			22-9-1762	From Major Commanding 102nd Foot (Queen's Royal Volunteers); to Lieut.-Col., 22nd Foot, 1764.
Gould, Paston			1-3-1762	From 23rd R.W.F.; to Lieut.-Col., 30th Foot, 1764.
Perrin, James		6-1-1762		From 65th Foot; not in 1765 list.
Smith, George		12-2-1762		From 34th Foot; retired, 1765.
Somerville, James		15-4-1762		From 6th Foot; died, 1764.
Davidson, Alexander		18-8-1762		From 114th Foot; retired, 1765.
Lloyd, ——	22-12-1761	30-10-1764		Died, 1765.
Mills, Samuel	4-3-1762			Not in 1765 list.
Hinde, George	22-3-1762	18-7-1766		To half-pay, 60th Foot, 1770.
Sutherland, James	2-4-1762	11-3-1767		To half-pay, 26th Foot, 1767.
Sutton, John	30-12-1763			Died, 1764.
O'Hara, Arthur	6-4-1764	8-10-1767		Died, 1772.

THE DURHAM LIGHT INFANTRY

Name.	Ensign.	Lieutenant.	Captain.	Major.	Lieut.-Colonel.	Colonel.	Remarks.
St. Clair (or Sinclair), John	6-4-1764	...	...	...	1-6-1764	...	Died, 1767.
Brush, Henry	6-4-1764	...	...	...	24-12-1762	...	Died, 1764.
Martin, Jonas (or Josias)	...	...	...	...	13-9-1769	...	From 22nd Foot; retired, 1769.
Reynolds, Lawrence	...	...	...	23-3-1764	...	...	Colonel, 19-2-1779. From 9th Foot.
James, Nathan	...	...	15-6-1764	...	...	...	From ——; not in 1767 list.
Munro, Duncan	...	6-4-1764	...	...	...	...	Not in 1767 list.
Mulcaster, Thomas	...	21-11-1764	...	...	...	...	From half-pay, 25th Foot; to half-pay, 1767.
Puleston, Thomas	...	12-10-1760	...	...	...	...	From half-pay, 76th Foot; to 54th Foot, 1765.
		22-11-1764					
Cunninghame, C—— Augustus	...	...	...	...	...	...	Surgeon, 6-4-1764. To half-pay, late 93rd Foot, 1765.
Church, Charles Cobbe	25-12-1764	...	...	...	...	...	From late 122nd Foot; to 23rd R.W.F., 1765.
	13-2-1762						
Wilson, Robert	25-12-1764	...	...	...	...	...	From late 72nd Foot; not in 1766 list.
Drakeford, Matthew	25-12-1764	23-1-1769	...	...	...	...	From late 107th Foot; not in 1781 list.
Goddard, James	...	4-1-1765	...	...	...	...	From half-pay, 67th Foot; died, 1765.
Dalrymple, Argyll	...	...	11-6-1765	...	...	...	From 1st Dragoon Guards; died, 1766.
Dickson, John	...	...	12-6-1765	...	...	...	From 47th Foot; to 81st Foot, 1782.
Green, Reuben John	...	...	...	...	...	...	Capt.-Lieut., 15-4-1762—25-12-1764.
MacIntosh, John	...	4-1-1765	...	...	...	...	From 42nd Foot; to 73rd Foot, 1778.
		5-1-1760					
Shewcraft, John	...	25-1-1765	...	...	...	...	From half-pay, 4th Foot; retired, 1770.
		15-7-1761					
Parke, Charles	...	17-6-1765	...	...	...	...	From half-pay, 8th Foot; died, 1766.
		28-1-1760					
Turnbull, John	...	10-10-1765	...	...	...	...	From half-pay, late 74th Foot; died, 1768.
		3-3-1763					
Lawder, William	6-9-1765	...	...	...	...	...	Retired, 1766.
Davies, Simon	2-10-1765	26-12-1770	...	...	...	...	From half-pay, late 106th Foot; retired, 1784.
Barker, Caleb	16-7-1762	...	...	...	...	...	Surgeon, 21-6-1765. From half-pay, late 93rd Foot; retired, 1775.
James, ——	...	...	?	...	...	...	From ——; date of appointment to 68th not traced; exchanged with John McDougall.

APPENDIX I

Name			
McDougall, John		14-3-1766	From half-pay, late 103rd Foot; to half-pay, 1768.
Effingham, Earl of, Thomas		4-9-1761	From Coldstream Guards; to half-pay, late 80th Foot, 1766.
Le Hunte, George		1-8-1766	From half-pay, late 80th Foot; to half-pay, late 111th Foot, 1767.
Sutherland, William		7-8-1766 28-11-1759	From half-pay, late 105th Foot; to 38th Foot, 1766.
	9-4-1766		
Dunbar, Joseph		30-5-1766	From 38th Foot; to half-pay, late 108th Foot, 1768.
Webb, John		2-8-1760 18-7-1766 1-8-1760	From half-pay, 51st Foot; to half-pay, 63rd Foot, 1775. Retired, 1768.
Hodgkinson, Joseph	6-12-1765		To 6th Foot, 1772.
Whiston, William	13-2-1766	4-10-1770	Died, 1767.
Crump, Joshua	18-7-1766		Chaplain, 28-11-1766. To half-pay, late 71st Foot, 1771.
Criggan, Claud			From half-pay, 23rd R.W.F.; died, 1767.
Kirkby, Henry		23-1-1767	
Bellenden, Hon. Robt.		4-3-1767 15-10-1761	From half-pay, late 111th Foot; not in 68th in 1769; succeeded as 6th Baron Bellenden, 1796; died, 13-10-1797.
Nugent, Anthony		28-6-1767	From 13th Dragoons; retired, 1775.
Adamson, John		13-4-1767	From half-pay, 26th Foot; retired, 1770.
Potts, William	11-3-1767	18-4-1770	Adjutant, 1777; Major in the Army, 1-3-1794; to 10th Foot, 1796.
Boyd, St. Lawrence	27-3-1767		To 38th Foot, 1767.
Osborne, Robt. Weir	19-8-1767	3-8-1782	From 38th Foot; retired, 1772.
	10-12-1762		
Bowyer, Henry	8-10-1767		To 19th Foot, 1776.
Lloyd, Watkin	9-12-1767	27-3-1772	Died, 1769.
Beswicke, Edward		27-5-1768	From 36th Foot; to half-pay, late 106th Foot, 1773.
Stewart, James (i)		10-6-1768 12-11-1778 25-7-1788 22-2-1783	Col., 1-3-1794. From 17th Foot; Maj.-Gen., 3-5-1796; Lieut.-Gen. 25-9-1803; but remained on regimental list as senior Lieut.-Col. until appointed Colonel, 1st Veteran Battalion, 30-6-1804.

173

THE DURHAM LIGHT INFANTRY

Name.	Ensign.	Lieutenant.	Captain.	Major.	Lieut.-Colonel.	Colonel.	Remarks.
Walsh, Samuel	...	8-1-1768	...	...	...	...	From half-pay, late 98th Foot; died, 1768.
Morton, William	...	26-11-1762 13-4-1768	...	...	...	...	From half-pay, late 108th Foot; to half-pay, late 108th Foot, 1770.
Farley, John Simon	21-4-1768	30-7-1762 30-3-1772	9-10-1778	1-1-1795 1-3-1794	1-3-1800 1-1-1798	...	Maj.-Gen., 4-6-1811; but remained on regimental list as senior Lieut.-Col. until 1815; died, 6-6-1821.
Schaw, John Bridges	...	...	6-10-1769	25-7-1788 17-11-1780	...	...	Colonel, 21-8-1795. From 17th Foot; retired, 1797.
McKenzie, Ronald	23-1-1769	7-6-1773	10-7-1776	...	...	...	Retired, 1778.
Thompson, William	5-5-1769	29-3-1775	20-11-1776	...	...	...	Adjutant, 1776; to 13th Foot, 1783.
Tymperley, Robert	...	...	25-12-1770	...	...	...	From "late of the Negroes at the Havanah"; retired, 1776.
Shaw (or Shawe), John	...	23-2-1770 15-1-1763	5-2-1762	...	...	...	From half-pay, 60th Foot; to 73rd Foot, 1777.
Jones, Thomas	...	25-12-1770 22-3-1762	...	...	...	...	From 74th Foot; died, 1772.
Crump, Byam	22-8-1770	...	...	...	...	...	Died, 1771.
Bayer, Rowland Otto	14-12-1770	...	...	...	...	...	Retired, 1775.
Storey, Anthony	26-12-1770	4-12-1775	...	...	...	...	Retired, 1777.
Mackay, George	30-4-1771	...	...	...	...	...	Killed in expedition in St. Vincent against the Carribs, 1772-1773.
Roberts, Charles	...	...	...	...	...	...	Chaplain, 6-5-1771. From half-pay, late 71st Foot; died, 1772.
Taylor, William (or Richard)	...	25-5-1772 10-12-1771	...	...	...	...	From 6th Foot; retired, 1775.
Byron, John	27-3-1772	10-7-1776	...	...	...	...	To 2nd Guards, 1773.
Brabazon, Malby	30-3-1772	...	31-3-1782	2-9-1795	...	...	Major, 1-3-1794; died end of 1795, or January, 1796; succeeded by Thomas Picton.
Hackman, James	20-5-1772	10-7-1776	...	...	...	...	Retired, 1776.
Green, Crispus	...	...	5-2-1773	...	...	...	Chaplain, 20-5-1772. Retired, 1775.
Colthurst, Nicholas	...	...	25-5-1772	...	...	...	From half-pay, late 106th Foot.
Byam, William	28-4-1773	20-11-1776	29-12-1781	...	...	...	From Volunteer; retired, 1782 or 1783; not in 1783 list.
Bigsby, James	5-7-1773	...	...	...	...	...	Not in 1776 list.
Ness, Robert	30-8-1773	14-12-1776	...	...	...	...	Not in 1782 list.
Burch, Joseph Randyll	6-2-1775	...	10-4-1779	...	...	...	Retired, 1777.

174

APPENDIX I

Creed, Francis	...	3-7-1775 27-7-1762	Capt.-Lieut. and Capt., 25-7-1788. From half-pay, 63rd Foot; retired, 1793.
Webster, Gilbert	29-3-1775	12-5-1777 12-11-1778	Retired, 1779.
Burvill, John	4-12-1775	...	To 72nd Foot, 1779.
Ironside, William	...	...	Chaplain, 23-3-1775. Retired, 1787.
Rose, ——	...	1-6-1778	Surgeon, 5-2-1775. Retired, 1785.
Forbes, Lord	7-6-1776	30-10-1780	Earl of Granard, 16-4-1780; retired, 1782; died, 9-6-1837.
Montgomery, Alexander	10-7-1776	1-6-1778	Not in 1782 list.
Stewart, Gilbert Shuckburgh	10-7-1776	1-6-1778 11-8-1789	Not in 1796 list.
Dillon, Luke (i)	14-12-1776	1-6-1778	To 98th Foot, 1785.
Lynch, Alexander	14-12-1776	1-6-1778 22-1-1783	To 36th Independent Company, 1781.
Campbell, Neil	5-3-1777	...	Retired, 1777.
Cowan, James	12-5-1777	1-6-1778	Not in 1780 list.
Smith, Hugh	15-12-1777	1-6-1778	Retired, 1781.
Breveter, Robert	...	2-6-1778	To a company of invalids in Ireland, 1780.
Cox, Sir Richard, Bart.	...	3-6-1778	Retired, 1782 or 1783.
Kelly, John (or Charles)	...	9-10-1778	Capt.-Lieut. and Capt., 8-3-1793. To 70th Foot, 1795.
Hill, Thomas	...	7-11-1778	From 52nd Foot; Adjutant, 1787; retired, 1791.
Montgomery, George	...	12-11-1778	Retired, 1784.
Power, George	...	12-11-1778	To an independent company, 1781.
Fox, John	5-6-1778	10-4-1779	To 24th Foot, 1781.
Sirr, Henry Charles	6-6-1778	8-3-1780	Retired, 1791; Acting Town Major, Dublin, 1796-98; Town Major, Dublin, 1798-1826; wounded and arrested Lord Edwd. Fitzgerald, 19-5-1798; died, 7-1-1841.
Gore, William	7-6-1778	12-9-1780	Retired, 1781.
Balaquier, John	9-10-1778	...	To half-pay, late 79th Foot, 1788.
Wilson, Hamilton	7-11-1778	...	Died, 7-3-1780.
Greaves, Robert	12-11-1778	30-10-1780	Retired, 1787.
Innes, William	12-11-1778	...	To an independent company, 1781
Daniel, Thos. Ahmuty	...	25-7-1778	Apparently declined appointment to the regiment and never joined.
McIntosh, John	...	10-4-1779	From ——; not in 1780 list.

175

THE DURHAM LIGHT INFANTRY

Name.	Ensign.	Lieutenant.	Captain.	Major.	Lieut.-Colonel.	Colonel.	Remarks.
St. Leger, Hon. Richard	…	…	…	…	…	…	Capt.-Lieut. and Capt., 19-1-1780. From 6th Foot; to 2nd Horse, 1785; M.P., Doneraile, 1777-83. From 72nd Foot; retired, 1781.
Jeffreyson, George	…	12-5-1779 14-10-1758	…	…	…	…	From a company of invalids in Ireland; not in 1783 list.
Shanley, Edmund	…	8-3-1780 20-1-1763	…	…	…	…	
Wilson, William	1-5-1779	1-9-1781	…	…	…	…	To half-pay, late 98th Foot, 1789.
Aldworth, P—— Rogers	12-8-1779	1-9-1781	…	…	…	…	To half-pay, 1783.
Matthews, P—— G—— Rook	8-3-1780	13-10-1781	…	…	…	…	To half-pay, 1783.
Beatty, Pakenham	8-3-1780	…	…	…	…	…	To an independent company, 1781.
Chaffer (or Chalfer), George	5-11-1782	20-8-1783	…	…	…	…	Quartermaster, 12-8-1779. Retired, 1789.
Greenless, James	12-9-1780	13-10-1781	…	…	…	…	To half-pay, 1783.
Leslie, Henry	5-2-1781	29-12-1781	…	…	…	…	To half-pay, 1783.
Dunroche, Henry	4-4-1781	5-11-1782	…	…	…	…	To half-pay, late 83rd Foot, 1784.
Wilson, John	26-5-1781	…	…	…	…	…	To half-pay, 60th Foot, 1785.
Roche, Benjamin	26-5-1781	5-11-1782	…	…	…	…	To half-pay, late 104th Foot.
Dalrymple, Knt., Sir Hew (or Hugh) Whiteford	…	…	…	…	21-9-1781	…	From 77th Foot; to 1st Foot Gds., 1783; signed convention of Cintra, 1808; General, 1-1-1812; created a baronet, 6-5-1815; died, 9-4-1830.
Cooper, Nathaniel	…	20-7-1781 28-5-1781	20-8-1783	…	…	…	From an independent company; to half-pay, 73rd Foot, 1788.
Reed, Thomas	…	19-11-1781 3-3-1776	…	…	…	…	From 24th Foot; to 103rd Foot, 1781.
Studdard, Richard	1-9-1781	31-3-1782	…	…	…	…	To half-pay, 1783.
Mahon, John	1-9-1781	3-8-1782	…	…	…	…	To half-pay, 1783.
FitzGerald, Lord Edwd.	…	…	…	…	…	…	Capt.-Lieut., 4-4-1782. From 19th Foot; to 90th Foot, 1783; Irish rebel; wounded and arrested by Major Sirr, 19-5-1798; died, 4-6-1798. (See H. C. Sirr.)
Baillie, George	…	13-4-1782 25-7-1778	…	…	…	…	From 5th Foot; to half-pay, 1783.
Mansell, William	25-2-1782	14-9-1782	…	…	…	…	To half-pay, 1783.
Thomas, Francis	29-6-1782	10-11-1784	…	…	…	…	Retired, 1786.
Lewis, Richard	29-6-1782	27-2-1783	…	…	…	…	To half-pay, 1783.
Copley, John	29-6-1782	…	…	…	…	…	Retired, 1785.

APPENDIX I

Name				Notes
Shanley, Francis	14-9-1782			To half-pay, 61st Foot, 1785. From Quartermaster, 5-11-1782.
Seddon, Thomas				From Serjeant; to "The Invalids," 1795.
De Burgh, Hon. John Thomas			28-5-1783	From 1st Foot Guards; to half-pay, late 71st Foot, 1785; succeeded as 13th Earl of Clanricarde, 8-12-1797; general ——; colonel, 66th Foot; died, 27-7-1808.
Dillon, Luke (ii)	27-2-1783	24-9-1787		Retired, 1784.
Fuller, Richard Thos.	10-3-1783			To 41st Foot, 1796.
Potts, John	2-4-1783			Adjutant, 1783; resigned commission, 1785.
Cuming, John Gordon		21-5-1783		From half-pay, late 104th Foot; to 16th Foot, 1783.
Chambers, Samuel		26-6-1783		From 2nd Dragoons; to half-pay, 1783.
Waugh, Daniel (or David)	7-4-1784 29-1-1783	21-2-1787		Capt.-Lieut. and Capt., 11-3-1795. From half-pay, late 83rd Foot; killed at St. Lucia, 22-4-1795.
Thompson, William	14-7-1784			Retired, 1785.
Bulwer, William Earle (or Erle)		6-10-1784		From 40th Foot; to 65th Foot, 1787; O.C. 106th Foot, 1794; died, July, 1807.
Gordon, Francis	6-10-1784			To half-pay, 16th Foot, 1785.
Montgomery, John	10-11-1784			Not in 1785 list.
Jones, Francis Hall	9-2-1785	6-2-1788		Retired, 1789.
Forsyth, Robert	21-2-1785			To 78th Foot, 1785.
Ferguson, David			15-6-1785 31-12-1781	From half-pay, late 71st Foot; died, 1788.
O'Meara, Daniel		11-5-1785 8-11-1781		From 98th Foot; Major in the Army, 1-3-1794; Lieut.-Col. in the Army, 3-5-1796; to 3rd West India Regt. 1797.
Taylor, Hon. Hercules Langford		17-8-1785 16-4-1785		From 2nd Horse; to 51st Foot, 1788; M.P. for Kells, 1781-1783 and 1783-1790; died, 20-5-1790.
Moneypenny, Francis	23-3-1785 25-7-1788			From half-pay, 16th Foot; died, 1791.
	16-4-1783			
Connor, Richard	6-4-1785 28-7-1789			From 78th Foot; retired, 1790.
	27-2-1784			
Abbott, Chas. Fredk.	4-5-1785 11-8-1789			Retired, 1793.

THE DURHAM LIGHT INFANTRY

Name.	Ensign.	Lieutenant.	Captain.	Major.	Lieut.-Colonel.	Colonel.	Remarks.
Archer, William	21-12-1785	...	...	...	...	...	To half-pay, Fish's late corps, 1788.
Wales, Robert	...	...	...	...	...	...	Surgeon, 15-6-1785. Died, 1792 or 1793.
Lucas, Robert	13-12-1786	28-5-1790	2-9-1795	...	...	...	To 6th West India Regt., 1804.
MacLean, Norman	...	...	13-2-1788	...	...	...	From half-pay, 73rd Foot; Major in the Army, 1-3-1794; died, 1796.
			2-8-1780				
Tufton, Hon. Charles Hamilton, Alexander Mark Ker	21-2-1787	28-10-1789	23-4-1795	12-3-1800	...	...	To 7th Foot, 1788.
	24-9-1787						To half-pay, 1802.
Meyrick, Thomas	...	...	25-9-1787	...	...	...	From half-pay, 28th Foot; to half-pay, 1787.
Sandys, James	...	25-9-1787	...	...	...	...	From half-pay, late 91st Foot; to 41st Foot, 1787.
Nesfeld, William	...	...	...	...	...	...	Chaplain, 5-10-1787. Retired, 1794.
Yate, William Baker	26-10-1787	...	...	...	...	...	From half-pay, late Waller's Corps; to half-pay, 1787; died, 8-9-1810.
Ironside, William	20-2-1788	16-6-1791	3-9-1795	...	...	...	Retired, 1801.
Gavin, William	...	...	30-3-1788	...	...	...	Retired, 1789.
			30-4-1787				
Rowley, George	...	27-8-1788	...	...	...	...	From half-pay, late 79th Foot; to an independent company, 1791.
		25-10-1783					
Stewart, John	...	30-3-1789	...	...	...	...	From half-pay, late 98th Foot; to 101st Foot, 1794.
		24-12-1785					
McArthur, John	30-4-1788	...	...	...	...	...	From half-pay, late Fish's Corps; to New South Wales Corps, 1789.
	20-10-1782						
Hinuber (or Hinaber), Adolphus Lewis	22-8-1788	13-9-1791	4-9-1795	13-7-1809	...	...	D.A.G., Minorca, 1800; D.A.G., West Indies, 1805; Lieut.-Col. in the Army, 6-2-1805; retired, 1812.
				23-6-1800			
Maxwell, John Shaw	24-10-1788	...	...	...	...	...	To 7th Foot, 1791.
Stewart, Isaac	28-7-1789	21-9-1791	...	...	...	...	Adjutant, 1791; died, 1795.
Donald, Robert	21-8-1789	...	...	...	...	...	To an independent company, 1791.
Ker, Walter	14-10-1789	...	...	...	...	...	To 34th Foot, 1791.
Willock, James	28-10-1789	...	...	...	...	...	To an independent company, 1791.
Nesbitt, George	28-5-1790	...	...	...	...	...	To an independent company, 1793.
Snell, William	16-2-1791	27-7-1793	...	...	...	...	To 115th Foot (Prince William's Regt.), 1794.
Raleigh, Francis	...	22-9-1791	...	...	...	...	From 2nd Foot; to 4th West India Regt., 1795.
Scott, John (i)	1-7-1791	10-10-1794	...	...	...	...	To 78th Foot, 1794.
White, Henry	10-8-1791	8-10-1794	...	...	...	...	To 32nd Foot, 1795.

APPENDIX I

Name			Notes
Malet, Francis Hodder	5-10-1791	9-10-1794	Wounded at St. Lucia, 22-4-1795; died, 1795.
Tharp, Thos. Partridge	19-10-1791	8-3-1793	To 82nd Foot, 1794.
Mettam, Thomas	7-12-1791		To 21st Foot, 1794.
Maxwell, William	25-1-1792		To 30th Foot, 1792.
Pigot (or Pigott), John	7-6-1792		From 30th Foot; to 85th Foot, 1794.
Blake, Robert Dudley	25-4-1792		
Erskine, William John	8-3-1793		Apparently never joined.
Gooch, William Thos.	6-8-1793		Apparently never joined.
Leigh, Henry	30-10-1793	11-3-1795	Retired, 1797.
	27-11-1793	23-4-1795	Capt.-Lieut. and Capt., 12-3-1800. Retired, 1804.
Henry, John			Surgeon, 15-2-1793. Promoted on Staff, 1796.
Mansell, John		26-3-1794	(See Appendix II.)
Dundas, Thomas		30-4-1794	(See Appendix II.)
Clarke, Alured		6-8-1794	(See Appendix II.)
Stuart (or Stewart), Hon. Charles		25-10-1794	(See Appendix II.)
Stewart, James (ii)	5-2-1794	11-5-1795	Capt.-Lieut. and Capt., 23-5-1800. Adjutant, 1795; to half-pay, 1802; again in the regiment as captain, 25-3-1803; to York Light Infantry Volunteers, 1806.
Carr, Henry William	12-3-1794	2-9-1795	Dangerously wounded at Goyave, 15-10-1795. To 83rd Foot, 1796.
Cox, William (i)	1-10-1794	3-9-1795	Capt.-Lieut. and Capt., 7-8-1800. To half-pay, 1802.
Lindores (or Lindow), John			Chaplain, 23-10-1794. The last regimental chaplain; not in 1798 list.
Trigge, Thomas		26-1-1796	(See Appendix II.)
Picton, Thomas			From half-pay, 12th Foot; Lieut.-Colonel, 22-6-1795; to 56th Foot, 1796; G.O.C. 3rd Division in Peninsula; G.C.B.; Lieutenant-General; killed at Waterloo, 18-6-1815.
Darling, Henry		25-3-1795	(See Appendix II.)
		30-5-1795	From 5th Foot; to be a permanent assistant in the Q.M.G.'s department, and a Major in the Army, 21-1-1803.

THE DURHAM LIGHT INFANTRY

Name.	Ensign.	Lieutenant.	Captain.	Major.	Lieut.-Colonel.	Colonel.	Remarks.
Humber, John	...	...	...	...	...	...	From Serjeant, 46th Foot; to 46th Foot, 1795. Qr.-Mr, 1-8-1795.
Blair, Robert Hunter	...	...	6-9-1795	...	...	...	From 117th Foot; killed in a duel in Ireland, 1799.
Boycott, Charles	...	...	Sept., 1795	...	...	...	From 117th Foot; to 34th Foot, 1795.
Roberts, Richard	...	...	18-11-1795 21-11-1793	...	...	...	From an independent company; retired, 1797.
Annesley, Arthur	...	...	9-12-1795	...	...	...	From 66th Foot; retired, 1796.
Thompson, Richard	...	...	...	25-7-1805	...	...	Capt.-Lieut. and Capt., 4-11-1795. From 37th Foot; wounded in Walcheren, 1809; retired, 1812.
Winnett, James	?	4-9-1795	...	26-8-1813 4-6-1813	...	...	Capt.-Lieut. and Capt., 3-8-1801. Date of appointment as Ensign, 68th, not traced; retired, 1829.
Reed, John (i)	...	6-9-1795	...	...	...	...	Capt.-Lieut. and Capt. 13-12-1801. From 78th Foot; Adjutant, 1798; to half-pay, 1803.
Ball (or Bell), Abraham	...	7-9-1795 28-8-1794	...	...	...	...	From Podmore's Regt.; previously half-pay, 80th Foot; retired, 1797.
Symes, Henry	...	8-9-1795 29-8-1784	...	...	...	...	From Podmore's Regt.; previously half-pay, 60th Foot; resigned, 1797.
Charlton, Richard	...	9-9-1795 30-8-1794	...	...	...	...	From Podmore's Regt.; previously half-pay, Elford's Corps; retired, 1797.
Hue, John	...	10-9-1795 1-9-1794	...	...	...	...	From Podmore's Regt.; previously in 2nd Troop of Horse Grenadier Guards (reduced, 1788); to half-pay, 93rd Foot, 1796.
Hale, G——	...	11-9-1795	...	...	...	...	From Podmore's Regt.; name does not appear in 68th in any Army List.
Pearse, W——	...	12-9-1795	...	...	...	...	From Podmore's Regt.; name does not appear in 68th in any Army List.
Summers, James	...	13-9-1795 12-3-1795	25-6-1803	...	...	...	From Podmore's Regt.; died in Walcheren, 9-9-1809.
Durand, John Hassell	...	14-9-1795 2-4-1795	...	...	...	...	From Podmore's Regt.; retired, 1796.
Delmé, William	...	10-10-1795	...	...	...	...	From 16th Foot; died, 1797.

APPENDIX I

Speed, William John	...	14-10-1795	...	From half-pay, Marines; to 1st West India Regt., 1797.
Cullen, Thomas ...	...	16-11-1781	...	From 12th Foot; died, 1796.
		18-11-1795		
Chalmley, Henry	...	3-11-1794	...	From 90th Foot; died, 1796.
		18-11-1795		
Reynolds, William Augustus	...	3-11-1794	...	From 61st Foot; retired, 1796.
		18-11-1795		
Jerson, —— ...	...	?	...	Name does not appear in 68th in any Army List; to 1st Foot, 1796. Qr.-Mr., 29-9-1795. From Qr.-Mr. died, 1796.
O'Connor (or Connor), Daniel	7-11-1795	6-1-1796	...	From 35th Foot; Quartermaster, 1797; Paymaster, 1798; died at Lisbon, 31-3-1812.
Wood, John	...	6-1-1796	...	From Volunteer, 68th; superseded, 1797.
Campbell, Peter ...	7-11-1795	20-1-1796	...	From Volunteer, 68th; to York Hussars, 1798.
Hebden, James	7-11-1795	20-1-1796	...	From 119th Foot; retired, 1797.
Montgomery, William	2-9-1795	...	...	From 119th Foot; previously half-pay, 2nd Foot; superseded, 1797.
Turner, Charles ...	3-9-1795	...	...	From Qr.-Mr., 135th Foot. To 3rd West India Regt., 1804.
	16-8-1786			
M'Carthy, Daniel	4-9-1795	17-6-1795	...	To 8th West India Regt., 1804.
M'Intyre, Duncan ...	5-9-1795	26-10-1796	...	To 55th Foot, 1797.
Humphreys, Nathaniel	6-1-1796	16-2-1797	...	To 5th Foot, 1796.
Loane, Boyle Octavius	12-1-1796	...	...	From 94th Foot; to 12th Garrison Battalion, 1804.
O'Mullen (or O'Mullane) Edward	20-1-1796	16-3-1797	...	From 117th Foot; to New South Wales Corps, 1797
Cox, William ...	20-1-1796	16-2-1797	...	Qr.-Mr., 12-8-1795. From Qr.-Mr.-Serjt.; died, 1797.
	16-9-1795			
Aird, David	8-7-1795	...	...	From 48th Foot; to 8th Foot, 1798.
Airy, George ...	...	...	1-5-1796	From 14th Foot; to half-pay, 129th Foot, 1801.
Armstrong, Richard	...	...	27-2-1796	From 31st Foot; died, 17-11-1801.
Edwards, Thomas	...	...	26-10-1796	Ensign, 68th; date not traced; to 87th Foot, 1798.
Isles, Ellis ...	?	26-4-1796	...	From 55th Foot; to 9th Veteran Battalion, 1810.
Devon, George ...	...	27-4-1796	13-5-1804	From 74th Foot; to 22nd Foot, 1796.
Maxwell, Alexander	...	3-5-1796	...	

THE DURHAM LIGHT INFANTRY

Name.	Ensign.	Lieutenant.	Captain.	Major.	Lieut.-Colonel.	Colonel.	Remarks.
Ahmuty, Thomas	...	4-5-1796	...	...	...	...	From 26th Foot; retired, 1796.
A——S—— Greenwood, ——	...	24-6-1796	...	...	...	...	From 4th West India Regt.; died, 1796.
Bell, Andrew Thomas	...	26-8-1796 31-7-1789	...	...	...	...	From half-pay, 93rd Foot; to 27th Foot, 1800.
Wardlow, John	...	5-10-1796	...	...	...	...	From 20th Foot; to 20th Foot, 1796.
Thomas, John	...	26-10-1796	...	...	...	...	From 20th Foot; retired, 1800.
Craskell, Thomas	...	2-11-1796 17-6-1780	...	...	...	...	From half-pay, Dunlop's Jamaica Corps; to 9th West India Regt. 1799.
McVicar, Douglas (or Dougald)	...	9-11-1796	...	...	...	...	From 85th Foot; to half-pay of an independent company, 1800.
Hollis, Joseph	17-6-1796	1-6-1797	...	...	...	...	From Volunteer, 9th Foot; retired, 1802.
Cornwall, John (or George)	26-10-1796	9-2-1797	...	...	...	...	Died, 28-7-1801.
Whitfield, Henry W——	21-12-1796	...	...	...	...	...	From S. Hants Militia; to 9th Foot, 1799.
McKnight, David	...	...	...	...	...	...	Surgeon, 18-7-1796; died, 1797.
Anstruther, Robert	...	...	...	...	31-8-1797	...	From 66th Foot; to 3rd Foot Gds., 1799; Brig.-Gen. in the Peninsula, 1808; died, 15-6-1808 (the day before the battle of Corunna from fatigue, and was buried close to Sir John Moore's place of burial.
Fitzgerald, Richard	...	...	4-1-1797	...	...	...	From 34th Foot; to half-pay of an independent company, 1799.
Cassidy, James	...	11-1-1797 1-12-1796	...	...	...	...	From 1st West India Regt.; to 1st West India Regt. 1804.
Bree, Robert Francis	23-2-1797	1-4-1797	...	...	...	...	Resigned, 1798.
Whitney, Boleyn Morris	...	1-5-1797	...	...	...	...	From 87th Foot; died, 1-8-1801.
Foley, P—— B——	...	1-9-1797	2-6-1801	...	...	...	From 65th Foot; to 4th West India Regt.
Beckwith, William	28-9-1797 6-4-1791	...	...	...	...	...	From New South Wales Corps; not in 1800 list.
Mathison, James Stewart	2-2-1797	...	...	...	...	...	To 92nd Foot, 1799.
Hewitson, Charles	9-2-1797 15-12-1794	5-3-1800	...	...	...	...	From late 121st Foot; died, 1801.
Stewart, Ralph	16-2-1797	6-3-1800	...	...	...	...	Died, 12-7-1801.

APPENDIX I

Name			Notes
Stewart, James (iii)	17-2-1797	7-3-1800	Died in St. Lucia, 12-8-1803 "of the bite of a serpent."
Ward, James	30-3-1797	...	To 67th Foot, 1797.
Dickson, Robert	1-6-1797	...	To 46th Foot, 1797.
Palmer, William (i)	1-7-1797	13-10-1798	From Kilkenny Militia; to 37th Foot, 1802.
Vaughan, George	1-10-1797	...	Retired, 1798.
Hutcheon, David	...	...	Surgeon, 23-2-1797. Surgeon to the Forces, 1803.
Murton, George	...	...	Asst.-Surgeon, 20-1-1797; Surgeon, 22-3-1800; died, 14-8-1801.
Hall, Townshend Monckton	...	1-9-1798	From 28th Foot; retired, 1800.
Thompson, William (iii)	...	...	From 87th Foot; retired, 1799.
Hickey, John	1-3-1798	...	Resigned, 1799.
Wade, E—— R——	1-4-1798	...	Resigned, 1799.
McDonnell, Joseph (or Alexander G. McDonell)	1-5-1798	15-3-1800	Died, 20-10-1801.
Ashworth, Charles	13-10-1798	12-1-1799	To 55th Foot, 1801. Colonel, 26-1-1797. From 3rd Foot Guards; to 60th Foot, 1800.
Cunynghame, David	...	...	From half-pay of an independent company; to 1st Foot Guards, 1800.
Marly, Thomas	...	9-2-1799 16-5-1793	16-8-1799 To 38th Foot, 1802.
Crookshank, Chichester	12-1-1799	26-3-1799	To 67th Foot, 1803.
Rochfort, Gustavus	15-4-1799	2-11-1799	25-11-1802 Maj., 4-6-1814; wounded at Vittoria, 21-6-1813; drowned, 22-4-1822, at the wreck of the "Albion" off the old Head of Kinsale.
Gough, William	29-6-1799	16-11-1799	13-5-1804 Adjutant, 1805; wounded at Vittoria, 21-6-1813; to 54th Foot, 1831.
Reed, John (ii)	26-3-1799	21-3-1800	12-5-1808 2-6-1825 28-7-1830 To 58th Foot, 1802.
Ashworth, Frederick	6-7-1799	23-4-1800	Died, 29-7-1801.
Wall, James	16-11-1799	29-8-1800	From 92nd Foot; to 70th Foot, 1804.
De Courcy, Hon. Gerard	14-12-1799	28-8-1800	
Hanbury, William	...	...	Qr.-Mr., 15-4-1799. From Serjt.-Major; died, 6-9-1805.
Eustace, Charles	...	...	Col.-Commandant, 7-3-1800. (See Appendix II.)

THE DURHAM LIGHT INFANTRY

Name.	Ensign.	Lieutenant.	Captain.	Major.	Lieut.-Colonel.	Colonel.	Remarks.
Napier, John Robert	...	...	...	...	8-2-1800 10-8-1796	...	From 60th Foot; to half-pay, 95th Foot, 1801.
Mannooch, Francis	...	...	...	27-2-1800	2-3-1800	...	From 1st Foot; retired, 1802.
Johnson, Robert (or William Johnston)	...	...	...	...	13-7-1809	6-4-1814	Colonel in the Army, 4-6-1814. (See Appendix II.)
Scott, George	...	...	...	1-3-1800	25-4-1808	...	From 64th Foot; to 8th West India Regt., 1804.
Wright, William	...	...	...	2-3-1800	...	...	From 54th Foot; to half-pay, 1802.
Irvine, Charles	...	...	1-3-1800	...	...	...	From half-pay, 30th Foot; to 62nd Foot, 1800; D.A.G., Jamaica, 1801.
Carey, Henry	...	...	2-3-1800	...	...	...	From 64th Foot; to half-pay, 1802.
			21-10-1795				
Soden, Mossom	...	...	5-3-1800	...	...	...	From 13th Foot; wounded in Walcheren, 1809; Major in the Army, 4-6-1811; died at Elvas, 24-4-1812.
			28-12-1799				
Williams, William	...	...	4-3-1800	...	...	...	From 54th Foot; Appointment cancelled.
Galway, Edward	...	...	6-3-1800	...	...	...	From 64th Foot; to 64th Foot, 1800.
Blakeney, Samuel	...	...	7-3-1800	...	...	...	From 6th Foot; died, 23-8-1803.
Arnot, Hugh (or Hugo)	...	...	8-3-1800	...	...	...	From 1st Foot; to 1st Foot Guards, 1801.
Portarlington, Earl of, Robert	...	...	24-3-1800	...	...	...	From 20th Foot; to 46th Foot, 1800.
Adamson, Wm. Brown	...	...	15-6-1800	...	...	...	From 62nd Foot; to 59th Foot, 1800.
			14-2-1800				
McCormick, Thomas	...	...	...	...	...	...	Capt.-Lieut. and Capt., 16-4-1800. From 54th Foot; to 54th Foot, 1800.
Napier, Charles	...	1-3-1800	...	...	...	...	From half-pay, 4th Foot; to Manningham's Rifle Corps, 1800.
Trench, Hon. Charles	...	2-3-1800	...	...	...	...	From 4th Dragoons; to 62nd Foot, 1801.
Scott, John (ii)	...	3-3-1800	...	...	...	...	From 64th Foot; to half-pay, 1802.
Hunt, Matthew	...	4-3-1800	...	...	...	...	From 13th Foot; to Royal York Rangers, 1807.
Tracey, William	...	8-3-1800	15-8-1805	...	...	...	From 13th Foot; died, 1805.
Bell, Thomas	...	9-3-1800	...	...	...	...	From 1st Foot; not in 1801 list.
Murray, Edward	...	11-3-1800	...	...	...	...	From 13th Foot; resigned, 1800.
Achmuty, Benjamin	...	13-3-1800	14-11-1805	...	...	...	From 13th Foot; to 70th Foot, 1806.

APPENDIX I

Atkinson, John		14-3-1800 23-10-1806 26-8-1805	From 16th Foot; to York Light Infantry Volunteers, 1805; again in the 68th from York Light Infantry Volunteers, 1806; died, 1808.
Spence, John Monk		16-3-1800	From 64th Foot; to 87th Foot, 1805.
Dexter, Christopher		17-3-1800	From 13th Foot; died, 26-8-1801.
Bowker, Thomas		18-3-1800	From 64th Foot; resigned, 1801.
Buist, Richard		20-3-1800	From 16th Foot; to half-pay, 46th Foot, 1802.
Weld, Richard		22-3-1800	From 54th Foot; not in 1805 list; doubtful if he ever joined 68th; probably was re-transferred to 54th Foot in 1800.
Stark, David		11-4-1800	From half-pay of an independent company; retired, 1800.
Patrickson, John Hill		3-6-1800	From half-pay, 104th Foot; died, 25-10-1801.
Campbell, Fredk. B——	18-1-1800 5-6-1800		Died, 29-7-1801.
Reid, Charles	18-1-1800 30-8-1800		From Kildare Militia; died, 7-8-1801.
Porter, James	? 23-10-1800		Ensign, 68th; date not traced; to 11th Foot, 1802.
Palmer, William (ii)	? 24-10-1800		Ensign, 68th; date not traced; to 37th Foot, 1802.
Crampton, Jeremiah	31-1-1800 25-10-1800		From Dublin City Militia; to 95th Foot, 1802.
Hempenstall, E—— L——	2-2-1800		From Wicklow Militia; died, 3-10-1800.
Ponsonby, John	3-2-1800 15-1-1801		From Dublin Militia; to half-pay, 1802.
Spence, Andrew	3-2-1800		From Dublin Militia; died, 2-4-1801.
Baylie, Henry	3-2-1800 25-6-1801		From Dublin Militia; resigned, 1801.
Baggs, Philip	4-2-1800 17-7-1801		From Meath Militia; to 37th Foot, 1802.
Shields, Thomas	4-2-1800 3-8-1801		From Meath Militia; to half-pay, 1802.
Williams, George	4-2-1800 3-8-1801		From Meath Militia; to 37th Foot, 1802.
Mockler, Henry	4-2-1800 10-8-1801		From Meath Militia; to 11th Foot, 1802.
McAlister, Donald	4-2-1800 11-8-1801		From Meath Militia; died, 11-8-1801.

THE DURHAM LIGHT INFANTRY

Name.	Ensign.	Lieutenant.	Captain.	Major.	Lieut.-Colonel.	Colonel.	Remarks.
Macawley, Arthur J——	7-2-1800	13-8-1801	...	...	...	...	From Antrim Militia; died, 1808 or 1809.
O'Hara, John	7-2-1800	7-9-1801	...	...	...	...	From Antrim Militia; died, 23-9-1801.
O'Rourke, Ambrose	7-2-1800	...	...	...	...	...	From Antrim Militia; died, 3-7-1801.
Henderson, Arthur	7-2-1800	...	...	...	...	...	From Antrim Militia; died, 23-7-1801.
Tenison (or Tennison), James	7-2-1800	...	...	...	...	...	From Antrim Militia; died, 3-9-1801.
Birchall, Robert	7-2-1800	...	...	...	...	...	From Antrim Militia; died, 27-6-1801.
Whitestone, Henry	8-2-1800	9-9-1801	...	...	...	...	From Clare Militia; to 37th Foot, 1802.
Baldwin, Edward	13-2-1800	...	...	...	...	...	Died, 30-7-1801.
Atkins, Robert	13-2-1800	...	...	...	...	...	Died, 14-7-1801.
Haggarty, James	14-2-1800	15-9-1801	...	...	...	...	Died, 23-9-1801.
Buchanan, B——	14-2-1800	...	...	...	...	...	Died, 22-7-1801.
O'Flaherty, John	16-2-1800	...	...	...	...	...	To 45th Foot, 1801.
Montgomery, John (ii)	17-2-1800	...	...	...	...	...	From Monaghan Militia; died, 22-6-1801.
Ramsay, George	20-2-1800	...	...	...	...	...	Died, 1-8-1801.
Compton, Francis	22-2-1800	...	...	...	...	...	Died, 29-8-1801.
Strangway, John	25-2-1800	...	...	...	...	...	Died, 19-9-1801.
Ormsby, Anthony	25-2-1800	...	...	...	...	...	Died, 24-7-1801.
Farrel, William	25-2-1800	25-9-1801	...	...	...	...	To 11th Foot, 1802.
Woods, George	25-2-1800	...	...	...	...	...	From Sligo Militia; to 70th Foot, 1801.
Brown, Thomas	1-3-1800	...	...	...	...	...	From South Mayo Militia; to 3rd Foot, 1801.
Blake, Henry	1-3-1800	...	...	...	...	...	From South Mayo Militia; to 3rd Foot, 1800.
Murphy, Michael	1-3-1800	3-10-1801	...	...	...	...	From Tipperary Militia; to half-pay, 1802.
Ledwith, William	3-3-1800	...	...	...	...	...	From Longford Militia; to 45th Foot, 1801.
Lynch, John	4-3-1800	...	...	...	...	...	To 11th Foot, 1801.
Gualy, Francis	15-3-1800	31-10-1801	...	...	...	...	From Dublin Militia; to 11th Foot, 1802.
Browne, Nicholas	16-3-1800	1-11-1801	...	...	...	...	From Dublin Militia; to half-pay, 1802.

APPENDIX I

Bennett, L—— H——	24-3-1800	…	…	From Armagh Militia; to "Rifle Corps," 1800.
Wolfe, Richard	30-3-1800	…	…	From Kildare Militia; died, 2-7-1801.
Dundas, John	2-4-1800	…	…	From Monaghan Militia; died, 18-7-1801.
Irvine, John	…	…	…	From Roscommon Militia; died, 24-10-1801.
Tuton, Charles	4-4-1800	9-11-1801	…	From Monaghan Militia; to 11th Foot, 1802.
Sheils (or Shiels), Wm.	17-4-1800	2-6-1801	…	From Louth Militia; died, 13-9-1801
Hobart, R—— Bayley	21-4-1800	…	…	From Carlow Militia; died, 21-10-1801.
Atkinson (or Allison), John Thomas	19-6-1800	…	…	Retired, 1800.
Drought, William	4-7-1800	…	…	From Queen's County Militia; to 4th Dragoon Guards, 1801.
Newton, W—— H——	13-11-1800	…	…	Appointment cancelled.
Crowder, James Allen	31-10-1801	20-11-1801	…	Adjt., 20-5-1800; died, 10-11-1803.
Gibson, William	…	…	…	Asst.-Surgeon, 5-4-1800; died, 1813.
Nash, James	…	…	…	Qr.-Mr., 20-5-1800. From Serjt.-Major, 63rd Foot; to half-pay, 1802.
Cole, John	…	…	…	Asst.-Surgeon, 23-5-1800; Surgeon, 25-6-1803. To the Staff, 1812.
Sharpe, John	…	…	…	Asst.-Surgeon, 16-10-1800. To 87th Foot, 1802.
Muston, John	…	…	…	Asst.-Surgeon, 30-10-1800; died, 19-9-1801.
Hicks, George	…	16-7-1800	…	From 34th Foot; to 1st Foot Gds., 1800.
Polson, William Gray	…	6-12-1800	…	From 59th Foot; retired, 1802.
Cumming, Henry	…	6-4-1797	…	From 56th Foot; to half-pay, 1802.
Dawson, Edward	22-1-1801	17-12-1800	…	To 12th Light Dragoons, 1801.
Vansittart, Geo. Henry	…	…	10-4-1801	Colonel, 26-1-1797. From half-pay, 95th Foot; to half-pay, 1802. Brigdr-General, Leeward Islands, 10-4-1801.
Cavan, Earl of, Richard	…	…	…	Colonel - Commandant, 18-6-1801. From Coldstream Guards; to half-pay, 1802.

187

THE DURHAM LIGHT INFANTRY

Name.	Ensign.	Lieutenant.	Captain.	Major.	Lieut.-Colonel.	Colonel.	Remarks.
Dale, Thurston	...	...	17-9-1801	...	...	...	From half-pay, late 129th Foot; to half-pay, 1802.
Fox, John	...	...	17-8-1799	...	...	...	From 1st Foot Guards; to half-pay, 1802.
			25-12-1801				
Bradford, Granville	...	18-4-1801	...	...	...	...	From 62nd Foot; superseded, 1802.
Duckworth, Geo. Henry	...	2-12-1799	...	...	...	...	From 39th Foot; to 11th Foot, 1801.
Sampson, John (or R. J.) S	...	25-6-1801	...	...	...	...	From 11th Foot; to half-pay, 1802.
Jones, Thomas	10-4-1801	25-8-1801	...	...	...	...	Cornet, 19-6-1798. From 12th Light Dragoons; to half-pay, 1802.
Perkins, Theophilus	4-6-1801	...	...	...	...	...	To 71st Foot, 1801.
Lennon, William	24-6-1801	25-6-1803	...	...	...	...	From 71st Foot; promotion to Lieutenant cancelled; to half-pay, 1803.
	13-11-1800						
Lear, John	...	...	...	...	...	...	Surgeon, 15-8-1801. From 8th West India Regt.; to 5th Foot, 1802.
Gledstanes, Nathaniel	3-10-1801	25-10-1803	13-7-1809	2-8-1830	...	...	Maj., 21-6-1817. Wounded, severely, at Nivelle, 10-11-1813; died at Athlone, 7-10-1830.
Wright, Edward	1-11-1801	...	...	...	...	...	Not in 1802 list.
Wren, Robert	2-11-1801	...	...	...	...	...	To 11th Foot, 1803.
Dunlop, William	3-11-1801	...	...	...	...	...	To 11th Foot, 1803.
Pepyatt, Thomas	19-11-1801	...	...	...	...	...	To half-pay, 1802; died, 5-2-1813.
Gillan, William	20-11-1801	25-4-1803	...	...	...	...	Not in 1805 list.
Dickson, Robert (ii)	27-11-1801	...	...	...	...	...	To half-pay, 8th West India Regt., 1803.
Hartle, Robert	...	...	...	...	...	...	Asst.-Surgeon, 22-11-1801. To 1st West India Regt., 1804.
Creagh, Andrew	...	13-12-1801	...	...	...	...	To 37th Foot, 1802.
Egan, Thomas	21-1-1802	21-1-1802	...	...	...	...	From 11th Foot; to 37th Foot, 1802.
Blakeney, H—— P——	18-2-1802	...	...	...	...	...	To half-pay, 1802.
Willis, H——	...	...	...	...	...	...	To half-pay, 1802.
Prendergast, James	...	17-3-1802	...	...	...	...	From 95th Foot; to half-pay, 1802.
Smyth, Robert	...	...	...	...	22-4-1802	...	From 52nd Foot; to half-pay, 1802.
Hanbury, John	...	...	3-6-1802	...	...	...	From 1st Foot Guards; to half-pay, 1802.
Hopwood, J—— D——	3-6-1802	...	...	...	...	...	To half-pay, 1802.
Darling, Wm. L——	...	23-6-1802	...	...	...	...	From 87th Foot; to half-pay, 1802.
Creighton, Charles	24-7-1802	...	...	...	...	...	To half-pay, 1802.
Cox, Sir John, Knt.	24-7-1802	...	...	...	...	...	To half-pay, 1803.

APPENDIX I

De Coulier, Joseph	...	25-12-1802	...	From half-pay, 46th Foot; not in 1805 list.
Kerr, Charles	...	15-5-1800	...	Paymaster; to half-pay, 1802.
Meyne (or Heyne), J——C——	...	...	...	Asst.-Surgeon, 25-6-1803. Not in 1808 list.
Greer, Samuel	...	25-8-1803	...	From half-pay, 8th West India Regt.; to 8th West India Regt., 1804.
Mackay, William	...	24-11-1803 25-5-1804	9-1-1812	Major, 21-1-1819. Wounded at Moresco, 20-6-1812; to half-pay, 60th Foot, 1821.
North, William	...	22-12-1803	8-11-1809 8-10-1830	Major, 22-7-1830. From 82nd Foot; wounded at Salamanca, 22-7-1812; retired, 1833.
Anton, James	...	25-11-1803	...	From 7th West India Regt.; to 70th Foot, 1806.
Reed, Thomas (ii)	...	25-11-1803 25-7-1802	...	To 70th Foot, 1804.
Melland, Wm. S——	...	21-1-1804	9-11-1809	From 14th Foot; retired, 1811.
Walker, Thomas	...	...	26-1-1804	From half-pay, 7th West India Regt.; to 8th West India Regt., 1806.
			6-12-1796	
Boyd, James	...	2-2-1804	...	From half-pay, 32nd Foot; to 9th Foot, 1804.
Leith, James U—— M——	...	3-2-1804	7-10-1812	Wounded at Ostis, 30-7-1813; killed at Oeyreguave, 23-2-1814.
Salmon, Henry	...	9-2-1804	...	Retired, 1806.
Irwin (or Irvine), Henry	...	12-9-1805	...	Wounded at Ostis, 30-7-1813; killed at Nivelle, 10-11-1813.
Bury	...	25-2-1804	4-6-1812	
Hawthorne, Robert	...	23-6-1804	...	From 60th Foot; to 4th Garrison Battalion, 1808.
			14-5-1804	
Bishop, James	...	25-5-1804	...	To 37th Foot, 1804.
Straker, James	...	26-5-1804	...	To 16th Foot, 1804.
Wahab, James	...	25-7-1804	...	From 64th Foot; to 3rd West India Regt.
Archdall (or Archdale), Henry Mervyn	...	25-9-1804 14-11-1805	26-8-1813	Wounded at Nivelle, 10-11-1813; to half-pay, 84th Foot, 1818; died, 1868.
Melville, Robert	...	25-10-1804	20-7-1805 19-8-1813	Retired, 1829.
Obins, Hamlet	...	26-10-1804	...	From 29th Foot; to 70th Foot, 1804.
		15-8-1804		
Brown, William	...	1-11-1804 28-11-1805	...	To 2nd Garrison Battalion, 1810.

THE DURHAM LIGHT INFANTRY

Name	Ensign	Lieutenant	Captain	Major	Lieut.-Colonel	Colonel	Remarks
North, James	...	30-11-1804	...	...	...	...	From 4th West India Regt.; to 46th Foot, 1806.
Hollis, John J——	...	1-12-1804	...	...	...	...	From 47th Foot; to Royal Regiment of Malta, 1809.
Frome, William	...	24-12-1804	...	...	...	...	From 1st West India Regt.; to 2nd West India Regt., 1806.
Kennedy, Simson	...	25-12-1804	8-10-1812	...	...	...	Major, 22-7-1830. From 38th Foot; to half-pay, unattached, 1832. Appointment cancelled.
Tathum, Joseph	26-12-1804	...	7-4-1825	15-10-1829	...	...	Wounded in Walcheren, 1809; to half-pay, unattached, 1833.
Menzies, James	18-4-1805	1-5-1806	...	...	...	...	From 7th Foot; to 93rd Foot, 1806.
Church, Edward	...	16-5-1805	...	...	...	...	From 82nd Foot; superseded, 1806.
Hutchinson, Felton N——	16-5-1805	...	...	...	...	...	
Coppinger, Edward	20-7-1805	...	...	...	...	...	Shown in Army List, 1806, as Ensign, 1-10-1804; superseded, 1806.
Smith, John	29-8-1805	...	...	...	...	...	To 44th Foot, 1808.
Castle, Thomas	12-9-1805	...	...	...	...	...	To 5th Garrison Battalion, 1806.
Tracie, James	28-11-1805	18-9-1808	...	...	...	...	Died in England, 24-12-1812.
De Lisle, George	5-12-1805	...	...	...	...	...	From 87th Foot; to Royal African Corps, 1806.
Hinds, John	23-9-1805	7-11-1809	...	...	...	...	Quartermaster, 21-9-1805. From Serjeant-Major; Adjutant, 1807; wounded at Vittoria, 21-6-1813; died, while adjutant, 25-3-1823.
	3-12-1807						Resigned, 1805.
Gledstanes, Albert	25-12-1805	...	5-7-1806	17-9-1812	2-6-1825	...	Lieut.-Col., 21-6-1813. From 70th Foot; wounded at Moresco, 20-6-1812; medal and two clasps (F.O.'s); C.B.; retired, 1830.
Hawkins, John P——	...	...	24-8-1804	...	...	...	
McDonald, George	...	6-2-1806	6-1-1814	...	...	...	From 93rd Foot; wounded and taken prisoner at Moresco, 20-6-1812; to 17th Foot, 1833.
Abbott, William	...	3-3-1806	31-3-1814	...	...	...	From 15th Foot; to half-pay, 39th Foot, 1818.
Ashley, William	...	21-8-1806	...	...	...	...	From 2nd West India Regt.; to 96th Foot, 1809.
Morris, Apollos	6-2-1806	...	...	...	...	...	To 66th Foot, 1808.
Anderson, Henry	1-5-1806	19-9-1808	21-6-1810	...	...	...	Killed at Vittoria, 21-6-1813.
Champain, William	3-7-1806	...	...	...	...	...	The first cadet to join 68th from the Military College; to 29th Foot, 1808.

APPENDIX I

Name				Notes
Garrett, George				Asst.-Surgeon, 4-9-1806. To 10th Veteran Battalion, 1807.
Twaddell, Robert	25-12-1806			From 8th West India Regt.; to 1st Foot, 1808.
Sorlie, Sholto	20-5-1802	25-12-1806 25-4-1806		From 46th Foot; wounded at Vittoria, 21-6-1813; to 2nd Veteran Battalion, 1814.
Burrell, James	13-11-1806	20-9-1808		To 25th Foot, 1810.
Archbold, George	20-11-1806	21-9-1808		From Royal African Corps; to half-pay, 43rd Foot, 1820.
Smyth, William	15-1-1807	22-9-1808	8-4-1825	Wounded in Walcheren, 1809; retired, 1830.
Nixon, James	25-8-1807	16-2-1809		From Durham Militia; died of the Walcheren disease, 30-8-1809.
Tyrrey, Michael Gould	25-10-1807	13-7-1809		From City of Cork Militia; to 8th Garrison Battalion, 1809
McGregor, Charles				Assist.-Surgeon, 23-7-1807. Died, 1809.
Crespigny, George Champion		17-11-1808 14-5-1807	8-10-1812	From 1st Foot; wounded in Walcheren, 1809; to 89th Foot, 1812; from 89th Foot, 1812; killed at Ostis, 30-7-1813.
Domville, Compton		1-12-1808 26-6-1806		From 1st Garrison Battalion; retired, 1810.
Jenkins, John	26-10-1807			From North Cork Militia; died of the Walcheren disease, 1809.
Jackson, Thomas (or Robert)	31-3-1808	8-11-1809	2-6-1825	From Limerick Militia; retired, 1831.
Todd, Adam	19-5-1808			From Dumfries Militia; died of the Walcheren disease, 1809.
Stapylton (or Stapleton), Henry	28-7-1808	9-11-1809		From Durham Militia; died, 26-2-1814, from wounds received at Oeyreguave, 23-2-1814.
Thompson, James	17-8-1808	19-4-1810		From Dumfries Militia; wounded in Walcheren, 1809; to 10th Royal Veteran Battalion, 1821.
Finucane, Frederick	22-9-1808	25-12-1811		Killed at Salamanca, 22-7-1812.
Wilson, John				Quartermaster, 3-12-1807. From Serjeant; died at Santo Martinho, 23-3-1813.
Rudsdell, George				Asst.-Surgeon, 10-12-1807. To 79th Foot, 1813.

THE DURHAM LIGHT INFANTRY

Name.	Ensign.	Lieutenant.	Captain.	Major.	Lieut.-Colonel.	Colonel.	Remarks.
Sherbrooke, John Cope	...	...	...	...	...	27-5-1809	(See Appendix II.)
Mends, Hugh Bowen	...	30-3-1809 27-11-1806	...	...	...	...	From 8th Garrison Battalion; wounded in Walcheren, 1809; to 22nd Foot, 1814.
Mackay, Honeyman	...	18-5-1809 30-6-1808	...	...	...	...	From 96th Foot; wounded at Vittoria, 21-6-1813; to 5th West India Regt., 1816.
Sloan, James	...	7-9-1809 29-1-1807	...	...	...	...	From 8th Garrison Battalion; to half-pay, 1820; died, 1840.
Grant, Patrick	...	16-11-1809	...	...	...	...	From 78th Foot; to half-pay, 52nd Foot, 1817.
Reed, William	16-2-1809	...	...	...	...	...	Died of the Walcheren disease, 1809.
Clarke, Robert	12-4-1809	26-12-1811	...	...	...	...	From Argyll Militia; wounded at Nivelle, 10-11-1813; to half-pay, 1819.
Stopford, Roger	13-4-1809	21-6-1810	...	...	...	...	From Durham Militia; killed at Nivelle, 10-11-1813.
Woodhams, J——	26-4-1809	...	...	...	...	...	From West Kent Militia; resigned, 1809.
Loftus, William	27-4-1809	...	...	...	...	...	From Durham Militia; resigned, 1811.
Caldow, John	2-11-1809	...	...	...	...	...	From Donegal Militia; to 5th Garrison Battalion, 1810.
							Retired on half-pay, 1829.
Carson, James	6-11-1809	4-6-1812	...	...	...	...	From Volunteer, 26th Foot; to 5th West India Regt., 1815.
Dawes, David	7-11-1809	7-10-1812	...	...	...	...	To 50th Foot, 1811.
Clarke, George	8-11-1809	...	...	...	...	...	To 96th Foot, 1812.
Nunn, Hay Macdowell	9-11-1809	...	...	...	...	...	Asst.-Surgn. 25-9-1806—30-11-1809.
Greenwell, W—— K——	...	...	...	...	...	...	From 71st Foot; resigned, 1812.
Miller, James	...	...	18-1-1810	...	...	...	Major, 25-7-1810; from 9th Veteran Battalion; died, 13-8-1812, from wounds received at Salamanca, 22-7-1812.
Bolton, William	19-4-1810	8-2-1810	...	...	...	...	From 25th Foot; died, 21-2-1820.
Gibson, William (ii)	...	8-10-1812	3-8-1830	...	...	...	From City of Cork Militia; retired, 1833.
Parvin, John Henry	4-10-1810	...	...	...	...	...	From City of Cork Militia; killed at Vittoria, 21-6-1813.

APPENDIX I

Name			
Mitchell, James	31-1-1811 16-8-1810	29-7-1813	From 50th Foot; died, 1830; was only a Lieutenant at the time of his death. Retired, 1812.
Fry, William	21-2-1811		Wounded at Nivelle, 10-11-1813; died, 1-5-1828.
Mendham, William	28-3-1811	30-1-1812	From Notts Militia; died at Niza, 6-8-1811.
Forbes, Henry	16-5-1811		From Durham Militia; wounded at Vittoria, 21-6-1813, and at Lazaca, 31-8-1813; to half-pay, 1818; restored to establishment, 1819; to half-pay, 4th Dragoon Guards, 1823.
Skene, David J——	3-10-1811	30-7-1813	
Spencer, Lord Charles	26-12-1811	27-8-1812	To 95th Foot, 1812.
Le Mesurier, Peter	...	22-3-1810	From 89th Foot; to half-pay, 103rd Foot, 1819.
Wood, Charles	...	17-9-1812	From 52nd Foot; D.A.A.G. in Peninsula; to 18th Light Dragoons, 1813.
Fowke, John	20-3-1812	19-8-1813	Wounded at Vittoria, 21-6-1813; to half-pay, 1819.
Kortwright, William	26-3-1812	...	To Coldstream Guards, 1812.
Ball, Robert	14-5-1812	26-8-1813	Wounded at Vittoria, 21-6-1813; to 71st Foot, 1815.
Pennefather, Kingsmill	4-6-1812	5-1-1814	Died, 1814.
Stretton, Severus William Lynan	11-6-1812	6-1-1814	From Nottingham Militia; wounded at Vittoria, 21-6-1813; to half-pay, 1819; restored to establishment, 1820; to half-pay, 64th Foot, 1825.
Connell, John	7-10-1812	3-3-1814	From Volunteer, 28th Foot; wounded at Ostis, 30-7-1813; to 67th Foot, 1814.
Perry, ——	8-10-1812	...	From Volunteer, 9th Foot; to 3rd Garrison Battalion, 1813.
Frazer, Archibald	...	...	Asst.-Surgeon, 25-6-1812; died, 1817.
Reid, James	...	...	Surgeon, 5-11-1812. From 51st Foot; died, 11-6-1832.
Warde, Henry	1-1-1813		(See Appendix II.)

THE DURHAM LIGHT INFANTRY

Name.	Ensign.	Lieutenant.	Captain.	Major.	Lieut.-Colonel.	Colonel.	Remarks.
Sheddon, Thomas	18-2-1813	30-1-1814	…	…	…	…	From Ayr Militia; wounded at Orthes, 27-2-1814; to half-pay, 1819.
Gibson, Joseph	28-7-1813	31-1-1814	…	…	…	…	From Volunteer, 51st Foot; wounded at Vera, 31-8-1813, and at Nivelle, 10-11-1813; died, 1816.
Hodges, C—— Bishop	29-7-1813	…	…	…	…	…	Appointment cancelled.
Church, ——	30-7-1813	…	…	…	…	…	From Volunteer, 95th Foot; to 95th Foot, 1813.
Berkeley, C—— B——	19-8-1813	14-4-1814	…	…	…	…	To half-pay, 92nd Foot, 1817.
Browning, Thomas	26-8-1813	17-10-1816	…	…	…	…	From Volunteer; wounded at Lazaca, 31-7-1813, and at Nivelle, 10-11-1813; to half-pay, 1819.
Wilson, John (ii)	27-8-1813	…	…	…	…	…	Resigned, 1814.
White, John Lewis	…	…	…	…	…	…	Paymaster, 25-2-1813. To half-pay, 81st Foot, 1818.
Ross, Nicholas	…	…	…	…	…	…	Quartermaster, 13-5-1813. From Quartermaster-Serjeant; to half-pay, 62nd Foot, 1818.
Barr, M——	…	…	…	…	…	…	Asst.-Surgeon, 9-9-1813. Died, 1813 or 1814.
Kearns, J——	5-1-1814	26-2-1818	…	…	…	…	From Serjeant-Major; wounded at Vittoria, 21-6-1813; to half-pay, 1819.
Macdonald, Donald	6-1-1814	7-4-1825	19-12-1826	…	…	…	To half-pay, 1831.
Blood, John (i)	3-3-1814	8-4-1825	6-8-1829	3-5-1833	…	…	From Volunteer, 59th Foot; to 7th Foot, 26-3-1825; to 68th Foot, 8-4-1825; to half-pay, Waggon Train, 1838.
Carson, George	30-3-1814	9-4-1825	…	…	…	…	From Volunteer; died, 11-5-1826.
Dillon, Edward	31-3-1814	…	…	…	…	…	Died, 1818.
Harvey, John	14-4-1814	…	…	…	…	…	To 37th Foot, 1825.
Black, Thomas	1-9-1814	…	…	…	…	…	From Sicilian Regiment; to half-pay, 19th Foot, 1823.
Saunders, Robt. Francis	24-2-1814	22-12-1814	…	…	…	…	From 67th Foot; to half-pay, 1819.
Williams, Richard	…	…	…	…	…	…	Asst.-Surgeon, 24-2-1814; Surgeon, 29-6-1832. To half-pay, 1838.
Ainslie, ——	Date not traced.	6-4-1815	…	…	…	…	Not in 1815 list.
Bristow, William	…	4-8-1813	…	…	…	…	From 71st Foot; to half-pay, 1819.
Moore, Henry	6-7-1815	…	…	…	…	…	Not in 1816 list.

APPENDIX I

Name	Date 1	Date 2	Notes
Lewis, Arthur G—	...	3-8-1815	From 5th West India Regt.; to half-pay, 1819.
Burgoyne, John Montagu (later Sir J. M. Burgoyne, Bart.)	17-10-1816	30-3-1814	To half-pay, 71st Foot, and, later, to Grenadier Guards, 1818; died, 17-3-1858.
Sutherland, Robert	...	17-4-1817	From half-pay, 92nd Foot; to half-pay, 1819.
Scott, George Erving	...	21-3-1811	From 52nd Foot; was at Waterloo, 18-6-1815; to half-pay, 1819.
Clifford, Henry	...	10-7-1817	Asst.-Surgeon, 3-10-1816—2-10-1817. From half-pay, 83rd Foot; to half-pay, 1819.
	...	10-2-1814	
Crotty, Francis C—	...	26-2-1818	From half-pay, 39th Foot; to 39th Foot, 1819.
		5-5-1814	
Craig, William Alexander	...	23-4-1818	From half-pay, 84th Foot; to 50th Foot, 1818.
Rowley, Robert Charles	15-1-1818	...	To 7th Foot, 1819.
Nason, George	22-1-1818	...	To half-pay, 1822.
	9-10-1815		
Douglas, Sholto	...	25-2-1818	From half-pay, 50th Foot; to half-pay, 1819.
Mair, Arthur	5-3-1818	...	To 47th Foot, 1823.
Read, Henry	...	...	Paymaster, 8-10-1818; Lieutenant in Army, 20-2-1811. From half-pay, 81st Foot; deserted, 1836.
Macbeath, George (i)	...	...	Qr.-Mr., 2-11-1809—19-2-1818. From Qr.-Mr., half-pay, 62nd Foot; had been previously a Lieutenant in 89th and in 1st Foot; died, 14-7-1835.
Kysh, Fredk. Wm.	...	18-2-1819	From half-pay, 3rd West India Regt.; to 5th Foot, 1819.
Pinckney, George	...	12-8-1819	From 5th Foot; to half-pay, York Chasseurs, 1820.
Eliot, George Augustus	...	16-12-1819	Brevet-Major, 19-12-1813. From half-pay, 103rd Foot; to Major, unattached, 1826.
Power, Manley	24-6-1819	...	To 32nd Foot, 1819.
Bennett, Henry Wm.	30-12-1819	...	From 32nd Foot; was at Waterloo, 18-6-1815; to half-pay, 16th Foot, 1824.
	14-1-1813		

THE DURHAM LIGHT INFANTRY

Name.	Ensign.	Lieutenant.	Captain.	Major.	Lieut.-Colonel.	Colonel.	Remarks.
Parker, Jonathan	...	...	4-5-1820	...	...	...	From half-pay, York Chasseurs; retired, 1829.
Hill, Edward Rowley	...	22-6-1820	31-3-1814	...	...	...	From half-pay, 43rd Foot; to half-pay, 1822.
		24-2-1814					
Maitland, Peregrine	15-6-1820	2-6-1825	...	...	...	...	To Captain of an unattached company, 1826.
Clarke, James	11-1-1821	...	...	...	...	...	To half-pay, 1822.
Hewett, John	...	...	12-4-1821	...	...	...	From half-pay, 60th Foot; to half-pay, 1821.
Duff, James	15-5-1823	20-7-1825	...	...	...	...	From Serjeant-Major; Adjutant, 1823; died, 1840.
Cogan, John Douglas	22-5-1823	...	...	...	...	...	From half-pay, 19th Foot; killed by lightning at Quebec, 9-6-1824.
	24-10-1821						
Smyth, Harry	10-7-1823	13-8-1825	15-10-1829	21-4-1843	...	...	Bt.-Lieut.-Col. Mortally wounded at Inkerman, 5-11-1854; died at Scutari.
Hunter, John	...	11-12-1823	...	...	...	...	From half-pay, 4th Dragoon Gds.; to Captain of an unattached company, 1826.
Smith, William	29-7-1824	28-1-1826	...	...	...	...	To Captain of an unattached company, 1827.
Bernard, Peter	8-8-1824	11-2-1826	5-11-1829	...	...	...	From half-pay, 16th Foot; to half-pay, unattached, 1831.
	29-1-1824						
Huey, Richardson Wm.	26-3-1825	19-12-1826	11-6-1830	13-10-1838	31-12-1847	...	The first compiler of 68th Standing Orders; to 1st Foot, 1852.
Forster (or Foster), William	7-4-1825	...	...	...	...	...	From half-pay, 48th Foot; to 23rd Foot, 1826.
	19-5-1814						
Fuller, William	7-4-1825	...	...	...	...	...	From half-pay, 67th Foot; to half-pay, unattached, 1826.
	22-2-1816						
Macpherson, Evan	8-4-1825	20-3-1827	21-4-1843	...	...	...	Adjutant, 1831; to half-pay, 14th Light Dragoons, 1846.
Johnstone, George	9-4-1825	...	...	...	...	...	To Lieutenant, unattached, 1826.
Durnford, Philip	10-4-1825	1-5-1828	9-8-1831	...	...	...	Retired, 1834.
Maclean, Archibald	2-6-1825	...	...	...	...	...	Retired, 1830.
Madeley, Houghton	13-8-1825	6-8-1829	...	...	...	...	Retired, 1830.
Walwyn, Richard	28-1-1826	...	...	...	...	...	To Lieutenant, unattached, 1826.
Bayly, Lancelot	11-2-1826	15-10-1829	28-6-1833	...	...	...	Retired, 1838.
Crawford, James	...	...	...	...	...	...	Asst.-Surgeon, 30-6-1825. To 24th Foot, 1829; died, 28-12-1855.
McNabb (or McNab), Allan	...	11-5-1826	...	...	...	...	From 74th Foot; to half-pay, Royal African Corps, 1828.

APPENDIX I

Name					
Ferguson, Henry Robt.	…	…	…	29-1-1826	From half-pay, 20th Light Dragoons; to Major, unattached, 1826.
North, Joseph	…	10-10-1826	11-6-1830	…	From Cape Corps (Infantry); to 80th Foot, 1836.
		15-9-1825			
Woolhouse, Andrew Mackason		2-11-1826	…	…	From half-pay, unattached; to half-pay, unattached, 1828.
		13-8-1825			
Boyle, Hon. Robert		14-11-1826	…	…	To 30th Foot, 1829.
Strachan, James McGill	19-12-1826	5-11-1829	13-12-1833	…	Retired, 1836.
Flint, Anstruther Chas.	28-12-1826	15-6-1830	8-4-1834	…	Retired, 1837.
Witham, George	20-3-1827	26-10-1830	11-7-1834	…	Retired, 1842.
Ring, Richd. Fitzgerald	…	25-11-1828	…	…	From Royal African Colonial Corps; died, 13-5-1831.
		9-6-1825			
Bouchette, John Francis	1-5-1828	26-11-1830	…	…	Retired, 1833.
Gillman, Wm. Henry	17-7-1828	14-5-1831	13-5-1836	…	Bt.-Major, 9-11-1846. From half-pay, unattached; retired, 1854, with rank of Colonel.
	1-7-1828				
Phipps, Richd. Leckonby	…	1-10-1829	3-5-1833	31-12-1847	Bt.-Major, 9-11-1846. From Royal Staff Corps; to half-pay, 1849.
Graham, Wm. Frederick Vernon	16-7-1829	31-12-1828	20-5-1836	…	Retired, 1838.
		9-8-1831			
Douglas, Archibald	…	6-8-1829	3-5-1833	…	Retired, 1833.
Macbeath, George (ii)	15-10-1829	31-5-1833	28-6-1836	9-3-1855	Bt.-Major, 9-11-1846; Bt.-Lt.-Col., 20-6-1854. To provisional battalion, 1857. C.B.; son of G. Macbeath (i.).
Reynardson, Edwd. Birch	5-11-1829	…	…	…	To 1st Foot Guards, 1830; commanded Grenadier Guards at Inkerman; died, 10-5-1896.
Vivian, Robert	…	…	30-11-1830	…	From half-pay, unattached; retired, 1836.
			13-5-1826		
Parkinson, Jas. Benners	11-6-1830	28-6-1833	15-9-1837	…	To half-pay, 1845.
Harris, William C———	12-6-1830	8-11-1833	19-1-1838	…	Retired, 1838.
Roe, Wm. Harriott	15-6-1830	…	…	…	Retired, 1833.
Hamilton, George	16-6-1830	…	…	…	To 55th Foot, 1836.
Surtees, Arthur	…	26-10-1830	…	…	To 14th Light Dragoons, 1832; died, 17-4-1833.
Denys, George Wm.	26-11-1830	13-12-1833	…	…	To half-pay, 15th Foot, 1837.
Barrow, Thomas	…	…	…	1-2-1831	From half-pay, Coldstream Guards; retired, 7-2-1831.
Keane, John	…	…	…	13-4-1831	(See Appendix II.)

THE DURHAM LIGHT INFANTRY

Name.	Ensign.	Lieutenant.	Captain.	Major.	Lieut.-Colonel.	Colonel.	Remarks.
Cross, John	...	...	...	...	8-2-1831	...	From 52nd Foot; was at Corunna, 16-1-1809; Busaco, 29-9-1810; Ciudad Rodrigo, 19-1-1812; Vittoria, 21-6-1813; Nivelle, 10-11-1813, etc.; also at Waterloo, 18-6-1815; wounded at Redinha, 12-3-1811, and at Waterloo; Lieutenant-Governor and Officer Commanding Forces in Jamaica, 1838; K.H.; retired, 1843; died, 27-9-1850.
Craufurd, Robt. Gregan	...	...	17-5-1831	...	...	...	From half-pay, unattached; retired, 1834.
Kinlock, John	...	...	5-4-1831 16-8-1831 9-8-1831	...	...	...	From 2nd Life Guards; retired, 1833; died, 1894, aged 87.
Mackenzie, Alex. Douglas (later, Alex. Douglas Douglas)	7-6-1831 8-6-1830	8-4-1834	...	...	...	...	From 58th Foot; retired, 1835.
Hill, Alfred Edward	9-8-1831	11-7-1834	18-5-1838 14-12-1832	...	...	...	Retired, 1842.
Mackinnon, Donald Hy. Aylmer	...	...	4-12-1832	...	...	...	From half-pay, unattached; retired, 1845.
Barlow, Robt. Hilaro	17-8-1832	26-6-1835	5-10-1838	...	...	...	Retired, 1845.
Fitzgerald, John	...	...	...	...	...	...	Asst.-Surgeon, 30-7-1832. Resigned, 1833.
Paulet, Lord William	...	...	...	18-1-1833 1-9-1830	21-4-1843	9-4-1864	Bt.-Col., 20-6-1854. (See Appendix II.)
Graham, Herbert (or R——)	...	...	4-5-1833 21-9-1832	...	...	...	From 17th Foot; retired, 1836.
Pringle, Norman	...	...	...	30-4-1833	...	...	From half-pay, 31st Foot; retired, 1833.
Mainwaring, Arthur	3-5-1833	13-5-1836	13-10-1838	...	...	...	Adjutant, 1835; to 66th Foot, 1841.
Napier, John Moore	31-5-1833	20-5-1836	...	...	...	...	To 62nd Foot, 1842.
Smyth, Henry	28-6-1833	28-10-1836	2-12-1842	12-5-1848	30-12-1853	...	Bt.-Col., 28-11-1854; C.O. in Crimea; C.B.; to 76th Foot, 1859; General, 29-9-1878; Colonel, 2nd Queen's, 25-3-1877.
Blount, Herbert	8-11-1833	15-9-1837	23-7-1844	24-11-1854	17-11-1857	...	Bt.-Lieut.-Col., 2-11-1855. Retired, 1859. Died, 10-5-1860.
Cross, William	29-11-1833	19-1-1838	4-7-1845	...	...	...	Adjutant, 1840; retired, 1847; subsequently Lieut.-Col., Armagh Militia; died, 1-8-1882.

APPENDIX I

Name				
Proctor, Henry A.—	13-12-1833			Not in 1839 list.
K—				
Burton, Edwd. William				Asst.-Surgeon, 21-6-1832—12-4-1833. To Hospital Staff, 1834.
Beale, Thomas Salwey	8-4-1834			Retired, 1837.
Johnston, John	11-7-1834	18-5-1838	16-12-1845	Adjutant, 1838; retired, 1846.
Carnegie, Charles Hay				Asst.-Surgeon, 14-3-1834—6-6-1834. From Hospital Staff; to 5th Dragoon Guards, 1836.
Leslie, Alexander				Asst.-Surgeon, 18-7-1834. To 17th Light Dragoons, 1841.
Hill, Percy	26-6-1835	5-10-1838		To Royal Canadian Rifle Regt., 1846.
Hilliard, Henry	24-4-1835			Lieutenant, 16-11-1809; Paymaster, 22-3-1821—5-2-1836. From 28th Foot; was at Waterloo, 18-6-1815; to half-pay, 1838.
Baxter, James				Quartermaster, 15-7-1835. From Serjeant-Major; to Royal Canadian Rifle Regt., 1845.
Taylor, Mascie Domville		5-8-1836		From 80th Foot; retired, 1841.
		18-12-1835		
Wynne, Heneage Griffith	13-5-1836	13-10-1838	30-1-1846 30-12-1853	
	10-7-1835			From 97th Foot; killed at Inkerman, 5-11-1854.
Cary-Elwes, Lincoln	20-5-1836	12-6-1840		Retired, 1844; died, 21-10-1869.
Horner, William W.	22-7-1836	10-9-1841		Retired, 1844.
Powell, Cornelius	28-10-1836			To 1st Dragoon Guards, 1839.
Irving, Charles				Asst.-Surgeon, 12-6-1835—1-4-1836. From 7th Foot; died, 1845.
Ouvry, Henry Aimé		3-11-1837	2-5-1845	From 12th Foot; to 3rd Light Dragoons, 1848.
		4-9-1835		
Madocks, John Edward	30-6-1837	·4-3-1842		Retired, 1838.
Grant, Peter Charles Stuart	15-9-1837			Retired, 1846.
Browne, William Barrington	19-1-1838			Retired, 1839.
Rhodes, William	18-5-1838	2-12-1842		Retired, 1847; M.P., Lower Canada; Minister of Agriculture for the Province of Quebec; died at Quebec, February, 1892.
Browne, Salwey	25-5-1838	21-4-1843	22-12-1846	Retired, 1849.
Tipping, Alfred	22-6-1838	30-5-1843	7-5-1847	To 1st Foot Guards, 1850.

Name.	Ensign.	Lieutenant.	Captain.	Major.	Lieut.-Colonel.	Colonel.	Remarks.
Beale, Walter Yonge	5-10-1838	...	...	...	...	...	To 10th Foot, 1842.
Jephson, Robert George	19-10-1838	...	...	...	...	...	To 10th Foot, 1842.
Carter, John Collis	...	...	...	...	...	...	Surgeon, 19-10-1838. To Medical Department, 1840.
Bridgman, Chas. Orlando	8-3-1839	...	...	...	...	...	Retired, 1842.
Elmslie, Graham	28-8-1839	...	...	...	...	...	To 49th Foot, 1842.
Bulkeley, Lempster	...	...	...	...	...	...	Captain, 9-1-1835; Paymaster, 10-5-1839. Not in list for April, 1840.
Carmichael, Wm. Hugh Hedges	12-6-1840	23-7-1844	14-5-1847	...	...	...	Adjutant, 1845; died, 1848.
Atkinson, Thomas	...	...	...	...	...	...	Surgeon, 6-11-1840. To Medical Department, 1844.
Kennedy, Arthur Edwd.	...	...	19-3-1841 12-6-1840	...	...	...	From half-pay; retired, 1847; Governor, in succession, of several colonies; knighted, 1868; died at sea, off Aden, 13-6-1883
Jenkinson, Geo. Samuel	...	3-8-1841 12-7-1839	...	...	...	...	From 11th Light Dragoons; to 8th Light Dragoons, 1843; succeeded his uncle in 1855 as 11th Baronet; M.P., N. Wilts., 1868-80; died, 1892.
Greer, Henry Harpur	10-9-1841	20-8-1844	31-12-1847	29-12-1854	18-2-1859	...	C.O. in New Zealand; C.B.; Lieut.-General, 1-7-1881. Died, 26-3-1886.
Campbell, Morris Robinson	...	...	...	...	...	...	Lieutenant, 19-12-1835; Paymaster, 20-8-1841. From 96th Foot; to half-pay, 1849.
Lucas, David	...	...	...	...	...	...	Asst.-Surgn., 20-12-1839—27-8-1841. From Medical Department; to 61st Foot, 1844.
Dalgety, James W.	...	...	15-4-1842 2-12-1837	...	...	...	From half-pay; to Royal Military College, 1844.
Noel, Hon. Henry Lewis	4-3-1842	2-5-1845	...	...	...	...	Retired, 1847; subsequently Officer Commanding Rutland Militia; died, 1898.
Cotton, Henry Calvely	29-4-1842 16-4-1842	4-7-1845	...	...	...	...	From 10th Foot; to Royal Canadian Rifle Regt., 1846.
Stewart, Houston	6-5-1842	16-12-1845	...	...	...	...	To 32nd Foot, 1846.
Stuart, Henry Boulton	20-5-1842	...	...	...	...	...	To 15th Foot, 1844.
Poulett, Hon. Vere (later, Viscount Hinton)	24-6-1842	...	...	...	...	...	Retired, 1845; subsequently Colonel, 1st Somersetshire Militia; died, 29-8-1857.

APPENDIX I

Name				Remarks
Storer, Thos. Whitmore	2-12-1842	23-1-1846	6-6-1854	Adjutant, 1847; invalided from the Crimea, and died 1856.
Verner, Richard	21-4-1843	...	...	Retired, 1844.
Stuart, Francis Coutts	30-5-1843	30-1-1846	31-3-1848	To 42nd Foot and half-pay, 1851; died, 1-8-1889.
Paul Amedée Gibbs, Edward	...	...	...	(See Appendix II.)
Nicol, Charles	...	21-4-1846	14-4-1848	21-2-1844 (See Appendix II.)
Hawker, Samuel Wm. Henry	19-1-1844	21-4-1846	14-4-1848	7-12-1844 To 6th Foot, 1850.
Leveson-Gower, John Edward	23-7-1844	31-7-1846	12-5-1848	To 50th Foot, 1848; died, 21-1-1892.
Dering, Edward Heneage	20-8-1844	...	...	From 15th Foot; to Coldstream Guards, 1846; died, Nov., 1892.
Morant, Horatio	20-8-1844	3-11-1846	21-10-1853 17-11-1857 2-12-1862	Bt.-Major, 26-12-1856. Wounded before Sevastopol, 21-10-1854; to half-pay, 1866; A.D.C. to the Queen. O.C. 3rd Brigade Depôt, Sunderland, 1873; O.C. 18th Brigade Depôt, Chester, 1876; Lieut.-General, 1885.
Hunter, Thomas	...	...	...	Surgeon, 23-7-1844—6-12-1844. To 4th Light Dragoons, 1850.
Finch, Hon. Daniel Greville	2-5-1845	22-12-1846	30-12-1853	To half-pay, 1857; afterwards Lieut.-Col., 24th Foot; died, 23-2-1882.
Kortright, Augustus	4-7-1845	...	...	Retired, 1846.
Carmichael, Henry Gossett Richard	16-12-1845	7-5-1847	...	Retired, 1852.
Alington, George Hugh	30-12-1845	14-5-1847	...	Died, 1853.
Doherty, Daniel	...	...	...	Quartermaster, 23-7-1841—11-4-1845. From Royal Canadian Rifle Regt.; to 44th Foot, 1847.
Woollcombe, William	...	...	...	Asst.-Surgeon, 28-3-1844. To half-pay, 1850.
Johnston, R—— Gudgeon	...	...	1846	From Royal Canadian Rifle Regt.; retired, 1846.
Trevillian, Maurice C——	...	...	1846	From half-pay, 14th Light Dragoons; retired, 1846.
Duberly, Henry	...	31-3-1846 15-4-1842	...	From 32nd Foot; to Paymaster, 8th Hussars, 1847.
Lyon, Edmund David	23-1-1846 14-11-1845	8-8-1847	...	From 8th Foot; retired, 1854.

THE DURHAM LIGHT INFANTRY

Name.	Ensign.	Lieutenant.	Captain.	Major.	Lieut.-Colonel.	Colonel.	Remarks.
Savage, Edmund Stuckeley	30-1-1846	31-12-1847	10-3-1854	18-2-1859	...	...	Bt.-Major, 6-6-1856. To 86th Foot, 1861.
Digby, John Bickerton	28-4-1846	...	...	...	...	...	Retired, 1847.
Stevenson, Wm. George	31-7-1846	31-3-1848	...	...	...	...	To Scots Fusilier Guards, 1849.
Croft, Stephen	28-8-1846	14-4-1848	25-8-1854	...	...	...	Retired, 1855.
Shuttleworth, Charles Ughtred	18-9-1846	12-5-1848	24-11-1854	2-12-1862	...	...	Bt.-Lieut.-Col., 21-3-1865. To half-pay, 1870.
Westropp, Ralph	3-11-1846	...	...	...	...	...	Retired, 1852.
Garforth, Wm. Francis Willoughby	22-12-1846	26-12-1851	...	...	...	...	To 7th Light Dragoons, 1852.
Jones, Harry Valette	30-3-1847	12-11-1847	6-11-1854	...	...	...	Retired, 1847.
Cassidy, John	...	14-4-1846	...	...	...	...	From 9th Foot; retired, 1863.
Seymour, Wm. Henry	7-5-1847	10-6-1852	29-12-1854	...	...	...	To 2nd Dragoon Guards, 1855; General; K.C.B. C.O. 2nd Dragoon Guards in Indian Mutiny; Inspector-General of Cavalry in Ireland, 1874-9; Colonel, 3rd Dragoon Guards, 1883; Colonel, 13th Hussars, 1891; Colonel, 2nd Dragoon Guards, 1894.
Nicol, Charles Samuel	14-5-1847	12-11-1852	...	...	...	...	Adjutant, 1849; retired, 1854.
Massey, Hon. Eyre Challoner Henry	8-10-1847	...	...	...	...	11-11-1895	To 7th Foot, 1851; Colonel of the Durham L.I., 1895. (See Appendix II.)
Falconar, James	4-11-1847	...	...	...	...	...	From Col.-Serjt., 92nd Foot; to 74th Foot, 5-11-1847.
Kirk, Chas. Edmonstone	5-11-1847	...	...	...	31-12-1847	...	To 7th Foot, 1852.
Burdett, Sir Robt., Bart.	...	...	...	...	...	...	Bt.-Col. From half-pay, unattached; retired on the same day that he was appointed to the regiment.
Phipps, Thos. Henry Leckonby Hele	31-12-1847	...	...	...	...	...	To 82nd Foot, 1851.
Russborough, Viscount; Joseph Henry	31-3-1848	...	...	...	...	...	A.D.C. to H.E. the Lord-Lieutenant of Ireland; retired, 1851; succeeded as 5th Earl of Milltown, 1866; died, 8-4-1871.
Lewis, John Edward	...	...	12-5-1848 13-7-1847	...	...	...	Bt.-Lieut.-Col., 26-12-1856. From Captain, unattached; to half-pay, 1857.
Needham, Henry	...	...	18-8-1848 30-12-1843	...	...	...	From 50th Foot; retired, 1854.

APPENDIX I

Name				
Hamilton, Thomas de Courcy	... ...	9-6-1848 10-4-1847	1-12-1854	...	From 90th Foot; Adjutant, 1850; V.C.; to half-pay, 1857; subsequently Lieut.-Col., 64th Foot; Major-General.
Trent, Harrison Walke John	14-4-1848	1-7-1853	29-12-1854	10-11-1869	7-10-1874	Bt.-Major, 21-3-1865; Bt.-Lieut.-Col., 31-8-1874; Col., 31-8-1879. Wounded at Te Ranga, 21-6-1864. Commandant, School of Musketry, and Inspector-General of Musketry, 1880-85; died, 1-8-1899.
Tryon, Thomas	12-5-1848	...	...	...	To 7th Foot, 1850.
Tunks, Thomas		...	...	...	Quartermaster, 14-4-1848. From Serjeant-Major; to half-pay, 1860.
Mercer, Douglas (later, Douglas Mercer-Henderson)	...	...	...	31-1-1850	(See Appendix II.)
Udny, John Augustus	...	...	18-8-1849	...	Major, 23-11-1841; Bt.-Lieut.-Col., 11-11-1851. From Grenadier Guards; to half-pay, 1854.
Somerville, Thos. Henry	...	...	8-2-1850 2-11-1849	12-12-1854	From 6th Foot; to half-pay, 1855.
Paterson, Augustus	...	...	24-9-1850 15-2-1850	...	From 42nd Foot; to 41st Foot, 1854.
White, Henry	12-4-1850	21-10-1853	29-12-1854	...	To 13th Light Dragoons, 1859.
Garforth, Frank	16-8-1850	30-12-1853	...	...	To 7th Light Dragoons, 1854.
Fitzroy, Cavendish Chas.	14-2-1851 22-11-1850	20-1-1854	29-12-1854	...	From 82nd Foot; A.D.C. to Earl of Carlisle when Lord-Lieutenant of Ireland; 5th Class Medjidie; to half-pay, 1869; promoted Brevet-Major (with date 28-10-1869) in 1874; died, 8-1-1894.
Hadley, William	...	...	...	...	Lieutenant, _____; Paymaster, 13-7-1849; invalided from the Crimea, and died, 1856.
Graves, John Stuart ...	...	...	...	...	Surgeon, 2-11-1841—20-4-1849. To Medical Staff, 1855.
Shiel, Thomas Wildrige	...	...	...	...	Assistant-Surgeon, 13-12-1850. To Medical Staff, 1856.
O'Leary, John Francis	...	...	...	...	Asst.-Surgeon, 21-2-1851. Killed before Sevastopol, 17-10-1854.
Barker, Fredk. Grote	12-12-1851	10-3-1854	...	...	Killed at Inkerman, 5-11-1854.
Vaughan, Herbert ...	26-12-1851	17-3-1854	20-2-1855	...	Adjutant, 1855; to half-pay, 1856; died at Worcester, 30-3-1914.
Edwards, Richd. Lloyd	23-1-1852	6-6-1854	13-4-1855	...	Killed in the Crimea, 11-5-1855.

203

THE DURHAM LIGHT INFANTRY

Name.	Ensign.	Lieutenant.	Captain.	Major.	Lieut.-Colonel.	Colonel.	Remarks.
Fuller, Chas. Travers	24-1-1852	...	...	...	14-9-1852	...	Retired, 1853.
Lennox, Lord Arthur	...	...	...	...	22-11-1842	...	From half-pay, 6th Foot; retired, 1853; M.P. for Chichester, 1831-46, and for Yarmouth, 1847; died, 15-1-1864.
Cator, John	30-7-1852	6-6-1854	23-11-1855	...	...	...	Wounded at Inkerman, 5-11-1854; to 10th Foot, 1856.
Smyth, Harry Edmond	23-11-1852	11-8-1854	...	...	...	...	Died of fever at Balaklava, 14-3-1855.
Battiscombe, Henry Lumsden	8-7-1853	11-8-1854	14-1-1856	...	...	...	Wounded before Sevastopol, January, 1855. To 6th Foot, 1856.
Wilkinson, Christopher Brice	11-10-1853	11-8-1854	26-2-1856	...	...	...	To Military Train, 1857; from Military Train, 27-11-1857.
Light, Hugo Shelley	21-10-1853	25-8-1854	17-11-1857	12-10-1870	...	...	Retired, 1871.
Henniker, Sir Brydges Powell, Bart.	30-12-1853	...	...	...	...	...	To Royal Horse Guards, 1854; subsequently in West Essex Yeomanry Cavalry; died, 12-7-1906.
Tucker, Aubrey Harvey	20-1-1854	6-11-1854	26-10-1862	13-11-1875	29-10-1879	...	2nd-Lieutenant, 13-9-1853; Colonel, 29-10-1883. From Ceylon Rifle Regiment; Legion of Honour; C.B.; O.C. 41st Regtl. District, 1885; died, 20-4-1907.
Morgan, Jonathan	10-3-1854	...	...	...	...	...	To 4th Foot, 1855.
Marshall, James	17-3-1854	6-11-1854	...	...	...	...	Killed in the Crimea, 8-6-1855.
Ramsey, Alexander	...	...	1853	...	...	...	From 42nd Foot; retired, 1853; name never in 68th in Army List.
Macdonald, Alexander	...	...	1854	...	...	...	From half-pay, 62nd Foot; retired, 1854; does not appear to have ever joined.
Herries, Wm. Lewis	...	...	7-7-1854	...	...	17-4-1854	(See Appendix II.)
Fitzgerald, Wm. Henry	...	...	9-12-1851	...	...	...	Bt.-Major, 9-10-1863; from half-pay, Canadian Rifle Regt.; retired, 1866.
Spratt, James	...	...	26-1-1855	7-10-1874	...	...	Bt.-Major, 10-1-1870. From 35th Foot; retired, 1876.
			12-1-1855				
Vicars, Edward Richd. Fox	5-5-1854	24-11-1854	17-5-1858	...	...	...	Died at Rangoon, 25-10-1862.
Deshon, Edward	6-6-1854	1-12-1854	...	...	...	...	Retired, 1861.
Grace, Sheffield	?	8-12-1854	15-6-1858	28-10-1871	...	...	From 11th Foot; half-pay, 1871; Lieut.-Colonel, h.-p., 1-10-1877.

APPENDIX I

Name				
Saunderson, Francis de Luttrell	28-7-1854	8-12-1854	11-2-1859	To 61st Foot, 1861.
Sparke, John Francis	23-8-1854	8-12-1854	22-2-1859	To 84th Foot, 1859.
Ethelston, Edmund Peel	24-8-1854	9-2-1855	...	To half-pay, 1862.
Seymour, John Hobart Culme	25-8-1854	9-2-1855	2-12-1862	To 82nd Foot, 1867; adjutant, Hon. Corps Gentlemen-at-Arms; died, 10-11-1887.
Blood, John	8-9-1854	9-2-1855	6-2-1863 31-10-1871	Retired, 1875.
Cox, John Ponsonby	...	2-3-1855	...	From Cape Mounted Rifles; to Captain, half-pay, 1868.
Clarkson, John (or Thomas) Reeder	14-12-1854	9-3-1855	27-7-1866	To 7th Foot, 1866.
Nicholletts, Gilbert Alfred	15-12-1854	9-3-1855	...	To 2nd Foot, 1869.
Thornton, Geo. Henry (Stanilaus Thornton in 1856-57 list)	5-1-1855	9-3-1855	...	Retired, 1861.
Thompson, Joseph	5-11-1854	15-3-1855*	...	*Cancelled, 26-6-1855. Died, January, 1855.
Villiers-Stuart, Henry John Richard	16-1-1855	15-3-1855	14-3-1868	To half-pay, 1870; Lieut.-Col., Waterford Artillery Militia, 1872. Died at Castlane, near Carrick-on-Suir, 10-5-1914.
Watson, Francis Gordon Digge	26-1-1855	12-5-1855	...	Retired, 1856; Lieut.-Col., Isle of Wight Artillery Militia, 1885.
Duesbery, Wm. Henry Thornton	22-2-1855	8-6-1855	...	Retired, 1865.
Brocas, Reginald	9-2-1855	9-10-1855	...	To 75th Foot, 1858.
Milligan, Harry Robt.	16-2-1855	23-11-1855	...	To 60th Foot, 1858.
Pownall, Chas. Ernest Beatty	24-4-1855	8-1-1856	25-4-1868	Retired, 1869.
Turnor, George	23-2-1855	14-1-1856	...	To 2nd Foot, 1857.
Cave-Brown-Cave, Bowyer Wenman	16-3-1855	...	...	Appointment cancelled, 18-5-1855.
Wilkinson, George Faulkner	28-3-1855	26-2-1856	...	To Military Train, 1860.
Gooch, George Cecil	29-3-1855	...	...	To 93rd Foot, 1855.
Annesley, Jas. O'Donel	30-3-1855	17-11-1857	...	To 25th Foot, 1860; died, 24-7-1884.
Johnston, Alexander	...	...	...	Asst.-Surgeon, 1-9-1854—22-9-1854. Invalided from the Crimea, and died at Portsmouth, 25-6-1856.
Thomson, Alexander Dingwall	11-5-1855	26-2-1856	...	To 16th Foot, 1857.

205

Name.	Ensign.	Lieutenant.	Captain.	Major.	Lieut.-Colonel.	Colonel.	Remarks.
Noble, Samuel Black	18-5-1855	23-3-1858	...	...	...	...	To 32nd Foot, 1858.
Kay, Wm. Algernon	5-6-1855	7-5-1858	10-11-1869	29-10-1879	...	...	Retired with rank of Lieut.-Colonel, 1880; now Sir W. A. Kay, 5th Bart, succeeded, 1907.
Covey, Charles	8-6-1855	22-6-1858	1-4-1870	26-5-1880	...	...	Adjutant, 1856; accidentally killed when pig-sticking near Allahabad, 22-3-1884.
Marshall, Arthur Francis	6-7-1855	22-6-1858	13-1-1869	...	...	...	From 9th Foot; died at Ahmedabad, 11-6-1875, when D.A.Q.M.G., Bombay Army.
Mackenzie, Henry Patrick Johnston	15-5-1855						
	6-7-1855	...	...	...	...	...	To 2nd Dragoon Guards, 1857.
Hardy, Robert Cope	20-7-1855	...	...	...	...	...	To Military Train, 1857.
Tew, Blackburne Cyril	27-7-1855	11-2-1859	...	...	...	...	Half-pay, Captain, 1868.
Harrison, Edward	23-11-1855	...	...	...	...	...	Lieutenant, 76th Foot, 1859.
Turnor, Wm. Weston	1-2-1856	26-10-1862	...	...	...	...	Half-pay, Captain, 1870.
Cavendish, Hy. George	26-2-1856	23-8-1859	...	...	...	...	Retired, 1862; died, 9-11-1865.
Bolden, Leonard	27-2-1856	23-4-1861	1-12-1869	...	...	...	Killed by a tiger near Mandalghur, E. Indies, 22-4-1877.
Briggs, John Pitts	28-2-1856	22-10-1861	...	...	...	...	Retired, 1861.
O'Leary, Thos. Connor	...	...	...	...	...	...	Surgeon, 9-2-1855—27-7-1855. From 59th Foot; to 45th Foot, 1859.
Kellett, Edwd. Young	...	...	...	...	...	...	Asst.-Surgeon, 28-4-1854—29-6-1855. From Staff; to Staff, 1857.
Corbett, Augustus Patrick Meyer	...	...	...	...	...	...	Asst.-Surgeon, 3-11-1854—29-6-1855. From Staff; to Staff, 1860.
Wolseley, Wm. Chas.	...	10-3-1857	...	...	...	...	From 16th Foot; to 6th Foot, 1857; died, 28-11-1878.
		29-4-1856					
Hughes, William	...	...	...	...	...	...	Lieutenant, 2-6-1849; Paymaster, 1-4-1856. To 82nd Foot, 1857.
Bernard, Luke Fitzgerald	...	...	...	...	...	...	Lieutenant, 3-5-1844. Paymaster, 29-5-1857. From 82nd Foot; to Royal Canadian Rifle Regt., 1857.
Mansel, Robt. Christopher	...	...	...	...	...	4-6-1857	(See Appendix II.)
Craig, Robert Guthrie	23-10-1857	...	...	...	...	...	Cornet, 21-2-1856. From Military Train; retired, 1867; Paymaster, 84th Foot, 1867.
Cathcart, Reginald Archibald Edwd.	17-11-1857	...	...	...	...	...	To Coldstream Guards, 1859; subsequently Sir R. A. E. Cathcart, sixth baronet.
Dewé, Henry	23-3-1858	...	...	...	...	...	Appointment cancelled, 1858.

APPENDIX I

Name				Remarks
Fereday, Fredk. Francis	…	…	…	Paymaster, 9-11-1855 — 29-12-1857. From Military Train; to 83rd Foot, 1867.
Williams, Clement	…	…	…	Asst.-Surgeon, 5-1-1855—14-8-1857. From Staff; to Staff, 1865.
Applin, Augustus Oliver	…	…	…	Asst.-Surgeon, 3-10-1857—6-11-1857. From Staff; to Staff, 1865.
Robley, Horatio Gordon	14-5-1858	26-11-1861	…	Half-pay, Captain, 1870; Lt.-Col., Argyll & Sutherland Highrs., 1883; Hon. Major-General.
Clayton, Richard	21-5-1858	5-9-1862	12-10-1870	Retired, 1871.
Hood, Charles Clifton	13-7-1858	2-12-1862	5-10-1872	Adjutant, 1870; retired, 1873.
Caldecott, Geo. Fowler	25-2-1859	6-2-1863	…	To 13th Foot, 1867.
Best, Thomas	…	…	…	Surgeon, 13-4-1852—23-8-1859; Surgeon-Major, 22-4-1862. From 46th Foot; to Staff, 1868.
Lloyd, Robert Clifford	…	…	8-7-1859	Colonel, 9-9-1859. From 76th Foot; retired, 1862.
Clement, Reynold Alleyne	13-5-1859 7-12-1858	…	…	From 13th Light Dragoons; retired, 1868; one of His Majesty's gentlemen-at-arms; secretary, Ascot Racecourse Committee; died, 2-10-1905
Oakley, George John Arata	23-9-1859	…	…	From 84th Foot; retired, 1866.
Howard, Alfred Gordon	21-10-1859	14-6-1864	…	To 86th Foot, 1867.
Palmer, Wm. Henry France	30-12-1859	26-5-1865	…	To 14th Hussars, 1868.
Burke, Bernard H——	31-7-1860	…	…	From Military Train; half-pay, Captain, 1870.
Codrington, Oliver	26-2-1858	…	…	Asst.-Surgn. 13-6-1859—26-10-1860. To Staff, 1864; re-appointed to 68th, 1865; re-appointed to Staff, 1872.
Sladden, Henry	…	…	…	Quartermaster, 4-5-1860. To 3rd Brigade Depôt, 1873; died, 1-1-1907.
Kirby, Joshua Henry	…	23-4-1861 1-6-1860	10-11-1869	Colonel, 10-11-1874. From 86th Foot; died at Belgaum, 30-6-1877 (Brigdr.-General, Bombay Army).
Casement, Thomas	17-9-1861 10-5-1861	…	…	From 61st Foot; to 64th Foot, 1867.

THE DURHAM LIGHT INFANTRY

Name.	Ensign.	Lieutenant.	Captain.	Major.	Lieut.-Colonel.	Colonel.	Remarks.
Johnson, Benjamin	...	18-2-1862 1-10-1858	...	...	...	...	Retired, 1864.
Clifford, Walter John Oliver	30-4-1861	...	...	...	...	...	Retired, 1867.
Greene, Wm. Sheppey	29-10-1861	14-3-1868	...	...	...	...	To 19th Hussars, 1869.
Busfield, Walter	26-11-1861	...	...	...	...	...	Retired, 1868.
Ilderton, Chas. Edward	5-9-1862	20-5-1868	31-10-1871	...	...	...	To 2nd Foot, 1872.
Pace, Fredk. William	2-12-1862 19-8-1862	...	...	...	...	...	From 72nd Foot; to Lieut., 31st Foot, 1868.
Woodward, Wm. Fredk.	6-2-1863	10-11-1869	7-10-1874	1-7-1881	...	...	Retired, 1888.
Molyneux, Herbert Chesshyre	14-6-1864	1-12-1869	31-3-1875	29-10-1884	...	...	Half-pay, 1875; Captain and Hon. Major, 1st Durham Militia (3rd D.L.I.), 1875-1885; died at Leamington, 24-10-1913.
Tyndall, Saml. Wm.	26-5-1865	28-5-1870	12-6-1875	1-7-1881	...	...	Half-pay, Lieut.-Colonel, 1887; died, 15-7-1888.
Shaw, George Kennedy	...	...	22-1-1867 12-3-1861	31-5-1876	1-7-1881	...	From 64th Foot; formerly in 60th Foot; died, 27-7-1884 at Kasauli (while Commandant of Convalescent Depôt there).
Rogers, Arthur Parry	...	30-3-1867 27-11-1866	2-8-1871	...	...	...	From 13th Foot; retired, 1872.
Woodland, Arthur Law	1-2-1867	12-10-1870	29-6-1875	23-3-1884	31-10-1896	...	Colonel, 31-10-1900; Adjt., 1872; O.C. 1st D.L.I. in S. Africa, 1899-1900; C.B.; O.C. 5/68th Regtl. District., 1901; to Border Record Office, 1905.
Mackenzie, Lawrence	...	...	...	...	...	...	Paymaster, 1-10-1864 — 1-1-1867. From 85th Foot; resigned, 1872.
Rhodes, Henry Brooke	...	25-12-1867 1-5-1866	28-10-1871	...	...	...	From 86th Foot; retired, 1871.
St. Aubyn, Wm. John	...	15-2-1868 9-1-1863	12-2-1873	...	...	...	From 14th Hussars; to 24th Foot, 1873.
Marx, George Francis	8-1-1868	2-8-1871	16-2-1876	...	...	...	Retired, 1877.
Williams, Thomas Anthony Hwfa	14-3-1868	28-10-1871*	...	...	...	...	*Antedated, 27-10-1871. To 15th Foot, 1872; secretary, Sandown Park Club.
Mason, Edwd. Snow	...	...	17-4-1867 26-2-1867	...	...	...	From 82nd Foot; retired, 1868.
Stanley, Albert Hamilton	25-4-1868	31-10-1871*	23-4-1877	...	...	...	*Antedated 27-10-1871. Retired, 1882; died, 3-1-1900.
Parke, Chas. Ethelston	20-5-1868	31-10-1871*	...	...	...	...	*Antedated, 27-10-1871. To Rifle Brigade, 1872.

APPENDIX I

Name			Notes
McGill, Edward	… …	…	Surgeon, 9-11-1867 — 16-9-1868. From Staff. Died at Armagh, 14-9-1869.
Spencer-Churchill, Chas. Henry	…	13-1-1869	Bt.-Lieut.-Col. From half-pay, 60th Foot; retired on the same day that he was appointed to the regiment.
Boulderson, Joseph	17-11-1869	31-10-1871	From 19th Hussars; retired, 1876.
Meadows, Robt. Wyatt	1-4-1869		Surgeon, 25-8-1865 — 20-10-1869. From Staff; appears last in Army List, July, 1876.
Tollemache, Hamilton James	1-12-1869	31-10-1871*	*Antedated, 27-10-1871. Retired, 1875. Subsequently Hon. H. J. Tollemache; Barrister-at-Law. Died, 16-6-1893.
Chisholm-Batten, James Forbes	24-11-1869	…	To 34th Foot, 1869; Paymaster, 1st D.L.I., January, 1886—October, 1888.
Spencer, Augustus Campbell	27-4-1870 8-2-1870	1-11-1871*	*Antedated, 28-10-1871. From 6th Foot; to 5th Lancers, 1873.
Clarke, James George	…	12-10-1870	From half-pay, 46th Foot; retired, 1870.
Tickell, Eustace Ashburner	12-10-1870	1-11-1871* 18-6-1877	*Antedated, 28-10-1871. Died at Sunderland, 2-7-1877.
Gordon, William	22-4-1871	9-2-1876 15-11-1883 31-10-1892	From 21st Foot; half-pay, 1896; Colonel; O.C. 1st Regtl. District, 1898; died at Threave, Castle Douglas, 11-4-1913.
Harris, James Archer	…	14-10-1871	From half-pay, late Military Train; retired, 1871.
Semple, Charles	…	14-10-1871	From half-pay, late 4th West India Regt.; to 93rd Foot, 1871.
Burton, William Conyngham Vandeleur	28-10-1871 5-6-1866	1-11-1871*	*Antedated, 28-10-1871. From 9th Foot; retired, 1877.
Ord, Harry St. George	…	31-10-1871 9-10-1869	From 93rd Foot; to 64th Foot, 1873.
Palliser, William	…	31-10-1871	From half-pay, late 18th Hussars; retired, 1871.

THE DURHAM LIGHT INFANTRY

Name.	Sub-Lieut.	Lieutenant.	Captain.	Major.	Lieut.-Colonel.	Colonel.	Remarks.
Mansel, Wm. Grenville	30-12-1871	30-12-1871	...	...	...	...	To Bengal Staff Corps, 1878.
Stewart, Norman Robt.	30-12-1871	30-12-1871	28-10-1879	...	...	...	To Bengal Staff Corps, 1879; Major-General, Indian Army; C.B.; now Sir N. R. Stewart, 2nd Baronet, succeeded, 1900.
Hilliard, John Chinnery	30-12-1871	30-12-1871	30-10-1879	28-7-1884	...	...	Half-pay, Lieut.-Colonel, 1891.
Burnett, Wm. Francis	...	...	...	...	...	...	Asst.-Surgeon, 31-3-1866—17-1-1872. From Staff; appears last in Army List, March, 1873.
Heatly, Charles Fade	...	...	...	...	...	...	Lieutenant, 7-7-1837; Hon. Major, 1-1-1860; Paymaster, 3-2-1872. From 18th Foot; retired, 1879.
Barnard, Lindsay Hy.	...	14-2-1872 13-7-1870	...	...	...	...	From Rifle Brigade; retired, 1873.
Fulton, Carré	...	14-8-1872 28-10-1871	15-8-1877	15-11-1883	...	...	From 15th Foot; retired, 1887; Hon. Lieut.-Colonel.
Crawford, Robt. Alexr.	...	...	19-10-1872 10-5-1871	1-7-1881	28-7-1884	...	Colonel, 28-7-1888. From 2nd Foot; half-pay, 1888; O.C. 100th Regtl. District, 1891; died at Buxton, 17-2-1903.
Thomas, Robt. Edwd. Neilson	2-11-1872	...	...	...	...	...	To 9th Foot, 1875.
Molloy, Oscar Frederick	...	...	...	...	...	...	Asst.-Surgeon, 1-4-1871 — 1-1-1873. From Staff; appears last in Army List, March, 1873.
Gunning, Robt. Henry	26-3-1873	...	...	...	...	...	To 60th Foot, 1874; O.C. 3rd Bn. King's Royal Rifle Corps; killed in action at Glencoe, Natal, 1899.
Lee, George Arthur	...	...	30-4-1873 25-3-1871	1-7-1881	27-8-1884	...	Colonel, 27-8-1888. From 24th Foot; half-pay, 1890; O.C. 16th Regtl. District, 1892; died at Folkestone, 11-9-1903.
Wiehe, Francis George Archibald	...	25-6-1873 28-10-1871	7-1-1880	29-10-1884	...	...	From 64th Foot; half-pay Lieut.-Colonel, 1894; Bt.-Colonel, 1898; Chief Instructor, School of Musketry, Hythe, 1894.
Meade, John de Courcy Dashwood	9-8-1873	...	...	...	...	...	To 89th Foot, 1873.
Briscoe, Benjamin	24-9-1873 9-3-1872	9-3-1872	...	...	...	...	From 37th Foot; to Bengal Staff Corps, 1878.

APPENDIX I

Name				Notes
Darwin, Chas. Waring	4-10-1873 9-8-1873	9-8-1874	22-7-1880	29-10-1884	From 87th Foot; Adjutant, 1875; half-pay, Lieut.-Colonel, 1894; Lieut.-Colonel and Hon. Colonel, 3rd (late 4th) D.L.I., 1905—1912. Chairman, Territorial Force Association of Co. Durham; C.B. Quartermaster, 6-12-1873; Hon. Captain, 6-12-1873. To 3rd D.L.I., 1882; retired, 1886; Hon. Major; died, 15-6-1913, at Hove.
Shea, William	...	...	...	...	From 49th Foot; to Bengal Staff Corps, 1878.
Yate, William Gordon	24-12-1873 12-11-1873	12-11-1873	...	...	To Lieut.-Colonel, Royal Irish Fusiliers, Sept., 1908; Director of Recruiting and Organization, Army Headquarters, 1911; Brigadier-General
Carleton, Frank Robt. Crofton	21-9-1874	21-9-1874	8-6-1881	28-7-1891	Half-pay, 1903; Bt.-Colonel; one of His Majesty's Gentlemen-at-arms. Bt.-Lieut.-Col. 8-7-1899; Colonel, 10-2-1904. O.C. 1st D.L.I. in S. Africa, 1900-1902; wounded at Vaal Krantz, 5-2-1900; appointed A.A.G., Bombay, 1904; C.B.
Paget, Alwyn de Blaquire Valentine	11-2-1875	11-2-1875	24-8-1881	21-10-1891	26-4-1899
FitzGerald, Herbert Swayne	11-2-1875	11-2-1875	5-7-1882	31-10-1892	31-10-1900
Way, Henry George	28-8-1875 13-6-1874	13-6-1874	...	...	From 99th Foot; to Madras Staff Corps, 1882.
Burn, Alexander Edwd. Pelham	28-8-1875 21-9-1874	21-9-1875	...	...	From 97th Foot; to Bengal Staff Corps, 1879.
Goad, Howard	10-9-1875	10-9-1875	...	...	To Bengal Staff Corps, 1881; Director-General, Army Remount Department, India, 1898-1908; C.S.I.
Seymour, Henry Wm.	10-9-1875	10-9-1875	...	...	To Bombay Staff Corps, 1880.
Drummond, Wm. Chas.	...	...	6-10-1875	...	From half-pay; late 95th Foot; half-pay, 1875.
Conran, James	...	...	23-10-1875 28-5-1870	...	From half-pay; late 5th West India Regt.; retired, 1880; Hon. Major.
Oldfield, Christopher Campbell	...	...	18-12-1875 7-8-1867	...	From half-pay; late 38th Foot; retired, 1876.
Hilliard, Arthur Courtney	...	26-2-1876 20-11-1875	15-11-1883	...	From 109th Foot; retired, 1889.
Preston, Richd. Wm.	29-8-1876 10-9-1875	...	...	...	From unattached list; to Madras Staff Corps, 1880.

THE DURHAM LIGHT INFANTRY

Name.	Sub-Lieut.	Lieutenant.	Captain.	Major.	Lieut.-Colonel.	Colonel.	Remarks.
Noel, Gerard Thomas	17-1-1877 14-6-1876	14-6-1878	28-7-1884	...	...	...	From 32nd Foot; retired, 1890; Major, 3rd (now 4th) D.L.I. in S. Africa, 1899-1900.
Beresford, John Blakeney de la Poer	17-1-1877 15-7-1876	...	...	...	...	...	From unattached list; to Madras Staff Corps, 1880.
Curling, William Kingsdown	10-2-1877 24-6-1876	24-6-1878	1-9-1884	27-8-1894	...	...	From 99th Foot; retired, 1896; Lt.-Colonel, Reserve of Officers.
Cartwright, Henry Aubrey	15-8-1877 11-10-1876	11-10-1876	23-3-1884	...	...	...	From 75th Foot; retired in 1892; served in S. African War, 1899-1902, in 7th Bn. Imperial Yeo.; Master, Wilton Foxhounds.
	2nd Lieut.						
Menzies, Wm. Maxwell	15-8-1877	7-1-1880 30-10-1879	6-9-1885	...	...	...	Promoted Lieut. in 106th Foot, and re-transferred at once to 68th Foot; died at Virginia Water, 22-2-1896.
Westropp, Wm. Keily	...	...	15-8-1877	...	...	...	From 41st Foot; half-pay Major, 1881.
Hervey-Bathurst, Claude	29-9-1877	7-1-1880	13-8-1886	...	...	...	To Essex Regt., 1886.
Murphy, Moore	31-10-1877	22-7-1880	...	...	...	...	From Serjeant-Major; appointed Quartermaster, School of Musketry, Hythe, 1882.
Ross, Walter Charteris	31-10-1877 29-9-1877	16-7-1880	5-11-1887	31-10-1896	...	...	From 2nd Foot; Adjutant, 1885; dangerously wounded at Bothaville, Orange River Colony, 5-11-1900; half-pay Lieut.-Col., 1903; C.B.
Kenyon-Slaney, Francis Gerald	1-5-1878	8-6-1881	28-11-1887	16-12-1896	...	...	Lieut., 106th, 2-2-1881; retired, 1899; Lieut.-Col., Reserve of Officers.
O'Callaghan, Herbert Pigott	15-1-1879 25-5-1878	1-7-1881	...	...	...	...	From 107th Foot; died at Fatehgarh, 10-11-1882.
Gunning, Charles Vere	9-7-1879	1-7-1881	5-7-1888	...	...	...	Adjutant, 1888; retired, 1896; Maj., Reserve of Officers, served in S. African War, 1899-1902; now Sir C. V. Gunning, 7th Baronet, succeeded 1906.
Vane, William Lyonel (later Hon. William Lyonel Vane)	11-2-1880 14-1-1880	1-7-1881	29-10-1888	14-9-1898	...	...	From 101st Foot; retired, 1902; Lieut.-Colonel and Hon. Colonel, 6th Battn. (late 2nd V.B.) Dur-

APPENDIX I

Name					Remarks
Robb, Fredk. Spencer Wilson	11-8-1880	1-7-1881	2-2-1889	26-4-1899	...ham L.I., 1903-1911. Vice-Chairman, Territorial Force Association of Co. Durham. Bt.-Major, 13-7-1898; Bt.-Lt.-Col. 16-11-1898. Adjutant, 1890; D.A.A.G., Soudan Campaign, 1898; A.A.G., Headquarters, 1902; Maj.-Gen.; C.B.; K.C.V.O.; 2nd Class Red Eagle of Prussia.
Mansel, George Clavell	25-8-1880 11-8-1880	1-7-1881	1-4-1889	9-8-1899 29-2-1904	Bt.-Col., 1-3-1907. From 48th Foot; half-pay, 1908; D.S.O.; died, 12-7-1910.
Wells, Cecil Grenville	10-11-1880	1-7-1881	...	...	Died at Allahabad, 21-11-1884.
Brett, Arthur	... ...	... ...	...	...	
Parke, Laurence	19-2-1881	1-7-1881	17-4-1889	31-10-1900	Paymaster, January, 1881. To 10th Hussars, 1884. Adjutant, 1887; retired, 1901; Lt.-Col., 7th Bn. Hampshire Regt.
Keane, George Wilfred	19-2-1881	1-7-1881	27-8-1890	...	Half-pay, 1898.

THE DURHAM LIGHT INFANTRY

OFFICERS.

2ND REGIMENT BOMBAY EUROPEAN LIGHT INFANTRY.

8TH OCTOBER, 1839, TO 29TH JULY, 1862.

N.B.—Officers, unless promoted on transfer, were gazetted with the dates of their ranks in former regiments.

Dates of promotion after 29th July, 1862, refer to 106th Light Infantry.

Name.	Ensign.	Lieutenant.	Captain.	Major.	Lieut.-Colonel.	Colonel.	Remarks.
Brooks, Geo. Benjamin	...	...	...	...	...	8-10-1839	(See Appendix II.)
Ottey, Philip Downing	...	...	...	...	8-10-1839	...	From 11th N.I.; appointed senior Lieut.-Colonel, but transferred at once to 5th N.I.
Wilson, George James	...	...	...	8-10-1839	8-10-1839	...	From 23rd N.I.; not in 1840 (2) list.
Powell, Stratford	...	...	...	28-6-1838	...	...	From 26th N.I.; not in 1845 list.
Foquett, William	...	...	...	8-10-1839	...	...	From 20th N.I.; not in 1842 list.
	...	...	...	28-6-1838	...	...	
Spencer, Henry	...	...	21-12-1826	1-4-1841	21-1-1846	...	From 25th N.I.; not in 1848 list.
Fawcett, John	...	...	2-4-1827	23-8-1844	...	...	From 6th N.I.; not in 1846 list.
	...	...	...	23-11-1841	...	...	
Macan, George	...	...	9-2-1829	10-10-1845	15-5-1850	...	From 15th N.I.; not in 1855 (2) list.
Wynter, Thomas Rose	...	...	13-9-1829	21-1-1846	...	...	From 14th N.I.; not in 1847 list.
Thornton, George	...	...	30-6-1829	2-11-1846	...	...	From 19th N.I.; not in 1847 (2) list.
Denton, Charles	...	...	19-6-1829	...	...	...	From 24th N.I.; not in 1845 list.
Wells, Charles Hotham	...	...	8-10-1839	...	...	...	From 26th N.I.; died, 5-10-1840.
	...	...	27-9-1834	...	...	...	
Le Mesurier, Alexander Peter	...	...	8-10-1839	24-11-1846	1851	...	From 23rd N.I.; not in 1855 (2) list.
Ramsey, John Skardon	...	...	21-5-1835	15-5-1850	27-3-1855	...	From 4th N.I.; C.O. in Persia, 1856-7; transferred to 11th N.I., 20-1-1857.
	...	...	8-10-1839	9-11-1846	20-6-1854	...	
	...	...	27-8-1835	...	...	...	
Wade, William	...	...	8-10-1839	...	...	...	From 1st European Regiment; not in 1841 list.
	...	...	4-1-1836	...	...	...	
Tucker, Francis	...	3-12-1824	8-10-1839	...	...	...	From 14th N.I.; not in 1847 list.
Nathaniel Burton	...	26-2-1837	...	...	...	...	

APPENDIX I

Name				
Gillanders, John	...	29-11-1825	8-10-1839	...	From 26th N.I.; Adjutant, 1-2-1840; not in 1850 list.
Bowman Mackenzie		14-5-1837			From 14th N.I.; not in 1858 list.
Shortreed, Robert	...	5-9-1826	1-4-1841	6-2-1852	
		4-1-1838			
Goldie, Alexander	...	5-7-1833	...	...	From 26th N.I.; not in 1840 (2) list.
		7-1-1839			
Gordon, John Glenny	...	7-12-1828	...	...	From 19th N.I.; not in 1842 list.
		8-6-1839			
Guerin, Edmund Arthur		9-5-1827	22-2-1844	27-3-1855	Bt.-Colonel, 25-11-1858. From 14th N.I. Adjutant, 9-12-1840.
			7-12-1839	11-11-1851	From 7th N.I.; Quartermaster, 19-6-1840.
Hibbert, John Riccardby	...	8-10-1827			
Bainbridge, Geo. Hobson	...	26-4-1832			From 6th N.I.; not in 1843 list.
Russell, John	...	23-7-1832	23-8-1844	12-10-1857	From 11th N.I.; not in 1840 (2) list.
Jones, Henry Charles	...	19-6-1833	3-1-1843	20-6-1854	From 24th N.I.; not in 1861 list.
Hendley, John Leslie	...	20-12-1835	24-1-1845	...	From 21st N.I.; not in 1845 list.
Christie, Charles Forbes	...	8-4-1836	24-1-1845	25-2-1860	From 21st N.I.; not in 1848 list.
Barr, Henry James	...	25-7-1836			Bt.-Lt.-Colonel, 19-1-1858. From 8th N.I.; this officer was, with A. E. Saunders, M. F. Gordon, and C. R. W. Harvey, in the 2nd Bombay European L.I. during the whole period that the regiment existed.
Saunders, Ambrose Edward	...	24-12-1837	10-10-1845	2-6-1860	Bt.-Lt.-Col, 14-3-1857. From 3rd N.I. (See H. J. Barr.)
Gordon, Michie Forbes	...	8-10-1839	21-1-1846	28-11-1854	From 11th N.I. (See H. J. Barr.)
			5-7-1844		
Willoughby, Henry John		8-10-1839	15-5-1846	...	From 24th N.I.; not in 1860 list.
De Vitré, James Dennis	19-6-1835	1-11-1839	...	...	Not in 1841 (2) list.
	21-12-1834				
Harvey, Chas. Robert Wood	24-2-1838	12-11-1839	2-11-1846	19-1-1858	Quartermaster and Interpreter, 21-7-1843. (See H. J. Barr.)
Evans, John Arthur	11-12-1835				
	21-1-1839	12-11-1839	24-11-1846	...	Not in 1855 (2) list.
	11-12-1835				
Whitehill, Charles Stephen	8-3-1839	12-11-1839	7-8-1847	...	
	10-12-1835				
Wiseman, James	19-7-1839	3-10-1840	...	...	Not in 1854 list.
Mackintosh	12-12-1837				
	20-10-1839				Not in 1844 (2) list.
Miles, Henry	...	12-12-1837	3-10-1840	...	...	Not in 1845 list.

215

THE DURHAM LIGHT INFANTRY

Name.	Ensign.	Lieutenant.	Captain.	Major.	Lieut.-Colonel.	Colonel.	Remarks.
Taylor, Robert	...	...	...	...	7-9-1831	...	From 5th N.I.; appointed senior Lt.-Col. in 1839, vice P. D. Ottey.
Kneller, Chas. Fredk.	8-10-1839	...	...	...	...	...	Not in 1841 list.
Peyton, John	8-10-1839	...	...	...	...	...	Not in 1841 list.
Eické, Detlev	12-11-1839	...	...	...	...	...	Not in 1841 list.
Stannus, Ephraim Gerrish	...	...	...	...	...	21-1-1826	(See Appendix II.)
Stalker, Foster	...	...	...	...	26-6-1838	13-6-1850 19-3-1849	C.B.; From 19th N.I.; appointed Lt.-Col. in 1840, vice G. J. Wilson; left in 1844; again in the regiment as senior Lt.-Col., early in 1846; left again the same year, and re-appointed senior Lt.-Col. in 1847. Maj.-Gen.; died, 14-3-1857.
Sandwith, Wm. Fleming	8-10-1839 22-7-1839	5-10-1840 19-10-1840	15-6-1848	...	...	...	Adjutant, 22-2-1844; not in 1854 list.
Shakespear, William Powlett			...	...	...	...	Died, 30-9-1844, from wounds received before the fort of Samanghur.
Brassey, Willoughby	12-11-1839 28-7-1839	1-4-1841	15-5-1850	...	...	...	Not in 1855 (2) list.
Bourchier, Chas. John	6-12-1839 3-8-1839	...	...	...	...	...	Not in 1843 list.
Dunsterville, John Bruce	24-3-1840 29-9-1839	...	...	...	...	...	Not in 1841 (2) list.
Walker, Chamberlen William	3-10-1840 10-3-1840	14-4-1842	...	...	...	...	Not in 1841 (2) list.
Campbell, Wellington	3-10-1840 10-3-1840	16-7-1842	...	...	...	...	Not in 1845 (2) list.
Campbell, Alexander Patrick	8-10-1840 13-8-1840	16-7-1842	6-2-1852	...	...	...	Killed, 31-12-1844, at Sassadroog.
Shewell, Henry	19-11-1840 28-8-1840	...	...	...	...	...	Instructor of Musketry, 24-3-1857.
Madden, Robt. James	19-11-1840 28-8-1840	...	...	...	...	...	Not in 1843 list.
Winfeld, John Philip	12-12-1840 22-10-1840	4-5-1843	15-11-1853	...	...	...	Not in 1856 list.
Close, Henry Edward Gordon	6-2-1841 22-10-1840	8-6-1843	...	...	...	...	Not in 1848 (2) list.
Tyacke, Henry Philip	17-3-1841 12-12-1840	30-11-1843	15-11-1853	30-7-1862	29-5-1866	...	Wounded at Sassadroog, 31-12-1844; To 106th L.I., 1862; retired, 1872.

APPENDIX I

Name					Notes
Cahill, Thos. Stanton	19-4-1840	...	...	...	Surgeon, 21-1-1841.
Pelly, Lewis	12-12-1840	...	...	...	Left 2nd Bombay European L.I., 1842; subsequently Lieut.-Gen., K.C.B., K.C.S.I.; M.P. for North Hackney, 1885-92; died, 22-4-1892. Adjutant, 6-2-1852; retired, 1857.
Saville, John Walter	23-12-1841	22-2-1844	22-2-1854	...	
	12-6-1841				
Church, Cockburn Fiske Gooding	5-1-1842	4-4-1844	...	...	Not in 1848 list.
Webb, John	16-10-1841	...	...	...	Not in 1843 list.
	14-4-1842				
	6-1-1842				
Aitchison, Charles Torrington	13-6-1842	23-8-1844	16-1-1855	...	Wounded at Panhala, 1-12-1844.
Miles, William	10-6-1842	...	...	...	Not in 1843 list.
	16-7-1842				
	11-6-1842				
James, Chas. Mardon Wallace	16-7-1842	...	...	...	Not in 1843 list.
	11-6-1842				
Bruce, Herbert	16-7-1842	13-9-1844	27-3-1855	26-4-1859	C.B. Although a Lt.-Col. in the Bombay Army, never held higher rank than Captain in the regiment.
	11-6-1842				
Thompson, Charles	16-7-1842	30-9-1844	3-7-1855	...	Wounded at Sarapur in 1844; not in 1846 list.
	18-6-1842				
Head, Michael George	19-11-1842	31-12-1844	...	...	Not in 1851 list.
	25-2-1842				
Davies, Charles	...	...	...	4-9-1837	Appointed Lieut.-Col. in 1843, vice F. Stalker; from 14th N.I.
Soames, George	10-5-1843	10-10-1845	...	...	Not in 1847 list.
	1-1-1843				
Westropp, James Edwd.	8-6-1843	?	23-11-1856	...	
	1-2-1843				
Walton, William Hervey	4-7-1843	10-4-1845	...	...	Not in 1847 (2) list.
	21-2-1843				
Jessop, Charles Scott	20-11-1843	21-1-1846	23-11-1856	...	
	1-8-1843				
Whittaker, Benjamin Robert	22-2-1844	21-1-1846	12-10-1857	...	
	5-9-1843				
Robertson, Henry Dundas	...	...	...	28-6-1838	Appointed Lt.-Col. in 1844, vice C. Davies; from 16th N.I.
Turquand, Leonard	1-4-1844	21-4-1846	...	...	Not in 1851 (2) list.
	8-12-1843				
Hassard, Robert Deey	27-8-1844	15-5-1846	12-10-1857	...	Adjutant, 17-2-1855.
	1-1-1844				

THE DURHAM LIGHT INFANTRY

Name.	Ensign.	Lieutenant.	Captain.	Major.	Lieut.-Colonel.	Colonel.	Remarks.
Frankland, Augustus Charles	13-9-1844 1-1-1844	13-7-1846	...	...	...	...	Killed at Khooshab, 8-2-1857.
Faure, Wm. Caldwell	30-9-1844 6-1-1844	...	...	...	...	...	Killed near Sassooly, 31-12-1844.
Turnbull, Walter	31-12-1844 1-2-1844	...	...	...	...	...	Not in 1846 list.
Heyman, Frederic James	4-1-1845 7-4-1844	...	...	...	...	...	Not in 1846 list.
Seton, Bruce	...	...	...	...	9-6-1845	...	Senior Lt.-Col. in 1846, vice F. Stalker; from 16th N.I.; died, 27-11-1876.
Capon, David	...	...	...	...	-12-1845 30-5-1836	...	Was nominally in the regiment from December, 1845, to February, 1846; name does not appear in 2nd European L.I. in Army List. Subsequently Colonel, 106th L.I.
Reid, Henry George Harris	10-10-1845 1-3-1845	7-8-1847	...	...	...	...	Died, 22-5-1857, at sea on the "Madge Wildfire" on passage from Persia to Karachi.
Moore, George	...	...	...	...	21-6-1838	...	Senior Lt.-Col. early in 1847; from 25th N.I.
Hickes, Frederick	12-6-1846	26-9-1847	3-7-1859	...	...	...	Not in 1857 list.
Ledwith, James Symes	13-6-1846	26-9-1847	...	...	...	...	Not in 1860 list.
Clifton, Edward Gerard	13-6-1846	15-6-1848	...	...	...	...	Not in 1854 list.
Laughton, Geo. Arnold	11-7-1846 3-7-1846	13-12-1849	3-7-1859	...	...	...	
Musgrave (or Mosgrove), Fredk. Johnson Moore	...	...	...	...	...	...	Asst.-Surgeon, 1846; not in 1847 (2) list.
Scott, Stanley	11-12-1846	16-4-1850	25-2-1860	...	...	...	Not in 1861 list.
Billamore, Geo. Reid	12-12-1846	15-5-1850	...	...	...	...	Asst.-Surgeon, 1847, vice F. J. M. Musgrave.
Davey, William	...	...	...	...	...	...	Appointed to the regiment as senior Lt.-Col., end of 1847; from 16th N.I.
Soppitt, Matthew	...	...	...	...	26-1-1838	...	
Cavaye, William	...	...	...	...	23-11-1841	...	Appointed to the regiment as junior Lt.-Col., end of 1847; was senior in 1849; from 23rd N.I.
Hobart, Wm. Arthur	14-1-1847	...	...	...	...	...	Not in 1849 list.
Robinson, Wm. Chas.	24-4-1847	16-1-1851	...	...	...	...	Not in 1861 list.

APPENDIX I

Name				Remarks
Hutcheon, David	24-4-1847	6-2-1852	19-12-1860	
Griffiths, Augustus Spottiswode	19-8-1847	25-11-1852		Quartermaster and Interpreter, 29-11-1855.
Berthon, Edward Park	26-9-1847			Not in 1854 list.
Ferguson, Alexander	10-2-1848	15-11-1853		
	10-8-1847			
Twyford, Dehany Chas. Edward	17-3-1848	15-11-1853		Died, 10-8-1857.
Watkins, Francis Wilmer	17-2-1848			Asst.-Surgeon, 5-1-1848.
Forbes, David			23-11-1841	Appointed to the regiment as junior Lt.-Col. in 1848, vice M. Soppitt; from 25th N.I.; not in 1850 list; to 3rd European Regiment. Surgeon, 17-5-1842; appointed to the regiment in 1848. Asst.-Surgeon, 3-6-1843; appointed in 1848 vice T. W. Watkins; not in 1850 list.
Barrington, William Boxwell				Died at Ahmedabad, 29-5-1856.
Bayne, Ronald				
Bowles, Alfred Arthur Loraine	13-12-1849	16-1-1855		
Hallett, Francis Amyot	13-12-1849	22-5-1854		Not in 1857 list.
Anderson, Francis	16-4-1850	27-3-1855		Not in 1857 list.
	10-12-1849			
Gillespie, Robert Rollo	25-6-1850	3-7-1855	30-7-1862	11-9-1868	13-8-1873	Adjutant, 18-1-1859; to 106th L.I., 1862; Maj.-Gen.; C.B.; died, 1890, when G.O.C. Mhow Divn.
	8-6-1849			
Pitcairn, Henry	16-1-1851			Not in 1852 list.
	12-12-1849			
Mildmay, Arthur George St. John	3-4-1851			Not in 1855 list.
Beatty, Thomas Berkeley	11-12-1847			
Gayer, James Arthur	6-2-1852	29-3-1856		Asst.-Surgeon, 7-7-1851. Not in 1853 list.
	10-12-1850			
Bowie, John Mortimer				Asst.-Surgeon, 27-11-1851. Not in 1853 list.
Utterson, Alfred	6-3-1853	20-8-1856		
	12-12-1851			
Lockett, Robt. Chas.	10-9-1853			Not in 1855 list.
	20-2-1852			
Kaye, Joseph				Asst.-Surgeon, 26-11-1852. Not in 1855 list.

219

THE DURHAM LIGHT INFANTRY

Name.	Ensign.	Lieutenant.	Captain.	Major.	Lieut.-Colonel.	Colonel.	Remarks.
Gillespie, Wm. Augustus	15-11-1853 13-6-1852	20-10-1856	...	...	...	...	
Gardyne, Evan Bruce	15-11-1853 9-12-1852	23-11-1856	30-7-1862	19-6-1872	...	...	To 106th L.I., 1862; to 6th Foot, 1873.
Watson, Robert Grant	15-11-1853 11-6-1853	23-11-1856	...	...	...	...	
Robertson, Elliot Larking	15-11-1853 9-12-1852	23-11-1856	30-7-1862	13-8-1873	5-9-1877	...	To 106th L.I., 1862; to half-pay, 1880.
Wright, Alexander	...	...	...	...	...	...	Surgeon, 6-9-1854; described as "Surgeon-Major" in 1861 list, but with same date (6-9-1854).
Thorp, Robt. Crossing, M.D.	...	...	...	...	...	...	Asst.-Surgeon, 8-2-1854. Not in 1856 (2) list.
Gould, John Henry	...	...	...	...	...	...	Asst.-Surgeon, 28-2-1854. Not in 1856 (2) list.
Campbell, Neil	...	...	...	...	18-8-1847	...	Appointed to the regiment as senior Lt.-Col. in 1855; from 16th N.I.
Hale, Joseph	...	...	...	...	30-11-1848	...	Appointed to the regiment as junior Lt.-Col. in 1855; from 21st N.I. Resigned, 2-9-1857.
Macready, Edward Neville Bourne	10-1-1855 9-12-1854	23-11-1856	...	...	...	...	
Phillips, Augustus Marshall	8-6-1855	27-12-1856	...	...	...	...	
Warden, Francis	28-6-1855 9-6-1855	8-2-1857	30-7-1862	13-5-1874	...	...	To 106th L.I., 1862; retired, 1877.
Adey, Arthur Wellesley George	...	...	...	...	...	...	Asst.-Surgeon, 13-1-1855. Not in 1857 list.
Woodcock, Elborough Martin	15-3-1856 4-2-1856	25-5-1857	...	...	...	...	Wounded at Khooshab, 8-2-1857.
Davidson, David	...	...	...	...	1-12-1854 1-12-1851	...	Bt.-Col., 28-11-1854. Appointed to the regiment as senior Lt.-Col. in 1857; from 13th N.I.
Stiles, Henry	...	...	...	...	25-12-1854	...	Bt.-Col., 28-11-1857. Appointed to the regiment as junior Lt.-Col. in 1857; from 7th N.I.
Jervis, Ernest Scott	6-12-1856	4-7-1857	30-7-1862	...	...	...	To 106th L.I., 1862; retired, 1866.
Edwards, Henry Bennett	13-12-1856	10-8-1857	...	...	...	...	
Shewell, Arthur Mark	14-12-1856	2-9-1857	...	...	...	...	
Ducat, Arthur William	14-12-1856	12-10-1857	30-7-1862	...	...	...	To 106th L.I., 1862; to 104th Foot, 1871.

APPENDIX I

Name				Remarks
Grant, Chas. Newel	20-4-1857	26-4-1859	...	...
Burnett, Francis Redfearn	12-6-1857	3-7-1859	28-5-1864	To 106th L.I., 1862; retired, 1868.
Mackenzie, George	13-6-1857	25-2-1860	...	...
Seton, William Samuel	20-7-1857	29-9-1860	...	...
Garrow, Wm. George Baker	4-8-1857	29-10-1860	...	...
Thorold, Harry Octavius	...	...	...	Asst.-Surgeon, 6-2-1858. Not in 1861 list. (See Appendix II.)
Parr, Thomas Cheese (or Chase)	...	...	...	15-3-1857
Caldecot, Cuthbert	12-12-1857	19-12-1860	30-10-1866	18-3-1856 To 106th L.I., 1862; died at Kasauli, 27-2-1870.
Stuart, Chas. Shepherd	...	...	...	17-6-1851 Bt.-Colonel, 28-11-1854; K.C.B.; appointed to the regiment as senior Lt.-Col. in 1860; from 1st Bombay Fusiliers (European).
Davis, Arthur Henry	19-9-1858	26-3-1861	4-7-1868	...
Gaitskell, John Henry	11-12-1859	1-1-1862	...	To 106th L.I., 1862; Adjutant, 1862; retired, 1873.
Elliot, Mowbray Lettson	24-8-1859	30-7-1862	28-2-1870	To 106th L.I., 1862; to 65th Foot, 1873.
French, Henry	27-2-1859	...	...	Attached.
Nicholson, Malcolm Hassells	27-10-1859	...	...	Attached.
	9-12-1859	...	...	
Hemsted, Edward	27-6-1860	...	...	Attached.
Douglas, Edmund Alexander	10-9-1860	...	...	Attached.

THE DURHAM LIGHT INFANTRY

OFFICERS.

106TH BOMBAY LIGHT INFANTRY.

30TH JULY, 1862 TO 30TH JUNE, 1881.

N.B.—Officers appointed on 30th July, 1862 and in 1863, unless promoted on transfer, were gazetted with the dates of their ranks in former regiments.

Dates of promotion after 30th June, 1881, refer to the Durham Light Infantry.

Name.	Ensign.	Lieutenant.	Captain.	Major.	Lieut.-Colonel.	Colonel.	Remarks.
Leith, Robt. William Disney	...	...	...	...	28-6-1862	29-5-1866	From 1st Bombay Fusiliers (European); half-pay, 1866; Lt.-Gen.; C.B.; Colonel, Worcestershire Regt.; died in the Isle of Wight, 1892.
Tyacke, Henry Philip	...	...	...	30-7-1862	19-6-1872		From 2nd Bombay European L.I.; retired, 1872.
Bolton, William Mainwaring Sloane	...	...	...	30-7-1862	19-6-1872		From 2nd Grenadier Regt. (N.I.); died at Morar, 12-8-1873.
Dawson, Edwd. Steer Kennet	...	...	23-11-1856	29-5-1866			From late 31st N.I.; died at Simla, 10-9-1868.
Jopp, D'Arcy William	...	...	11-12-1860	...	...		From late 31st N.I.; resigned, 1866.
Kirkland, Nugent	...	...	30-7-1862	11-9-1868	13-8-1873		From late 29th N.I.; retired, 1868.
Gillespie, Robt. Rollo	...	...	30-7-1862	11-9-1868	13-8-1873		From 2nd Bombay European L.I.; Maj.-Gen.; C.B.; died when G.O.C., Mhow Division, 1890.
Coghlan, Edward	...	...	30-7-1862	...	...		From 4th N.I.; died at Delhi, 6-5-1868.
Maunsell, George	...	...	30-7-1862	19-6-1872	...		From 11th N.I.; half-pay, 1866.
Gardyne, Evan Bruce	...	...	30-7-1862	19-6-1872	...		From 2nd Bombay European L.I.; to 6th Foot, 1873.
Robertson, Elliot Larkins	...	...	30-7-1862	13-8-1873	5-9-1877		From 2nd Bombay European L.I.; half-pay, 1880.
Warden, Francis	...	...	30-7-1862	13-5-1874	...		From 2nd Bombay European L.I.; retired, 1877.
Jervis, Ernest Scott	...	...	30-7-1862	...	...		From 2nd Bombay European L.I.; retired, 1866.

222

APPENDIX I

Name				
Ducat, Alfred William	…	30-7-1862	…	From 2nd Bombay European L.I.; to 104th Foot, 1871.
Wilmot, George Washington	…	30-7-1862	…	From 11th N.I.; died in India, 27-5-1864.
Burnett, Francis Redfearn	3-7-1859	28-5-1864	…	From 2nd Bombay European L.I.; retired, 1868.
Anstruther, Robert Durham	13-7-1860	13-2-1866	…	From 10th N.I.; retired, 1874.
Sangster, Thos. Henry	7-10-1860	29-5-1866	…	From 4th N.I.; to 66th Foot, 1866.
Wright, John	10-11-1860	30-10-1866*	…	*Antedated, 19-9-1866. From 15th N.I.; died at Agra, 31-7-1871.
Caldecot, Cuthbert	19-12-1860	30-10-1866	…	From 2nd Bombay European L.I.; died at Kasauli, 27-2-1870.
Garlick, John William	12-6-1861	7-5-1867	5-9-1877	From Lieutenant, unposted, Bombay; half-pay, 1879.
Sangster, David James Kilgour	25-6-1861	…	…	From 2nd Lieutenant, 4th N.I.; to 53rd Foot, 1864.
Gaitskell, John Henry	1-1-1862	4-7-1868	…	From 2nd Bombay European L.I.; Adjutant, 1862; retired, 1873.
Girardot, Geo. Chas.	1-1-1862	11-9-1868	31-10-1877	21-7-1880	From Ensign, unposted; half-pay, 1884; hon. Major-General.
Peyton, Edwd. Gilbert	1-1-1862	18-11-1868	…	From Ensign, unposted; retired, 1873.
Elliot, Mowbray Lettson	30-7-1862	28-2-1870	…	From 2nd Bombay European L.I.; to 65th Foot, 1873.
Bulkeley, Henry Wm. Conynghame	30-7-1862	19-6-1872	23-7-1879	1-7-1881 D.L.I.	From Ensign, unposted; half-pay, 1881.
Gleig, Charles Fleming	30-7-1862	15-3-1873	…	From Ensign, unposted; to 22nd Foot, 1873.
Heathcote, Charles Lechmere	30-7-1862	19-11-1873	21-7-1880	From Ensign, unposted; half-pay, 1881.
Hill, Herbert Byron	30-7-1862	…	…	From Ensign, unposted; reverted to Bombay General List, Infantry.
Hancock, Arthur Percival	7-1-1861	28-5-1864	…	From Ensign, unposted; resigned, 1865.
Hunter, Fredk. Mercer	8-6-1861	25-7-1865	…	From Ensign, unposted; to Bombay Army, 1869.
McNair, Alfred Lionel	27-8-1861	13-2-1866	…	From Ensign, unposted; to Bombay Staff Corps, 1866.
Coulson, George John	21-12-1861	29-5-1866	…	From Ensign, unposted; to Bombay Staff Corps, 1866.

THE DURHAM LIGHT INFANTRY

Name.	Ensign.	Lieutenant.	Captain.	Major.	Lieut.-Colonel.	Colonel.	Remarks.
Maurice, Arthur Corbet	27-2-1862	30-10-1866*	...	...	...	...	*Antedated, 20-7-1866. From Ensign, unposted; to 101st Foot, 1868.
Mackey, Francis	...	...	...	...	...	...	Quartermaster, 30-7-1862. From Qr.-Mr.-Serjt., 2nd Bombay European L.I. Died at Jhansi, 1-1-1873.
Capon, David	...	...	...	...	...	30-9-1862	(See Appendix II.)
Hepworth, David	...	...	...	...	...	...	Paymaster, 12-8-1862. Late Indian Forces; to 3rd Brigade Depôt, 1878.
Winslow, James	20-11-1860	30-10-1866*	...	...	...	...	*Antedated, 19-9-1866. Appointed to 106th, 1863, from Madras General List; retired, 1871.
Coker, Edmund Rogers	8-6-1861	30-10-1866	30-5-1874	12-2-1881	24-8-1881	...	Commanding Battalion, 27-8-1884; Colonel, 24-8-1885. Appointed to 106th, 1863, from General List, Infantry, Madras Army; while on General List was attached to 74th Highlanders at Bellary; Adjt., 14-2-1874. C.O., 2nd D.L.I., Egypt, 1885; D.S.O.; half-pay, 1887; died at Taunton, 11-3-1914.
Bailey, Henry	2-10-1861	30-10-1866	29-8-1874	...	...	...	Appointed to 106th, 1863, from Bengal General List; retired, 1877.
Bird, Guy Golding	4-1-1862	7-5-1867*	...	...	...	...	*Antedated, 14-3-1867. Appointed to 106th, 1863, from Madras General List; to 20th Foot, 1868.
Flood, Stephen	...	...	...	...	...	...	Asst.-Surgn., 1-10-1862—17-11-1863. From Staff; to Staff, 1868.
Folliott, William	...	...	...	...	...	...	Asst.-Surgn., 1-10-1862—17-11-1863. From Staff, to 20th Hussars, 1871.
Churchill, George Frederic	8-3-1864	19-12-1867*	...	...	...	...	*Antedated, 17-5-1867. To Bengal Staff Corps, 1870.
Young, Henry Roberts	...	31-5-1864 4-6-1860	...	...	...	...	From 2nd Bengal N.I.; to 81st Foot, 1865.
Ainsworth, William	...	14-6-1864 19-4-1864	13-5-1874	...	...	...	From 53rd Foot; Adjutant, 1868; retired, 1878.
Christie, Walter Henry	23-8-1864	...	...	...	...	...	From 16th Foot; to Commissariat Department, 1867.
Crerar, James	5-7-1864	...	...	...	...	...	Surgeon, 6-5-1855—28-6-1864. From Staff; to Staff, 1868.

APPENDIX I

Name					Notes
Stuart-Menteith, Wm. Augustus Claude	...	...	4-2-1865	...	From 81st Foot; half-pay Captain, 1870.
Moorhouse, Henry Alexander Bruce	25-7-1865	22-10-1861 4-7-1868	...	...	Retired, 1873.
Bingham, Edward Henry	13-2-1866	11-9-1868	...	...	To Bengal Staff Corps, 1870.
Westropp, Robt. G——	...	...	27-7-1866 2-6-1865	...	From 66th Foot; died, 29-5-1874.
Mallandaine, James John	29-5-1866	11-9-1868	14-3-1877	...	To 60th Foot, 1877.
Unwin, Wm. Heathcote	...	7-8-1866 18-5-1858	...	...	From 56th Bengal N.I.; appointment cancelled, 9-11-1866.
Wyllie, Wm. Hutt Curzon	30-10-1866	18-11-1868*	...	...	*Antedated, 5-10-1868. To Bengal Staff Corps, Sept., 1870; subsequently Lt.-Col., Indian Army. K.C.I.E., C.V.O.; assassinated, 1-7-1909, at the Imperial Institute, London, by a native Indian student.
Jamieson, Alister Wm.	9-11-1866	18-11-1868	...	...	To Bengal Staff Corps, 1871.
Harrington, Robt. Nicholai	18-12-1866	...	...	...	To 104th Foot, 1867.
Kittoe, Markham Robinson	6-7-1867	10-2-1869	...	...	Retired, 1874.
Dawson, Frederick	...	22-1-1868 17-11-1863	31-10-1874	1-7-1881	From 20th Foot; retired, 1883; hon. Lieut.-Colonel.
Ferguson, William	...	...	...	...	Surgeon, 9-3-1867—11-4-1868. From Staff; to Staff, 1870.
Reynolds, Henry Chas.	...	20-5-1868 15-6-1867	16-12-1874	1-7-1881	From 101st Foot; half-pay, Lt.-Col., 1886.
Compigné, Henry Mapleton	8-7-1868	18-1-1870	17-3-1877	...	Paymaster, November, 1878. To Army Pay Department, 1878; to 13th Regtl. District, 1881.
Dempster, Cathcart	9-7-1868	28-2-1870	...	...	To Bengal Staff Corps, 1875.
Pooley, Geo. Richd.	10-7-1868	23-3-1870	...	...	Retired, 1875.
James, Walter Wilson	11-7-1868	1-11-1871*	31-10-1877	1-7-1881	*Antedated, 28-10-1871. Half-pay, Lieut.-Colonel, 1890.
McNamara, Wm. Henry	...	...	...	...	Asst.-Surgn., 1-10-1867—7-11-1868; Surgeon, May, 1874. From Staff; appears last as Asst.-Surgeon, March, 1873; re-appears as Surgeon, May, 1874; appears last as Surgeon, August, 1878.

THE DURHAM LIGHT INFANTRY

Name.	Ensign.	Lieutenant.	Captain.	Major.	Lieut.-Colonel.	Colonel.	Remarks.
Deane, Geo. Wm.	3-2-1869 13-1-1869	1-11-1871*	…	…	…	…	*Antedated, 28-10-1871. From 101st Foot; to Bengal Staff Corps, 1874.
Mackenzie, Thomas Harding	3-2-1869	1-11-1871*	…	…	…	…	*Antedated, 28-10-1871. To Bombay Staff Corps, 1873.
Gubbins, Charles Edgeworth	4-2-1869	1-11-1871*	…	…	…	…	*Antedated, 28-10-1871. To Bengal Staff Corps, 1874.
Biggs, John William Forbes	5-2-1869	1-11-1871*	…	…	…	…	*Antedated, 28-10-1871. To 109th Foot, 1874.
Maxwell, Henry St. Patrick	6-2-1869	1-11-1871*	…	…	…	…	*Antedated, 28-10-1871. To Bengal Staff Corps, 1872; C.S.I.
Bignell, Edwd. Duncan Frederick	7-7-1869	1-11-1871*	…	…	…	…	*Antedated, 28-10-1871. To 22nd Foot, 1873. (See Appendix II.)
Barlow, Maurice	…	1-11-1871*	…	…	…	18-12-1869	*Antedated, 28-10-1871. To 54th Foot, 1873.
Brice, Hugh Munbee	6-7-1870	1-11-1871*	…	…	…	…	*Antedated, 28-10-1871. To 17th Foot, 1873.
Harris, Wm. Octavius	6-7-1870	1-11-1871*	…	…	…	…	*Antedated, 28-10-1871. (See Appendix II.)
Cadogan, Hon. George	…	…	…	…	…	9-8-1870	Surgeon, 2-1-1867—22-10-1870. From Staff; appears last in April, 1874.
Kelly, James	…	…	…	…	…	…	Asst.-Surgeon, 1-10-1867—15-2-1871. From Staff; appears last in March, 1873.
Macmullen, Richard	…	…	…	…	…	…	From 104th Foot; retired, 1874.
	Sub-Lieut.						
Richardson, Robert Campbell	…	…	19-8-1871 28-11-1868	…	…	…	
Brownrigg, Robt. Henry Francis Reade	24-4-1872	24-4-1872	14-12-1878	14-5-1883	…	…	Adjutant, 16-7-1874; died, 17-4-1884 at Didsbury, near Manchester.
Lloyd, Edward	…	…	…	1-2-1873	…	…	From 6th Foot; to half-pay, 1874.
Connell, Patrick	…	…	…	…	…	…	Qr.-Mr., 23-4-1873. From Serjt.-Major; to 4th D.L.I., 1881; retired, 1884.
Westloe, Frederick Henry (later Fredk. Henry Whitby)	9-8-1873	9-8-1873	23-7-1879	20-1-1884	27-8-1894	…	Bt.-Col., 27-8-1898. To A.A.G., Madras, 1899; hon. Brig.-Gen.; died, 4-1-1914.
Thackwell, Edward Loftus Roche	9-8-1873	…	…	…	…	…	To 7th Foot, 1873.
Pechell, Edward	…	…	27-8-1873 7-11-1868	…	…	…	From 22nd Foot; retired, 1880; hon. Major; died, 11-11-1880.
Rodney Cecil	…	25-8-1873	13-11-1879	1-9-1884	…	…	
Parker-Jervis, Charles Edward	…	28-10-1871					From 54th Foot; half-pay, Lt.-Col. 1891.

APPENDIX I

Name				Notes
Pitman, Harry Bromley	...	13-9-1873	...	From 65th Foot; retired, 1874.
Boyle, Andrew Thomas	...	15-12-1869	...	From 17th Foot; retired, 1877.
	6-11-1873			
Leeds, George Lewis	20-10-1869	...	...	From half-pay, 37th Foot; retired, 1874.
	8-4-1874			
Loftus-Tottenham, Beresford Stuart Crichton	13-5-1874	...	...	From 14th Hussars; to 10th Hussars, 1875.
	28-2-1874	15-2-1868		
Haly, William O'Grady	11-7-1874	...	17-5-1874	(See Appendix II.)
Thackwell, Joseph Edward Lucas	24-7-1872	24-7-1872	...	From 45th Foot; to 5th Lancers, 1874.
Douglas, Sholto Claud	2-12-1874	...	...	Resigned, 1879.
Davidson, Jame ...	2-12-1874	...	...	To 8th Hussars, 1875.
Rosseter, Henry Donald	11-2-1875	2-2-1881	8-10-1890	Died at Poonah, 24-8-1896.
Moore, Maurice George	13-6-1874	...	...	To 88th Foot, 1875.
Jameson, Wm. Henry	13-6-1874	...	...	To 3rd Foot, 1875.
Younghusband, George William	21-9-1874	...	...	To 34th Foot, 1875.
Norton, Reuben ...	20-11-1875	20-6-1883	...	Retired, 1893; Lt.-Col. and hon. Colonel 3rd Battn. Suffolk Regt. 1897. Hon. Lieut.-Colonel in the Army, 1903.
Joy, Frank Leslie ...	20-11-1875	...	...	Died at St. Leonards-on-Sea, 14-1-1878.
Bisset, John Jarvis ...	13-11-1875	...	2-11-1875	(See Appendix II.)
Ferguson, Arthur Hill Ringland		...		From half-pay, 1st West India Regt.; to half-pay, Captain, 1875.
Edwards, Robert Lloyd	5-1-1876	...	...	From 45th Foot; to Rifle Brigade, 1876.
	20-11-1875			
Davison, Geo. Markham	28-1-1876	14-3-1883	11-4-1894	Bt.-Colonel, 26-4-1906. From unattached list; retired, 1906.
	13-6-1874			
Napier, Archibald Lennox Milliken	28-1-1876	...	...	From unattached list; to 69th Foot, 1876.
	11-2-1875			
Lawley, Hon. Richard Thompson	28-1-1876	...	...	From unattached list; to 7th Hussars, 29-1-1876; succeeded as 4th Baron Wenlock, 1912; C.B.
	11-2-1875			
Wickham, Richd. Wm.	1-4-1876	...	26-4-1903	From 6th Dragoon Guards; resigned, 1879.
	23-4-1875			
Coulton, Philip Beaumont Gruneisen	11-4-1876	6-8-1876	...	From 8th Hussars; resigned, 1876.
Dwyer, Lambart Francis William	13-6-1874	5-1-1870	...	From half-pay, 17th Foot; retired, 1877.

227

Q 2

THE DURHAM LIGHT INFANTRY

Name.	Sub-Lieut.	Lieutenant.	Captain.	Major.	Lieut.-Colonel.	Colonel.	Remarks.
Saunders, George Morley	16-1-1877	26-8-1876	20-1-1884	11-4-1894	...	...	Retired, 1903.
Knox, Fredk. Chas. Northland	24-6-1876	...	...	...	...	...	From unattached list; to 85th Foot, 1877.
	2nd Lieut.						
Sebright, Guy Thomas Saunders	5-9-1877	...	...	...	...	...	To Coldstream Guards, 1877.
Berwick, Wm. Alexander	...	15-8-1877	22-3-1879	...	...	...	From half-pay, 42nd Foot; half-pay, Captain, June, 1878; restored to establishment, March, 1879; retired, 1882.
		28-10-1871	29-6-1878				
Peyton, Charles Talbot	...	...	31-10-1877	1-7-1881	27-8-1890	...	From 10th Foot; to half-pay, 1894; Bt.-Col.; died, 24-5-1913.
Pearson, Thomas Horner	...	...	19-12-1877	...	...	...	From 43rd Foot; retired, 1881.
			30-11-1873				
Allan, Crawford Lewin	...	...	29-12-1877	24-8-1881	...	...	From 60th Foot; half-pay, Lt.-Col., 1888.
			11-11-1876				
Warden, Edmund Jas. Peach	30-1-1878	...	...	...	...	...	To 13th Foot, 1878.
Wood, Wm. Stuckey	3-4-1878	1-11-1878	...	...	...	...	To 77th Foot, 1878.
Purdon, David Wm.	1-5-1878	...	...	...	...	...	To Madras Staff Corps, 1883.
Forbes, Wm. Lachlan	1-5-1878	...	...	...	...	...	To 7th Foot, 1879.
Maunsell, John Drought	25-5-1878	5-2-1879	29-10-1884	...	...	...	To Army Pay Department, 1885.
Gilbert, Edwd. Foot	...	...	21-8-1878	...	...	...	From half-pay, 49th Foot; to half-pay, 1879.
			28-6-1871				
Moss, Gilbert Winter Zwilchenbart	21-8-1878	...	...	...	...	...	To 7th Foot, 1879.
Johnson-Smyth, Thos. Roger	14-9-1878	30-4-1879	12-2-1885	25-8-1896	...	...	Killed in action at Vaal Krantz, S. Africa, 5-2-1900.
Talbot, Edward Lister Kay	5-10-1878	23-7-1879	...	...	...	...	Resigned, 1883.
Thomas, Henry	8-3-1879	13-11-1879*	...	...	...	...	*Antedated, 30-10-1879. From 1879; Serjt.-Major; Adjutant, D. A. Commy.-Gen. 1881. Dismissed the Service, 1883.
Honywood, Arthur	13-8-1879	...	...	...	...	...	To 66th Foot, 1879.
Bulkeley, Thomas Mowbray Martin	13-8-1879	...	...	...	...	...	To 73rd Foot, 1879.

APPENDIX I

Trelawny Hemphill, Fitzroy	14-1-1880	...	To 25th Foot, 1880.
Parsons, Clement Geo.	14-1-1880	...	To 22nd Foot, 1880.
Kerr, Schomberg	31-1-1880	...	To 25th Foot, 1880.
Noble, George John	21-7-1880	...	From 13th Hussars; transfer cancelled, 24-8-1880.
Templer, Lawrence Gwynn	14-1-1880 23-10-1880 18-6-1881	...	Resigned, 1887.
Bush, John Ernest	23-10-1880 1-7-1881 7-2-1900 15-8-1906		Bt.-Col., 15-8-1909; Adjutant, 1884; half-pay, 1910; O.C. York and Durham Infantry Brigade (Terr. Force), 1911.
Binyon, Alfred Ernest	23-10-1880 1-7-1881	...	Adjutant, 1881; died at Gibraltar, 14-4-1884.
Gall, Herbert Ray	18-12-1880 17-12-1879	...	From half-pay, 5th Foot; to 96th Foot, 1881.
Ruddach, John Warner	2-2-1881 27-8-1890*	...	*Cancelled, 2-12-1890. From 54th Foot; retired, 1891.
Gardiner, Richd. John	19-2-1881 1-7-1881 27-8-1890	...	Retired, 1899; in Royal Garrison Regt., July, 1901—Sept., 1902; Major in the Army, Oct., 1902; Captain and Hon. Major, 4th Royal Dublin Fusiliers, 1906; died, April, 1914.
Fryer, Alfred Charles	12-3-1881 18-5-1881	...	From 61st Foot; to 19th Foot, 1881.
Tetley, Arthur Joshua	1-12-1880	...	From half-pay, 47th Foot; half-pay, 1882.

THE DURHAM LIGHT INFANTRY

OFFICERS.—THE DURHAM LIGHT INFANTRY (1ST AND 2ND BATTALIONS).

1ST JULY, 1881, TO MARCH, 1914.

For further particulars concerning the first seventy-three Officers, refer to 68th and 106th lists.

Name.	2nd Lieut.	Lieutenant.	Captain.	Major.	Lieut.-Colonel.	Colonel.	Remarks.
Paulet, Lord W.	...	...	...	...	...	9-4-1864	From 68th.
Bisset, J. J.	...	...	...	...	...	2-11-1875	From 106th.
Tucker, A. H.	...	...	...	...	29-10-1879	...	From 68th.
Girardot, G. C.	...	...	...	...	21-7-1880	...	From 106th.
Shaw, G. K.	...	...	...	...	1-7-1881	...	From 68th.
Bulkeley, H. W. C.	...	...	...	...	1-7-1881	...	From 106th.
Covey, C.	...	...	...	26-5-1880	...	...	From 68th.
Coker, E. R.	...	...	...	12-2-1881	...	...	From 106th.
Crawford, R. A.	...	...	...	1-7-1881	...	...	From 68th.
Lee, G. A.	...	...	...	1-7-1881	...	...	From 68th.
Woodward, W. F.	...	...	...	1-7-1881	...	...	From 106th.
Dawson, F.	...	...	...	1-7-1881	...	...	From 68th.
Reynolds, H. C.	...	...	...	1-7-1881	...	...	From 106th.
Tyndall, S. W.	...	...	...	1-7-1881	...	...	From 68th.
Peyton, C. T.	...	...	...	1-7-1881	...	...	From 106th.
James, W. W.	...	...	...	1-7-1881	...	...	From 106th.
Woodland, A. L.	...	...	29-6-1875	...	...	...	From 68th.
Gordon, W.	...	...	9-2-1876	...	...	...	From 68th.
Stanley, A. H.	...	...	23-4-1877	...	...	...	From 68th.
Westropp, W. K.	...	...	15-8-1877	...	...	...	From 68th.
Fulton, C. L.	...	...	15-8-1877	...	...	...	From 68th.
Allan, C. L.	...	...	29-12-1877	...	...	...	From 106th.
Brownrigg, R. H. F. R.	...	...	14-12-1878	...	...	...	From 106th.
Berwick, W. A.	...	...	22-5-1879	...	...	...	From 106th.
Whitby, F. H.	...	...	23-7-1879	...	...	...	From 106th.
Hilliard, J. C.	...	...	30-10-1879	...	...	...	From 68th.
Parker-Jervis, C. E.	...	...	13-11-1879	...	...	...	From 106th.
Wiehe, F. G. A.	...	...	7-7-1880	...	...	...	From 68th.
Darwin, C. W.	...	...	22-7-1880	...	...	...	From 68th.
Ruddach, J. W.	...	...	2-2-1881	...	...	...	From 106th.
Rosseter, H. D.	...	...	2-2-1881	...	...	...	From 106th.
Tetley, A. J.	...	...	18-5-1881	...	...	...	From 106th.
Carleton, F. R. C.	...	...	8-6-1881	...	...	...	From 68th.

APPENDIX I

Paget, A. de B. V.	...	11-2-1875	From 68th.
FitzGerald, H. S.	...	11-2-1875	From 68th.
Davison, G. M.	...	13-6-1875	From 106th.
Way, H. G.	...	28-8-1875	From 68th.
Goad, H.	...	10-9-1875	From 106th.
Norton, R.	...	20-11-1875	From 106th.
Hilliard, A. C.	...	26-2-1876	From 68th.
Saunders, G. M.	...	26-8-1876	From 106th.
Cartwright, H. A.	...	15-8-1877	From 68th.
Noel, G. T.	...	14-6-1878	From 68th.
Curling, W. K.	...	24-6-1878	From 106th.
Purdon, D. W.	...	1-11-1878	From 68th.
Maunsell, J. D.	...	5-2-1879	From 106th.
Johnson-Smyth, T. R.	...	30-4-1879	From 106th.
Talbot, E. L. K.	...	23-7-1879	From 106th.
Menzies, W. M.	...	30-10-1879	From 68th.
Thomas, H.	...	30-10-1879	From 106th.
Barker, R. B.	...	13-11-1879	From 106th.
Murphy, W. J.	...	17-11-1879	From 68th.
Hervey-Bathurst, C.	...	7-1-1880	From 106th.
Payne, A. T.	...	17-3-1880	From 68th.
Ross, W. C.	...	16-7-1880	From 68th.
Murphy, M.	...	22-7-1880	From 106th.
Kenyon-Slaney, F. G.	...	18-6-1881	From 106th.
Templer, L. G.	...	1-7-1881	From 68th.
O'Callaghan, H. P.	...	1-7-1881	From 68th.
Gunning, C. V.	...	1-7-1881	From 106th.
Vane, W. L.	...	1-7-1881	From 106th.
Robb, F. S. W.	...	1-7-1881	From 68th.
Mansel, G. C.	...	1-7-1881	From 68th.
Bush, J. E.	...	1-7-1881	From 106th.
Binyon, A. E.	...	1-7-1881	From 106th.
Wells, C. G.	...	1-7-1881	From 68th.
Parke, L.	...	1-7-1881	From 68th.
Keane, G. W.	...	1-7-1881	From 68th.
Gardiner, R. J.	...	1-7-1881	From 106th.
Brett, A.	...	...	Paymaster, Jan., 1881. From 68th.
Compigné, H. M.	...	...	Paymaster, Nov., 1878. From 106th.
Connell, P.	...	...	Quartermaster, 23-4-1873. From 106th.
Shea, W.	...	...	Quartermaster, 6-12-1873. From 68th.

231

THE DURHAM LIGHT INFANTRY

Name.	2nd Lieut.	Lieutenant.	Captain.	Major.	Lieut.-Colonel.	Colonel.	Remarks.
Weldon, William	...	...	...	...	...	...	Qr.-Mr., 7-1-1882. From Qr.-Mr.-Serjt. Retired, 1883.
Sitwell, Francis Honorius Sisson	...	28-1-1882	27-8-1890	1-1-1902*	...	...	*Cancelled, 24-6-1902. Retired, 1902.
Triphook, Simon Bagge	...	...	...	...	...	...	From half-pay; died at Ardmore, Co. Waterford, 17-10-1887.
Bagwell-Purefoy, Wilfred	...	10-5-1882	...	26-4-1882 1-7-1881	...	...	To 3rd Hussars, 1883.
Buck, William Tennant	...	10-5-1882	28-7-1891	27-8-1901	...	...	Retired, 1910.
Byrne, John William	...	...	...	...	...	...	Qr.-Mr., 20-9-1882. From Serjeant-Major; to 4th D.L.I., 1885; to 3rd D.L.I., 1886. Died at Barnard Castle, 22-1-1892.
Deane, James	...	10-3-1883	...	...	...	...	To Royal Highlanders, 1883.
de Lisle, Henry de Beauvoir	...	10-3-1883	1-10-1891	1-1-1902	...	...	Bt.-Lt.-Col., 2-1-1902; Adjt., 1892; wounded, 14-8-1900 in operations west of Pretoria; to 5th Dragoon Guards, 1902; to 1st (Royal) Dragoons, 1903; Brigadier-General; C.B., D.S.O.
Mead, Harold Richard	...	10-3-1883	...	...	...	...	To Bombay Staff Corps, 1888.
MacCartie, Joseph FitzGerald	...	10-3-1883	...	...	...	...	Died in Burmah, 12-5-1886, from wounds received, 8-5-1886, while attached to 26th Bengal N.I.
MacLaren, Thomas Geo.	...	10-3-1883	...	...	...	...	To King's Own Borderers, 1884.
Vanrenen, Adrian John Hebron	...	10-3-1883	...	...	...	...	To Scottish Rifles, 1884.
Sheehan, Thos. Vaughan	...	...	...	...	...	...	Qr.-Mr., 15-8-1883; Hon. Captain, 15-8-1893. To 4th D.L.I., 1886; retired, 1893.
Searle, Charles Thomas Arnaud	...	25-8-1883	...	...	...	...	To Bengal Staff Corps, 1889.
Burn, Wm. Augustus Farquhar	...	25-8-1883	...	...	...	...	To Middlesex Regt., 1883.
Shaw, Alexander James	...	19-12-1883	...	...	...	...	To Madras Staff Corps, 1887.
Cooper, Edmund Saffery	...	19-12-1883	...	...	...	...	To Bengal Staff Corps, 1889.
Long, Sidney Seldon	...	30-1-1884	...	...	...	...	To Army Service Corps, 1890; temp. Brigdr.-General, 1913.
Wilson, Chas. Edward	...	6-2-1884	1-10-1891	2-8-1902	29-2-1908	...	Colonel, 4-10-1911; Adjutant, 1889; to half-pay, 1912.
Baker, Alfred William	...	6-2-1884	19-4-1893	...	...	...	Died at Jebba, West Africa, 26-12-1898.

APPENDIX I

Name				Notes
Biddulph, Nicholas Trafalgar	14-5-1884	11-4-1894	26-4-1903	Retired, 1909.
Ward, Geo. Alexander	2-7-1884	...	...	From Serjeant, D.C.L.I.; to Madras Staff Corps, 1887.
Pratt, Ernest St. George	23-8-1884	11-4-1894	7-5-1903	15-8-1910 Bt.-Maj., 29-11-1900; Bt.-Lt.-Col., 23-7-1910; Adjt., 1892; Assistant Director, War Office, 1913; D.S.O.
Tweddell, Francis	23-8-1884	...	...	To Bengal Staff Corps, 1888.
Mathew, Chas. Massy	23-8-1884	11-4-1894	8-9-1903	To Army Ordnance Department, 1904; C.B., D.S.O.
Ridgway, Albert Brutton	...	...	...	Paymaster, Oct., 1884. Appears last in Army List, Aug., 1885.
Stockdale, Eustace Hervey	22-11-1884	...	...	From South Staffordshire Regt.; died at Allahabad, 19-9-1886.
Berkeley, Robert Bruce	23-8-1884	...	...	To Bengal Staff Corps, 1888.
Moss, Thomas	7-2-1885	...	...	To Bombay Staff Corps, 1888.
Mure, William Caven Lockhart	6-5-1885	...	...	To Bombay Staff Corps, 1889.
Byrne, Joseph Magee	9-5-1885	...	...	Qr.-Mr., 24-6-1885; Hon. Captain, 24-6-1895; Hon. Major, 1-1-1903. To 4th (now 3rd) D.L.I., 1893; proceeded to S. Africa with 3rd (now 4th) D.L.I. 1900; retired, 1905; recruiting duty, Co. Durham, 1906.
Fenton, Arthur FitzGerald	29-8-1885	...	...	To Bengal Staff Corps, 1888.
Cary-Elwes, Lincoln Edmund	29-8-1885	11-4-1894	3-11-1903	Retired, 1905; D.S.O.
Sugden, William	...	...	...	Paymaster, Sept., 1885. Last appears in Army List for June, 1886.
Luard, Charles Camac	2-9-1885	13-2-1895	30-5-1904	29-2-1912 Adjt., 1896. Bt.-Maj., 26-6-1902.
McMahon, Bernard Wm. Lynedoch	25-11-1885	26-4-1896	10-6-1905	28-7-1913 Adjt., 1896. Bt.-Maj., 29-11-1900.
Goring-Jones, Michael Derwass	30-1-1886	6-5-1896	15-8-1906	
Purvis, Herbert John Edward	30-1-1886	...	...	To Bombay Staff Corps, 1890.
Cragg, Albert Charles	28-4-1886	...	...	Resigned, 1890.
Dowdall, Laurence Richard	...	...	...	Paymaster, July, 1886. Appears last in Army List, July, 1890.

THE DURHAM LIGHT INFANTRY

Name.	2nd Lieut.	Lieutenant.	Captain.	Major.	Lieut. Colonel.	Colonel.	Remarks.
Gordon, Harry Laurence	...	25-8-1886	...	...	...	...	To Bombay Staff Corps, 1889.
Qualtrough, Wm. John	...	...	...	...	...	...	Qr.-Mr., 1-9-1886; Hon. Captain, 1-9-1896. Retired, 1898.
Harrison, Claude Edwd.	...	...	13-11-1886 19-3-1885	...	...	...	From Essex Regt.; resigned, 1887.
Chisholm-Batten, James Forbes	...	...	...	...	...	...	Paymaster, Dec., 1886. Formerly Ensign, 68th L.I. Appears last in Army List, Oct., 1888. To Indian Staff Corps, 1892.
Ford, Chas. Annesley Wilbraham	14-9-1887	3-7-1889	...	...	...	...	Retired, 1902.
D'Arcy-Hildyard, Robt. Maxwell	14-9-1887	20-11-1889	25-8-1896	...	...	...	Died at Monte Carlo, 12-2-1893.
Lascelles, Alexander Charles	16-11-1887	20-11-1889	...	...	...	...	To Bengal Staff Corps, 1890.
Dunsford, Francis Pearson Shaw	16-11-1887	...	...	...	...	...	From Serjeant, Lancashire Fus.; retired, 1899.
Iremonger, Edgar Asshton	21-12-1887	20-11-1889	31-10-1896	...	...	...	To Indian Staff Corps, 1893.
Eardley-Wilmot, Ernest	11-2-1888	12-3-1890	...	...	...	...	To Indian Staff Corps, 1891.
Lloyd, Wm. Edmund Eyre	11-2-1888	...	...	...	...	...	To Bengal Staff Corps, 1890.
Birch, Fredk. Wm.	11-2-1888	...	...	...	...	...	*Antedated, 27-8-1890. To Indian Staff Corps, 1893.
Lees, Clarence Edward	28-8-1888	24-9-1890*	...	...	...	...	*Antedated, 27-8-1890. Resigned, 1896; Lt.-Col., 2nd V.B. Royal Scots Fusiliers, 1896; Hon. Col., 2nd V.B. Royal Scots Fus., 1906. Retired, 1913.
Robertson-Glasgow, Robert Purdon	22-8-1888	24-9-1890*	...	...	...	...	
Bell, Robert Francis	22-8-1888	27-8-1890	16-12-1896	26-6-1907	...	...	Colonel, 9-6-1886. (See Appendix II.)
Upcher, Russell	...	...	...	...	31-10-1888 9-6-1882	11-9-1908	Severely wounded at Vaal Krantz, 5-2-1900; to half-pay, 1901; D.S.O.; died at Bishop Cleeve, Cheltenham, 18-5-1911.
Lascelles, Walter Chas.	28-11-1888	25-2-1891	1-1-1897	...	...	...	To Army Service Corps, 1892.
Grey, Charles William	29-12-1888	25-2-1891	...	...	...	...	Retired, 1912.
Saville, Robert Charles	30-1-1889	10-5-1891	1-4-1897	29-2-1908	...	...	Died at Newcastle-on-Tyne, 29-7-1894.
Casement, Joshua Bernard	30-1-1889	22-6-1891	...	...	...	...	*Antedated, 28-7-1891; Bt.-Major, 29-11-1900.
Cumming, Hanway Robert	8-6-1889	15-8-1891*	24-11-1897	...	...	...	

APPENDIX I

Name				Notes
Harter, Oswald Birley	8-6-1889	15-8-1891	19-1-1898	…	To Army Ordnance Department, 1909.
Hales, Ernest Baseley	8-6-1889	1-10-1891*23-11-1898 28-9-1909		15-8-1910	*Antedated, 19-9-1891. Temporary half-pay, 1909; from half-pay, 28-9-1909; retired, 1911.
Bridge, Walter Sydney	26-6-1889	3-2-1892	…	…	From Serjeant, 6th Dragoon Gds.; resigned, 1893; Captain, Reserve of Officers, 11-9-1901.
Young, David Coley	21-9-1889	…	…	…	To Indian Staff Corps, 1893.
Morant, Hubert Horatio Shirley	16-10-1889	19-11-1892	9-8-1899	23-5-1910	Served with Egyptian Army, 1898-1908; has Medjidie 4th Class and Osmanieh, 4th Class.
Simson, Henry	1-3-1890	…	…	…	Died at Poonah, 15-8-1892.
Tucker, Aubrey Chas.	29-11-1890	15-3-1893	9-8-1899	…	Retired, 1907; Captain and Hon. Major, 3rd Battn. Welsh Regt., 1908.
Owen-Lewis, Francis	18-2-1891	15-3-1893	…	…	To Indian Staff Corps, 1896.
Bridges, Arthur Holroyd	25-3-1891	…	…	…	To Indian Staff Corps, 1893; served with 1st D.L.I. in South Africa, 1899-1900.
Crosthwaite, Joseph Arthur	9-9-1891	19-4-1893	9-10-1899	24-6-1911	
Anderson, Robt. Holme	10-10-1891	11-4-1894	…	…	To Indian Staff Corps, 1896.
Bacon, Anthony Edwd. Mortimer	10-10-1891	11-4-1894	21-10-1899	…	Retired, 1902; Captain, 4th (now 3rd) D.L.I., 1902.
Loring, Charles Buxton	7-11-1891	10-6-1894	…	…	To Indian Staff Corps, 1895.
Holder, Arthur John	5-12-1891	10-6-1894	…	…	Died at Mhow, 3-8-1894.
Wilkinson, Henry Benfield Des Voeux	9-1-1892	30-7-1894*11-11-1899		29-2-1912	*Antedated, 20-7-1894.
Oakes, Horace Charles	12-3-1892	4-8-1894*	…	…	*Antedated, 30-7-1894. To Indian Staff Corps, 1897.
Parkes, James Arthur	…	…	…	…	Q.M., 31-12-1887—16-3-1892; Hon. Capt., 31-12-1897. From 3rd Bn. Scottish Rifles; 3rd D.L.I.; retired, 1900.
Stewart, Archibald Francis	28-9-1892	4-8-1894	…	…	To Indian Staff Corps, 1899.
Martin, Frank	28-9-1892	13-2-1895	…	…	To Indian Staff Corps, 1895.
Mander, D'Arcy Wentworth	17-12-1892	12-2-1896	14-1-1900	2-12-1912	To Indian Staff Corps, 1898.
Fairfax, Bryan Charles	8-3-1893	26-4-1896	19-2-1900*	…	*Antedated, 7-2-1900. Retired, 1914.

235

THE DURHAM LIGHT INFANTRY

Name.	2nd Lieut.	Lieutenant.	Captain.	Major.	Lieut.-Colonel.	Colonel.	Remarks.
Blake, Edward Algernon Cleader	26-4-1893	6-5-1896	7-2-1900	28-7-1913	...	...	Wounded at Vaal Krantz, 5-2-1900; Adjt., 1901; Bt.-Maj., 22-8-1902.
Robb, Alexander Kirkland	20-5-1893	21-5-1896	19-2-1900	23-8-1913	...	...	
Ainsworth, William John	19-7-1893	23-7-1896	11-9-1901*	...	...	...	*Antedated, 2-7-1901. Adjutant, 1901; D.S.O.
Liebrecht, John Henry	...	...	...	...	...	...	Qr.-Mr., 4-10-1893; Hon. Captain, 29-11-1900. From Serjeant-Major; to half-pay, 1903.
Moore, Edward Du Pré Herford	2-6-1894	25-8-1896	11-9-1901	...	...	...	
Cochrane, George Leslie	13-6-1894	31-10-1896	11-9-1901	...	...	...	Retired, 1910; Captain, 3rd (late 4th) D.L.I., 1910.
Fyers, Wm. Augustus	...	...	...	...	...	26-5-1894	(See Appendix II.)
Corbett, Chas. Clarence	10-10-1894	...	...	...	...	...	Died at Mhow, 21-1-1896.
Carter, Frederic Hugh	10-10-1894	...	...	...	...	...	Died at Mhow, 15-9-1895.
Lang, Eustache Arthur	10-10-1894	14-4-1897*26-11-1901	...	...	...	...	*Antedated, 22-3-1897. To Army Pay Department, 1905.
Hall, Ralph Ellis Carr	12-12-1894	28-7-1897	...	...	...	...	To Indian Staff Corps, 1896.
Davies, John Murray	6-3-1895	16-12-1896	26-11-1901	...	...	...	Died, 31-8-1898, at Poona.
Northey, William	28-9-1895	28-7-1897	...	...	...	...	D.S.O.
Way, Arthur Strachan	26-2-1896	...	...	...	...	...	Killed at Tabaksberg, S. Africa, 29-1-1901.
Gregory, Godfrey Levinge	25-3-1896 29-2-1896	...	...	...	...	...	From Royal Irish Regt.; resigned, 1898.
Tyndall, Robert	12-8-1896 6-6-1896	4-12-1897	22-1-1902	...	...	...	From South Staffordshire Regt.
Gibson, William	12-8-1896	19-1-1898	29-3-1902	...	...	...	Retired, 1911.
Ashburner, Lionel Forbes	16-9-1896*	24-11-1897	...	...	...	...	*Antedated, 16-1-1895, 18-5-1896. From Indian Staff Corps; to Royal Fusiliers, 1901; D.S.O., M.V.O., 4th Class.
Cartwright, Alfred Leonard	23-9-1896	29-3-1898	24-5-1902	...	...	...	From Serjeant, Northmbd. Fus.
Soltau-Symons, Lionel Culme	9-12-1896	1-9-1898	5-2-1908 19-2-1902	...	...	...	Wounded at Inniskilling Hill, S. Africa, 24-2-1900. To R. Warwickshire Regt., 19-2-1902; from R. Warwickshire Regt., 5-2-1908.
Unthank, John Salusbury	9-12-1896	23-11-1898	24-5-1902	...	...	...	
Duncan, Henry Clare	20-2-1897	19-8-1899	...	...	...	...	To Indian Staff Corps, 1901.

APPENDIX I

Name				Notes
Irvine, Alfred Ernest	24-3-1897	9-10-1899	5-6-1903	...
Thresher, Edward Burnaby	15-5-1897	21-10-1899	...	... Adjutant, 1900; died at Standerton, S. Africa, 9-4-1901.
Brereton, David Lloyd	28-7-1897	11-11-1899	12-6-1903	...
Watts, Herbert Ponsonby	1-12-1897	7-12-1899	...	... To Indian Staff Corps, 1901. (See Appendix II.)
Gipps, Reginald	...	...	...	17-12-1897 Killed at Vaal Krantz, 5-2-1900.
Shafto, Chas. Duncombe	16-2-1898	14-1-1900	...	... Adjutant, 1905.
Tyler, Roper Maxwell	16-2-1898	7-2-1900	12-6-1903	...
Jeffreys, John William	4-5-1898	7-2-1900	31-7-1903	... Wounded at Vaal Krantz, 5-2-1900; wounded at Roberts' Drift, Vaal River, 6-9-1901; Adjutant, 1904.
Matthews, Claud Leonard	4-5-1898	19-2-1900	22-1-1904	... Adjutant, 1907.
Wallace, Arthur Wm. Baillie	18-5-1898	18-4-1900	13-5-1905	...
Long, Thomas Francis	...	...	...	... Qr.-Mr., 28-9-1888; Hon. Captain, 28-9-1908; Hon. Major, 28-9-1913. From Serjt.-Maj.; to 4th (now 3rd) D.L.I., 1905; retired, 1914.
Maughan, Francis Gilfrid	4-1-1899	1-8-1900	30-5-1904	... Adjutant, 1908.
Lambton, Ronald Robt.	20-5-1899	30-1-1901*	...	... *Antedated, 2-11-1900. Wounded at Vaal Krantz, 5-2-1900; killed near Blood River Poort, South Africa, 17-9-1901.
Leather, Kenneth John Walters	27-9-1899	15-3-1901	...	... *Antedated, 21-1-1901. Resigned, 1904; Major, 4th D.L.I., 1912.
Rasbotham, Roger Egerton	18-10-1899	15-3-1901*	...	... *Antedated, 30-1-1901. Killed at Eden Kop, S. Africa, 16-6-1901.
Nickalls, Patteson Womersley	18-10-1899	10-4-1901	...	... Resigned, 1901.
Appleby, Ernest Walton	18-10-1899	23-6-1901*	...	... *Antedated, 15-3-1901. Wounded at Vaal Krantz, 5-2-1900; resigned, 1902.
Dent, Wilfrid Harry	...	...	11-11-1899	... From Yorkshire Rgt.; retired, 1907.
Hamilton-Grace, Raymond Sheffield	20-1-1900	23-6-1901*	10-6-1905	... *Antedated, 30-5-1901. To 18th Hussars, 1909.
Whitby, Henry Frank	20-1-1900	3-7-1901*	...	... *Antedated, 23-6-1901. To Indian Army, 1904.
Phillips, Lionel	21-2-1900	3-7-1901*	...	... *Antedated, 25-6-1901. To Indian Army, 1905.
Bowers, Arthur Hugh Maunsell	21-2-1900	13-7-1901*	29-1-1909	... *Antedated, 3-7-1901.

Name.	2nd Lieut.	Lieutenant.	Captain.	Major.	Lieut.-Colonel.	Colonel.	Remarks.
Preston, Hon. Jenico Edward Joseph	7-3-1900	...	...	...	...	...	Appointment cancelled, 1900.
Evans, David Howard	7-3-1900	...	...	...	...	...	Appointment cancelled, 1900.
Butler, Hon. Lesley James Probyn	28-3-1900	...	...	...	...	...	To Irish Guards, 1901.
Splaine, Wm. Young	...	...	...	...	...	...	Qr.-Mr., 10-3-1900. 3rd (now 4th) D.L.I.; from Q.M.S.; retired, 1910.
Franklyn, Henry Arden	18-4-1900	23-9-1901	...	...	...	...	*Antedated, 11-9-1901. Resigned, 1906.
Lavie, Henry Ernest	18-4-1900	23-9-1901	26-4-1909	...	...	...	*Antedated, 13-7-1901.
Wood, John Hardy	21-4-1900	19-2-1902	2-6-1909	...	...	...	*Antedated, 23-9-1901.
Lovering, Wm. Reginald	11-8-1900	19-2-1902	29-3-1912	...	...	...	Removed from the Service for absence without leave, 7-4-1914.
Hare, Harry Vivian	11-8-1900	19-2-1902	29-3-1912	...	...	...	Adjutant, 1911.
Garsia, Aubrey Christie Haly	15-1-1901	26-11-1901	...	...	...	...	From 4th New Zealand Contingent; died in Kashmir, 8-7-1905.
Coddington, Hubert John	5-1-1901	26-4-1902	1-1-1913	...	...	...	*Antedated, 29-3-1902. Wounded at Leeuw Kop, South Africa, in (or about) August, 1901.
Whittingham, Charles Herbert	27-2-1901	26-4-1902	...	...	...	...	From Col.-Serjt., Gren. Gds.; retired, 1908; is in Egyptian Slavery Suppression Department.
Turner, Robert Villiers	9-3-1901	24-5-1902	27-5-1914*	...	...	...	*Antedated, 7-4-1914. From unattached list.
Hartley, Alan Fleming	8-1-1901	5-6-1903	...	...	...	...	From unattached list; to Indian Army, 1905.
Blewitt, Baker Arthur Rawson	9-3-1901	12-6-1903	...	...	...	...	From unattached list; to Indian Army, 1905.
Richardson, Henry	4-5-1901	12-6-1903	...	...	...	...	From unattached list; retired, 1910; Captain, 3rd D.L.I., 1910.
Greenwell, Wm. Basil	4-5-1901	31-7-1903	27-5-1914*	...	...	...	*Antedated, 7-4-1914. Adjt., 1913.
Hudson-Kinahan, Geo. Frederick	4-5-1901	22-1-1904	27-5-1914	...	...	...	
Festing, Hubert Wogan	11-5-1901	14-7-1904*	...	...	...	...	*Antedated, 30-5-1904. Adjt., 1910.
Peareth, John Twisden	26-6-1901	...	...	...	...	...	Resigned, 1904.
Manger, Edwd. Vincent	3-8-1901	6-8-1904*	...	...	...	...	*Antedated, 14-7-1904.
Rowlandson, Christopher Orlebar	14-9-1901	6-8-1904*	...	...	...	...	*Antedated, 14-7-1904. To half-pay, 1907; died, 16-4-1909.
Palk, Wilmot Lawrence Lancelot	14-9-1901	6-8-1904	...	...	...	...	Resigned, 1905; formerly Midshipman, R.N.

APPENDIX I

Gillespie, John Gilbert	19-10-1901	19-10-1904*	…	*Antedated, 18-8-1904. Resigned, 1908; Lieutenant, Warwickshire Yeomanry, 1911.
Taylor, Henry Jefferys	4-12-1901	19-10-1904	…	
Woodhouse, Percy St. John Rance	18-1-1902	14-1-1905	…	To Indian Army, 1906.
Godsal, Walter Hugh	18-1-1902	13-5-1905*	…	*Antedated, 10-5-1905. Adjt., 1913.
St. John, Hon. Rowland Tudor	18-1-1902	10-6-1905	…	*Antedated, 13-5-1905.
Phillips, George Wm. Fisher	29-1-1902	8-7-1905	…	*Antedated, 10-6-1905.
Shirreff, Charles Richd.	23-4-1902	9-7-1905	…	Resigned, 1906.
Jackson, Hugh Nicholas	30-4-1902	…	…	To Indian Army, 1904.
Lascelles, Reginald Geo.	30-4-1902	…	…	Drowned at Cannanore, Madras, 16-8-1904.
Hartcup, Wm. Richard Monyns	30-4-1902	7-10-1905	…	
Dallas, Alister Grant	…	22-10-1902 27-11-1901	…	From 16th Lancers; half-pay, Lieut.-Colonel, 1907.
Freel, Joseph	…	…	…	Qr.-Mr., 21-2-1903; Hon. Captain, 21-2-1913. From Serjt.-Major.
Smyth-Pigott, Bernard Cecil	26-9-1903	23-6-1906	…	Resigned, 1905.
James, Walter	26-9-1903	…	…	*Antedated, 30-9-1906. Resigned, 1910.
Shafto, Frederic Chas. Duncombe	17-2-1904	19-12-1906*	…	Resigned, 1906.
Morton, Herbert Henry Powys	4-6-1904	…	…	
McCullagh, Herbert Rochfort	3-12-1904	25-6-1908	…	
Congreve, Chas. Ralph	28-1-1905	19-9-1908	…	
Wyllie, Wm. Thomas	20-5-1905	30-12-1908	…	
Gilpin, Ernest Henry	20-5-1905	2-6-1909	…	
Clements, Thomas	…	…	…	Qr.-Mr., 10-5-1905. From Serjt.-Major; to 3rd D.L.I., 1914.
Warren, John Frederick	16-8-1905	8-1-1910	…	
Smith, Robert Cecil	16-8-1905	23-2-1910	…	To Indian Army, 1908.
Shute, Cyril Aveling	16-8-1905	…	…	From Royal Garrison Regt.
Birt, Ernest William	…	13-9-1905 7-11-1903	…	
Fordyce, Ernle Lawrence Dingwall	29-11-1905	…	…	To Indian Army, 1910.

THE DURHAM LIGHT INFANTRY

Name.	2nd Lieut.	Lieutenant.	Captain.	Major.	Lieut.-Colonel.	Colonel.	Remarks.
Coote, Mervyn Chidley	29-11-1905	1-4-1910	...	...	...	...	To Indian Army, 1910.
Twist, Wilfrid Bernard	23-5-1906	10-4-1910	...	...	...	...	
Churchill, John Atherton	23-8-1906	...	...	...	...	...	
de Bunsen, Arnold George	29-12-1906	17-7-1911	...	...	...	...	From Manchester Regt.
Boxer, Hugh Caldwell	...	6-3-1907	...	...	...	...	
Hayes, Geoffrey ...	4-5-1907	4-1-1912	...	...	...	...	From Lancashire Fusiliers.
Stoker, Robert John Graham	...	29-1-1908 5-10-1901	2-6-1909	...	...	...	
Harter, John George	2-9-1908	4-3-1912	...	...	...	...	
Spooner, Reginald Frederick	28-11-1908	29-3-1912	...	...	...	...	Resigned, 1913.
Grey-Wilson, William Arthur	6-2-1909	23-10-1912	...	...	...	...	
Clifton, Arthur John ...	13-10-1909	6-9-1913 2-10-1912	...	...	...	...	From Bombr., R.F.A.; to A.S.C., 18-10-1912; from A.S.C., 6-9-1913.
Rountree, Arthur Noel	6-11-1909	23-8-1913	...	...	...	...	
Whan, Samuel	...	...	...	...	...	...	Qr.-Mr., 19-3-1910. From Serjt.-Major; 4th D.L.I. Resigned, 1912.
Vandeleur, John Beauclerk	6-4-1910	...	...	...	...	...	
Hasted, John Ord Cobbold	20-4-1910	7-11-1913	...	...	...	...	
Swetenham, Edmund	20-4-1910	...	...	...	...	...	
Norton, Leopold Grantly	28-5-1910	...	...	...	...	...	
Drysdale, John Ebenezer	24-8-1910	23-10-1912	...	...	...	...	From unattached list, Terrl. Force; to Army Service Corps, 1913.
Parke, Walter Evelyn	6-11-1909	...	...	...	...	...	
Yate, Victor Alexander Campbell	16-8-1911 20-9-1911	...	...	...	...	...	
Green, Charles Henry	14-2-1912	...	...	...	...	...	
Ferguson, John Frederick	14-2-1912	...	...	...	...	...	
Bradford, Roland Boys	22-5-1912	...	...	...	...	...	
Smith, Percival Arnold	22-5-1912	...	...	...	...	...	
Carr-Ellison, Thomas Fenwicke Clennell	4-9-1912	...	...	...	...	...	
Conant, Nigel Cecil Peter	4-12-1912	...	...	...	...	...	

APPENDIX I

Lysaght-Griffin, Edward	3-9-1913	...
Henry Lysaght		
Stanuell, Chas. Martin	24-1-1914	...
Beart, Chas. Wm.	25-2-1914	...
Lambert-Shea, Joseph Patrick	... ...	Qr.-Mr., 25-3-1914. From Serjeant-Major.

241 R

[APPENDIX II.

COLONELS OF THE 68TH REGIMENT OF FOOT.

(i.) JOHN LAMBTON.

Appointed 22nd April, 1758.

JOHN LAMBTON, fourth son of Ralph Lambton, Esq., of Lambton, Co. Durham, by his marriage with Dorothy, daughter of John Hedworth, Esq., of Harraton, Co. Durham; born 26th July, 1710.

Ensign and Lieutenant, Coldstream Guards, 12th October, 1732; Lieutenant and Captain, 1739; Captain and Lieutenant-Colonel, 24th January, 1746; was Quartermaster from 1742 to 1745.

Was present with the Coldstream Guards at the battle of Fontenoy, 30th April (11th May, N.S.), 1745.

When senior Captain and Lieutenant-Colonel of the Coldstream Guards was appointed Colonel of the newly-formed 68th Regiment in April, 1758, and held that appointment for the rest of his life. Commanded the 68th in person in the three expeditions to France in 1758.

Major-General, 26th February, 1761; Lieutenant-General, 30th April, 1770; General, 20th November, 1782.

General Lambton married, on 5th September, 1763, Lady Susan Lyon, eldest daughter of Thomas, 8th Earl of Strathmore, and by her, who died in 1769, was the father of two sons and two daughters; his elder son, William Henry, was father of the first Earl of Durham; his younger son was the celebrated Ralph Lambton.

In 1761, on the death of his eldest brother, Henry, who was M.P. for Durham City, General Lambton was elected M.P. in his place, and continued to represent Durham City continuously in five Parliaments, until he retired in February, 1787.

In 1774, in consequence of the death of both his other brothers, General Lambton became the head of the Lambton family. Died 22nd March, 1794.

APPENDIX II

(ii.) JOHN MANSELL.

Appointed 26th March, 1794.

JOHN MANSELL was appointed Cornet, 3rd Dragoon Guards, in 1753 or 1754, and served in that regiment for nearly thirty years; Lieutenant in the light troop 25th December, 1755; Captain, 20th January, 1759; Major, 11th May, 1770; Lieutenant-Colonel, 27th April, 1775; Colonel in the Army, 16th May, 1782; Major-General. Died April, 1794.

(iii.) THOMAS DUNDAS.

Appointed 30th April, 1794.

THOMAS DUNDAS was born 30th June, 1750. Cornet, King's Dragoon Guards, 25th April, 1766; Captain, 63rd Foot, 20th May, 1769; Major, 65th Foot, 20th January, 1776; Lieutenant-Colonel, 80th Foot (Royal Edinboro' Volunteers), 17th December, 1777—[the 80th was disbanded in 1783]—Brevet-Colonel, 20th July, 1782. M.P. for Orkney and Shetland, 1771, 1774, and 1784. Joint Commissioner for arranging the capitulation at York Town, 1781. Major-General, 1793. Died 3rd June, 1794, at Guadaloupe, where he was in command. There is a monument to him in the north transept of St. Paul's Cathedral.

(iv.) ALURED CLARKE.

Appointed 6th August, 1794.

ALURED CLARKE was born in 1745. Ensign, 50th Foot, 20th March, 1759; Lieutenant, 50th Foot, 1760; Captain, 5th Foot, 1767; Major, 54th Foot, 1771; Lieutenant-Colonel, 54th Foot, 1775; exchanged to 7th Foot, 1777; Colonel, 1st 60th, 8th July, 1791; to

68th, 1794; to 5th Foot, 25th October, 1794; to 7th Foot, 23rd August, 1801.

Lieutenant-Governor of Jamaica, 1782-90. Present at the capitulation of Cape Colony, 16th March, 1795. Commander-in-Chief, Bengal, 1797. Commander-in-Chief, India, 1798-1801. K.B.

Promoted to Field-Marshal on the accession of H.M. King William IV. Died 16th September, 1832.

(v.) HON. CHARLES STUART.

Appointed 25th October, 1794.

The Hon. CHARLES STUART, fourth son of John, 3rd Earl of Bute; born January, 1753.

Ensign, 37th Foot, 1768; Captain, 35th Foot, 1773; Lieutenant-Colonel, 26th Foot, 1777, with which regiment he served during the American War. Employed in the Mediterranean, 1794-5, and made himself master of Corsica. Captured Minorca, 7th November, 1798, and somewhat later La Vallete, Malta. To 26th Foot, as Colonel, 25th March, 1795. K.B.; Major-General, 1793; Lieutenant-General, 1798. Died at Richmond Lodge, 25th March, 1801.

(vi.) THOMAS TRIGGE.

Appointed 25th March, 1795.

THOMAS TRIGGE was appointed Ensign, 12th Foot, 6th October, 1757; Lieutenant, 26th August, 1759; Captain, 14th March, 1765; Major, 17th November, 1773; Lieutenant-Colonel, 6th June, 1778. All his regimental service was in the 12th Foot. Served in Corsica, 1794. Lieutenant-Governor of Portsmouth. Commander-in-Chief in Leeward Islands, 1798. Captured (i.) St. Bartholomew, (ii.) St. Martin, (iii.) St. John, (iv.) St. Thomas, and (v.) St. Croix, 1801. Lieutenant-General of Ordnance, 1804.

APPENDIX II

Major-General, 12th October, 1793; Lieutenant-General, 1st January, 1798; General, 25th September, 1803. K.B.; to 44th Foot, as Colonel, 27th May, 1809.

(vii.) JOHN COAPE SHERBROOKE.

Appointed 27th May, 1809.

JOHN COAPE SHERBROOKE was born 1764. Ensign, 4th Foot, 7th December, 1780; Lieutenant, 4th Foot, 22nd December, 1781; Captain, 85th Foot, 6th March, 1783; to 33rd Foot, 23rd June, 1784; Major, 33rd Foot, 30th September, 1793; Lieutenant-Colonel, 33rd Foot, 24th May, 1794. Served in the Netherlands, 1794, and in Mysore, 1799; commanded the right column at the storming of Seringapatam, 4th May, 1799; General Officer Commanding, 1st Division, in the Peninsula, 1809; Lieutenant-Governor of Nova Scotia, 1814; Governor-General of Canada, 1816-18; Major-General, 1st January, 1805; Lieutenant-General, 4th June, 1811; General, 27th May, 1825. G.C.B.; had medal for Talavera.

Colonel, Sicilian Regiment, 1807; Colonel, 3rd West India Regiment. To 33rd Foot, as Colonel, 1st January, 1813. Died 14th February, 1830.

(viii.) HENRY WARDE.

Appointed 1st January, 1813.

HENRY WARDE was born 7th January, 1766. Ensign and Lieutenant, 1st (Grenadier) Guards, 1783; Lieutenant and Captain, 6th July, 1790; Captain and Lieutenant-Colonel, 11th October, 1794; Colonel in the Army, 1st January, 1801. Wounded at Valenciennes, 1793. Officer Commanding Brigade of Guards, in Spain, 1808. Took part in capture of Mauritius, 1810; Governor of Mauritius, 1811-13; Governor of Barbadoes, 1821-7.

THE DURHAM LIGHT INFANTRY

Major-General, 25th April, 1808; Lieutenant-General, 4th June, 1813; General, 22nd July, 1830. G.C.B.; to 31st Foot, as Colonel, 12th April, 1831. Died 1st October, 1834.

(ix.) JOHN KEANE.

Appointed 13th April, 1831.

JOHN KEANE, second son of Sir John Keane, 1st Bart., of Belmont, Co. Waterford; born 6th February, 1781. Received first commission as Captain, 124th Foot, 12th November, 1794; subsequently in 44th, 60th, and 13th Foot; Brevet-Colonel, 5/60th, 1812.

Present at reduction of Martinique, 1809; Officer Commanding a brigade of 3rd Division, at Vittoria, Pyrenees, and Toulouse, 1813-14; at New Orleans, 8th January, 1815; Commander-in-Chief, Bombay, 1834-9; took Ghazni and occupied Kabul, 1839. Major-General, 4th June, 1814; Lieutenant-General, 22nd July, 1830. G.C.B., G.C.H.; created a peer (Baron Keane of Ghazni and Cappoquin). Appointed Colonel, 68th, from Colonel 94th Foot; afterwards Colonel 43rd Light Infantry. Died at Burton Lodge, Hants, 26th August, 1844.

(x.) WILLIAM JOHNSTON.

Appointed 6th April, 1838.

WILLIAM JOHNSTON was born 1773. Ensign, 18th Foot, 3rd June, 1791; Lieutenant, 18th Foot, 7th January, 1794. Served in 18th when it was sent, in 1793, to Toulon, as part of a force which held that town for two months against an enemy of four times its numbers; it was in this siege that the great Napoleon first made the acquaintance of the British soldier, and received a deep bayonet wound in his left thigh. Lieutenant Johnston, as he then was, proceeded with the 18th to Corsica, where he was wounded, and where he was temporarily

APPENDIX II

a Captain in Smith's Corsican Regiment. Captain, 4th April, 1795; was in Tuscany 1797, but returned to England and went on half-pay in 1798; while on half-pay served in a yeomanry corps against the rebels in Ireland, 1798.

Became Captain, 9th Foot, and purchased majority in 68th, 27th February, 1800; Lieutenant-Colonel, 25th April, 1808; commanded 68th in Walcheren and the Peninsula; severely wounded at Vittoria; Colonel, 4th June, 1814; Major-General, 27th May, 1825; Lieutenant-General, 28th June, 1838; K.C.B. Medal for Peninsula, with two clasps. Died at Southampton, 23rd January, 1844.

(xi.) EDWARD GIBBS.

Appointed 21st February, 1844.

EDWARD GIBBS was appointed Ensign, 59th Foot, 14th October, 1798; Lieutenant, 52nd Foot, 28th October, 1799; Captain, 24th February, 1803; Major, 4th February, 1808; Lieutenant-Colonel, half pay, 6th February, 1812; Lieutenant-Colonel, 52nd Light Infantry, 4th April, 1813; Colonel and A.D.C. to the King, 27th May, 1825; Major-General, 10th January, 1837. Governor of Jersey, 1844; C.B., K.C.H.

Served at Ferrol, 1800; Sicily, 1806-7; Corunna, Ciudad Rodrigo, Badajoz, Vittoria, etc., and Antwerp, 1813. Lost his left eye at Badajoz. To 52nd Light Infantry, as Colonel, 7th December, 1844.

(xii.) CHARLES NICOL.

Appointed 7th December, 1844.

CHARLES NICOL was appointed Ensign, 16th Foot, 24th June, 1795; Lieutenant, 16th Foot, 31st August, 1795; Captain, 16th Foot,

THE DURHAM LIGHT INFANTRY

26th August, 1799; Captain, 84th Foot, 14th September, 1809; Lieutenant-Colonel, 66th Foot, 13th June, 1811; Colonel in the Army, 27th May, 1825; Major-General, 10th January, 1837; Lieutenant-General, 9th November, 1846; C.B.; Commanding Officer, 66th Foot, in Peninsula; General Officer Commanding a division, under Sir D. Ochterlony, in Nepal War.

(xiii.) DOUGLAS MERCER (later DOUGLAS MERCER HENDERSON).

Appointed 31st January, 1850.

DOUGLAS MERCER was appointed Ensign and Lieutenant, 3rd Foot Guards, 24th March, 1803; Lieutenant and Captain, 20th March, 1806; Captain and Lieutenant-Colonel, 20th December, 1813; Colonel in the Army, 22nd July, 1830. Served with 3rd Foot Guards in Hanover, 1805, Walcheren, and in Peninsula; was at Waterloo, 15th June, 1815. Major-General, 23rd November, 1841; Lieutenant-General, 11th November, 1851; C.B.

(xiv.) WILLIAM LEWIS HERRIES.

Appointed 17th May, 1854.

WILLIAM LEWIS HERRIES was appointed Cornet, 19th Light Dragoons, 23rd January, 1801; Lieutenant, 19th Light Dragoons, 17th March, 1803; to 9th Light Dragoons, 14th April, 1804; Captain King's Dragoon Guards, 19th October, 1809; Captain, Meuron's Regiment, 18th June, 1812; Major, 2nd June, 1814; Lieutenant-Colonel, half-pay, 31st July, 1817; Colonel, 10th January, 1837; D.Q.M.G. in Mediterranean.

Major-General, 9th November, 1846; Lieutenant-General, 20th June, 1854; C.B., K.C.H. Served in Buenos Ayres, 1808, Walcheren, and in Peninsula. Lost his left leg at Bayonne, 14th April, 1814.

APPENDIX II

(xv.) ROBERT CHRISTOPHER MANSEL

Appointed 4th June, 1857.

ROBERT CHRISTOPHER MANSEL was appointed Ensign, 10th Foot, 29th January, 1807; Lieutenant, 10th Foot, 25th January, 1808; Captain, 53rd Foot, 8th July, 1813; to 93rd Foot, 1820; Major, 19th April, 1821; to 96th Foot, 9th June, 1825; Lieutenant-Colonel, half-pay, 10th June, 1826.

Major-General, 11th November, 1851; Lieutenant-General, 26th October, 1858; K.H. Served with 10th Foot in the Mediterranean, and with 53rd Foot in Peninsula. Severely wounded at Toulouse, 10th April, 1814. Died 8th April, 1864.

(xvi.) LORD WILLIAM PAULET.

Appointed 9th April, 1864.

LORD WILLIAM PAULET, fourth son of Charles Ingoldsby, 13th Marquis of Winchester, by his marriage with Anne, second daughter of J. Andrews, Esq., of Shotley Hall, Northumberland; born 7th July, 1804.

Educated at Eton. Received his first commission in the Army as Ensign, 85th Light Infantry, 1st February, 1821; Lieutenant, 7th Fusiliers, 23rd August, 1822; then served again in the 85th, and then in 63rd Foot, and in 21st Fusiliers.

Captain, 12th February, 1825; Major, 10th September, 1830; Lieutenant-Colonel, 21st April, 1843; Colonel, 20th June, 1854; Major-General, 13th June, 1858; Lieutenant-General, 8th December, 1867; General, 7th October, 1874; Field-Marshal, 10th July, 1886.

On 18th January, 1833, Lord William exchanged to the 68th, in which regiment he served for ten years as a major, and for nearly five years as lieutenant-colonel commanding.

Was A.A.G. of the cavalry division in the Crimea, and was present at the Alma, Inkerman, Sevastopol, and Balaklava, at which last-named action he had his hat shot off.

THE DURHAM LIGHT INFANTRY

On 23rd November, 1854, was appointed to the command of the Bosphorus, Gallipoli, and the Dardanelles; after the fall of Sevastopol was appointed to the command of the Light Division. At the conclusion of the war was awarded the medal, with four clasps, the C.B., officer of the Legion of Honour, 3rd class Medjidie, Sardinian, and Turkish Medals.

Lord William commanded the 1st Infantry Brigade at Aldershot from 1856 to 1860, and the South-Western District at Portsmouth from 1860 to 1865; he was Adjutant-General of the Army from 1865 to 1870.

After being Colonel of the 87th Fusiliers for a short period, he was appointed colonel of the 68th in April, 1864, and held that appointment until his death.

Lord William died 10th May, 1893, at his residence, 18, St. James's Square, London, and was buried at Amport St. Mary, Hants, 13th May; his funeral was attended by H.R.H. the Duke of Cambridge, and by the 68th—the whole battalion—in review order, with band and colours.

The welfare of his regiment was its colonel's first thoughts, and he was always ready to use his influence for the benefit of all ranks.

Lord William became a K.C.B. 1865, and a G.C.B. 1870. He was unmarried.

COLONELS COMMANDANT OF THE 68TH REGIMENT OF FOOT.

During the period, 1800—1802, that the regiment was divided into two battalions, there was a "colonel commandant," junior to the colonel, on the strength.

(i.) CHARLES EUSTACE.

Appointed 7th March, 1800.

CHARLES EUSTACE was appointed to the 68th from "Senior Captain, 33rd Foot (25th November, 1775), and Lieutenant-General (26th June, 1799)."

APPENDIX II

Major in the Army, 29th August, 1777; Lieutenant-Colonel in the Army, 18th March, 1779; Colonel in the Army, 18th October, 1787; Major-General, 20th December, 1793. D.Q.M.G. in Ireland. Died 10th June, 1801.

(ii.) RICHARD, 7TH EARL OF CAVAN.

Appointed 18th June, 1801.

RICHARD, 7TH EARL OF CAVAN, was born 10th September, 1763. Appointed Ensign, Coldstream Guards, 2nd April, 1779; Lieutenant, Coldstream Guards, 27th July, 1781; Captain and Lieutenant-Colonel, 23rd August, 1793. When appointed to the 68th was 1st Major, Coldstream Guards, and a Major-General (18th June, 1798).

Wounded at Valenciennes, 3rd January, 1793. Commanded a brigade in the Ferrol Expedition and before Cadiz, 1800. Commanded a brigade of Guards at Alexandria, September, 1801, and from October, 1801, was G.O.C. in Egypt.

A Knight of the Crescent, and one of the six officers, besides Admiral Viscount Nelson, who received the diamond aigrette. Lieutenant-General, 30th October, 1805; General, 4th June, 1814.

To half-pay, on reduction, 1802. Colonel 2nd West India Regiment, 27th September, 1805, and eventually Colonel, 45th Foot. Died 21st November, 1837.

COLONELS OF THE 2ND BOMBAY EUROPEAN LIGHT INFANTRY.

(i.) GEORGE BENJAMIN BROOKS.

Appointed 8th October, 1839.

GEORGE BENJAMIN BROOKS, son of J. B. Brooks. Nominated a Cadet by the Lord Lieutenant of Ireland; arrived in Calcutta 5th

January, 1801, and appointed to the 1st Battalion 7th Bombay Native Infantry, then in Egypt.

Ensign, 6th March, 1800; Lieutenant, 26th May, 1800; Brevet-Captain, 3rd August, 1809; Captain, 25th December, 1812; Major, 4th July, 1821; Lieutenant-Colonel, 1st May, 1824; Brevet-Colonel, 1st December, 1829; Colonel (2nd Bombay European Light Infantry), 8th October, 1839; Major-General, 28th March, 1838; Lieutenant-General, 11th November, 1851; General, 30th August, 1860.

Brigade-Major in Pindaree War. Transferred to 11th Bombay Native Infantry, 1818. Appointed to command Marine Battalion, 1823; to 24th Bombay Native Infantry, 1824; to 13th Bombay Native Infantry, 1830; and later to 2nd Bombay Native Infantry.

Transferred to the left wing of the Bombay European Regiment, 18th April, 1835, and to the 1st Bombay Native Infantry, 1836.

Commanded the Field Force in Upper Sind, September, 1840, to July, 1841; and was presented by the officers engaged at Peer Chutra with the sword, etc., of the chief captured there.

Removed, as Colonel, to the 20th Bombay Native Infantry, 1840. Returned to England, 1841, and remained unemployed. Died at Windsor, 4th October, 1862.

(ii.) EPHRAIM GERRISH STANNUS.

Appointed ———, 1840.

EPHRAIM GERRISH STANNUS, son of Ephraim Stannus, of Comus, Co. Tyrone; born 1784.

E.I.C. Cadet, 1799; Ensign, 6th March, 1800; Lieutenant, 26th May, 1800; Captain, 6th July, 1811; Major, ———, 1818; Lieutenant-Colonel, 31st October, 1822; Colonel, 5th June, 1829; Major-General, 28th June, 1838.

Was in the Bombay European Regiment in the early part of his career, then commanded 9th Bombay Native Infantry; Colonel of 10th Bombay Native Infantry, 1829 to 1840. Served in Kathiawar, and in Pindaree War.

APPENDIX II

Private Secretary to Mountstuart Elphinstone, Governor of Bombay. First British Resident in the Persian Gulf, 1823 to 1826. Lieutenant-Governor of East India College, Addiscombe, 1834 to 1850. C.B., knighted 1837. Died 21st October, 1850.

(iii.) FOSTER STALKER.

Appointed 15th May, 1850.

FOSTER STALKER, son of Joshua Stalker, born 20th February, 1798.

Arrived at Bombay 15th August, 1819, and was posted to 10th Bombay Native Infantry. Cadet, 1818; Ensign, 10th April, 1819; Lieutenant, 11th April, 1819; Captain, 5th August, 1825; Major, 30th June, 1830; Lieutenant-Colonel, 26th June, 1838; Colonel, 19th March, 1849; Major-General, 28th November, 1854.

Served in 4th Native Infantry, and transferred to 19th Bombay Native Infantry, 1824. Staff Officer with Mahi Kantha Field Force, 1825.

Tried, with others, for the murder of Captain Urquhart for "being present and aiding Dr. Malcolmson in a duel," and found "Not guilty."

Commanded 19th Bombay Native Infantry at the capture of Ghazni, 1839. Received 3rd Class of Order of Durani Empire from Shah Sujah. Transferred to 14th Bombay Native Infantry, 1843; to 1st Grenadier Regiment, 1844; to 2nd Bombay European Light Infantry, 1845; to 26th Bombay Native Infantry, 1845; and back to 2nd European Light Infantry, 1846.

Commanded 2nd Infantry Brigade of Field Force, 1848; was present at siege and capture of Multan, 1849; commanded Rajputana Field Force, 1849; commanded Persian Expeditionary Force, October, 1856, to January, 1857. C.B., A.D.C. to the Queen. Died in Persia, 14th March, 1857.

THE DURHAM LIGHT INFANTRY

(iv.) THOMAS CHEESE (OR CHASE) PARR.

Appointed 15th March, 1857.

THOMAS CHEESE (OR CHASE) PARR was born 31st August, 1802. Cadet, 1818; arrived at Bombay 4th August, 1819, and was posted to 4th Bombay Native Infantry.

Ensign, 4th February, 1819; Lieutenant, 5th February, 1819; Captain, 4th September, 1827; Major, 19th October, 1839; Lieutenant-Colonel, 21st January, 1846; Brevet-Colonel, 20th June, 1854; Colonel, 18th March, 1856; Major-General, 13th October, 1857; Lieutenant-General, 6th February, 1870; General, 10th February, 1876.

Served with 7th Bombay Native Infantry in Arabia, 1821, and was transferred to that regiment 1824, having in the meantime been in the 10th Bombay Native Infantry; as a captain was in both the 7th and 2nd Native Infantry. Commanded the Marine Battalion, 1833-35, and 7th Bombay Native Infantry during operations in Southern Mahratta country, 1845, and from 1835 to 1846. Transferred to 28th Bombay Native Infantry, 1846; to 1st European Regiment, 1846; to 10th Native Infantry, 1847; to 7th Native Infantry, 1849; to 2nd Native Infantry, 1850; and to 6th Native Infantry, 1853. Was not transferred to the 106th Light Infantry in July, 1862, but remained in the Army List as "Colonel of the cadre of the former 2nd Bombay European Light Infantry." Died at Bickley 15th June, 1883.

COLONELS OF THE 106TH LIGHT INFANTRY.

(i) DAVID CAPON.

Appointed 30th September, 1862.

DAVID CAPON, son of Colonel J. Capon, H.E.I.C.S.; born 16th August, 1793. Arrived at Bombay 26th May, 1810; posted to 1st Bombay Native Infantry (Grenadiers). Ensign, 26th May, 1810;

APPENDIX II

Lieutenant, 27th May, 1815; Captain, 5th November, 1821; Major, 21st August, 1829; Lieutenant-Colonel, 30th May, 1836; Brevet-Colonel, 9th November, 1846; Major-General, 20th June, 1854; Lieutenant-General, 25th January, 1861.

Served with 2nd Battalion 1st Bombay Native Infantry at Palanpur, 1813, and at the storming of the fort at Mudelanghur. Transferred to 2nd Bombay Native Infantry, 1824; to 22nd Native Infantry, April, 1837; to 18th Native Infantry, June, 1837; to 20th Native Infantry, 1838; to 16th Native Infantry, January, 1839; and to 24th Native Infantry, September, 1839.

Officer Commanding at Aden, 1839, and commanded at the repulse of the Arabs, who attacked Aden, 11th November, 1839.

Transferred to 10th Native Infantry, December, 1839; to 11th Native Infantry, July, 1840; to 24th Native Infantry, October, 1840; to 12th Native Infantry, 1843; to 2nd Native Infantry, 1844; to 2nd European Light Infantry, December, 1845; and to 27th Native Infantry, February, 1846.

Commanded 1st Infantry Brigade, Bombay Column, at Multan, 1848-9, and at Gujerat, 21st February, 1849.

Appointed Colonel, 23rd Bombay Native Infantry, 26th February, 1848. K.C.B. Died 17th December, 1869.

(ii.) MAURICE BARLOW.

Appointed 18th December, 1869.

MAURICE BARLOW was appointed Ensign, 85th Foot, 21st July, 1814; Lieutenant, 85th Foot, 23rd March, 1815; Captain, 3rd Foot, 20th December, 1821; Major, 3rd Foot, 12th June, 1828; to 14th Foot, 25th June, 1830; Brevet-Lieutenant-Colonel, 23rd October, 1841; Lieutenant-Colonel, 14th Foot, 24th December, 1847; Colonel in the Army, 20th June, 1854; Major-General, 26th October, 1858; Lieutenant-General, 24th April, 1866; General, 21st March, 1874.

Served in Crimean War; Knight of the Legion of Honour; 3rd

THE DURHAM LIGHT INFANTRY

Class Medjidie. Colonel, 3rd West India Regiment, 8th June, 1863, to 17th December, 1869.

Transferred to 14th Foot, as Colonel, 9th August, 1870. Died at Florence, 12th May, 1875.

(iii.) HON. GEORGE CADOGAN.

Appointed 9th August, 1870.

HON. GEORGE CADOGAN, second son of 3rd Earl Cadogan; born 2nd December, 1814. Ensign and Lieutenant, Grenadier Guards, 22nd February, 1833; Lieutenant and Captain, Grenadier Guards, 9th January, 1838; Captain and Lieutenant-Colonel, Grenadier Guards, 6th August, 1847; Colonel in the Army, 28th November, 1854. Served in the Crimean War; Knight of the Medjidie, and Commander, 1st Class, of St. Maurice and Lazare.

Major-General, 3rd June, 1862; Lieutenant-General, 25th October, 1871. K.C.B. Transferred as colonel to 71st Foot, 1874. Died 27th January, 1880.

(iv.) WILLIAM O'GRADY HALY.

Appointed 17th May, 1874.

WILLIAM O'GRADY HALY was appointed Ensign, 4th Foot, 17th June, 1828; Lieutenant, 4th Foot, 19th June, 1831; to 47th Foot, 11th October, 1831; Captain, 47th Foot, 25th April, 1834; Major, 47th Foot, 19th May, 1846; Lieutenant-Colonel, 47th Foot, 27th December, 1850; Colonel in the Army, 28th November, 1854. Exchanged to 38th Foot, 1860. Wounded at Inkerman, 5th November, 1854. Major-General, 12th January, 1865; Lieutenant-General, 26th May, 1873; C.B.; General Officer Commanding a division in Bengal, 1870. Transferred as Colonel to 47th Foot, 1875.

APPENDIX II

(v.) JOHN JARVIS BISSETT.

Appointed 2nd November, 1875

JOHN JARVIS BISSETT was appointed Ensign, Cape Mounted Riflemen, 7th February, 1840; Lieutenant, 16th February, 1844; Captain, 1st April, 1847; Brevet-Major, 15th September, 1848; Brevet-Lieutenant-Colonel, 28th May, 1853; Brevet-Colonel, 28th November, 1854; Major-General, 8th March, 1857.

Changed his name from John T—— Bissett to John Jarvis Bissett, 1849. Officer commanding a brigade at Gibraltar, 1870.

Was continually in Cape Mounted Rifles until promoted to rank of Major-General. Served with distinction in South Africa. General. K.C.M.G., C.B. Died 1894.

COLONELS OF THE DURHAM LIGHT INFANTRY.

(i.) LORD WILLIAM PAULET.

LORD WILLIAM PAULET (1st Battalion), from Colonel, 68th Light Infantry.

(ii.) JOHN JARVIS BISSETT.

JOHN JARVIS BISSETT (2nd Battalion), from Colonel, 106th Light Infantry.

On the death of Lord W. Paulet, Sir J. J. Bissett became Colonel of both battalions.

(iii.) WILLIAM AUGUSTUS FYERS.

Appointed 26th May, 1894.

WILLIAM AUGUSTUS FYERS was appointed Ensign, 40th Foot, 17th October, 1833; Lieutenant, 40th Foot, 20th May, 1836; Captain, 40th Foot, 7th May, 1847; 4th Foot, 1851; Rifle Brigade,

THE DURHAM LIGHT INFANTRY

1852; Major, Rifle Brigade, 2nd October, 1855; Lieutenant-Colonel, Rifle Brigade, 26th December, 1856; Colonel in the Army, 8th June, 1864; Major-General, 23rd August, 1869; Lieutenant-General, 1st July, 1881; K.C.B.

With 40th in Afghanistan, 1841-2, and with Rifle Brigade in Crimea and Indian Mutiny. Died 10th November, 1895.

(iv.) EYRE CHALLONER HENRY MASSEY, 4TH BARON CLARINA.

Appointed 11th November, 1895.

EYRE CHALLONER HENRY MASSEY, 4TH BARON CLARINA, eldest son of 3rd Baron Clarina, born 29th April, 1830.

Ensign, 68th Light Infantry, 8th October, 1847; Lieutenant, 7th Foot, 21st November, 1851; Captain, 95th Foot, 14th January, 1853; Major, 95th Foot, 17th November, 1857; Brevet-Lieutenant-Colonel, 95th Foot, 20th July, 1858; Colonel in the Army, 3rd April, 1865; Major-General, 1st March, 1870; Lieutenant-General, 5th November, 1885; General, 28th January, 1891.

With 95th in Crimea and Indian Mutiny. When a Major in 95th commanded 106th Light Infantry for some time. General Officer Commanding Dublin District, 1881-6.

Knight of Legion of Honour, Turkish Medal, Medjidie, etc.; C.B. Died 16th December, 1897.

(v.) REGINALD GIPPS.

Appointed 17th December, 1897.

REGINALD GIPPS, son of Sir George Gipps, R.E., Governor of New South Wales, 1838-46. Born 1831. Ensign and Lieutenant, Scots Fusilier Guards, 10th April, 1849; Lieutenant and Captain, 30th June, 1854; Captain and Lieutenant-Colonel, 2nd February,

APPENDIX II

1858; Colonel in the Army, 5th January, 1871; Major-General, 1st July, 1881; Lieutenant-General, 2nd December, 1889; General, 26th May, 1894.

Served in Crimea with Scots Fusilier Guards; twice wounded. Medal with four clasps, Legion of Honour, 5th Class Medjidie, and Turkish Medal. Military Secretary to H.R.H. the Duke of Cambridge and to Viscount Wolseley when they were Commanders-in-Chief. G.C.B. Died 11th September, 1908.

(vi.) RUSSELL UPCHER.

Appointed 11th September, 1908.

RUSSELL UPCHER, third son of Henry Ramey Upcher, Esq., of Sheringham Hall, Norfolk. Born 3rd February, 1844; educated at Harrow.

Ensign, 24th Foot, 21st November, 1862; Lieutenant, 29th October, 1866; Captain, 31st October, 1871; Brevet-Major, 11th November, 1878; Lieut.-Colonel, 9th June, 1882; Colonel, 9th June, 1886; Major-General, 6th July, 1898.

Major-General Upcher served continuously in the 24th for twenty-five years, commanding the second battalion of that regiment at the end of his career in it. He served with distinction in South Africa, 1877-8-9, being in command of the troops at the battle of Quintana in the Zulu campaign, and in command of the first battalion of the 24th after the battle of Isandhlwana; mentioned in despatches four times; medal, with clasp; and promoted to rank of Brevet-Major.

Served in Burmese campaign, 1885-9; mentioned in despatches; medal, with two clasps; D.S.O.

Appointed to command 1st Battalion Durham Light Infantry, 31st October, 1888, and filled this appointment for the regulation period of four years.

Commanded the 5th and 68th Regimental Districts, 1894 to 1898; C.B.

[*APPENDIX III.*

LIEUTENANT-COLONELS.

DURING the latter part of the eighteenth century, and the earlier part of the nineteenth, it was not unusual for officers to remain on the regimental list of lieutenant-colonels after they had become general officers, and consequently had ceased to perform regimental duty; also, at different periods, two lieutenant-colonels have been borne on the strength of a regiment or battalion; as these two facts are apt to occasionally give rise to confusion as to who was the senior effective officer doing regimental duty, a complete list is now given with the dates of appointment in the regiment as lieutenant-colonel.

68TH REGIMENT.

(i.) William Adey. 22nd April, 1758. Sole Lieutenant-Colonel.

(ii.) David Wedderburn. 22nd September, 1762. Sole Lieutenant-Colonel.

(iii.) Jonas Martin. 1st June, 1764. Sole Lieutenant-Colonel.

(iv.) Lawrence Reynolds. 13th September, 1769. Sole Lieutenant-Colonel.

(v.) Sir Hew Whitefoord Dalrymple, Knight. 21st September, 1781. Sole Lieutenant-Colonel.

(vi.) Hon. John Thomas De Burgh. 23rd May, 1783. Sole Lieutenant-Colonel.

(vii.) David Ferguson. 15th June, 1785. Sole Lieutenant-Colonel.

(viii.) James Stewart. 25th July, 1788. Was sole Lieutenant-Colonel until 1795, when he became a Brigadier-General, but remained on the regimental list as senior Lieutenant-Colonel up to 1804.

APPENDIX III

(ix.) John Bridges Schaw. 1st September, 1795.
(x.) Robert Anstruther. 31st August, 1797.
(xi.) David Cuninghame. 16th August, 1799.
(xii.) John Robert Napier. 8th February, 1800.
} *

(xiii.) John Simon Farley. 1st March, 1800, on augmentation. Was sole Lieutenant-Colonel from 1804 to 1809, when he became a Brigadier-General, but remained on the regimental list as senior Lieutenant-Colonel up to 1815.

(xiv.) Francis Mannooch. 2nd March, 1800, on augmentation. Was a junior Lieutenant-Colonel; retired in 1802.

(xv.) George Henry Vansittart. 10th April, 1801. Was a junior Lieutenant-Colonel; to half-pay when the 2nd Battalion was reduced.

(xvi.) Robert Smyth. 22nd April, 1802. Was a junior Lieutenant-Colonel; to half-pay 22nd July, 1802.

68TH LIGHT INFANTRY.

(xvii.) William Johnston. 13th July, 1809. Nominally junior Lieutenant-Colonel, under J. S. Farley up to 1815, then sole Lieutenant-Colonel up to 1825.

(xviii.) John P———. Hawkins. 2nd June, 1825. Sole Lieutenant-Colonel.

(xix.) John Reed. 20th July, 1830. Sole Lieutenant-Colonel.

(xx.) Thomas Barrow. 1st February, 1831. Was only seven days in the Regiment.

(xxi.) John Cross. 8th February, 1831. Sole Lieutenant-Colonel.

(xxii.) Lord William Paulet. 21st March, 1843. Sole Lieutenant-Colonel.

---

* These four officers were, in succession, nominally junior Lieutenant-Colonels under James Stewart, who was extra-regimentally employed.

THE DURHAM LIGHT INFANTRY

(xxiii.) Sir Robert Burdett, Bart. 31st December, 1847. Never joined, retired at once.

(xxiv.) Richardson William Huey. 31st December, 1847. Sole Lieutenant-Colonel.

(xxv.) Lord Arthur Lennox. 14th September, 1852. Sole Lieutenant-Colonel.

(xxvi.) Henry Smyth. 30th December, 1853. Sole Lieutenant-Colonel, and latterly senior of two.

(xxvii.) George Macbeath. 9th March, 1855. Junior Lieutenant-Colonel; never commanded.

(xxviii.) Herbert Blount. 17th November, 1857. Junior Lieutenant-Colonel; never commanded.

(xxix.) Henry Harpur Greer. 18th February, 1859. Senior Lieutenant-Colonel.

(xxx.) Robert Clifford Lloyd. 17th May, 1857. Junior-Lieutenant-Colonel, from 76th Foot; never commanded.

(xxxi.) Horatio Harbord Morant. 2nd December, 1862. Junior Lieut-Colonel; never commanded.

(xxxii.) Joshua Henry Kirby. 10th November, 1869. Sole Lieutenant-Colonel.

(xxxiii.) Harrison Walke John Trent. 7th October, 1874. Sole Lieutenant-Colonel.

(xxxiv.) Aubrey Harvey Tucker. 29th October, 1879. Sole Lieutenant-Colonel.

2ND REGIMENT BOMBAY EUROPEAN LIGHT INFANTRY.

The dates given are those of rank in the Bombay Army, but the order of succession is that of appointment to the rank of Lieutenant-Colonel in the 2nd Bombay European Light Infantry.

(i.) Philip Downing Ottey. Appointed 8th October, 1839, but transferred at once to 5th Native Infantry.

(ii.) Robert Taylor. 7th September, 1831. The first Commanding Officer.

(iii.) George James Wilson. 8th October, 1839. Junior Lieutenant-Colonel.

APPENDIX III

(iv.) Foster Stalker. 26th June, 1838. Junior Lieutenant-Colonel, vice G. J. Wilson, in 1840.

(v.) Charles Davies. 4th September, 1837. Vice F. Stalker, in 1844.

(vi.) Henry Dundas Robertson. 28th June, 1838.

(vii.) David Capon. 30th May, 1836. Was in the regiment December, 1845, to February, 1846.

(viii.) Foster Stalker. 26th June, 1838. Now (1846) a second time in the regiment as senior Lieutenant-Colonel.

(ix.) Bruce Seton. 9th June, 1845. Became senior in 1846, vice F. Stalker.

(x.) Henry Spencer. 21st January, 1846.

(xi.) George Moore. 21st June, 1838. Senior early in 1847.

(xii.) Foster Stalker. 26th June, 1838. Now (1847) a third time in the regiment as senior, vice G. Moore.

(xiii.) Matthew Soppitt. 26th January, 1838. Senior Lieutenant-Colonel in 1848.

(xiv.) William Cavaye. 23rd November, 1841. Senior Lieutenant-Colonel in 1849.

(xv.) David Forbes. 23rd November, 1841. Junior Lieutenant-Colonel in 1849 and 1850.

(xvi.) George Macan. 15th May, 1850. Senior in 1852.

(xvii.) Alexander Peter Le Mesurier. ——, 1851. Junior Lieutenant-Colonel; never commanded.

(xviii.) Neil Campbell. 18th August, 1847. Senior in 1855.

(xix.) Joseph Hale. 30th November, 1848. Junior Lieutenant-Colonel; never commanded.

(xx.) John Skardon Ramsey. 20th June, 1854. Senior in 1856. Was Commanding Officer in Persia.

(xxi.) David Davidson. 1st December, 1851. Senior in 1857.

(xxii.) Henry Stiles. 25th December, 1854. Junior Lieutenant-Colonel; never commanded.

(xxiii.) Sir Charles Shepherd Stuart, K.C.B. 17th June, 1851. Senior in 1861.

(xxiv.) Edmund Arthur Guerin. 29th September, 1860.

THE DURHAM LIGHT INFANTRY

106TH BOMBAY LIGHT INFANTRY.

The dates given (except that of Lieutenant-Colonel Leith) are those of appointment to the rank of Lieutenant-Colonel in the 106th Light Infantry.

(i.) Robert Wm. Disney Leith. 28th February, 1862.
(ii.) Henry Philip Tyacke. 29th May, 1866.
(iii.) William Mainwaring Sloane Bolton. 19th June, 1872.
(iv.) Robert Rollo Gillespie. 13th August, 1873.
(v.) Elliot Larkins Robertson. 5th September, 1877.
(vi.) George Charles Girardot. 21st July, 1880.

THE DURHAM LIGHT INFANTRY.

The dates given are those of appointment to the rank of Lieutenant-Colonel in the Durham Light Infantry.

(i.) 1. Aubrey Harvey Tucker. 29th October, 1879. From 68th Light Infantry.
(ii.) 2. George Charles Girardot. 21st July, 1880. From 106th Light Infantry.
(iii.) 1. George Kennedy Shaw. 1st July, 1881. Junior Lieutenant-Colonel; never commanded.
(iv.) 2. Henry William Cuninghame Bulkeley. 1st July, 1881. Junior Lieutenant-Colonel; never commanded.
(v.) 2. Edmund Rogers Coker. 24th August, 1881. Commanding Officer, 2nd Battalion, 27th August, 1884.
(vi.) 1. Robert Alexander Crawford. 28th July, 1884. Commanding Officer, 1st Battalion, 29th October, 1884.
(vii.) 2. George Arthur Lee. 27th August, 1884. Commanding Officer, 2nd Battalion, 24th August, 1887.
(viii.) 1. William Frederick Woodward. 29th October, 1884. Junior Lieutenant-Colonel; never commanded.
(ix.) 1. Russell Upcher. 31st October, 1888.
(x.) 2. Charles Talbot Peyton. 27th August, 1890.
(xi.) 1. William Gordon. 31st October, 1892.

APPENDIX III

(xii.) 2. Frederick Henry Whitby. 27th August, 1894.
(xiii.) 1. Arthur Law Woodland. 31st October, 1896.
(xiv.) 2. Alwyn de Blaquiere Valentine Paget. 26th April, 1899.
(xv.) 1. Herbert Swayne FitzGerald. 31st October, 1900.
(xvi.) 2. George Markham Davison. 26th April, 1903.
(xvii.) 1. George Clavell Mansel. 29th February, 1904.
(xviii.) 2. John Ernest Bush. 13th August, 1906.
(xix.) 1. Charles Edward Wilson. 29th February, 1908.
(xx.) 2. Ernest St. George Pratt. 15th August, 1910.
(xxi.) 1. Charles Camac Luard. 29th February, 1912.
(xxii.) 2. Bernard William Lynedoch McMahon. 28th July, 1913.

ADJUTANTS.

68TH REGIMENT.

(i.) George Munro. 22nd July, 1758.
(ii.) Humphrey Hopper. 18th September, 1765.
(iii.) Charles William Este. 11th March, 1767.
(iv.) William Thompson. 10th July, 1776.
(v.) William Potts. 12th July, 1777.
(vi.) Thomas Hill. 12th December, 1787.
(vii.) Isaac Stewart. 4th May, 1791.
(viii.) James Stewart. 1st July, 1795.
(ix.) John Reed (i.). 14th July, 1798.
(x.) James Allen Crowder. 20th May, 1800. Adjutant of 2nd Battalion and, after its reduction, of the single battalion.
(xi.) John Reed (ii.). 26th February, 1805.
(xii.) John Hinds. 3rd December, 1807.

68TH LIGHT INFANTRY.

(xiii.) James Duff. 15th May, 1823.
(xiv.) Evan Macpherson. 30th August, 1831.

THE DURHAM LIGHT INFANTRY

(xv.) Arthur Mainwaring. 30th January, 1835.
(xvi.) John Johnston. 1st June, 1838.
(xvii.) William Cross. 15th December, 1840.
(xviii.) Wm. Hugh Hedges Carmichael. 17th January, 1845.
(xix.) Thomas Whitmore Storer. 30th March, 1847.
(xx.) Charles Samuel Nicol. 16th March, 1849.
(xxi.) Thomas de Courcy Hamilton. 23rd August, 1850.
(xxii.) Herbert Vaughan. 2nd February, 1855.
(xxiii.) Hugo Shelley Light. 27th August, 1855.
(xxiv.) Charles Covey. 28th September, 1856.
(xxv.) Charles Clifton Hood. 4th November, 1870.
(xxvi.) Arthur Law Woodland. 19th October, 1872.
(xxvii.) Charles Waring Darwin. 13th November, 1875.
(xxviii.) Charles Vere Gunning. 22nd July, 1880.

2ND REGIMENT BOMBAY EUROPEAN LIGHT INFANTRY.

(i.) John Bowman Mackenzie Gillanders. 1st February, 1840.
(ii.) Edmund Arthur Guerin. 9th December, 1840.
(iii.) William Fleming Sandwith. 22nd February, 1844.
(iv.) Willoughby Brassey. 11th December, 1845.
(v.) Henry Shewell. 1st February, 1847.
(vi.) John Walter Savile. 6th February, 1852.
(vii.) Robert Deey Hassard. 17th February, 1855.
(viii.) Robert Rollo Gillespie. 18th January, 1859.

106TH LIGHT INFANTRY.

(i.) John Henry Gaitskell. 10th September, 1862.
(ii.) William Ainsworth. 11th April, 1868.
(iii.) Edmund Rogers Coker. 14th February, 1874.
(iv.) Robert Henry Francis Reade Brownrigg. 16th July, 1874.
(v.) Henry Thomas. 8th March, 1879.
(vi.) Alfred Ernest Binyon. 4th June, 1881.

APPENDIX III

THE DURHAM LIGHT INFANTRY.

(i.) 1. Charles Vere Gunning. 22nd July, 1880. From 68th Light Infantry.
(ii.) 2. Alfred Ernest Binyon. 4th June, 1881. From 106th Light Infantry.
(iii.) 2. John Ernest Bush. 15th April, 1884.
(iv.) 1. Walter Charteris Ross. 22nd July, 1885.
(v.) 1. Laurence Parke. 4th June, 1887.
(vi.) 2. Charles Edward Wilson. 15th April, 1889.
(vii.) 1. Frederick Spencer Wilson Robb. 13th August, 1890.
(viii.) 2. Henry de Beauvoir de Lisle. 1st July, 1892.
(ix.) 1. Ernest St. George Pratt. 19th November, 1892.
(x.) 2. Charles Camac Luard. 1st July, 1896.
(xi.) 1. Bernard William Lynedoch McMahon. 19th November, 1896.
(xii.) 1. Edward Burnaby Thresher. 19th November, 1900.
(xiii.) 2. William John Ainsworth. 15th March, 1901.
(xiv.) 1. Edward Algernon Cleader Blake. 10th April, 1901.
(xv.) 1. Claud Leonard Matthews. 10th April, 1904.
(xvi.) 2. Roper Maxwell Tyler. 1st February, 1905.
(xvii.) 1. Arthur William Baillie Wallace. 10th April, 1907.
(xviii.) 2. Francis Gilfrid Maughan. 2nd February, 1908.
(xix.) 1. Hubert Wogan Festing. 10th April, 1910.
(xx.) 2. Harry Vivian Hare. 2nd February, 1911.
(xxi.) 1. William Basil Greenwell. 10th April, 1913.
(xxii.) 2. Walter Hugh Godsal. 17th November, 1913.

[*APPENDIX IV.*

REGIMENTAL MUSIC.

It is not widely known that the system of having a definite march authorised for each individual regiment is quite a modern one; before the introduction of this system, a regiment marched past to any air that the commanding officer, for the time being, chose to select; in the case of some corps, however, the 14th West Yorkshire Regiment being one of the best known examples, the same air had been continuously played for many years.

Also, until H.R.H. the Duke of Cambridge became Commander-in-Chief, the National Anthem was played in a variety of arrangements and in different keys.

Up to about 1867, when regiments were brigaded for ceremonial purposes, each regiment was played past the saluting point by its own band; but, when about this time the system of massing the bands of a brigade was introduced, it became necessary to have definite marches for each regiment, so that bands could be prepared to play the marches of other regiments at short notice.

Accordingly regiments were ordered to send the scores of their marches to the Royal Military School of Music at Kneller Hall for approval; the 68th sent up "I'm Ninety-five," which appears to have been in use since the Crimean War, but it was rejected, and "The Light Barque" was substituted—at the bidding, it is believed, of H.R.H. the Duke of Cambridge. From that time "The Light Barque" (originally spelt "Bark") has been the march of the 68th, and from 1882 the authorised march of all battalions of the Durham Light Infantry.

The 68th, however, when parading alone, still continued to march past in quarter-column to "I'm Ninety-five."

Although there is considerable difference of opinion on the subject, there is little doubt that "The Light Barque" was played by the 68th in ante-Crimean days, and that the use of "I'm Ninety-five" came about through close association with the Rifle Brigade in the Crimea.

APPENDIX IV

"Mony Musk" was played for marching past in double time, and the first eight bars of "Prince Regent" slow march for the general salute.

The final order fixing the regimental marches of infantry was not issued until 1882.

No information has, so far, been found concerning the airs played for parade purposes by the 2nd Bombay European Light Infantry, but in the 106th Light Infantry "Paddy Carey" was for some years the recognised march; about the end of 1878, or commencement of 1879, "Ap Shenkin" was substituted, and continued to be used until "The Light Barque" was ordered to be used instead; "Garry Owen" was played for marching past in quarter column, either "Mony Musk" or "The Keel Row" for marching past in double time, and "The Garb of Old Gaul" for the slow march; the first eight bars of "Gemma di Vergy" were used for the general salute, but were discontinued in 1903, when the 2nd Battalion proceeded to Aldershot, in favour of the general salute used by the brigade, of which the battalion formed a part; in the last year or two the "Prince Regent" slow march has been played by the 2nd Battalion as well as by the 1st.

There is a march, now known as "The 68th Slow March," concerning which nothing has been found beyond the fact that it was played by the band of the 68th many years ago; for a long time it was lost sight of, but a copy of it was found in Edinburgh by the late Colonel W. Gordon about twenty years ago; it is now played by the bands of both the 1st and 2nd Battalions.

The Durham Light Infantry does not have a monopoly of "The Light Barque," as the same air, with a slightly different arrangement, under the name of "Off! off, said the Stranger," is also the march of the Royal Irish Rifles, having been the march of the 1st Battalion (the 83rd Regiment) prior to 1881.

THE DURHAM LIGHT INFANTRY

"The Light Bark."

Written by Miss A. Mahony. Composed expressly for Madame Vestris (b. 1797, d. 1856) by G. T. Craven.

"Where the trembling moon-beams lit the horizon's verge a sail floated silently along, so small at first you might have taken it for the simple bark of the earliest navigator just risen from the wave."

Verse 1.

Off, said the stranger, off, off, and away;
And away flew the light bark, o'er the silv'ry bay,
We must reach, ere to-morrow, the far distant wave,
The billows we'll laugh at, the tempest we'll brave.
The young roving lovers, their vows have been given
Unsmiled o'er by mortals, but hallowed in Heaven;
One was Italy's daughter, I knew by her eye,
It wore the bright beam that illumines the sky.

Verse 2.

Off, said the stranger, off, off, and away;
And away flew the light bark, o'er the silv'ry bay,
And she has forsaken her palace and halls
For the chill breeze, and the light which falls
O'er the pure wave, from the Heavens above,
And their guiding star was the bright star of love.
Off, said the stranger, off, off, and away;
And away flew the light bark o'er the silv'ry bay.

The above was probably composed between 1820 and 1830; a fifth edition was published in October, 1831, by H. Falkner, 3, Old Bond Street, London.

[APPENDIX V.

FREEMASONRY.

(i.) There was an Irish Masonic Lodge, No. 714, in the 68th; it was constituted by warrant from the Grand Lodge of Ireland on 1st April, 1790; subsequently there was an English (Atholl) Lodge in the regiment; the date of the warrant of constitution of the latter was 22nd June, 1810, and the number was 348.

After the union of the Atholl (or Ancient) and Modern Grand Lodges, the lodge of the 68th was, in 1814, re-numbered No. 446, and in 1832 was again re-numbered No. 297; in 1835 it was named the "Durham Faithful Lodge." The lodge ceased to exist in 1844.

During the Peninsular War the lodge was at the depot at home; while the depot was at Brabourne Lees the lodge met at the barracks there; while at Hythe, in 1813, it met at the Duke's Head in Market Street; other meeting places are not recorded. No article connected with the lodge can now be found.

(ii.) There was a Scottish Masonic Lodge, No. 320, under a warrant of constitution dated 3rd February, 1813, in the Durham Militia; it was consecrated on 24th June, 1813, at Auchtermuchty, and was named the "St. Cuthbert Durham Militia Lodge." It subsequently bore the number 249.

It obtained an English warrant on 12th March, 1825; its number then was 800; it was re-numbered No. 530 in 1832, and was erased on 7th March, 1838.

In 1820 it met at the Turk's Head, in 1822 at the Lambton Arms, in 1825 at the Blue Bell, and in 1835 at the Goliah's Head [sic], all these inns being at Barnard Castle.

In and about 1820 there was very acute friction between this lodge, and the other lodge then existing in Barnard Castle—the Lodge of Concord—chiefly on account of the former initiating persons not of a military character; this ill-feeling eventually came to an end, and there was complete harmony between the two when the St. Cuthbert Lodge was regularly constituted under its English warrant on 6th June, 1825, at the Blue Bell Inn by the officers of the Lodge of Concord; from this time onwards the lodge appears to have been a town lodge.

[*APPENDIX VI.*

THE DURHAM LIGHT INFANTRY CLUB.

THE dinner club, like other institutions, was one of gradual development; when the officers of the 68th first held an annual dinner cannot now be ascertained; the late Lieutenant-General Morant records in his diary that the 68th dinner took place on 30th May, 1861, at The Thatched House.

The existing club dates from 24th May, 1864, when the annual dinner was held at the St. James's Hotel, Piccadilly, and eleven officers, all of them late of the 68th—the regiment was on active service in New Zealand at the time—were present; Colonel Smyth, C.B., was in the chair; it was then resolved to establish a club, consisting of officers serving at that time, or who had previously served, in the 68th, and that the club should meet at least once a year and dine together in London at a time fixed upon by the committee; the committee appointed on that day consisted of Lieutenant-Colonel Lewis, Major McPherson, and Captain Harris.

The qualification for membership remained the same until 1897, when the officers, past and present, since 1st July, 1881, of the 2nd Battalion Durham Light Infantry, were invited to join; the officers of the 2nd Battalion accepted the invitation.

In a few years' time the qualification was further extended to officers who have served, or are serving, in the 3rd and 4th Battalions Durham Light Infantry since 1st January, 1903; but with this condition, that subaltern officers of the 3rd and 4th Battalions will cease to be members of the club on retiring from the regiment.

For many years the dinner was held at Willis's Rooms, but for the last twenty years it has been held at the Hotel Metropole, Northumberland Avenue.

Colonel A. L. Woodland, C.B., is the present president of the committee.

[APPENDIX VII.

DURHAM LIGHT INFANTRY COTTAGE HOMES.

THE collection for these homes commenced with a contribution of £75 8s. 4d. from all ranks of the 1st Battalion, under the command of Lieutenant-Colonel H. S. Fitzgerald, C.B., at Eden Kop, Transvaal, in 1901. Colonel Woodland, C.B., commanding 68th Regimental District, at once organised a collection in the county of Durham; letters of appeal, signed by Lord Durham and Colonel Woodland, were sent to the local newspapers, and a territorial committee was formed; the result was that, in due course, a total sum, including a grant of £178 0s. 3d. from the Prince Christian Victor Memorial Fund, of £1,997 1s. 11d., was raised.

In October, 1901, Colonel J. G. Wilson, C.B., offered to build a cottage on his estate at Manfield, near Darlington, for the Durham Light Infantry, in memory of his son and brother, who had fallen in the South African War; a month later Colonel Wilson was himself killed, but his family carried out his wishes as regards a cottage for the Durham Light Infantry, as well as one for the York and Lancaster Regiment.

In 1902 a valuable site at Western Hill, close to the city of Durham, was presented by Mr. W. Lishman, and two cottages were built upon it; the first is a memorial to H.H. Prince Christian Victor of Schleswig-Holstein, and the second is dedicated to the memory of the officers and men of the Durham Light Infantry who lost their lives in South Africa. Privates Coulthard and Norwood, who had both been wounded at Vaal Krantz, were the first occupants of the cottages at Durham. In a few years' time, owing to its situation and to various difficulties that arose as to the selection and subsequent maintenance of occupants of the cottage at Manfield, the regiment was reluctantly compelled to give up its interest in it. The two cottages at Durham, on the other hand, have amply fulfilled the object for which they are intended; occupation of them is open to men of any battalion of the Durham Light Infantry whose disablement occurred during actual military employment. The cottages are under the management of a committee, of which Colonel C. W. Darwin, C.B., is the present president.

[*APPENDIX VIII.*

"THE DURHAM LIGHT INFANTRY GAZETTE" AND "THE BUGLE."

WHEN the 68th embarked for India in December, 1857, the regiment was in two ships, the "Argo," sailed 19th, and the "Australasian," sailed 22nd; the left wing on the "Argo" had a printing press, and started a paper called "The Argo"; the first number appeared on 4th January, 1858, at the Island of St. Vincent, where the two ships met; the right wing on the "Australasian" then commenced a similar paper, in manuscript; it was called "The Sea, or Floating Gentleman's Magazine"; the first number appeared on the 20th January, 1858, and the first two numbers were printed at the Cape; two more were printed at Madras, and here the "Argo" appeared with six numbers all printed on board ship.

The voyage across the Bay of Bengal to Rangoon afforded material for a final number of "The Sea."

The Regiment being once more united at Rangoon at the end of March, 1858, these two papers were united, under the name of "The Durham Light Infantry Gazette, or the Wanderers' Magazine," the first number of which appeared on 25th June, 1858. The motto "Coelum non animum mutant, qui trans mare currunt" (Horace, Epistles, book I., No. XI.) was adopted for the paper. "The Durham Light Infantry Gazette" was a most successful paper, but it only lasted for a few years.

In the 2nd Battalion, a paper called "The Bugle" was started on 10th May, 1894. The origin of this paper was that it was the custom in the battalion to insert at the end of daily orders notices concerning sport, competitions, etc.; these notices increased to such an extent that a whole sheet became daily necessary for them; Lieutenant-Colonel Peyton then decided to institute a weekly paper for the purpose, and during the remainder of his period of command wrote most of the weekly notes himself. "The Bugle" continued until 10th November, 1900.

[*APPENDIX IX.*

THE 2ND BATTALION DURHAM LIGHT INFANTRY POLO CLUB IN INDIA, 1888-1899.

(Contributed by Brigadier-General H. de B. de Lisle, C.B., D.S.O.)

THE organisation of a Polo Club in an infantry battalion presents considerable financial difficulties, consequently much opposition on the part of senior officers was brought forward at a mess meeting in 1888, when the proposal was introduced.

Captain W. C. Ross, who had then recently returned to India, where he had previously served in the 1st Battalion, rendered invaluable assistance by his support and advice, and was responsible for originating the rules in the battalion, which later proved so successful.

At that time only a few officers played polo, and none of them had ever played in a tournament; a few years, therefore, were required before the Polo Club could be tested by results.

In 1891 the first success was gained at Quetta, and this local tournament, though insignificant in itself, added greatly to the interest taken in polo throughout the battalion. On reaching Mhow early in 1892 every officer became a playing member, and polo was then recognised as the chief sport for officers, as football was for the men of the battalion.

The financial difficulty was overcome as follows:—In India the barracks for the non-commissioned officers and men are usually situated some distance from the officers' mess and bungalows; every officer required a pony on which to ride to barracks, etc., and most officers kept two, even if they did not play polo; few, if any, of these hacks were good enough for polo, but were only fit as a conveyance from the mess to barracks or to the club.

In those days untrained Arab ponies could be bought in Bombay for £20 to £30, and, when fit and trained, would be suitable for second-class tournaments, and would then be worth their initial price plus the cost of their keep for one year, a matter of about £20.

THE DURHAM LIGHT INFANTRY

It was therefore calculated that if officers kept one pony each, these would replace the hacks in use, the officers could play polo on them, and as the ponies were to be the property of the club, their normal increase in value would be an asset to the club; in short, the profit on ten ponies would be about £200 in one year. In practice, it was found that the club could provide good untrained ponies to as many officers as wanted them, and the profit on each pony averaged £20.

The difficulty regarding ponies having been overcome as described above, the next question was that of players; unless a player commences polo before the age of thirty, he seldom reaches tournament form; it was therefore necessary to train newcomers to replace those who did not show signs of improvement; a riding school was made in which beginners could train their ponies, while unconsciously teaching themselves to ride. Practice on the ground took place every afternoon, and recruit-officers were able to join in this practice after the usual afternoon parades. On polo days the recruit-officers were allowed to play instead of attending the usual afternoon parade, the commanding officer rightly thinking that though a young officer might take a little longer to pass the severe test in drill, which was then demanded, he would be the better officer if he was at the same time taught to be a good rider and skilful at games. The results were excellent; young officers became good riders in six months, and in a year were playing in tournaments, in spite of the fact that many of them had never ridden before joining the battalion.

By the end of 1893 the polo team of the battalion was mounted on good ponies; the members of it were all good riders and played well together, winning the Jubbulpore tournament with ease.

From that date the career of the polo club was one of unprecedented success; each season brought out one more good player, who replaced older men, until 1898, when the team was as good as, if not better than, any team which has competed in India.

In 1894, after winning the infantry tournament, another asset was added to the efficiency of the 2nd Durham Light Infantry polo. Prior to that date polo depended more on individual skill than on combined play; the older members of the team set to work to study the

APPENDIX IX

science of the game, basing all calculations on the fact that the ball travels faster than a pony can gallop; if accurate passing, on the lines of association football, were practised, it was calculated that even on slower ponies, a team would still be able to win; on equally fast ponies, this system of play, then a novelty, would always defeat the old style of individual play; after working at this for a year, the result was very decisive.

In fourteen consecutive tournaments the team was successful; these included all the first-class tournaments in India; the inter-regimental three times, the infantry four times, the championship and the open cups at Poona, Bombay, and Jodhpore.

The following is a list of polo tournaments won:—

1.	Quetta Open Tournament	1891	Quetta.
2.	Barnard Challenge Cup	1893	Jubbulpore.
3.	Infantry Cup	1894	Lucknow.
4.	Barnard Challenge Cup	1894	Jubbulpore.
5.	7th Hussars Cup	1894	Mhow.
6.	Infantry Cup	1895	Lucknow.
7.	*Durham Light Infantry Cup	1895	Jubbulpore.
8.	Mhow Cup	1895	Mhow.
9.	Infantry Cup	1896	Lucknow.
10.	Inter-regimental Cup	1896	Umballa.
11.	Bombay Open Cup	1896	Bombay.
12.	Jodhpore Open Cup	1896	Jodhpore.
13.	†Infantry Cup	1897	Lucknow.
14.	Inter-regimental Cup	1897	Meerut.
15.	Poona Open Cup	1897	Poona.
16.	Championship	1898	Lucknow.
17.	Inter-regimental Cup	1898	Meerut.

A noticeable feature of the success of the Polo Club, and of the main principle upon which it was initiated—" to encourage polo in the battalion "—lies in the large number of players which represented it in these seventeen successful tournaments; eighteen officers played

---

* Presented by the battalion to replace the Barnard Cup, won outright.

† A team of subalterns represented the battalion.

in the various tournaments, with an average of eight tournaments each.

To compare the merits of the various players would be invidious; it was not by individual play that the tournaments were won, but by the excellent system of combined play, in which every member of the team performed his share and played for his side. From Captain (now Brigadier-General) de Lisle's book on "Polo in India," it appears that Mr. (now Major) Wilkinson was the best player. In a chapter on "Some famous Players of the past" Captain de Lisle writes on page 249 of his book:—

"By far the best of all the players, however, was Mr. Wilkinson, of the Durham Light Infantry. In India I have never met a No. 2 who could be so absolutely depended on, and I look on him as a model whom forwards would do well to copy. He began by playing No. 1 for his team, and when put back to No. 2, his knowledge of No. 1 play enabled him to change with his first forward whenever the game made this desirable. Being also a very strong, as well as a fine, horseman, and always training his own ponies, he made them perfect, and could send them along as if he were riding an artistic finish. Although he had not a naturally good eye, from constant practice he could score with certainty, even when driving his pony along. Moreover, he could pick up a ball passed at right angles, and make a goal, when galloping at it, with a single stroke. No doubt he was much helped by having confidence in his backs, and so could place himself in position to pick up a ball passed back, but the fact that his backs could always be confident that a good back-hander would change defence into attack, and before the striker could turn, the ball was flying down the ground, and the opposite backs riding their best to try and catch Mr. Wilkinson."

Captain de Lisle then, on page 250, comments on the fact that some men can play polo with much accuracy, but fail to attain proficiency at other games of skill, and after stating that Mr. Wilkinson did not excel at cricket, billiards, racquets, etc., concludes by saying: "He [Mr. Wilkinson] was nevertheless the best shot with a polo stick when going at the fastest pace I ever met. He required twice the amount of practice other players put in, but when wound up he had not his equal as No. 2."

APPENDIX IX

It would perhaps be even more difficult to compare the merits of the many famous ponies which were trained in the battalion; fifteen years ago ponies were advertised for sale with the remark, "trained by the Durham Light Infantry," which gave them an added value. After this lapse of time the names will be but names, and will not convey anything to anyone except the owners; when it is realised that, without counting private ponies, over 400 ponies passed through the club, a selection is even more difficult.

If the prize were to be given to the pony which played in the greatest number of tournaments, it would be easily won by Captain de Lisle's bay mare "Mary Morrison," which, after a short racing career, was put to polo, and played in nineteen tournaments. In 1898 this famous pony was taken to England, and in 1902 was given to Captain Hardress-Lloyd for breeding; though twenty years of age she had a foal, which was taken to America in 1910 by Captain Lloyd when he played in the America Cup recovery team.

If the prize were awarded for looks, it would be won by the white Arab "Snow," a silver statuette of which adorns the mess table of the 2nd Durham Light Infantry; this pony was a winner of thirty-one races, mostly steeplechases, before beginning polo, and ended an honourable career at stud in Australia; his stock was snapped up in India five years ago, partly owing to memory of the sire, and partly because they were found to be so temperate and easy to train.

If we turn to those which brought in the longest prices, we must mention "Aaron" and "Princess" (both sold for £200), "Orson," "Scarborough," "Greymiss," "Finesse," "Greyling," "Solon," "Scimitar," "Soapsuds," and "Khaled," all of which were at the top of the first-class.

One interesting point about ponies in connection with finance is worthy of remark; as long as the team confined its ambitions to second-class tournaments, the best, as well as the indifferent, ponies could be sold each year, and, as a result, the profit of the club, after paying all expenses, including entries and rail fares, increased annually about £200; as soon as we began to play in first-class tournaments, ten or twelve of the best ponies had to be retained each year, and, as a result, the funds of the club decreased £200

THE DURHAM LIGHT INFANTRY

each of the last three years; the difference in the expense of first-class and second-class polo would therefore appear to be £400 annually.

When the battalion left India for Burma, a year had not passed before the war in South Africa had absorbed all the polo team, three of whom accompanied the Burma Mounted Infantry, and one, who was at the Staff College at the time, went from England on special service.

The record that the members of the Polo Club made in South Africa is no uncertain recommendation of the value of sporting training; all were mentioned in despatches, some of them several times; two were awarded the C.B., three the D.S.O., and two were promoted to brevet rank.

[*APPENDIX X.*

MEMORIALS TO THOSE WHO HAVE LOST THEIR LIVES ON ACTIVE SERVICE.

Monument in Durham Cathedral.
No. 1 (white marble).

In memory of
officers of the 68th (The Durham) Light Infantry,
Major Heneage Griffith Wynne,
Captain Richard Lloyd Edwards,
Lieut. Frederick Grote Barker,
Lieut. James Marshall,
Asst. Surgeon John Francis O'Leary,
who were killed in action in the Crimea.
Lieut.-Colonel Harry Smyth,
who died at Scutari of wounds received in action.
Lieut. Harry Edmund Smyth,
who died in the Crimea of fever.
Captain Thomas Whitmore Storer,
Paymaster William Hadley,
Asst. Surgeon Alexander Johnston,
who were invalided from the Crimea, and
died shortly afterwards.
And of
6 serjeants, 13 corporals, 4 buglers,
and
235 privates of the Regiment,
who were killed in action
or died of wounds or disease in the East
during the Russian War, 1854-55-56.
This tablet is erected by the officers of the Regiment, and by officers
who formerly served in it.

N.B.—Names of N.C.Os. and men are *not* given.

THE DURHAM LIGHT INFANTRY

There is a monument in Leeds Parish Church which was "Erected by their Fellow Townsmen to 'Lieut. Marshall, 68th, and various N.C.Os. and men of different regiments,' natives of Leeds, who lost their lives in the Crimean War." It bears the following names of members of the 68th Durham Light Infantry:—

Lieutenant James Marshall.
Serjeant William Blythe.
Corporal James Thackray.
Private Isaac Abbott.
  „ Thomas Abbott.
  „ William Anderson.
  „ Benjamin Beck.
  „ Robert Fossey.
  „ George Foster.
  „ John France.
  „ Thomas Fletcher.
  „ James Greenwell.
Private George Langworthy.
  „ Thomas Levitt.
  „ Joseph Merritt.
  „ Thomas Parker.
  „ Charles Peat.
  „ John Riley.
  „ John Simmons.
  „ George Swales.
  „ Joseph Smith.
  „ Charles Folley.
  „ Charles Ward.
  „ Isaac Walton.

The Colours, which were carried by the 68th through the Crimean War, are placed above this monument.

In 1899 hatchments were placed by the inhabitants of New Plymouth, New Zealand, in the parish church of St. Mary in that town in memory of the soldiers and sailors of Her Majesty's Forces who lost their lives in New Zealand in 1864-1865; an oil painting of the colours to be inserted in the hatchment, in memory of the 68th, was presented for this purpose by Colonel A. L. Woodland.

MONUMENT IN DURHAM CATHEDRAL.

No. 2 (brass).

In memory of the officer, non-commissioned officers and men of the 2nd Battalion Durham Light Infantry, who died whilst serving in Egypt and the Soudan, between 25th February, 1885, and 6th January, 1887.

APPENDIX X

Captain Richard Brock Barker.

Colour-Serjeant O. H. Keisten.

Serjeant T. Dale.	Private H. Garman.
„ J. Hamer.	„ T. Handley.
„ D. Hayes.	„ B. Hawkins.
Lance-Serjeant N. Livick.	„ J. Heeney.
Corporal T. Inett.	„ J. Johnson.
„ N. Murray.	„ M. Jones.
Lance-Corporal H. Harvey.	„ J. Lee.
„ „ T. Hughes.	„ J. Lucas.
„ „ E. Murphy.	„ J. McDonald (i.).
Bugler W. Chartres.	„ J. McDonald (ii.).
Private H. Barrett.	„ W. McDonald.
„ T. Bayliss.	„ W. Mackey.
„ G. Bell.	„ S. Mason.
„ J. Black.	„ M. Melia.
„ C. Carter.	„ H. Minter.
„ W. Chapman.	„ G. Morrow.
„ T. Christie.	„ H. Recardo.
„ F. Cox.	„ J. Rhind.
„ J. Cranson.	„ J. Roach.
„ T. Davis.	„ J. Smith.
„ T. Dodd.	„ R. Smith.
„ E. Drew.	„ J. Sweeney.
„ D. Duggan.	„ E. Tucker.
„ A. Dutton.	„ A. Turner.
„ H. Eteson.	„ T. Whitehurst.
„ J. Evans.	„ W. Wilson.
„ H. Feeley.	„ R. Young.

Canteen Steward R. Grafton.

This tablet is erected by their comrades—officers, non-commissioned officers and men—of the 2nd Battalion.

THE DURHAM LIGHT INFANTRY

Monument in Durham Cathedral Churchyard.

A Runic Cross (stone).

To the memory of the officers, non-commissioned officers and men of the Durham Light Infantry, who were killed in action, or died of wounds or disease in the South African Campaign.

1899—1902.

"Faithful Unto Death."

Erected 1905.

The Durham Light Infantry.

1st Battalion.

Major T. R. Johnson-Smyth.
Lieut. and Adjt. E. B. Thresher.
Lieut. C. Duncombe-Shafto.
    „   R. R. Lambton.
    „   R. E. Rasbotham.

Serjeant J. Haigh.	Private H. Hick.
„ W. Hardwick.	„ W. Horsman.
„ W. Kirkwood.	„ W. Howard.
„ W. Sykes.	„ J. Hudson.
„ R. Turner.	„ E. Hutchinson.
Corporal J. Melia.	„ W. Ingrey.
„ S. Nicholson.	„ T. Jackson.
Lance-Corporal R. Andrew.	„ A. Johnson.
„ „ H. Hamblin.	„ G. Johnstone.
„ „ W. Ismay.	„ S. Lascelles.
„ „ E. Morgan.	„ J. Logan.
„ „ M. Naitby.	„ D. Maher.
„ „ G. Weston.	„ G. Manser.
„ „ H. Wilson.	„ T. Marley.
Bugler K. Cumming.	„ T. McEwan.
„ R. Iles.	„ H. McDermott.
„ W. Lamb.	„ J. Parker.

DURHAM LIGHT INFANTRY
SOUTH AFRICAN WAR MEMORIAL.
Durham Cathedral Churchyard.

APPENDIX X

Bugler F. Witts.
Private W. Armour.
" J. Arkless.
" W. Ashmore.
" W. Bassett.
" W. Beadnell.
" W. Blair.
" W. Budd.
" W. Burnell.
" F. Collins.
" W. Collins.
" J. Cox.
" J. Cresswell.
" T. Critchley.
" T. Davis.
" G. Davis.
" J. Dixon.
" J. Elliot.
" J. Fawcett.
" H. Fletcher.
" W. Forfit.
" S. Frost.
" J. Gascoigne.
" H. Gettle.
" A. Gilbey.
" D. Graham.

Private W. Pell.
" G. Plotnicki.
" R. Rigg.
" W. Rose.
" J. Rowing.
" R. Rowntree.
" W. Rousham.
" A. Royal.
" E. Ryan.
" J. Ryan.
" J. Sellars.
" H. Shearman.
" W. Sherman.
" G. Styles.
" A. Tennett.
" W. Turner.
" H. Vernon.
" H. Wass.
" H. Walker.
" G. White.
" J. Whitehead.
" G. Wilson.
" J. Witts.
" W. Woods.
" E. Yoxall.

2nd Battalion.

Lieut. A. S. Way.

Corporal G. Meadon.
Lance-Corporal W. Clements.
" " W. C. Pickett.
Private G. E. Cartwright.
" J. Coan.
" T. Coyle.

Private J. Durkin.
" S. Holt.
" J. Lorrison.
" R. Watson.
" G. H. Woolan.

THE DURHAM LIGHT INFANTRY

3rd Battalion.

Colonel R. B. Wilson.
Lieut. F. H. A. Sowerby.
2nd Lieut. J. C. Williams.

Serjeant A. A. Gunton.
„ J. Graham.
„ J. Slater.
„ W. Watson.
Lance-Corporal J. Marrion.
„ „ H. Reynolds.
Private T. Byrnes.
„ G. Dalkin.
„ J. W. Dent.
„ J. Forrest.
„ J. Goodwin.
„ P. Handley.
„ E. Holmes.

Private O. Laffey.
„ H. Lain.
„ D. Marshall.
„ G. McClone.
„ W. McHugh.
„ C. Morris.
„ A. Nobes.
„ P. Scullion.
„ J. Stanton.
„ W. Taylor.
„ C. Thompson.
„ T. Wall.
„ W. Wright.

4th Battalion.

Corporal C. Woodcock.
Private T. Bradley.
„ C. Connor.
„ J. Connor.
„ W. Doyle.
„ F. Duffy.
„ J. Monaghan.

Private J. Finneran.
„ E. Harwood.
„ J. Kell.
„ W. Mason.
„ J. McLaughlin.
„ C. Quinn.

The Durham Light Infantry, Volunteer Battalions.

1st. Private J. Morris.
2nd. Privates J. Armstrong, N. Bishop, W. Eyles.
3rd. Bugler A. Orr.
4th. Corporal T. Usworth, Private I. Eland.
5th. Privates E. Dixon, S. Jones.

APPENDIX X

Monument in Durham Cathedral.
No. 3 (brass).

To the glory of God and in affectionate memory of
Lieutenant Charles Duncombe-Shafto,
1st Battalion Durham Light Infantry,
who was killed in action at Vaal Krantz
on the 5th February, 1900.
This memorial is erected by his brother-officers.

There is a stone pillar on the site of the battle of Vaal Krantz erected to the memory of those officers, non-commissioned officers and men of the 1st Battalion Durham Light Infantry who were killed, or died of wounds received, at the battle; the ground on which it stands was given by the landowner. The following names are on the pillar:—

Major T. R. Johnson-Smyth.
2nd Lieutenant C. Duncombe-Shafto.

Serjeant T. W. Haigh.   Private W. Howard.
   „   W. Hardwick.   „   J. Hudson.
Lance-Corporal E. Morgan.   „   G. Manser.
Bugler R. Cumming.   „   A. Nobes.
   „   W. Lamb.   „   T. Rose.
   „   F. Witts.   „   J. Rowing.
Private W. Blair.   „   E. Ryan.
   „   J. Fawcett.   „   H. Sellars.
   „   H. Fletcher.   „   A. Thirkell.
   „   D. Graham.

[*APPENDIX XI.*

THE 3RD AND 4TH BATTALIONS DURHAM LIGHT INFANTRY.

As it is not within the province of this book to trace the descent of the Militia from the ancient fyrd, nor even from the trained bands of a later period, it will suffice to give a short account of the Special Reserve from the middle of the eighteenth century, as it is from that time that the present 4th Battalion assumed its present shape, and from that time has had a continuous existence.

Owing to the strain placed upon the regular forces of the kingdom by the Seven Years' War, an act for the re-constitution of the Militia (30, Geo. II., cap. 25) was passed in 1757.

The newly constituted regiment of Durham Militia was not actually formed until 1759, when Henry, 2nd Earl of Darlington,[*] was appointed colonel; the head-quarters were at Barnard Castle, and the strength was 369 men, furnished by the different wards as under:—

Chester, 105; Darlington, 131; Easington, 59; Stockton, 45; Norhamshire, 11; and Islandshire, 18.

It is an interesting fact that one, William Herschel, in after years the celebrated astronomer, was the first bandmaster of the regiment.

---

[*] The assertion frequently made that this officer had been present at Dettingen and Fontenoy, and that he had been wounded at the former battle, is certainly in part, and probably, in its entirety, inaccurate. The Hon. Henry Vane, as he then was, was born in 1726, and received his first commission in the army, in the Grenadier Guards, on 11th May, 1745, i.e., in the same month that the battle of Fontenoy was fought. The confusion is between him and his uncle, the Hon. Gilbert Vane, who was also in the Grenadier Guards, and who was wounded at Fontenoy.

APPENDIX XI

The regiment was embodied on 22nd February, 1760, and in November, 1761, was at Pontefract, consisting of eight companies, with a strength of 23 officers, 16 serjeants, 16 drummers, and 396 rank and file; it was disembodied in 1763.

The House of Commons Journal for 1761-4 contains an estimate, dated 28th January, 1763, for £332 15s. 0d. for the march of the Durham Militia; this march was evidently the return to Barnard-Castle for disembodiment, but there is not any indication as to the place from which the march commenced, nor as to the dates on which it was begun and concluded.

The officers in 1761 were:—

Col. Henry, Earl of Darlington.
Lieut.-Colonel Robert Shafto.
Major Ralph Gowland.
Captain Nathaniel Pewterer.
   „   Timothy Hutchinson.
   „   Frederick Vane.
   „   John Bulman.
   „   Bartholomew Bowser.
Lieutenant John Taylor.
   „   Crosier Surtees.
   „   Robert Robinson.
   „   Robert Hutchinson.

Lieutenant Christopher Bell.
   „   William Norton.
   „   John Forster.
   „   William Forster.
Ensign James Benning.
   „   Thomas Cattrick.
   „   Anthony Bowser.
   „   Anthony Surtees.
   „   Charles Beaumont.
   „   Thomas Woodifield.
   „   William Garth.

Adjutant———. Quartermaster———. Surgeon———.
Agent: Mr. Drummond, Spring Garden.

The establishment in 1763 was (eight companies) 28 officers and 448 non-commissioned officers and men.

The whole of the Militia was embodied on 26th March, 1778; the Durham Regiment, according to the late Major R. W. Atkinson's history, was quartered at Sunderland, Hartlepool, and South Shields, but according to the "Army List" of 1778 it was quartered at Scarborough and Whitby. The officers in this year were:—

THE DURHAM LIGHT INFANTRY

Colonel Earl of Darlington.
Major John Taylor.
Captain Robt. Robinson.
    ,,   Robt. Hutchinson.
    ,,   James Benning.
    ,,   Thos. Caterick Greene.
Captain-Lieut. William Benning.
Lieutenant Thos. Drake.
    ,,   William Usher.
    ,,   Thos. Richardson.
Lieutenant Thos. Stout.
    ,,   Geo. Newsham.
    ,,   Thos. Coates.
Ensign John Smith.
    ,,   Lord Viscount Barnard.
Adjutant Samuel Castle.
Quartermaster Ambrose Castle.
Surgeon Thos. Stout.
Chaplain Rev. Mr. Lipscomb.
Paymaster Robt. Preston.

The regiment now appears to have consisted of only six companies. The uniform was "red, faced with purple, and silver-laced buttonholes."

Ensign Viscount Barnard was only twelve years old at this time.

The following notice as to precedence of regiments of Militia deserves attention:—

"No rank having been established for the several corps of Militia, it was this year settled by drawing lots.

"London, 1st June, 1778.

"At a meeting of the Lord Lieutenants of the several counties of England and Wales at the St. Alban's Tavern on this day, the following numbers were drawn:—

* * *

Durham, 44.

* * *

" etc., etc."

In the above notice it will be observed that only England and Wales are mentioned; the Irish Militia was not formed until 1793, and the Scottish Militia four years later.

Major Atkinson states, in his history, that in May, 1779, the Durham Militia was once again at Barnard-Castle; the regiment remained embodied until 1783.

In 1782 the Durham Militia again drew the number 44.

WILLIAM HARRY, 1ST DUKE OF CLEVELAND.
When a young man in the Uniform of the Durham Militia. Probably about 1790.

APPENDIX XI

Colonel the Earl of Darlington died on 10th September, 1792, and was succeeded in the command by William Harry, 3rd Earl of Darlington, and subsequently 1st Duke of Cleveland.

There is, at Raby Castle, a portrait of the latter, when quite a young man, in the uniform of the Durham Militia; the purple facings have disappeared, and are now replaced by buff, or pale yellow—the exact shade is not very distinct. The device on the buttons is an earl's coronet above the letters "D.M."*

At the end of 1792 the Durham Militia was again embodied, and was not disembodied for nearly ten years; its stations and movements were as under:—

1st Jan.,	1793.	Whitby (six companies), 7 officers, 13 serjeants, 13 corporals, 12 drummers, and 244 privates; total 289, all ranks.
1st March,	1793.	Whitby (four companies) and Stockton (two companies).
1st Jan.,	1794.	Whitby (four companies) and Scarborough (two companies).
1st July,	1794.	Scarborough (six companies).
1st June,	1795.	Malton.
1st July,	1795.	Fulwell Camp.
Oct.,	1795.	Head-quarters at Newcastle-on-Tyne; one company at Morpeth, one at North Shields, and one at Tynemouth.
1st Nov.,	1795.	Morpeth and Alnwick.
1st April,	1796.	Doncaster, en route to Yarmouth.
1st May,	1796.	Yarmouth, where it remained for one year; there was a detachment at Lowstoff [sic].
1st May,	1797.	Commenced to march to Hull.
17th May,	1797.	Arrived at Hull.
1st May,	1798.	York.
1st June,	1798.	Hull.

---

* A regimental colour, date uncertain, but probably of the last few years of the eighteenth century, has the Earl of Darlington's arms and the words "Durham Militia" on it.

THE DURHAM LIGHT INFANTRY

1st July,	1798.	Burstwick Camp.
1st Nov.,	1798.	Stamford, en route to Colchester.
1st Dec.,	1798.	Colchester Barracks.
9th Sept.	1799.	To Chelmsford Barracks, whence detachments were sent to Purfleet and Brentwood.
28th Oct.,	1799.	Now increased to twelve companies, the regiment left Chelmsford in three divisions for Newark
1st Nov.,	1799.	Stilton.
19th Nov.,	1799.	Newark, with a detachment at Peterborough.
26th Dec.,	1799.	Left Newark for Peterborough.
1st Jan.,	1800.	Peterborough.
14th Feb.,	1800.	Whittlesea, a detachment at Wisbech.
13th May,	1800.	Wisbech, en route to Yarmouth.
19th May,	1800.	Arrived at Yarmouth, where it remained for nine months; a detachment at Lowestoft.
19th Feb.,	1801.	Left Yarmouth.
17th March,	1801.	Arrived at Sunderland, and remained there for one year.
March,	1802.	Marched to Tynemouth.
May,	1802.	Returned to Barnard-Castle, and was disembodied.

In April, 1796, the strength of the regiment was (six companies) 14 officers, 20 serjeants, 20 corporals, 12 drummers, and 375 privates; but in the following December the establishment was raised to twelve companies, eight of which were to consist of 110 men each, and the remaining two—the flank companies—of 150 men each. The actual strength in 1797 was about 800; in 1798 it was about 1,200.

On 19th April, 1797, H.R.H. the Duke of York inspected the regiment.

In October, 1797, a party of 300 prisoners of war was escorted by 6 officers and 210 non-commissioned officers and men of the Durham Militia from Barton-on-Humber to Norman Cross, near Peterborough; there were about that time barracks for two regiments of infantry, and accommodation for a large number of prisoners of war at Norman Cross.

Towards the end of 1799 so many men had volunteered for the Regular Army that the regiment was reduced to 439 of all ranks.

APPENDIX XI

In March, 1803, the Government decided to call out the Militia, so the Durham Regiment was soon again embodied; it was called out early in May, and then consisted of eight companies, 14 officers, 26 serjeants, 9 drummers, and 401 rank and file. It remained embodied for eleven years; during that period its stations and movements were as under:—

1st June,	1803.	Sunderland.
1st Aug.,	1803.	Hull.
1st Jan.,	1804.	Beverley; now ten companies, with a strength of 27 officers and 773 non-commissioned officers and men.
14th Feb.,	1804.	Back to Hull.
1st Aug.,	1804.	Spalding, en route to Chelmsford.
14th Aug.,	1804.	Chelmsford Barracks.
1st Jan.,	1805.	Maldon; strength 791, all ranks.
14th April,	1805.	Danbury Barracks (5 miles east of Chelmsford).
1st July,	1805.	Huntingdon.
14th July,	1805.	Norman Cross Barracks (6 miles South of Peterborough).
1st Dec.,	1805.	Colchester.
1st Feb.,	1806.	Weeley Barracks (12 miles east of Colchester).
1st June,	1806.	Woodbridge Barracks, where it remained until March, 1808.
1st April,	1808.	Liphook, en route to Portsmouth.
1st May,	1808.	Portsmouth, where it remained until October, 1810.
17th Oct.,	1810.	Left Portsmouth.
16th Nov.,	1810.	Arrived at Sunderland.
20th Feb.,	1812.	Left Sunderland for Scotland.
4th March,	1812.	Arrived at Musselburgh.
25th Jan.,	1813.	Auchtermuchty, en route to Perth.
25th Feb.,	1813.	Perth, with several detachments, where the regiment stayed for one year.
25th Feb.,	1814.	Glasgow.
24th July,	1814.	Marched from Glasgow for Barnard-Castle.
6th Aug.,	1814.	Arrived at Barnard-Castle, and was disembodied eight days later.

THE DURHAM LIGHT INFANTRY

While at Portsmouth a guard of the regiment, on one of the prison ships, distinguished itself in suppressing a rising of the prisoners on board; the officer in command of the guard had temporarily left the ship for orders, and the responsibility then rested upon Serjeants James Allan and Anthony Hutchinson, both of whom faced the seriousness of the situation with firmness and decision.

Also, while at Portsmouth, a considerable number of men of the Durham and Shropshire Militias volunteered into the 43rd Light Infantry, the 53rd Regiment, and the 68th Light Infantry.

In 1809 the regiment volunteered for active service in Spain.

While at Musselburgh the regiment was on one occasion brigaded with the 1st Battalion of the 25th Regiment and the 42nd Highlanders for the purpose of being reviewed by Viscount Cathcart, who was then Commander-in-Chief in Scotland; his lordship was pleased to say that he considered the Durham Militia to be the smartest of the three regiments.

Serjeant-Major Charles Simpson, who was serjeant-major of the regiment for over thirty years, attained that rank on 10th May, 1814, while at Glasgow.

As the "local Militia," which existed from 1808 to 1816, is occasionally confused by some people with the "general Militia," it may perhaps not be out of place to state here that there were two regiments of local Militia in Co. Durham, the 1st consisting of ten companies, the 2nd of eight companies, and that neither of them had any relationship to the regiment of the general Militia, which is the subject of this chapter.

The officers in 1812 were:—

		Date.	Age.
Colonel William Harry, Earl of Darlington...		23-12-1792	45
Lieutenant-Colonel James O'Callaghan	...	9-5-1805	58
Major William Byers		9-5-1805	32
Captain Richard Lipscomb		8-5-1798	55
„	Henry Doubleday	18-5-1803	33
„	Joshua Rowley Gunthorpe	20-5-1803	31
„	William Hill	4-6-1804	32
„	William Greenwell	31-7-1806	34
„	William Hunter Burne	25-11-1806	23

APPENDIX XI

	Date.	Age.
Captain James Allan Wright	4-3-1807	23
„ Daniel O'Callaghan	25-6-1810	38
Lieutenant Thomas William Hill, P.M.	11-3-1803	39
„ William Horsley, S.M.	26-7-1803	29
„ Robert Moses	2-4-1806	31
„ George Nelson	7-2-1809	33
„ William Evans	30-5-1809	24
„ William Charles Sharp	26-3-1810	34
„ George Blakiston Robinson	10-2-1811	21
„ Nicholas Horsley	21-9-1812	20
„ Thomas Ilderton Ferrier	21-9-1812	—
Ensign Alexander Thompson	1-1-1812	19
„ James Mann	25-4-1812	19
„ Magnus Hodgson	4-6-1812	28
„ William McCarthy	15-8-1812	24
„ Francis Beaumont	25-9-1812	—
„ Charles Dixon	15-12-1812	28
Adjutant James Simpson, Lieutenant	21-3-1810	45
Quartermaster James Horner	10-5-1810	38
Paymaster Thomas William Hill	25-12-1797	39
Surgeon Leonard Fosbrooke	14-1-1809	44
Assistant Surgeon William Horsley	1-5-1809	29

Some points in this list are worthy of attention; it will be observed that paymaster and the assistant surgeon also figure in the list of combatant officers, but the surgeon and the other regimental staff officers do not. The ages of the officers are entirely lacking in graduation; the major is twenty-three years younger than the senior captain, and the last-joined ensign is five years older than two of the captains, etc.

An epaulet and breast-plate, originally worn by Captain W. H. Burne, are still in existence, in the possession of his present living representative; the button on the epaulet bears a Royal Crown—in the place of the earl's coronet of former days—the words "DURHAM MILITIA," and the figures "25," which indicate the order of precedence of the regiment at this period; the breast-plate is made of silver, is oval, and has engraved upon it the letters "D.M.," with a crown above, and the figures "xxv" below them.

THE DURHAM LIGHT INFANTRY

The regiment was again embodied at Barnard-Castle on 14th July, 1815; although it included twenty-five officers in its numbers, it was very weak, and could only muster 18 serjeants, 9 drummers, and 156 rank and file; it marched from Barnard-Castle on 22nd August, and arrived at Newcastle on the 26th. In the middle of September it moved to Tynemouth, but in November was back again in Newcastle, and on the 28th started for Glasgow, where it arrived on 11th December, and where it stayed until February, 1816; there were 232 non-commissioned officers and men in the regiment in December, 1815.

On 12th February, 1816, the regiment marched from Glasgow, and, having arrived at Barnard-Castle on the 26th of the same month, was disembodied two days later.

From that time until 1885 the regiment, or, to be more exact, the 1st Durham Militia, as it was called after 1853, did not serve out of the county of Durham.

The following paragraph appears in "The Glasgow Star" of 27th July, 1814:—"The first division of the Durham Militia has marched from this garrison. The orderly behaviour of the regiment during its stay in Glasgow is highly commended."

The regiment was called out for annual training up to 1825, then in the course of the next few years on only one or two occasions, after which it shared the fate of the whole of the Militia Force in being allowed to fall into decay until 1852. During this period, however, a permanent staff, with practically no duties to perform, was kept up. On 5th December, 1833, the staff consisted of Captain and Adjutant James Simpson, whose service amounted to 52 years and 294 days; Serjeant-Major Charles Simpson (son of the adjutant), whose service amounted to 32 years and 280 days; 12 serjeants, a drum-major, and 4 drummers.

Captain James Simpson, who had enlisted at the age of thirteen, was now sixty-six years old.

Colonel the Duke of Cleveland died on 29th January, 1842, and was succeeded as colonel by his son Henry, 2nd Duke of Cleveland.

On 31st December, 1844, the staff only consisted of Serjeant-Major Charles Simpson, who then had nearly forty years' service, and six serjeants, three of whom had over thirty years' service.

APPENDIX XI

The uniform of Mr. John Bowes, of Streatlam Castle, who was lieutenant-colonel at this period, is now in the Bowes Museum, Barnard-Castle; the facings are white, and the device on the buttons is a crown above the letters " D.M."

On 30th June, 1852, " an Act to consolidate and amend the laws relating to the Militia in England " was passed; the result was that the Durham Militia once more commenced a real and active existence.

In the following month, by an Order in Council, the county of Durham was ordered to furnish 1,096 men in 1852 and 666 in 1853, but, as the ballot was dispensed with, these numbers were not reached.

The Durham Militia was assembled at Barnard-Castle in November and December in two divisions, the one succeeding the other, for three weeks' training, assisted by a party of non-commissioned officers and men of the 28th Regiment.

In 1853 it was resolved that the Militia of the County of Durham should be divided into three regiments, two of infantry and one of artillery; the head-quarters of the first regiment of infantry to be at Barnard-Castle, of the second regiment of infantry at Durham, and of the artillery at Bishop Auckland; the head-quarters of the last-named were, however, moved later to Hartlepool.

The original regiment was henceforth known as the 1st or South Durham Militia, and the new regiment of infantry as the 2nd or North Durham Militia; both wore red with white facings; the proceedings of the artillery do not come within the scope of this book.

On 1st July, 1853, the South Durham Regiment consisted of (eight companies) 24 officers, 12 serjeants, 14 corporals, 4 drummers and 657 privates; and the North Durham Regiment consisted of (eight companies) 14 officers, 1 serjeant-major, and 179 men; but it must be remembered that the latter corps had not then been completely formed.

The number of companies in the North Durham Militia was soon varied; in 1855 it was reduced to six, and in 1860 to four; in 1861 it was again raised to eight, and in 1890 to ten.

During the Crimean War both regiments were embodied; the 1st from December, 1854, to May, 1856, at Barnard-Castle; the 2nd from March, 1855, to May, 1856, being quartered until August,

1855, at Durham, then at Sunderland, and during the last few months of the embodiment at Burnley.

On 1st July, 1855, both regiments were, from various causes, very weak in numbers; the 1st consisted of 389 all ranks, and the 2nd of only 241 all ranks; but these numbers were, in both cases, soon increased.

In 1860 Henry, second Duke of Cleveland, relinquished the colonelcy of the 1st Durham Militia, which had been held continuously by him, his father, and grandfather for over a century.

On 11th December, 1868, the 1st Durham Militia was informed by the Right Hon. E. Cardwell, then Secretary of State for War, that Her Majesty had approved of the regiment being made a fusilier regiment.

In 1869 an Act of Parliament was passed empowering the Crown to place the Militia under the general officers during training; and in 1871 another Act was passed revesting in the Crown the jurisdiction of the Lords-Lieutenant over the Militia; in the following year county store houses, etc., were transferred to the Crown.

No important changes in name or organization took place until July, 1881, when the 1st Durham (Fusilier) Militia became the 3rd Battalion of the Durham Light Infantry and the 2nd (North) Durham Militia became the 4th Battalion; their order of precedence thus became altered, for the former had previously ranked as the 3rd Regiment and the latter as the 43rd Regiment in the Militia Forces; at the same time the uniform of both battalions was assimilated to that of the two regular battalions of the Durham Light Infantry; head-quarters of the 3rd Battalion remained at Barnard-Castle, where they still are; head-quarters of the 4th Battalion remained at Durham until January, 1884, when they were moved to Newcastle-on-Tyne.

The 3rd Battalion was embodied from 9th March, 1885, to 29th September in the same year, and during that period was quartered at Colchester.

During the war in South Africa, 1899-1902, both battalions were embodied at different periods and had their first experience of active service; the 3rd was granted, as an honour, the words "South Africa, 1900-01," and the 4th "South Africa, 1902."

APPENDIX XI

The 3rd Battalion was embodied from 5th December, 1899, to 12th June, 1901; shortly after its embodiment it proceeded to South Africa with a strength of 30 officers and 796 non-commissioned officers and men and arrived at East London on 3rd February, 1900; during its service in South Africa the battalion was employed in guarding the lines of communication in Cape Colony and in the Orange Free State, escorting convoys, and in garrisoning Dewetsdorp for about six months, etc., etc.

The following were mentioned in Lord Roberts's despatch of 4th September, 1901:—

Colonel R. B. Wilson. Serjeant-Major A. Anderton.
Major E. S. V. Grimshawe. Qr.-Mr.-Serjt. R. W. Storey.
Captain T. G. Sowerby. Colour-Serjeant A. Chivers.
Captain H. J. Sowerby. Colour-Serjeant T. Taft.
Captain E. C. Sowerby. Serjeant T. Beeby (4th D.L.I.).
Serjeant T. Sweeney.

Colonel R. B. Wilson was awarded the C.M.G., Captain and Hon. Major H. J. Sowerby the D.S.O., and Serjeants T. Beeby and T. Sweeney received the D.C.M.

Colonel R. B. Wilson, Lieutenant F. H. A. Sowerby, 2nd Lieutenant J. C. Williams and twenty-six non-commissioned officers and men lost their lives in South Africa from various causes.

Quartermaster J. M. Byrne and 90 non-commissioned officers and men of the 4th Battalion joined the 3rd a few days before the latter sailed for South Africa.

The 4th Battalion was embodied twice, on the first occasion from 23rd January, 1900, to 4th December, 1900, when it was quartered at Aldershot, and on the second occasion from 6th January, 1902, to 3rd October, 1902, when it served in South Africa; on the latter occasion, after having spent about three weeks in York, the battalion sailed from Southampton in s.s. "Canada"—strength, 31 officers and 821 non-commissioned officers and men—and arrived at Capetown on 18th February; it was then conveyed by rail to Orange River Station, Cape Colony; it furnished detachments for duty at Kimberley, Belmont, Modder River, Schmidt's Drift, Barkley West, Daniel's Kiul, Boshoff, Slip Klip Drift, and Windsorton

Road; it was also employed on the line of blockhouses from Orange River to Modder River, with one company on the Orange River Bridge; a company of mounted infantry was also formed; this company was employed on convoy duty between Kimberley, Boshoff, and Christiana.

The battalion embarked at Port Elizabeth on 3rd September on s.s. "Roslin Castle," and disembarked at Southampton on 2nd October.

Serjeant T. Beeby gained the D.C.M.

The casualty list did not include any officers; sixteen non-commissioned officers and men lost their lives; of this number two were killed in action, three died from wounds received in action; ten died from disease, and one was drowned in the Vaal River.

Since the South African War the ordinary routine has been carried out in both battalions with few incidents calling for special mention.

In 1908 the enumeration was altered; the 3rd Battalion became the 4th, and the 4th became the 3rd; also, the whole of the Militia, under the new designation "Special Reserve," became more closely connected with the Regular Army.

On 1st June, 1912, new colours were presented to the 3rd Battalion at Whitley Bay by the Earl of Durham, K.G., replacing the original colours, which had been presented by the Marchioness of Londonderry; the honours of the regular battalions were inscribed on these colours.

On 4th July, 1912, the 4th Battalion marched from Deerbolt Camp, near Barnard-Castle, to Raby Castle, where, after an attack had been practised in the park, it was entertained by Lord and Lady Barnard; it then, in the afternoon of the same day, marched back to Deerbolt Camp.

Present establishment, 3rd Battalion, 34 officers, 663* non-commissioned officers and men; 4th Battalion, 31 officers, 780 non-commissioned officers and men.

Present strength.—3rd Battalion, 19 officers, 507* non-com-

---

*Exclusive of 41 privates, of the regular establishment, who would rejoin the home battalion (regular) on mobilization.

APPENDIX XI

missioned officers and men; 4th Battalion, 14 officers, 567 non-commissioned officers and men.

There are eight companies in each battalion.

COLONELS OF THE DURHAM MILITIA FROM 1759 TO 1853.

(i.) Henry, 2nd Earl of Darlington. 26th October, 1759. Formerly in Grenadier and in Coldstream Guards. Died 10th September, 1792.

(ii.) William Harry, 3rd Earl of Darlington. 23rd December, 1792. Subsequently 1st Duke of Cleveland. Was also Colonel of the Durham Fencible Cavalry, 1794—1799. Died 29th January, 1842.

(iii.) Henry, 2nd Duke of Cleveland. 16th May, 1842. Formerly in 7th Hussars, 2nd Life Guards, and 75th Foot.

LIEUTENANT-COLONELS OF THE DURHAM MILITIA FROM 1759 TO 1853.

(None before 1761.)

(i.) Robert Shafto, in 1761-2-3.

(None 1778—1781, nor, apparently, until 1794.)

(ii.) Calverley Bewicke. 8th June, 1794.

(iii.) James O'Callaghan. 9th May, 1805.

(iv.) John Bowes. 14th September, 1835.

1ST OR SOUTH DURHAM MILITIA, LATER 3RD BATTALION DURHAM LIGHT INFANTRY; NOW 4TH BATTALION DURHAM LIGHT INFANTRY.

Colonels (or Honorary Colonels).

(i.) Henry, 2nd Duke of Cleveland. 16th May, 1842. Resigned 1860.

(No Colonel from 1860 to 1873.)

THE DURHAM LIGHT INFANTRY

(ii.) Charles Freville Surtees. 15th March, 1873. Late Captain 3rd Hussars. Died 1906.

(iii.) Henry De Vere, 9th Baron Barnard. 23rd December, 1906. Formerly in Northampton and Rutland Militia.

Lieutenant-Colonels.

(i.) John Bowes. 14th September, 1835.

(ii.) Poulett Henry Somerset (late Coldstream Guards). 1st March, 1856.

(iii.) William Maude. 15th March, 1858.

(iv.) Charles Freville Surtees (late 3rd Hussars). 21st December, 1870.

(v.) John Frederick Gales. 30th April, 1873.

(vi.) William Dale Trotter. 28th October, 1874.

(vii.) George Sowerby (Honorary Colonel). 18th December, 1875.

(viii.) Charles James Briggs (Honorary Colonel). 2nd August, 1888.

(ix.) Richard Bassett Wilson (Hon. Colonel). 3rd July, 1893.

(x.) Edward Salusbury Vaughan Grimshawe (Hon. Colonel). 22nd March, 1901.

(xi.) Harry John Sowerby, D.S.O. (Honorary Colonel). 22nd March, 1907.

(xii.) William Hylton Briggs. 22nd March, 1912.

2ND OR NORTH DURHAM MILITIA, LATER 4TH BATTALION DURHAM LIGHT INFANTRY, NOW 3RD BATTALION DURHAM LIGHT INFANTRY.

Honorary Colonels.

(No Honorary Colonel before 1862.)

(i.) George Henry Robert Charles William, 2nd Earl Vane, Subsequently 5th Marquis of Londonderry. 12th March, 1862. Died 6th November, 1884.

(No Honorary Colonel from 1884 to 1892.)

(ii.) James John Allison, C.B.. 20th August, 1892.

APPENDIX XI

(iii.) Charles Stewart, 6th Marquis of Londonderry, K.G., G.C.V.O., C.B., V.D., A.D.C.   7th June, 1899.

Lieutenant-Colonels.

(i.) G. H. R. C. W. Viscount Seaham (later 2nd Earl Vane). 6th May, 1853.

(ii.) Edward Johnson.   27th February, 1862.

(iii.) Augustus Samuel Bolton (late 31st Foot).   2nd March, 1868.

(iv.) James John Allison (Honorary Colonel).   1st July, 1874.

(v.) Edward Leadbitter-Smith (Honorary Colonel).   5th October, 1892.

(vi.) Mark Henry Lambert (Honorary Colonel).   24th November, 1897.

(vii.) Charles Waring Darwin (Honorary Colonel) (late 1st Battalion Durham Light Infantry).   21st January, 1905.

(viii.) Richard Henry Wingfield Cardiff.   6th January, 1912.

[*APPENDIX XII.*

THE 5TH, 6TH, 7TH, 8TH AND 9TH BATTALIONS DURHAM LIGHT INFANTRY.

On the revival of the Volunteer Force in 1859 steps were taken for the formation of corps in the county of Durham, but there were many delays and no corps came into existence until the 1st (or Stockton) Corps was officially formed in February, 1860. By February, 1861, the following Rifle Corps—so called from the weapon, which at that time was coming into general use—were established in the county of Durham, which, in point of precedence as regards rifle corps, was No. 64 :—

Number.	Place.	Commanding Officer.
1st.	Stockton.	Captain R. Thompson (late Lieut., 48th Madras N.I.).
2nd.	——	——
3rd.	Sunderland.	Captain T. E. Chapman.
4th.	Bishop Auckland.	Captain W. Trotter.
5th.	——	——
6th.	South Shields.	Captain J. Williamson.
7th.	Durham.	Captain J. Fogg-Elliot.
8th.	Gateshead.	Captain G. H. L. Hawks.
9th.	Blaydon.	Captain J. Cowen.
10th.	Beamish.	Captain J. Joicey.
11th.	Chester-le-Street.	Captain P. S. Reid.
12th.	Middleton-in-Teesdale.	Captain H. G. Bainbridge.
13th.	Birtley.	Captain E. M. Perkins.
14th.	Felling.	Captain W. W. Pattinson.
15th.	Darlington.	Captain G. J. Scurfield.
16th.	Castle Eden.	Captain R. C. Bewicke.
17th.	Wolsingham.	Captain T. H. Bates.
18th.	Shotley Bridge.	Captain J. B. Richardson.
19th.	Hartlepool.	Captain G. W. Jaffrey.
20th.	Stanhope.	Captain J. T. Roddam.

APPENDIX XII

There was also a company at Barnard Castle, with headquarters nominally at Startforth, on the Yorkshire side of the Tees; it was formed in March, 1860, and was called the 7th North York; in December, 1863, it became the 21st Durham Rifle Volunteers, and was transferred to the 2nd Administrative Battalion Durham Rifle Volunteers.

The 2nd and 5th Durham Rifle Volunteers must have had a very brief existence, if they ever had any existence at all, as neither of them are mentioned in any Army List.

These corps were entirely new institutions and had no connection whatever with the Volunteer corps which had been in existence in the county at the time of the Napoleonic wars.

In August, 1861, these corps were grouped into administrative battalions as under:—

1st Administrative Battalion of Durham Rifle Volunteers
(7th, 10th, 11th, 13th, and 14th).
Commanding Officer: Lieutenant-Colonel E. M. Perkins.
Head-quarters: Durham.

2nd Administrative Battalion of Durham Rifle Volunteers
(1st, 4th, 12th, 15th, 16th, 17th, 18th, 19th, and 20th).
Commanding Officer: Lieutenant-Colonel W. Trotter.
Head-quarters: Bishop Auckland.

3rd Administrative Battalion of Durham Rifle Volunteers
(6th, 8th, and 9th).
Commanding Officer: Lieutenant-Colonel G. H. L. Hawks.
Head-quarters: Gateshead.

The 3rd Durham Rifle Volunteers at Sunderland was an independent battalion, under the command of Major Lord Adolphus Vane-Tempest.

In December, 1861, the 1st, 15th, 16th, and 19th Durham Rifle Volunteers were taken from the 2nd Administrative Battalion, and formed into a new administrative battalion, numbered the 4th, with head-quarters at Stockton-on-Tees. In the following May, Major

THE DURHAM LIGHT INFANTRY

G. J. Scurfield, from the 2nd Administrative Battalion, was promoted to be Lieutenant-Colonel, and appointed to the command of the new battalion.

In April, 1862, the position was:—

	Number of Companies.	Enrolled Members.
1st Administrative Battalion (7th, 10th, 11th, 13th, and 14th Durham Rifle Volunteers)	11	770
2nd Administrative Battalion (4th, 12th, 17th, 18th, and 20th Durham Rifle Volunteers)	7	407
3rd Administrative Battalion (6th, 8th, and 9th Durham Rifle Volunteers)	6	399
4th Administrative Battalion (1st, 15th, 16th, and 19th Durham Rifle Volunteers)	7	419
3rd (Sunderland) Durham Rifle Volunteers	5	296

Head-quarters of the 1st Administrative Battalion were moved from Durham to Chester-le-Street in July, 1862.

The present five battalions of the Territorial Force have an unbroken descent from these five battalions, although the order of precedence has been altered.

In 1863 the Lord Lieutenant (the Earl of Durham) decided that the Volunteer Corps in Co. Durham should be clothed in rifle green instead of in the various uniforms previously worn.

It is not possible to give here a detailed account of these infantry battalions in the County of Durham; such an account would fill the pages of a large volume; some of the original corps only lasted for a few years, the battalions have had varying periods of prosperity and adversity, head-quarters have not always remained in the same place, old companies occasionally disappeared and new ones took their places, and the location of companies was frequently changed.

In 1880—

The 4th Administrative Battalion became the 1st Durham Rifle Volunteers.

The 2nd Administrative Battalion became the 2nd Durham Rifle Volunteers.

APPENDIX XII

The 3rd Durham Rifle Volunteers remained the 3rd Durham Rifle Volunteers.

The 1st Administrative Battalion became the 4th Durham Rifle Volunteers.

The 3rd Administrative Battalion became the 6th Durham Rifle Volunteers.

But later in the year (in November) the 6th Durham Rifle Volunteers was renumbered the 5th Durham Rifle Volunteers.

In December, 1887—

The 1st Durham Rifle Volunteers became the 1st Volunteer Battalion Durham Light Infantry.

The 2nd Durham Rifle Volunteers became the 2nd Volunteer Battalion Durham Light Infantry.

The 3rd Durham Rifle Volunteers became the 3rd Volunteer Battalion Durham Light Infantry.

The 4th Durham Rifle Volunteers became the 4th Volunteer Battalion Durham Light Infantry.

The 5th Durham Rifle Volunteers became the 5th Volunteer Battalion Durham Light Infantry.

All the five battalions supplied contingents to the three "Special Service Companies," which, in succession, served in the South African War with the 1st Battalion Durham Light Infantry, and all bear as an honour the words, "South Africa, 1900-02."

On 1st April, 1907, the strength was:—

	Officers.	N.C.O.'s and Men.
1st Vol. Batt. Durham L.I.	29*	1077*
2nd ,, ,, ,, ,,	37	1107
3rd ,, ,, ,, ,,	20	672
4th ,, ,, ,, ,,	32	1158
5th ,, ,, ,, ,,	34	821

At this time the 1st and 3rd Battalions wore scarlet with white facings, the 5th wore scarlet with dark green facings, and the 2nd and

---

* Of these numbers 9 officers and 231 non-commissioned officers and men belonged to three companies which were recruited at Middlesbrough, in the North Riding of Yorkshire.

THE DURHAM LIGHT INFANTRY

4th wore rifle uniform. On the transfer to the Territorial Force on 1st April, 1908, the 4th, now the 8th Battalion Durham Light Infantry, adopted scarlet, so the 2nd, now the 6th Battalion Durham Light Infantry, remains the only battalion in rifle green; the white facings of other battalions were changed to dark green.

On 1st April, 1908—

The 1st Volunteer Battalion Durham Light Infantry became the 5th Battalion Durham Light Infantry.

The 2nd Volunteer Battalion Durham Light Infantry became the 6th Battalion Durham Light Infantry.

The 3rd Volunteer Battalion Durham Light Infantry became the 7th Battalion Durham Light Infantry.

The 4th Volunteer Battalion Durham Light Infantry became the 8th Battalion Durham Light Infantry.

The 5th Volunteer Battalion Durham Light Infantry became the 9th Battalion Durham Light Infantry.

A comparative table of the number and location of companies on the last day of the Volunteer Force and on the first day of the Territorial Force is now given.

31st March, 1908. 1st Vol. Bn. Durham L.I. Head-quarters: Stockton-on-Tees.		1st April, 1908. 5th Bn. Durham L.I. Head-quarters: Stockton-on-Tees.	
	Companies		Companies
Stockton	5	Stockton	3
Darlington	3	Darlington	3
Middlesbrough (Yorks)	3	Castle Eden	2
Castle Eden	1		
Total	12	Total	8

APPENDIX XII

2nd Vol. Bn. Durham L.I. Head-quarters: Bishop Auckland.		6th Bn. Durham L.I. Head-quarters: Bishop Auckland.	
	Companies		Companies
Bishop Auckland	3	Bishop Auckland	2
Shildon	1	Spennymoor	1
Spennymoor	2	Crook	1
Barnard Castle	1	Stanhope	1
Crook	1	Barnard Castle	1
Stanhope	1	Consett	2
Consett	2		
Total	11	Total	8

3rd Vol. Bn. Durham L.I. Head-quarters: Sunderland.		7th Bn. Durham L.I. Head-quarters: Sunderland.	
	Companies		Companies
Sunderland	7	Sunderland	6
		South Shields	2
Total	7	Total	8

4th Vol. Bn. Durham L.I. Head-quarters: Durham.		8th Bn. Durham L.I. Head-quarters: Durham.	
	Companies		Companies
Durham	4	Durham	2
Stanley	1	Chester-le-Street	1
Beamish	1	Birtley	1
Sacriston	1	Beamish	1*
Birtley	1	Stanley	1*
Chester-le-Street	1	Washington	1
Washington	1	Hamsteels	1
Houghton-le-Spring	1		
Total	11	Total	8

N.B. — The company at Washington will shortly be moved to Houghton-le-Spring.
* Both now at Stanley.

THE DURHAM LIGHT INFANTRY

5th Vol. Bn. Durham L.I. Head-quarters: Gateshead.	Companies	9th Bn. Durham L.I. Head-quarters: Gateshead.	Companies
Gateshead	4	Gateshead	4
Blaydon	4	Felling	1
Felling	1	Chopwell	1
South Shields	3	Blaydon	2
Total	12	Total	8

The state on 29th April, 1914, was :—

	Establishment.		Strength.	
	Officers.	Other Ranks.	Officers.	Other Ranks.
5th Bn. Durham Light Infantry	30	981	25	868
6th ,, ,, ,, ,,	30	985	28	897
7th ,, ,, ,, ,,	30	976	28	840
8th ,, ,, ,, ,,	30	980	29	1026
9th ,, ,, ,, ,,	30	975	28	937

HONORARY COLONELS AND LIEUTENANT-COLONELS OF THE 5TH, 6TH, 7TH, 8TH, AND 9TH BATTALIONS.

5TH BATTALION.

Honorary Colonels.

    (i.) H. G. Duke of Cleveland, K.G. 5th November, 1864.
    (ii.) G. J. Scurfield. 21st July, 1892.
    (iii.) Sir S. A. Sadler, Knight, V.D. 23rd December, 1896.
    (iv.) Rowland Burdon, V.D. 29th September, 1911.

APPENDIX XII

Lieutenant-Colonels.

    (i.) G. J. Scurfield. 1st February, 1862.

        (No Lieutenant-Colonel from 1871 to 1876)*

    (ii.) S. A. Sadler (Honorary Colonel). 10th August, 1876.

    (iii.) R. Ropner (Honorary Colonel), V.D.. 22nd December, 1896.

    (iv.) R. Burdon (Honorary Colonel). 15th February, 1899.

    (v.) J. Harris. 15th February, 1904.

    (vi.) H. Bowes. 2nd September, 1905.

    (vii.) J. R. Hanson. 1st April, 1908.

    (viii.) G. O. Spence. 15th August, 1910.

6TH BATTALION.

Honorary Colonels.

    (i.) R. Duncombe-Shafto. 21st November, 1863.

    (ii.) Sir W. Eden, Bart., T.D. 2nd May, 1896.

Lieutenant-Colonels.

    (i.) W. Trotter. 15th April, 1861.

    (ii.) C. L. Wood. 12th March, 1866.

    (iii.) J. Jobson. 20th March, 1872.

    (iv.) M. Headlam. 10th August, 1880.

    (v.) W. Watson (Honorary Colonel). 10th January, 1885.

    (vi.) H. J. Trotter, M.P. 8th January, 1887.

    (vii.) Sir W. Eden, Bart. 20th February, 1889. (Formerly in 8th Hussars.)

    (viii.) D. Armstrong (Honorary Colonel), V.D. 13th May, 1896.

    (ix.) Hon. W. L. Vane (Honorary Colonel). 27th June, 1903. (Formerly in 1st Battalion Durham Light Infantry.)

    (x.) H. C. Watson, V.D. 15th July, 1911.

---

* From October, 1871, to July, 1872, Major G. M. Watson was senior officer; there was then neither a lieutenant-colonel nor a major; and from July, 1872, to August, 1876, the battalion was saved from coming to an end by the exertions of the Adjutant, Major R. Thompson.

THE DURHAM LIGHT INFANTRY

7TH BATTALION.

Honorary Colonels.

    (i.)   E. T. Gourley. 10th July, 1869.
        (No Honorary Colonel from 1874 to 1881.)
        E. T. Gourley. 19th January, 1881.
        (No Honorary Colonel, 1885 to 1905.)
    (ii.) T. Reed, V.D. 22nd November, 1905.
    (iii.) G. W. Viscount Boyne. 26th April, 1913. (Formerly in 3rd Battalion Northumberland Fusiliers.)

Lieutenant-Colonels.

    (i.)   Lord Adolphus Vane-Tempest, M.P. (formerly in Scots Fusilier Guards). Major Commanding, 14th July, 1860; Lieutenant-Colonel, 23rd June, 1862.
    (ii.) E. T. Gourley. 10th November, 1865.
    (iii.) W. B. Ferguson. 14th January, 1869.
        E. T. Gourley. 1874. (With original date, 10th November, 1865.)
    (iv.) T. Reed. 19th January, 1881.
    (v.)   A. Peters. 4th January, 1896.
    (vi.) J. T. C. Bolam. 6th January, 1903.
    (vii.) W. J. Evans. 20th February, 1904.
    (viii.) E. Vaux, D.S.O., V.D. 9th September, 1911.

8TH BATTALION.

Honorary Colonels.

    (i.)   G. F. D'A. Earl of Durham. 29th July, 1863.
        (No Honorary Colonel from 1879 to 1905.)
    (ii.) J. G. Earl of Durham, K.G., V.D. 25th October, 1905.

Lieutenant-Colonels.

    (i.)   E. M. Perkins (Hon. Colonel). 15th April, 1861.
    (ii.) J. Joicey (Hon. Colonel). 2nd November, 1871.
    (iii.) J. Monks (Hon. Colonel). 5th October, 1881.
    (iv.) C. Rowlandson (Hon. Colonel). 23rd June, 1883.

APPENDIX XII

(v.) C. Perkins (Hon. Colonel). 17th March, 1894.
(vi.) J. Humble, V.D. (Hon. Colonel). 20th September, 1902.
(vii.) J. Turnbull, V.D. 19th September, 1908.
(viii.) W. C. Blackett. 20th October, 1912.

9TH BATTALION

Honorary Colonel.

(i) Hon. W. H. James (later Baron Northbourne). 11th September, 1891. (Originally dated 11th September, 1895, date altered in Army List for December, 1899).

Lieutenant-Colonels.

(i.) G. H. L. Hawks. 1st June, 1861.
   (No Lieutenant-Colonel from 1872 to 1876.)
(ii.) Jos. A. Cowen. 5th November, 1876.
(iii.) W. B. Proctor. 1st January, 1896.
(iv.) W. B. McQueen, V.D. 19th February, 1902.
(v.) C. H. Scott. 26th July, 1902. (Was at first junior of two lieutenant-colonels, and did not command the battalion until 19th February, 1908.)
(vi.) F. R. Simpson. 26th July, 1911.

POSTSCRIPT

As will have been noticed by the reader, this record of the Durham Light Infantry was closed at the end of May, 1914, and had the present war not taken place would have been published before now. The war has unfortunately delayed the publication of the book for several months; a considerable amount of time was necessarily required for final arrangements, and for printing the proofs, etc., etc. When the latter were completed, the war broke out, and as the compiler returned to military duty away from his home he was unable to correct them for nearly three months.

Some of those who are interested in the production of the book suggested further delay until the present war had been concluded, and the share taken in it by the Durham Light Infantry recorded; but no one knows how long the war may last, and even if it were soon terminated some considerable time would elapse before the necessary literary material could be collected and arranged.

It has been finally decided to proceed with the publication of the book in its present form, and it is hoped that, if the war comes to an end within a reasonable period of time, it may be possible to compile a short supplement recording the performances of the several battalions of the Durham Light Infantry during the present crisis, and to present a copy gratis to each of the original subscribers.

W. L. V.

1st December, 1914.

INDEX

A.

Adey, Lt.-Col. W., date of commission, 5; in Cherbourg expedition, 7.
Africa, South, war in, 1899-1902. (*See* Durham L.I., 1st Bn.).
Aiguillon, Duc d', defeat of British troops by, at St. Cas, 7, 8.
Ainsworth, Lieut. (Capt.) W. J., on plague duty at Sholapur, 134; with Mounted Infantry at Sannah's Post, 143; escape of, from Boer captivity, 144; awarded D.S.O. for services in S. Africa, 154.
Aitchison, Lieut. (Capt.) C. T., wounded at Panhala, 110; at the taking of Shorapur, 115.
Alderson, Col. E. A. H.; in command of Mounted Infantry in S. Africa, 147.
Alexander, Sir James, reference to book by, 96, 99.
Allen, Pte., mentioned in despatches, 141.
Alma, battle of the, 83.
Alten, Maj.-Gen. C. von, in command of a brigade in Portugal, 45, 46; transferred to Wellington's Light Division, 47; at Nivelle, 59.
Anderson, Capt. H., killed at Vittoria, 55.
Anderson, Maj.-Gen. H. S., inspection of 1/Durham L.I. by, at Mhow, 130.
Angus, Capt., in action at Goyave (Grenada), 28.
Anson, Adm. Lord, in command of Cherbourg expedition, 6.
Antigua, island of, 11 *et seq*.
Appleby, 2nd Lieut. E. W., wounded at Vaal Krantz, 138; on service with Mounted Infantry in S. Africa, 145, 146.
Archdale, Capt. H. M., wounded at Nivelle, 60.
Arundel, bad relations between inhabitants and officers at, 44.
Ashburner, Lieut. (Capt.), with Mounted Infantry at Sannah's Post, 143; mentioned in Lord Kitchener's despatches, 151; awarded D.S.O., 154.
"A Soldier's Journal," reference to, 3, 5, 6, 7.
Atkinson, Pte., mentioned for gallant conduct, 150.
Atkinson, Serjt. J., mentioned in despatches, 152.

B.

Bainbridge, Lt.-Col. E. G. T., at Sannah's Post, 143.
Baker, Pte. J., taken prisoner at Moresco, 50.
Baker, Col.-Serjt. R., noted for gallantry, 64.
Baker, Pte. W., mentioned in despatches, 141.
Balaklava, battle of, 83.
Ball, Ens. R., wounded at Vittoria, 56.
Band, establishment of a regimental, in 1821, 67; in 1846, 76.
Bargate, Pte. R., killed at Nivelle, 60.
Barker, Lieut. F. G., killed at Inkerman, 83.
Barker, Capt. R. B., died in Egypt, 126.
Barnard, Maj.-Gen. W. O., inspection of 1/Durham L.I. by, at Aldershot, 134.
Barnes, Maj.-Gen., in action near Echalar, 57, 58.

INDEX

Barré, Lt.-Col. Isaac, raised the first of the regiments numbered 106, 106.

Barron, Mr., wounded by mutineers of the 8th W. India Regt., 35.

Battiscombe, Lieut. H. L., wounded before Sevastopol, 87.

Beabeck, Pte., wounded at De Jager's Drift, 151.

Beauchamp, Pte. A., killed near Sassooly, 110.

Bedford, Col.-Serjt. H., mentioned in despatches, 154.

Bell, Maj.-Gen. J., inspection of 68th Regt. by, at Rangoon, 94.

Bell, Pte. J., mentioned in despatches, 152; awarded D.C. Medal, 155.

Bell, Capt. R. F., mentioned in Lord Roberts' despatches, 152.

Belts, method of wearing, in 1784, 22.

Belvidere (Grenada), retreat from, 26.

Bennett, Pte. G., awarded D.C. Medal, 142, 155.

Bentinck, Lt.-Gen. Sir H. J. W., in the Crimea, 87, 88.

Beresford, Marshal, at Nivelle, 59; at Orthes, 61; at Bordeaux, 62.

Berkshire Regt., Royal, 1st Bn., in the Nile expedition, 125.

Bernewitz, Maj.-Gen. H. de, in command of a brigade of the Peninsular army, 46; inspections of 68th Light Infantry by, 47, 54; at Salamanca, 51.

Birbeck, Pte., wounded at De Jager's Drift, 145.

Blake, Lieut. (Capt.) E. A. C., wounded at Vaal Krantz, 138; mentioned in Lord Kitchener's despatches, 154; specially promoted, 155.

Blakeney, Gen. Sir E., inspections of 68th Light Infantry by, at Dublin, 77; at Galway, 79.

Bligh, Lt.-Gen. E., in the Cherbourg expedition, 7, 8.

Bolden, Capt. L., killed by a tiger near Mandalgarh, 104, 118.

Bolton, Lt.-Col. W. M. S., died at Morar, 119.

Bombay Presidency Rifle Association, 128.

Boscawen, Maj.-Gen., in the Cherbourg expedition, 6.

Bothaville, defeat of De Wet at, 148, 149.

Bounty, rate of, for volunteering in the W. Indies, 37; for extension of service in India, 152.

Bowes, Lieut. H., in S. Africa with a "special service" company of Volunteers, 139.

Bowman, Lieut. J. B., in S. Africa with a "special service" company of Volunteers, 139.

Boys, enlistment of, 54.

Brereton, Brig.-Gen., in command at St. Lucia, 37.

Breslin, Pte. D., killed at Sassadroog, 110.

Bridges, Lieut. A. H., mentioned in Sir Redvers Buller's despatches, 141.

Bright, Corpl. A., awarded medal for services in the Punjab, 111.

Bright, Lt.-Gen. Sir R. O., inspection of 68th Light Infantry by, at Meerut, 105.

Broadwood, Brig.-Gen. R. G., description by, of action at Sannah's Post, 143.

Brooks, Brev.-Maj.-Gen., appointed Colonel of the 2nd Bombay European Regt., 108.

Brough, Lt.-Col. R. W., at the storming of Panhala, 110.

Brown, Bugler H., killed by lightning, 68.

Browne, Maj.-Gen., inspection of 68th Light Infantry by, at Canterbury, 75.

Browne, Pte. G., noted for gallantry, 64.

Browning, Ens. T., severely wounded at Nivelle, 60.

Budd, Pte., killed at De Jager's Drift, 145, 151.

Bugle-Majors, first appointment of, 43.

INDEX

Buller, Gen. Sir Redvers, at Laing's Nek, 139; despatches by, 140, 141.
Bultitude, Lce.-Corpl. A., mentioned in despatches, 141.
Bulwer, Maj. Wm. Earle, raised the second of the regiments numbered 106, 107.
Burdett, Sir Francis, committal to the Tower of, 43.
Burgos, Wellington's retreat from, 52, 53.
Burrows, Pte. S., awarded the Sardinian medal for the Crimea, 92.
Bushire, capture of, 113.
Butler, Maj.-Gen. Sir C., inspections of 68th Light Infantry by, 93, 100.
Butler, Brig.-Gen. W., in the Nile expedition, 125; inspection of 2/Durham L.I. by, at Akasheh, 126.
Byrne, Pte. (Corpl.), awarded the V.C. for gallantry at Inkerman, 91; noted for distinguished conduct in the Maori war, 98; awarded D.C. Medal, 99.

C.

Caffrey, Pte., noted for gallantry, 98.
Cambridge, H.R.H. the Duke of, presentation of new colours to 1/Durham L.I. by, 94, 127; inspection of 1/Durham L.I. by, 129; funeral of, 157.
Cameron Highlanders, the, in the Nile expedition, 125.
Campbell, Lieut. A. P., killed at Sassadroog, 110, 111.
Campbell, Gen. Sir G., inspection of 68th Light Infantry by, at Mullingar, 78; at Galway, 79.
Campbell, Maj.-Gen. Sir John, killed at the Redan, 87.
Capon, Pte., wounded at De Jager's Drift, 145, 151.
Captain-Lieutenant and Captain, abolition of rank of, in 1803, 37.
Carr, Lieut. H. W., wounded at Goyave, 27.
Carribs, operations against the, 15.
Carson, Ens. G., in Canada, 66.
Carter, Brig.-Gen. F. C., inspections of 2/Durham L.I. by, at Fermoy, 158, 160.
Carthew, Maj.-Gen. M., inspection of 68th Light Infantry by, at Rangoon, 95.
Casement, Capt. T., wounded at the Gate Pah, 98.
Castles, Serjt., wounded in action with Maoris, 99; awarded D.C. Medal, *ibid.*
Cathcart, Lt.-Gen. Hon. Sir G., in the Crimea, 82; killed at Inkerman, 84, 86.
Cator, Lieut. J., wounded at Inkerman, 83.
Cavioll, Pte. M., noted for gallantry, 64.
Challis, Pte., at the Bombay Presidency Rifle Association meeting, 128.
Chaplains, abolition of regimental, 29; the provision of, in garrisons and fortresses, 30.
Charity Fund, institution of a regimental, 66.
Chasseurs Britanniques, in the combat of Vera, 58; at Nivelle, 60.
Cherbourg, the 1758 operations against, 6 *et seq.*
Chevrons, the introduction of, 36.
Childers, Rt. Hon. H. C. E., Secretary of State for War, 121.
Church, the carrying of arms by troops to, in Ireland, 77.
Chute, Maj.-Gen. Ireton, inspection of 68th Light Infantry by, at Otahuhu, N.Z., 99.
Clarina, Lord, Colonel of the Durham L.I., 117.
Clarke, Lieut. R., severely wounded at Nivelle, 60.
Clery, Lt.-Gen. Sir C. F., in S. Africa, 135.
Clothing, cost of articles of, in 1759, 9; in 1776, 18.
Cochrane, Lieut. G. L., mentioned in Sir Redvers Buller's despatches, 140.

INDEX

Cochrane-Johnstone, Brig.-Gen. Hon. A. J., Governor of Dominica, 34.

Coddington, 2nd Lieut. H. J., wounded at Leeuw Kop, 147.

Cogan, Ens. J. D., killed by lightning, 68.

Coker, Col. E. R., awarded D.S.O., 126.

Colenso, battle of, 136.

Colour-Serjeant, institution of rank of, 56.

Connaught, H.R.H. the Duke of, presents the Khedive's Star to men of 2/Durham L.I., 127; bids farewell to 2/Durham L.I. at Poona, 128.

Connaught Rangers, presentation of colours to 1st Battalion at Delhi by H.M. King George V., 159.

Connor, Ens. D., in action at Goyave, 27.

Cook, Capt. J., in S. Africa with a "special service" company of Volunteers, 150.

Cooper, Col. C. D., on service in Natal, 139.

Corcoran, Pte. M., killed at Sassadroog, 110.

Corkvey, Pte. P., noted for gallantry, 64.

Cormick, Pte. M., awarded D.C. Medal, 87.

Cottle, Pte. J., awarded D.C. Medal, 142, 155.

Coughlan, Corpl. J., awarded D.C. Medal, 87.

Counties, regimental recruiting by, 20.

Covey, Lieut. (Major) C., at the Gate Pah, 97; mentioned in despatches, 98; accidentally killed, 122.

Cox, Lieut. J. S., at the Gate Pah, 97.

Crawford, Pte. J., mentioned in despatches, 141.

Creilly, Pte. T., noted for gallantry, 64.

Crespigny, Capt. (Major) G. C., wounded in the Walcheren expedition, 42; killed at Ostiz, 57.

Crump, Col.-Serjt. J., mentioned in despatches, 140, 152.

Cumming, Lieut. (Major) H. R., on plague duty at Sholapur, 133; mentioned in despatches, 140, 152; specially promoted for services in S. Africa, 155.

Currie, Col.-Serjt. L., noted for gallantry, 64.

D.

Dailey, a deserter to the enemy, 26.

Dalhousie, Countess of, presents colours to the 68th Light Infantry in 1825, 68.

Dalhousie, George 9th Earl of, in command of Wellington's 7th Division, 53; proceeds home, 59; resumes command, 62; inspection of 68th Light Infantry by, at Quebec, 68.

Daly, Pte. M., killed at Reshire, 112.

Davies, Pte. F., mentioned in despatches, 141.

Davison, Gen. K. S., inspection of 1/Durham L.I. by, at Nasirabad, 158; at Delhi, 160.

Deacon, Pte. J., awarded D.C. Medal, 87.

Deery, Col.-Serjt. L., killed at Nivelle, 60; noted for gallantry, 64.

de Lamotte, Maj.-Gen. P., in operations against the Ghadkarries, 110.

Delany, Serjt. E., noted for gallantry, 64.

Delany, Serjt. P., wounded at Inkerman, 92; awarded French war medal, *ibid*.

Delhi, the Coronation Durbar at, 159, 160.

de Lisle, Lieut. (Lt.-Col.) H. de B., with mounted infantry up the Nile, 123; recommended for the V.C., 124; capture of a nuggar, 125; awarded the D.S.O., 126; with mounted infantry in S. Africa, 149; severely wounded,

INDEX

ibid.; in command of 2nd Cavalry Brigade and of Australian Commonwealth Brigade, 150; nominated C.B., *ibid.;* 154; specially promoted, 155.

Desmond, Pte. D., noted for gallantry, 111.

Deveran, Pte. T., killed at Kooshab, 113.

Devonshire Regt., 2nd Bn., in S. Africa, 135.

De Wet, Gen., defeat at Bothaville of, 148, 149.

Disney-Leith, Col. R. W., appointed to command of 106th Light Infantry, 116.

Doña Maria, combat at, 57.

Donohue, Corpl., awarded French Crimean medal, 92.

Douglas, Gen. Sir C., inspection of 2/Durham L.I. by, at Aldershot, 156; at Longmoor, 162.

Doyle, Sir Conan, on the battle of Vaal Krantz, 138.

Doyle, Pte. J., killed at Reshire, 112.

Drum-Majors, first appointment of, 43.

Duff, Lieut. J., died in Jamaica, 73.

Duff, Col.-Serjt. J., mentioned for gallantry, 64.

Duncan, Maj.-Gen. J., inspection of 2/Durham L.I. by, 134.

Duncan, Serjt. R., noted for gallantry, 64.

Duncombe-Shafto, 2nd Lieut. C., killed at Vaal Krantz, 138.

Dundas, Maj. W., in operations against Carribs, 15.

Dunn, Serjt., killed at Salamanca, 52.

Durham Cathedral, deposition of old colours in, 162.

Durham, Earl of, presents colours to 2/Durham L.I., 161; at deposition of old colours in Durham Cathedral, 162.

Durham, James Francies, an Arab child of the regiment, 125.

Durham Light Infantry, 1st Battn.:
Arms and equipment; method of wearing belts in 1784, 22; pikes issued to serjeants instead of halberts, 24; serjeants' pouches, 70; issue of percussion arms, 75; weight of knapsack, 95; issue of the Lee-Metford rifle, 129.

Colours, description of, in 1758, 5; price of new, presented in 1772, 14; left behind on embarkation for the Peninsula, 44; award of Peninsular honours, 67; new colours presented in 1825, 68; Crimean honours sanctioned, 90; new colours presented by H.R.H. the Duke of Cambridge in 1857, 94; also in 1888, 127; honours for war in S. Africa, 157; new colours presented by H.M. King George V. at Delhi in 1911, 159, 160.

Establishment and strength; on formation, 2; in 1758, 6; in 1759-60, 9; in 1764, 11; in 1770, 12; in 1772, 15; in 1773, 16; in 1775, 17; in 1782, 20; in 1785, 24; in 1795, 29; in 1797, 30; in 1799, 31; in 1801, 33; in 1802, 36; in 1806, 37; in 1808, 40; in 1809, 41; in 1811, 45; in 1812, 48; in 1813, 54, 60; in 1814, 61, 62, 65; in 1821, 67; in 1825, 68; in 1826-27, *ibid.;* in 1834, 72; in 1838, *ibid.;* in 1842, 74; in 1846, 77; in 1849, 79; in 1851, 80; in 1854, 81; in 1855, 87; in 1856, 93; in 1857, 94; 1858-59, 94, 95; in 1866, 99; in 1867, 100; in 1869, *ibid.;* in 1872, 103; in 1887, 126; in 1897, 132; in 1899, 135; in 1906, 158; in 1913, 163; in 1914, 165.

Formation of regiment as 2nd Bn. Royal Welch Fuzileers, 1, 3.

Light Infantry Companies, establishment of, in 1770, 13.

Motto "Faithful," origin of the, 15.

Pay of various ranks in 1756, 2.

Second Battalion; formation of, in 1800, 31; stations and movements at home, 31, 32; in the W. Indies, 33 *et seq.;* absorption of, into 1st Battalion, 36.

INDEX

Stations and movements at home, 3, 5, 8, 9, 10, 11, 16, 17, 19, 20 *et seq.;* 29 *et seq.;* 38 *et seq.;* 43, 62, 64, 68, 70, 71, 75 *et seq.;* 93, 99 *et seq.;* 126 *et seq.*

Statistics of age, height, nationality and service of men in 1770, 12; in 1812, 48; in 1813, 54; in 1863, 95; in 1895, 130.

Title, changes in, to 68th Regt. of Foot, 3, 4; to 68th Light Infantry, 39; to 1/Durham L.I., 105.

Uniform in 1758, 5; in 1770, 12; prices of articles of, 1759, 9; cost of hats in 1776, 18; shoulder straps to be of colour of facings, 22, 23; introduction of the stock, 24; pattern of serjeants' sashes, 31; abolition of hats, *ibid.;* changes ordered in 1802, 35; alterations on conversion to Light Infantry, 40; colour of buglers' coats, 35, 46; colour of facings in 1816, 66; changes in 1809, 1819, and 1823, 67; dress of L.I. officers in 1826, 68; colour of cap lines, 69; regulations of 1829, 69, 70; lace and facings in 1832, 71; changes in 1834, 72; colour of serjeants' sashes, 74; changes in 1849, 79; change of facings from green to dark green in 1861, 95; changes in 1871, 100; helmet adopted in 1877, 104; changes in 1881, 105; in 1896, 131; field service cap authorized for officers in 1897, 132; change of facings from white to dark green, 155.

War and foreign services; operations against Cherbourg and St. Malo, 6; at St. Cas, 7, 8; at Antigua, 11 *et seq.;* operations against the Carribs, 15; garrison duty at Gibraltar, 24; at St. Lucia, *ibid.;* operations against the "Brigands," 25; on active service in Grenada, 26 *et seq.;* in the W. Indies, 33 *et seq.;* at the capture of Morne Fortuné, 36, 37; in the Walcheren expedition, 41 *et seq.;* in the Peninsula, 44; at Sabugal, 46; in the Salamanca campaign, 50; at El Retiro, 52; in the retreat from Burgos, 53; at Vittoria, 55; at Ostiz, 56; at Echalar, 57; at Vera, 58; at Nivelle, 59, 60; at Orthes, 61; at Bordeaux, 62; casualties in, and rewards for services during the Peninsular war, 63; services in Canada, 66 *et seq.;* at Gibraltar, 72; in the W. Indies, 72, 73; in Canada, 74; in Malta, 80, 81; in the Crimea, 82; at the Alma, Balaklava, Inkerman, and Sevastopol, 83 *et seq.;* honours and rewards for the Crimea, 87, 88, 90 *et seq.;* in the Ionian Islands, 90, 93; in Burma, 94, 95; in New Zealand, 95; attack on the Gate Pah, 96 *et seq.;* in India, 103 *et seq.;* 121 *et seq.;* in the S. African war, 1899-1902; at Colenso, 136; at Spion Kop, 137; at Vaal Krantz, 137; at Monte Christo, 138; at Pieters Hill, 139; list of officers and others mentioned in despatches, 140, 141, 142, 151, 152; the 2/Durham L.I. mounted infantry company in S. Africa, 143, 144; organization and work of various bodies of mounted infantry, 145 *et seq.;* honours and rewards, 154, 155; embarkation for India and subsequent movements, 153, 155 *et seq.;* winning of the Commander-in-Chief's cup for rifle shooting, 158; at the Delhi Coronation Durbar, 159, 160; on a punitive expedition across the Indian frontier, 164.

Warrants relating to the regiment, 4, 13, 14.

Durham Light Infantry, 2nd Battalion:

Arms and equipment; issue of Snider rifle, 119; of Martini-

INDEX

Henry rifle, *ibid.;* of new valise equipment, 119; of Lee-Metford rifles, 130; of the short Lee-Enfield rifle, a new sword-bayonet, web equipment, and a light entrenching tool, 158; of the short Lee-Enfield rifle, Mark III, 162.

Colours; presentation of first set of, 111; honours granted for the campaign in Persia, 115, 116; presentation of new colours in 1860, 116; new colours presented by the Princess Royal in 1874, 119; honours authorized for the S. African war, 157; presentation of new colours by the Earl of Durham in 1912, 161.

Establishment and strength in 1839, 108; in 1850, 111; in 1856, 112; in 1859, 115; in 1862, 116; in 1868, 118; in 1873, 119; in 1880, 120; in 1885, 122; in 1888, 127; in 1902, 156; in 1909, 158; in 1912, 161; in 1914, 165.

Formation of regiment in 1839 as the 2nd Bombay European Regt., 107, 108.

Stations and movements in the East up to 1873, 108, 109, 114 *et seq.*

Stations and movements at home, 119, 120, 121, 156 *et seq.*

Title, change of, to 2nd Regt. Bombay European L.I., 108, 109; to 2nd European Regt., Bombay L.I., 112; to 106th Bombay L.I., 116; to 2nd Bn. Durham L.I., 105, 120.

Uniform in 1839, 108; change of facings from pale buff to white, 109; wicker helmets adopted for Indian service, 115; mess dress for officers, 119; various changes in 1878, 120; change of facings from white to dark green, 155.

War services before 1873, and war and foreign services after that year; operations against the Ghadkarries, 109, 110, 111; campaign in Persia, 112, 113; the Indian Mutiny, 114, 115; at Malta and Gibraltar, 121; in Egypt, 122; at the battle of Ginniss, 125; honours and rewards for Egypt, 126; in India, 126 *et seq.;* successes at meeting of Bombay Presidency Rifle Association, 128; on plague duty at Poona, 132; at Bombay, 134; move to Burma, 134; with the Burma-China Boundary Commission, 136, 142; embarkation for India, 142; work of the mounted infantry company in S. Africa, 143, 144.

Dury, Maj.-Gen., in the Cherbourg expedition, 6; at St. Cas, 8.

Dutton, Corpl. J., awarded D.C. Medal, 87.

E.

Echalar, action of, 57.

Edwards, Capt. R. L., killed before Sevastopol, 88, 89.

8th W. India Regt.; mutiny of the, 34, 35.

18th Native Infantry, presentation of new colours to, at Delhi by H.M. King George V., 159.

85th Regt., in the Walcheren expedition, 41.

82nd Regt., in combat of Vera, 58; at Nivelle, 60.

Ellice, Gen. Sir R., inspection of 68th Light Infantry by, 80.

Elliot, Maj.-Gen., in the Cherbourg expedition, 6.

Elliott, Maj.-Gen. Sir E. L., inspection of 1/Durham L.I. by, at Lucknow, 158.

El Retiro, capture of fort, 52.

Elwes, Capt. L. E. C., mentioned in despatches, 141, 152; awarded D.S.O. for services in S. Africa, 154.

Ensign, rank of, abolished in 1871, 119.

Ensor, Lieut. H., with a "special service" company of Volunteers in S. Africa, 150, 153.

INDEX

Este, Capt. C. W., disagreement between, and the Lt.-Governor of Guernsey, 23.
Evelyn, Maj.-Gen., review of 68th Regt. by, at Newcastle, 17.

F.

"Faithful," origin of regimental motto, 15.
Farrell, Pte. E., died from snake-bite, 37.
Faure, Ens. W. C., killed near Sassooly, 110.
Ferris, Pte. W., awarded French Crimean medal, 92.
51st Regt., in the combat of Vera, 58; at Nivelle, 60.
Finns, Corpl. P., wounded at Inkerman and awarded French Crimean medal, 92.
Finucane, Lieut. F., killed at Salamanca, 52.
Fitzgerald, Lt.-Col. H. S., wounded at Vaal Krantz, 138; mentioned in despatches, 140, 141; nominated C.B., 154.
Fletcher, Serjt. A., awarded medal for services in the Punjab, 111.
Fletcher, Pte. W., awarded the D.C. Medal, 87; decorated with the Legion of Honour, 91.
Flood, Maj.-Gen. Solly, inspection of 2/Durham L.I. by, 127.
Flower, Serjt., wounded at Colenso, 136.
Flushing, siege and capitulation of, 42.
Fogarty, Pte. W., killed near Sassooly, 110.
Forbes, Ens. H., died at Niza, 45.
Forbes, Maj.-Gen. T., inspection of 68th Light Infantry by, at Nasirabad, 104.
Forge, Bugler J., noted for gallantry, 164.
Forrest, Pte. E., noted for gallantry, 111.
46th Regt., at Inkerman, 84.
14th Regt., at the Gate Pah, N.Z., 97.

Fowke, Ens. J., severely wounded at Vittoria, 56.
Francies, S.-M., wins cup at the Bombay Presidency Rifle Association meeting, 128.
Frankfort de Montmorency, Maj.-Gen. Visct, inspection of 1/Durham L.I. by, 131, 132.
Frankland, Lieut. A. D., killed at Kooshab, 113.
Franklin, Pte. A., mentioned in despatches, 141.
Freel, S.-M. J., mentioned in despatches, 152; awarded D.C. Medal, 155.
Frost, Pte., killed at De Jager's Drift, 145, 151.

G.

Gaitenby, Lce.-Serjt., mortally wounded at Villiersdorp, 147.
Galahar, Pte. T., killed at Kooshab, 113.
Galloway, Lce.-Cpl., wounded at Villiersdorp, 147.
Garrett, Maj.-Gen., in the Crimea, 88; inspection of 68th Light Infantry by, at Sevastopol, 90.
Garvock, Maj.-Gen. Sir J., inspection of 68th Light Infantry by, at Manchester, 100.
Gate Pah, N.Z., assault of the, 96 et seq.
"Gentleman's Magazine," quoted, 20, 21.
George III., H.M. King, review of a detachment of the 68th Regt. by, 16.
George V., H.M. King, presentation of new colours by, at Delhi, 159, 160.
Gettle, Pte., killed at Hart's Hill, 138.
Gibbons, S.-M. J., wounded at Inkerman and awarded French Crimean medal, 92.
Gibson, Ens. J., wounded at Vera, 58; wounded at Nivelle, 60.
Gibson, 2nd Lieut. W., with the Tirah expedition, 133.

INDEX

Gillanders, Capt. J., in operations against the Ghadkarries, 109; at the storming of Panhala, Samanghur, and the Pettah of Rangna, 110.

Gillespie, 2nd Lieut. J. G., with mounted infantry in S. Africa, 147.

Gillespie, Lt.-Col. R. R., at the presentation of new colours, 119.

Ginniss, battle of, 125.

Gledstanes, Capt. (Major) R., severely wounded at Nivelle, 60; in Canada, 66.

Goldie, Brig.-Gen. T. L., in the Crimea, 82; mortally wounded at Inkerman, 84, 86.

Gomm, Gen. Sir W. M., inspection of 68th Light Infantry by, in Jamaica, 73.

Gordon, Maj., in suppression of mutiny of the 8th W. India Regt., 34.

Gordon Highlanders, presentation of new colours to 2nd Battn. at Delhi by H.M. King George V., 159.

Gossett, Maj.-Gen. M. M. E., inspection of 1/Durham L.I. by, at Dublin, 132, 134.

Gough, Maj.-Gen. Sir C. J. S., inspection of 1/Durham L.I. by, 125.

Gough, Capt. H. de la P., brilliant services of, with mounted infantry in S. Africa, 144, 145.

Gough, Capt. W., severely wounded at Vittoria, 56.

Goyave, Grenada, evacuation of, 26; Col. Schaw's report on, 27, 28.

Grace, Lieut. S., awarded Sardinian medal for the Crimea, 92.

Graham, Maj.-Gen. (Lt.-Gen.), in the Walcheren expedition, 42; at Salamanca, 50, 51.

Grant, Maj.-Gen. J. T., inspection of 68th Light Infantry by, at Poona, 103.

Grant, Lieut. T., taken prisoner at St. Cas, 8.

Greaves, Lt.-Gen. Sir G., inspection of 2/Durham L.I. by, at Mhow, 130.

Green, John, author of "Vicissitudes of a Soldier's Life," 38, 40, 42, 43, 44, 55, 56, 58, 63, 65.

Greer, Col. H. H., at the Gate Pah, N.Z., 96 et seq.; mentioned in despatches and nominated C.B., 98.

Grenada, revolt in, 26.

Grierson, Lt.-Gen. Sir J. M., inspection of 2/Durham L.I. by, at Colchester, 161; at the 1912 manœuvres, 162.

Griffen, Corpl., with the Tirah expedition, 133.

Grinfield, Lt.-Gen. W., at St. Lucia, 36.

Groves, Lieut., killed at Sannah's Post, 143.

H.

Hackman, Lieut. J., murder of Miss Ray by, 17, 18.

Hagan, Pte. W., died from plague, 134.

Haggerty, Col.-Serjt. T., noted for gallantry, 64.

Haigh, Serjt., with the Tirah expedition, 133.

Halkett, Col., King's German Legion, 46.

Hall, Pte., mentioned in despatches, 140.

Hamilton, Capt. (Major) A. M. K., in action at Goyave, 27; in suppression of mutiny of the 8th W. India Regt., 34.

Hamilton, Capt. T. de C., awarded the V.C., 88, 91; decorated with the Legion of Honour, 91.

Harman, Brig.-Gen., inspection of 2/Durham L.I. by, at Wellington, 156.

Harrington, Corpl. G., awarded the D.C. Medal, 87.

Harris, Pte., wounded at Kalespruit, 146.

Hart, Maj.-Gen. A. F., at battle of Colenso, 136.

INDEX

Hart's Hill, attack on, 138.
Harter, Capt. O. B., mentioned in Sir Redvers Buller's despatches, 140.
Harwood, Pte. J., awarded the D.C. Medal, 87.
Hats, abolition of, in favour of caps, 31.
Hautois, Lt.-Col. de, at Vera, 58.
Havelock, Brig.-Gen. H., in the Persian campaign, 113.
Hawke, Adm. Sir E., in the blockade of Brest, 5.
Hawkins, Corpl. H., awarded the D.C. Medal, 155.
Hawkins, Capt. (Lt.-Col.) J. P., severely wounded at Moresco, 50; at battle of Ostiz, 57; at Vera, 58; mentioned in despatches, 59; awarded Peninsular medal and nominated C.B., 63; in Canada, 66.
Heath, Brig.-Gen. H. N. C., inspection of 2/Durham L.I. by, at Colchester, 160.
Hedley, Pte., wounded at Villiersdorp, 147.
Height, standard of, for infantry in 1803, 36; in 1827, 69.
Helmet, adoption of the, in 1877, 104.
Hibbert, Pte. W., mentioned in despatches, 141.
Highland L.I., presentation of new colours to 1st Battn. at Delhi by H.M. King George V., 159.
Hildyard, Maj.-Gen. H., at Colenso, 136; at Vaal Krantz, 137.
Hill, Gen. Sir R., at Nivelle, 59.
Hinds, Col.-Serjt. G., noted for gallantry, 64.
Hinds, Lieut. J., wounded in the Walcheren expedition, 42; severely wounded at Vittoria, 56.
Hinuber, Lieut. A. L., mentioned in despatches, 26; Brevet-Lt.-Col., 44.
Honner, Brig.-Gen. R. W., in the Persian expedition, 112.
Honourable E. India Company, extinction of the, 115.

Hoole, Serjt. T., noted for gallantry, 64.
Hope, Gen. Sir J., in the Peninsula, 47; at Nivelle, 59; inspection of 68th Light Infantry by, at Quebec, 74.
Horsford, Brig.-Gen. Sir A., inspection of 68th Light Infantry by, at Aldershot, 100.
Harton, Pte. E., mentioned in despatches, 141, 143; awarded the D.C. Medal, 155.
Hotham, Lieut., at the Gate Pah, N.Z., 97.
Houston, Maj.-Gen. W., in Portugal, 45.
Howe, Commodore, in the Cherbourg expedition, 6.
106th (Barré's) Regt.; origin, services and disbandment of the, 106.
106th (Bulwer's) Regt., origin, services and disbandment of the, 106, 107.
106th Light Infantry. See Durham L.I., 2nd Battn.
106th Regt., Winnipeg L.I.; affiliation of, to Durham L.I., 165.
Hurrell, Pte. C., noted for gallantry, 64.
Hutchinson, Pte. C., awarded the D.C. Medal, 87.
Hynes, Col.-Serjt. T., noted for gallantry, 64.

I.

Iles, Serjt., mentioned in despatches, 141.
Inglis, Maj.-Gen. W., in the Peninsula, 55; at Ostiz, 56; at Echalar, 57; at Vera, 58; mentioned in despatches, 58; at Nivelle, 59; wounded, 60; at Orthes, 61.
Inkerman, battle of, 83, 84.
Iremonger, Lt. E. A., on plague duty at Poona, 132.
Irvine, Capt. H. B., wounded at Ostiz, 57; killed at Nivelle, 60.
Ismay, Pte., mentioned in despatches, 141.

INDEX

J.

Jacob, Brig.-Gen. J., in the Persian campaign, 113.
Jefferies, Pte. W., killed at Nivelle, 60.
Jeffreys, Lieut. J. W., with mounted infantry in S. Africa, 146.
Jenkins, Ens. J., died from Walcheren fever, 43.
Jenner, Lt.-Col. J. V., with mounted infantry in S. Africa, 147.
Jessop, Capt. C. S., at the taking of Shorapur, 115.
Jones, Capt. H. C., at the storming of Samanghur, 110.
Jones, Brig.-Gen. M. L., inspection of 2/Durham L.I. by, at Cork, 158.
Jones, Corpl. W., mentioned in despatches, 154.
Johnson, Sergt., mentioned in despatches, 141.
Johnson-Smyth, Maj. T. R., killed at Vaal Krantz, 138; mentioned in Sir Redvers Buller's despatches, 141.
Johnston, Lt.-Col. W., severely wounded at Vittoria, 56; awarded Peninsular medal and nominated C.B., 63.
Juan Manoz, skirmish near, 53.

K.

Kaine, Pte. W., noted for gallantry, 64.
Kays, Maj. W. S., with mounted infantry in S. Africa, 146.
Kearns, S.-M., wounded at Vittoria, 56.
Kelly, Corpl., mentioned in despatches, 140.
Kelly, Pte. T., noted for gallantry, 64.
Kelly, Col.-Serjt. W., noted for gallantry, 64.
Kelly, Pte. W., killed at Nivelle, 60.
Kiddle, Maj., murdered by Was tribesmen, 142.

Kinglake's "History of the Crimean War," quoted, 84 *et seq*.
King's Royal Rifle Corps, 3rd Bn., at Colenso, 136; at Vaal Krantz, 137, 138.
Kirby, Maj. J. H., at the Gate Pah, N.Z., 97.
Kitchener, F.-M. Lord, despatches by, 151.
Kohlapur, rising of native troops at, 114.
Kooshab, battle of, 113.

L.

Ladysmith, relief of, 139.
Laing, Mr., killed by mutineers of the 8th W. India Regt., 35.
Laing's Nek, evacuation of, by Boers, 139.
Lambert, O.R. Serjt. T., awarded medal commemorating the proclamation of H.M. Queen Victoria as Empress of India, 104.
Lambton, Col. J., letter of service issued to, in 1758, 4; date of commission, 5; in the Cherbourg expedition, 7; at Antigua, 11.
Lambton, Lieut. R. R., wounded at Vaal Krantz, 138; killed at De Jager's Drift, 145; mentioned in Lord Kitchener's despatches, 151.
Lancaster, Corpl. J., awarded medal for services in the Punjab, 111.
Larkin, Pte. B., killed at Nivelle, 60.
Lascelles, Lieut. A. C., death of, 129.
Lascelles, Capt. W. C., wounded at Vaal Krantz, 138; mentioned in Lord Roberts' despatches, 152; awarded D.S.O., 154.
Leather, 2nd Lieut. K., with mounted infantry in S. Africa, 145.
Lee, Pte. T., noted for gallantry, 64.

INDEX

Lee-Metford rifle, issue of the, in 1891, 129.
Leek, Lce.-Serjt. E., mentioned for gallantry, 111.
Le Gallais, Col., killed at Bothaville, 148.
Leigh, Ens. H., in action with Grenada insurgents, 26.
Leith, Capt. J. U. M., wounded at Ostiz, 57; killed at Oeyreguave, 61.
Light Infantry, description of dress of, in 1808, 40.
Lennox, Maj.-Gen. W., inspection of 2/Durham L.I. by, at Alexandria, 122.
Liebrecht, Lt. & Qr.-Mr. J. H., mentioned in despatches, 141, 152; specially promoted Hon. Captain, 155.
Lindsley, Pte., with the Tirah expedition, 133.
Littlejohn, Serjt. W. H., mentioned in despatches, 152; awarded D.C. Medal, 155.
Liu, Gen., Burma-China Boundary Commissioner, 136.
Lloyd-Payne, Brig.-Gen. R., inspection of 2/Durham L.I. by, at Cork, 157.
Loot, value of, taken at Vittoria, 56.
Lorne, Maj.-Gen. Marquis of, review of 68th Regt. by, 10.
Loughlin, Serjt. J., noted for gallantry, 64.
Lovering, 2nd Lieut. W. R., with mounted infantry in S. Africa, 146.
Lowry-Cole, Gen. Sir G., at Vera, 58.
Luard, Capt. C. C., with mounted infantry in S. Africa, 143; specially promoted Major, 155.
Lucas, Pte. S., awarded D.C. Medal, 87.
Lucking, Pte. F., mentioned in despatches, 141.
Lyttelton, Maj.-Gen. Hon. N. G., in S. Africa, 135; at Vaal Krantz, 138.

M.

Macbeath, Lt.-Col. G., before Sevastopol, 88; awarded the Sardinian medal for the Crimea, 92.
McCallum, Pte. T., noted for gallantry, 64.
Macdonald, Lieut. G., wounded and taken prisoner at Moresco, 50, 51.
McEwen, Pte. M., noted for gallantry, 64.
McGlenchy, Pte. J., noted for gallantry, 64.
McGowan, Pte., with the Tirah expedition, 133.
McGready, Pte. M., noted for gallantry, 64.
Mackay, Ens. G., killed in Carrib operations, 15.
Mackay, Lieut. H., wounded at Vittoria, 56.
Mackay, Capt. W., receives 22 bayonet wounds at Moresco, 50.
McKay, Mrs., murdered by mutineers of 8th W. India Regt., 35.
McKay, Serjt., killed by mutineers of 8th W. India Regt., 35.
McLean, Maj. N., covers retreat from Belvedere, Grenada, 26.
McLeod, Pte. D., killed at Panhala, 110.
McMahon, Capt. B. W. L., mentioned in Sir Redvers Buller's despatches, 140, 141; mentioned in Lord Roberts' despatches, 152; specially promoted Major, 155.
McMahon, Pte. C., mentioned in despatches, 152.
Macpherson, Maj.-Gen. Sir H. T., inspection of 1/Durham L.I. by, 122.
Madrid, entry of Wellington into, 52.
Magner, Pte. J., awarded the Sardinian medal for the Crimea, 92.
"Magnificent," H.M.S., fired on by mutineers of 8th W. India Regt., 34.

INDEX

Maitland, Sir P., inspection of 68th Light Infantry by, at Kingston, Canada, 68.

Malcolm, Col. G., at the taking of Shorapur, 115.

Malet, Lieut. F. H., in action near Choiseul, St. Lucia, 25.

Mansel, Maj. G. C., mentioned in Sir Redvers Buller's despatches, 141; awarded the D.S.O., 154.

Mansfield, Sir W., presentation of new colours by, to 2nd European L.I., 116.

Marker, Maj. T. J., with mounted infantry in S. Africa, 147.

Marlborough, third Duke of, in command of the Cherbourg expedition, 6.

Marmont, Marshal, at Salamanca, 50.

Marshall, Capt. A. F., died from cholera, 103.

Marshall, Lieut. J., killed before Sevastopol, 89.

Martyr, Lt.-Col. C. G., with mounted infantry in S. Africa, 143.

Mary, H.M. Queen, Coronation of, 160.

Mason, Pte., killed at Ginniss, 125.

Massey, Lt.-Col. Hon. E. C. H., in temporary command of 106th Light Infantry, 116.

Matthews, Lieut. C. L., wounded at Vaal Krantz, 138; mentioned in Sir Redvers Buller's despatches, 141; on duty with mounted infantry, 145; wounded at Roberts' Drift, 146, 150; mentioned in Lord Roberts' despatches, 152.

Maughan, Capt. F. G., at the Coronation of H.M. King George V., 160.

Mellor, Pte., mentioned in despatches, 141.

Mendham, Lieut. W., severely wounded at Nivelle, 60.

Menzies, Lieut. J., wounded in the Walcheren expedition, 42.

Militia, volunteers from the, into line regiments, 38.

Miller, Pte. A., mentioned in despatches, 152.

Miller, Maj. J., died of wounds received at Salamanca, 51.

Minahan, Pte. T., killed at Nivelle, 60; noted for gallantry, 64.

Mitchell, Pte. J., awarded the French Crimean medal, 92.

Mitchell, Pte. R., noted for gallantry, 64.

Monte Christo, battle of, 138.

Montgomery, Maj.-Gen. G. S., inspection of 68th Light Infantry by, at Nasirabad, 114.

Moore, Pte., wounded near Eden Kop, 150.

Morant, Lt.-Gen. H., diary of, 77; severely wounded before Sevastopol, 83; remarks by, on the battle of Inkerman, 84; in action with Maoris, 99.

Moresco, the taking of, 50.

Morne Fortuné, siege of fort, 25; capture of, 36.

Morse, Maj.-Gen., presentation of colours by, to 2nd European L.I., 111.

Mostyn, Maj.-Gen., in the Cherbourg expedition, 6.

Moulton, Pte. A., awarded D.C. Medal, 87.

Mounted Infantry, organization and operations of the, in S. Africa, 145 *et seq.*

Murphy, Pte. E., noted for gallantry, 64.

Murray, Brig.-Gen., inspection of 68th Light Infantry by, at Mian Mir, 104.

Murray, Serjt. J., noted for gallantry, 98; awarded the V.C., 99.

Murrey, Pte. T., commended for gallantry, 64.

Mutiny, manifestations of, in various regiments in 1783, 20, 21.

Mutlow, Pte. C., killed at Sassadroog, 110.

Myers, Lce.-Serjt., with the Tirah expedition, 133.

INDEX

N.

Nairne, Lt.-Gen., inspection of 1/Durham L.I. by, at Mhow, 130.

Naitby, Lce.-Corpl. M., killed at Vereeniging, 147.

Napier, Sir Charles, in Sind, 109.

Napier, Gen. T. E., inspection of 68th Light Infantry by, at Limerick, 80.

Napier, Sir W., on the battle of Ostiz, 57; on the battle of Nivelle, 60.

Nattrass, Corpl., killed by lightning, 68.

Neal, Corpl. A., mentioned in despatches, 152; awarded D.C. Medal, 155.

New Zealand, war against the Maoris in, 96 *et seq*.

Nicholls, Brig.-Gen., defeats insurgents at St. Andrew's Bay, Grenada, 29.

Nicholson, Maj.-Gen. M. H., inspection of 2/Durham L.I. by, 131.

Nicholson, Pte., mentioned in despatches, 141.

Nicholson, Corpl. S., killed at Kroomdrai, 146, 150.

Nicholson, Pte. W., noted for gallantry, 111.

Nightingale, Miss Florence, relations of, with Pte. Robert Robinson, 90.

Nightingale, Serjt. J., mentioned in despatches, 152.

19th Punjabis, presentation of new colours to, by H.M. King George V. at Delhi, 159.

95th Regt., in the Walcheren expedition, 41.

Nivelle, battle of, 59.

Nixon, Lieut. J., died from Walcheren fever, 43.

Noble, Col.-Serjt. A., mentioned in despatches, 141, 152; awarded D.C. Medal, 155.

Noble, Pte. W., mentioned for gallantry, 111.

Noble, Serjt. W., awarded for services in the Pun

Norcott, Col., in command gade in Natal, 138.

North, Capt. W., wounded manca, 52.

Northey, Lieut. (Capt.) W tioned in Sir Redvers despatches, 142; on d mounted infantry, 14(tioned in Lord Kitchen patches, 154; award D.S.O., *ibid*.

Northumberland Fusiliers, tation of new colours tc at Delhi by H.M. King V., 159.

O.

O'Brien, Serjt. M. J., ment despatches, 154; awar D.C. Medal, 155.

O'Callaghan, Lieut. H. T., Fatehgarh, 121.

O'Connell, Ens. J., wou Ostiz, 57.

Ogden, Pte. J., awarded t Medal, 87; decorated Legion of Honour, 91.

O'Leary, Asst.-Surgeon J. F before Sevastopol, 83.

Orthes, battle of, 61, 62.

Ostiz, battle of, 56, 57.

Outram, Gen. Sir J., in com Persian expeditionary 113.

P.

Paget, Maj. A. de B. V., o1 duty at Poona, 132; Tirah expedition, 133.

Pakenham, Maj.-Gen. Sir spection of 68th Light by, at Portsmouth, 76.

Palmer, Ens., wounded at Pah, N.Z., 98.

Panhala, capture of fortress

Paris, Mr., at Gate Pah, N

Parke, Capt. L., mentione Redvers Buller's des 141.

INDEX

Parker, Pte. J. S., awarded D.C. Medal, 142, 155.
Paulet, F.-M., Lord Wm., at Glasgow, commanding detachment in aid of civil power, 72; at Jamaica, 73; at review of 68th Light Infantry by Duke of Wellington, at Walmer, 75; funeral of, 129.
Pay, rates of regimental, in 1756, 2.
Pegg, Lce.-Corpl., with the Tirah expedition, 133; died, 134.
Pendlebury, Col.-Serjt. W., mentioned in despatches, 152.
Percussion arms, issue of, in 1844, 75.
Perwin, Lieut. J. H., killed at Vittoria, 55.
Pettah of Rangna, storming of the, 110.
Pickford, Pte. S., mentioned in despatches, 143; awarded D.C. Medal, 155.
Picton, Brig.-Gen. T., at capture of Morne Fortuné, 37.
Pikes, serjeants ordered to carry, instead of halberts, 24.
Pilcher, Brig.-Gen. T. D., at Sannah's Post, 143; inspection of 2/Durham L.I. by, at Aldershot, 157.
Pratt, Capt. E. St. G., mentioned in Sir Redvers Buller's despatches, 141; on duty with mounted infantry, 146; mentioned in Lord Kitchener's despatches and awarded the D.S.O., 154; specially promoted Major, 155.
Pratt, Corpl., mentioned in despatches, 141.
Prescott, Lieut. J. J. W., mentioned in Sir Redvers Buller's despatches, 140.
Prize Money, long deferred payment of, 66.
Pulteney, Maj.-Gen. W. P., at manœuvres in Ireland, 159; inspection of 2/Durham L.I. by, at Fermoy, 160.
Puxley, Capt., in suppression of mutiny of 8th W. India Regt., 34.

Q.

Queue, introduction of the, in 1802, 35.
Quinn, Pte., mentioned in despatches, 151; specially promoted Corporal for gallantry, 155.

R.

Raglan, Lord, on the Russian sortie from Sevastopol, 89.
Ramsey, Lt.-Col. J. S., mentioned in despatches, 113, 114.
Ramsey, Maj. T. B., with mounted infantry in S. Africa, 147.
Rand, Mr., chairman of Plague Committee in India, 132, 133.
Rasbotham, Lieut. R. E., killed near Eden Kop, 150; mentioned in Lord Kitchener's despatches, 151.
Rathborne, Capt., with mounted infantry up the Nile, 123.
Ray, Miss Martha, murder of, by Lieut. Hackman, 18.
Rea, Pte. T., noted for gallantry, 64.
Reed, Capt. J., wounded at Vittoria, 56.
Reid, Pte., wounded at Roberts' Drift, 146.
Reid, Ens. W., died from Walcheren fever, 43.
Reilly, Pte. J., noted for gallantry, 64.
Reilly, Pte. T., killed at Sassadroog, 110.
Reshire, taking of fort of, 112.
Revell, Capt. T., taken prisoner at St. Cas, 8.
Richardson, Capt. C., in the Walcheren expedition, 41.
Rifle Brigade, 1st Bn., at Colenso, 136; at Vaal Krantz, 137, 138.
Ripon, Marquis of, at the Lahore Durbar, 105.
Ritson, Lieut. J. R., in S. Africa with a "special service" company of Volunteers, 139.

INDEX

Robb, Lieut. A. K., with the Tirah expedition, 133; recommended for the D.S.O., *ibid*.
Roberts, F.-M., Lord, inspection of 1/Durham L.I. by, at Dublin, 131; despatches by, 151, 152.
Robinson, Pte., with the Tirah expedition, 133.
Robinson, Pte. R., relations of, with Florence Nightingale, 90.
Robson, Pte. J., awarded D.C. Medal, 142, 155.
Ross, Pte. C., awarded French Crimean medal, 92.
Ross, Lt.-Col. W. C., severely wounded at Bothaville, 148; mentioned in despatches and nominated C.B., 149, 154.
Rosseter, Maj. H. D., death of, 131.
Rottenburg, Maj.-Gen. Baron de, instructs the 68th Regt. in light infantry exercises, 40; in the Walcheren expedition, 41, 42.
Rowlandson, 2nd Lieut. C. O., with mounted infantry in S. Africa, 147.
Royal, Pte., killed at De Jager's Drift, 145, 151.
Royal Highlanders, presentation of new colours to 2nd Battn. at Delhi by H.M. King George V., 159.
Royal Scots, in suppression of mutiny of 8th W. India Regt., 34; in the St. Lucia expedition, 36.
Royal Welch Fuzileers, 3; description of uniform in 1758, 5.
Ryan, Maj., at the Gate Pah, N.Z., 97.

S.

Sackville, Lord George, in the expedition against Cherbourg, 6.
St. Andrew's Bay, Grenada, defeat of insurgents at, 29.
St. Cas, defeat of British at, 7, 8.
St. Clair, Pte., noted for gallantry, 150; mentioned in despatches, 151; specially promoted Corporal, 155.
St. Malo, 1758 operations against, 6.
St. Vincent, operations against the Carribs of, 15.
Salamanca, campaign and battle of, 50 *et seq*.
Salmon, Serjt., wounded at De Jager's Drift, 145, 151.
Samanghur, the storming of, 110.
Sanderson, Bugler H., awarded D.C. Medal, 87.
Sannah's Post, action at, 143.
Sant, Qr.-Mr.-Serjt., awarded D.C. Medal, 87.
Sarasiddhi, Capt., Siamese Army, 135.
Sassadroog, action in the defile of, 110.
Saunderson, Lieut. F. de L., awarded Sardinian medal for the Crimea, 92.
Scarlett, Maj.-Gen. Hon. Sir J. Y., inspection of 68th Light Infantry by, at Portsmouth, 94.
Schaw, Lt.-Col. J. B., in suppression of the revolt in Grenada, 26 *et seq*.
"Scots Magazine" quoted, 21.
Scott, Maj. G., in suppression of mutiny of 8th W. India Regt., 34.
Scottish Rifles, 2nd Bn., at Colenso, 136; at Vaal Krantz, 138.
Seaforth Highlanders, presentation of new colours to 1st Bn. at Delhi by H.M. King George V., 159.
Second-Lieutenant, rank of, abolished in 1881, 105.
2nd (South Canterbury) Regt., N.Z., affiliated to Durham L.I., 163.
Sedgewick, Pte., wounded near Eden Kop, 150.
Seery, Col.-Serjt. W., noted for gallantry, 64.
Serjeant-Major, pay of, in 1813, 56.
Seven Years' War, operations during the, against the French coasts, 6.
70th Regt., at the Gate Pah, N.Z., 97.

INDEX

.st Regt., in the Walcheren expedition, 41.

ıakespear, Lieut. W. P., fatally wounded before Samanghur, 110.

ıaw, Lt.-Col. G. K., died at Kasauli, 122.

ıea, Col.-Serjt. J. P. L., mentioned in despatches, 141, 152; awarded D.C. Medal, 155.

ıeddon, Ensign T., severely wounded at Orthes, 61.

ıeridan, Pte. P., noted for gallantry, 64.

ıield, Pte. M., killed at Kooshab, 113.

ıipley, Col., at capture of Morne Fortuné, 36.

ıirreff, 2nd Lieut. C. R., with mounted infantry in S. Africa, 147.

ıorapur, taking of the fort of, 115.

ıuttleworth, Maj. C. U., at the Gate Pah, N.Z., 97; mentioned in despatches, 98.

am, H.R.H. the Crown Prince of, 135.

ıms, Pte. J., awarded French Crimean medal, 92.

ıth L.I. (see Durham L.I.), 1st Battalion.

ıth Regt., at the Gate Pah, N.Z., 97.

st Regt., in operations against the " Brigands " of St. Lucia, 25.

ıth Regt., in the St. Lucia expedition, 36.

ıene, Ens. (Lieut.) D. J., wounded at Vittoria, 56; severely wounded at Vera, 58.

ıadden, Col.-Serjt. H., gallant conduct of, before Sevastopol, 83; awarded D.C. Medal, 87; recommended for the V.C. and decorated with the Legion of Honour, 88, 91.

Small Books," introduction of, 65.

nith, Pte. T., noted for gallantry, 98.

Smyth, Lt.-Col. H., wounded at Inkerman, 83; died at Scutari, 90; decorated with the Legion of Honour, 91; awarded Sardinian medal for the Crimea, 92.

Smyth, Lieut. W., wounded in the Walcheren expedition, 42.

Snider Rifle, issue of the, 119.

Soden, Capt. M., wounded in the Walcheren expedition, 42; died at Elvas, 47.

Soltau-Symons, Lieut. (Capt.) L., wounded at Inniskilling Hill, 139; on duty with mounted infantry, 146; mentioned in Lord Roberts' despatches, 152.

Somers, Capt. J., died from Walcheren fever, 43.

Sorlie, Lieut. S., wounded at Vittoria, 56.

Soult, Marshal, at Nivelle, 60.

Spencer, Brig.-Gen. Hon. A., in the Crimea, 88.

Spion Kop, battle of, 137.

Stalker, Maj.-Gen. F., in command of Persian expeditionary force, 112, 113.

Stansfield, Pte., mentioned in despatches, 141.

Stapylton, Lieut. H., mortally wounded at Oeyreguave, 61.

Starkey, Pte. W., noted for gallantry, 64.

Starkie, Corpl. W., awarded D.C. Medal, 87.

Staro, Bugler T., noted for gallantry, 64.

Staunton, Col. G., in the Crimea, 88; inspection of 68th Light Infantry by, at Sevastopol, 90.

Steele, Lce.-Corpl. C., mentioned in despatches, 143; awarded D.C. Medal, 155.

Stevenson, Lt.-Gen. Sir F., G.O.C. in Egypt, 123; at Firket, 125; presentation of Egyptian war medals by, 126.

Stevenson, Maj.-Gen. N., inspection of 1/Durham L.I. by, at Bradford, 127.

INDEX

Stewart, Col. J., in operations against the "Brigands" of St. Lucia, 24, 25.
Stewart, Lieut. J. C., died from snake-bite, 37.
Stockdale, Lieut. E. H., died from typhoid, 126.
Stock, introduction of the, 24.
Stopford, Lieut. R., killed at Nivelle, 60.
Strangways, Capt. E. S., in S. Africa with a "special service" company of Volunteers, 153.
Stretton, Ens. S. W. L., severely wounded at Vittoria, 56.
Stuart, Lieut., wounded at the Gate Pah, N.Z., 98.
Stuart, Serjt., with mounted infantry up the Nile, 123; gallant conduct at Ambigole Wells, 124; awarded D.C. Medal, *ibid.*, 126.
Suddes, Pte., wounded at Villiersdorp, 147.
Sullivan, Col.-Serjt. D., noted for gallantry, 64.
Sutherland, Mr., killed by Was tribesmen, 142.
Swann, Pte. A., mentioned in despatches, 141.
Sweeny, Pte. E., noted for gallantry, 64.
Sweeny, Pte. O., noted for gallantry, 64.
Sykes, Serjt. W., killed at Roberts' Drift, 146, 150.
Symonds, Lce.-Corpl., with the Tirah expedition, 133.

T.

Tame, Pte. W., awarded D.C. Medal, 87.
Thacker, Corpl. T., mentioned for gallantry, 111.
3rd W. India Regt., in the St. Lucia expedition, 36.
Thomas, Serjt., mentioned in despatches, 141.
Thompson, Lieut. C., wounded at Sarapur, 110.

Thompson, Maj. R., loses his right arm in the Walcheren expedition, 42.
Thomson, Ens. J., wounded in the Walcheren expedition, 42.
Thresher, Lieut. E. B., mentioned in Sir Redvers Buller's despatches, 142; in Gough's Mounted Infantry, 144; died from enteric fever, 150.
Tilley, Col.-Serjt. H., mentioned in despatches, 141, 152, 154.
Todd, Ens. A., died from Walcheren fever, 43.
Torrens, Brig.-Gen. A. W., in the Crimea, 82; severely wounded at Inkerman, 84, 86.
Tothwell, Corpl. W., noted for gallantry, 64.
Trenchard, Capt. H. M., with mounted infantry in S. Africa, 147.
Trent, Capt. H. W. J., at the Gate Pah, N.Z., 97; mentioned in despatches and promoted Major, 98; in Bombay, 103.
Trigge, Gen. Sir T., Colonel of the 68th Light Infantry, 40.
Trimnell, Serjt., with the Tirah expedition, 133.
Trumpet-Majors, first appointment of, 43.
Tucker, Lieut. A. H., decorated with the Legion of Honour, 91.
Tudor, S.-M., noted for gallant conduct, 98; awarded D.C. Medal, 99.
Turnbull, Capt. J., in S. Africa with a "special service" company of Volunteers, 139; mentioned in Sir Redvers Buller's despatches, 141.
12th Regt., at the Gate Pah, N.Z., 97.
20th Hussars, in the Nile expedition, 125.
21st Native Infantry, disarming of the, 114.
27th Native Infantry, disarming of the, 114.
Tyacke, Lieut. H. P., wounded at Sassadroog, 110.

INDEX

U.

Unthank, Lt. J. S., with mounted infantry in S. Africa, 146.

V.

Vaal Krantz, battle of, 137, 138.
Vane, Maj. Hon. W. L., with Col. Wing's column in S. Africa, 151; mentioned in Lord Roberts' despatches, 152; mentioned in Lord Kitchener's despatches, 153; in command of detachment proceeding to attend the coronation of H.M. King Edward VII., 153; mentioned in Lord Kitchener's final despatch, 153.
Vaughan, Gen. Hon. Sir J., on affairs in St. Lucia, 25.
Vera, combat of, 58.
Vieuxfort, St. Lucia, skirmish at, 25.
Villares, action of, 50, 51.
Vittoria, battle of, 55.
Volunteers, "special service" companies of, in S. Africa, 139, 140, 150, 153.

W.

Waiton, Col.-Serjt. C., mentioned in despatches, 140, 152, 154.
Walcheren, 1809 expedition to, 41 et seq.
Waldegrave, Maj.-Gen., in the Cherbourg expedition, 6.
Walker, Maj.-Gen. G. T., in the Peninsula, 59; wounded at Orthes, 62.
Wallace, 2nd Lieut. A. W. B., mentioned in Sir Redvers Buller's despatches, 141.
Wallace, Lt.-Col. J., in operations against the Ghadkarries, 109, 110.
Walsh, Pte. W., mentioned for gallantry, 111.
Warberton, Pte. J., awarded D.C. Medal, 126.

Ward, Col.-Serjt. R., mentioned in despatches, 154; awarded D.C. Medal, 155.
Ward, Pte. W., killed at Samanghur, 110.
Warwick, Lieut. F. S., in S. Africa with a "special service" company of Volunteers, 150.
Was, operations against the, 142.
Watkins, Ven. H. W., at deposition of old colours in Durham Cathedral, 162.
Watson, Serjt. T., awarded French Crimean medal, 92.
Waugh, Capt. D., killed near Choiseul, 25.
Way, Lieut. A. S., at Sannah's Post, 143; killed at Kaffir's Kraal, 144; awarded the D.S.O., 154.
Webster, Col., in action at Goyave, 27.
Wellington, Duke of, at Salamanca, 50, 51; at El Retiro, 52; at Vittoria, 55; despatch relating to combat of Vera, 58; at Nivelle, 59, 60; inspection of 68th Light Infantry by, at Walmer in 1844, 75.
Wells, Lieut. C. G., died at Allahabad, 122.
Welsh, a deserter to the enemy, 26.
Wemyss, Gen. T. J., inspection of 68th Light Infantry by, at Galway, 79.
West Indies, excessive mortality amongst troops in the, 33, 37.
West Kent Regt., Royal, 1st Bn., in the Nile expedition, 125.
West Surrey Regt., 2nd Bn., in S. Africa, 135; at Vaal Krantz, 138.
West Yorkshire Regt., 2nd Bn., in S. Africa, 135.
Wheeler, Pte. P., noted for gallantry, 64.
White, Gen. Sir G., inspection of 2nd Durham L.I. by, at Quetta, 129.
White, Pte. H., killed at Panhala, 110.

333

INDEX

White, Pte., wounded at Roberts' Drift, 146.
Wiggin, Maj. E. A., with mounted infantry in S. Africa, 146.
Wilkie, Maj.-Gen., inspection of 2/Durham L.I. by, at Cairo, 126.
Wilkinson, Capt. H. B. Des V., with mounted infantry in S. Africa, 149; noted as qualified for staff employment, 155.
Wilkinson, Maj.-Gen. H. C., inspections of 1/Durham L.I. by, 126, 129.
Willcocks, Lt.-Gen. Sir J., inspection of 1/Durham L.I. by, at Nowshera, 163.
Williams, Col.-Serjt., mentioned in despatches, 141.
Williams, Pte. M., mentioned in despatches, 141.
Wilmot, Capt. G. W., killed by a tiger, 118.
Wilson, Lt.-Col. C. E., at the Delhi Durbar, 159.
Wilson, Qr.-Mr. J., died at Santo Martinho, 54.
Wilson, Lieut. P. P., in S. Africa with a "special service" company of Volunteers, 153.
Winchester, Marquis of, entertainment by, of officers 1/Durham L.I., 129.
Winnett, Maj., at Drummond's Island, Canada, 66.

Wolfe-Murray, Brig.-Gen. Sir J., inspection of 2/Durham L.I., by, at Wellington, 156.
Wolseley, F.-M. Viscount, inspection of 1/Durham L.I. by, at Buttevant, 130.
Women, presence of, with troops on active service, 42, 54.
Wood, Maj.-Gen. Sir E., inspections of 1/Durham L.I. by, 127, 130.
Wood, Paymaster J., died at Lisbon, 47.
Woodcock, Ens. E. M., wounded at Kooshab, 113.
Woodland, Col. A. L., at Vaal Krantz, 137, 138; invalided home, 140; mentioned in despatches, 140, 141; nominated C.B., 154.
Wrightson, Serjt., with the Tirah expedition, 133.
Wyndham, Sir C. A., Crimean diary of, 86, 89.
Wynne, Maj. H. G., killed at Inkerman, 83.

Y.

Yellow Fever, devastating effect of, 26.
York, visit to Dublin of T.R.H. the Duke and Duchess of, 132.

www.ingramcontent.com/pod-product-compliance
Lightning Source LLC
Chambersburg PA
CBHW081415230426
43668CB00016B/2244